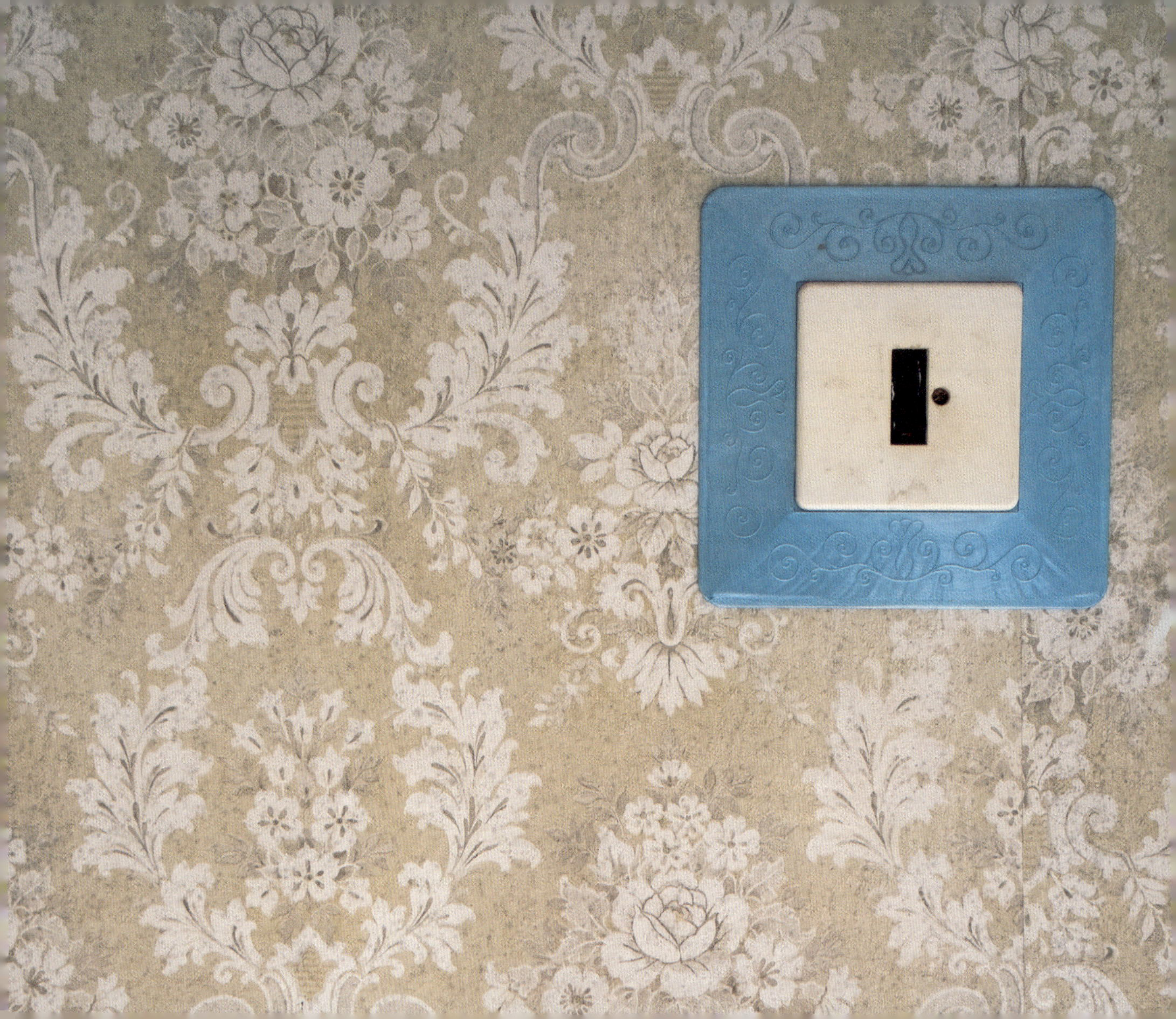

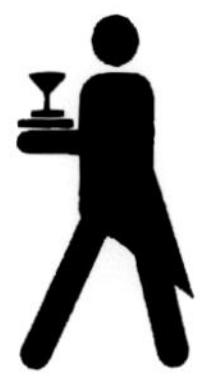

SOCIALIST HOTELS

ELENA AMABILI

INTRODUCTION BY
CAROLINE EDEN

FUEL

INTRODUCTION CAROLINE EDEN

Stationed by the stairs, or the lift, the job of the *dezhurnaya*, or floor lady, is to ensure that, on her watch, no improper activity takes place inside the hotel. Like a gallery attendant, the floor lady is silent but always watching. If you need a kettle, or an extra towel, it is her you must ask (nicely).

The first floor lady I met was at the Hotel Vakhsh (p232) in Dushanbe, Tajikistan's capital. I'd arrived long after midnight, and while the nearby cash machines had failed me (not unusual in 2009), that didn't faze the receptionist. Gazing over her spectacles into the deserted lobby - Soviet-looking and solemn, with its framed portrait of President Emomali Rahmon and a red-carpeted staircase flanked by triumphal columns - she offered a solution, with a flick of her cherry-red hair: 'No money? You can leave jewellery as a deposit.'

The neo-classical façade was deceiving. On stepping through the eerie and silent corridors any initial grandiosity quickly dissipated, to be replaced by an air of resignation and flaking paint.

The floor lady, exquisitely coiffed and vigilant despite the hour, met me at the top of the stairs and unlocked a guest room revealing a rug, a radiator and a single bed covered in a fleecy leopard-print velour throw. Ushering me inside, she opened another door to a cupboard-sized bathroom with cracked tiles and a hosepipe for a shower. Handing over the key, she then left without saying a word. For the rest of the night, as I slept, she would watch and wait, dressed in her hotel-issue uniform.

Come daylight, it was clear that the Hotel Vakhsh, named after one of Tajikistan's rivers, had two distinct assets: an unbeatable position right by the city's opera house, and an interesting history. A commemorative plaque, attached to an exterior wall, briefly told its story in Russian: in the 1940s the hotel had operated as a hospital treating wounded Soviet soldiers and officers. Bullet holes, pockmarking the same wall, acted as a less formal reminder that later, during Tajikistan's nasty civil war of the 1990s, the hotel had taken on another role as the headquarters of the opposition.

History, a certain atmosphere, a good location and a dash of uniqueness. By booking a stay in a hotel such as the Vakhsh, you are buying - and not for very much money - access to another world. Overnighting in some of the more dilapidated socialist hotels, usually beset with wiring and plumbing issues, is a bit like how I imagine sleeping in a museum would feel: not exactly comfortable but intriguing. And while many are best suited to those able to turn a blind eye to cracked walls and saggy furniture dating back decades there are other, if less obvious, benefits.

These ageing hotels do not offer guests high-tech gadgetry such as touchscreen panels, key cards and Bluetooth speakers which, installed for convenience, often end up being infuriating and glitchy to use. Rather, the socialist hotel presents a satisfyingly analogue stay, even if that involves bringing your own bath plug as these were, and still are, seldom supplied. They are usually pleasingly solidly built, too, with significant weight and structure, meaning less chance of hearing your neighbours through thin walls, or enduring the sounds of heels on floorboards above you at night.

A shared lexicon, and things in common, can be found even across vast distances, and this brokers a particular sense of comfort for the guest that can only come from familiarity.

The building itself may well have a stark blockish façade, concrete vertebrae or recessed upper stories but depending

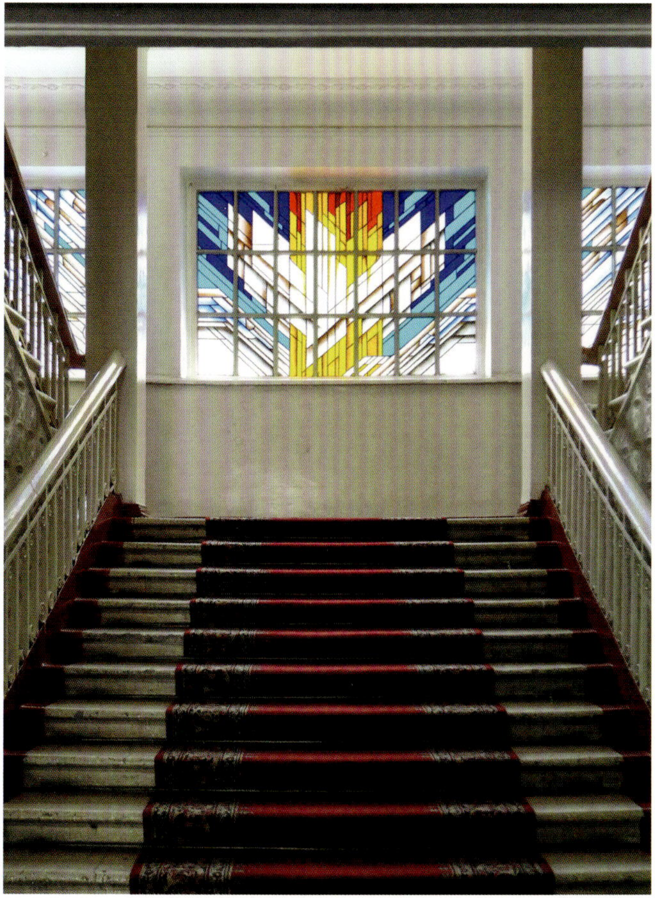

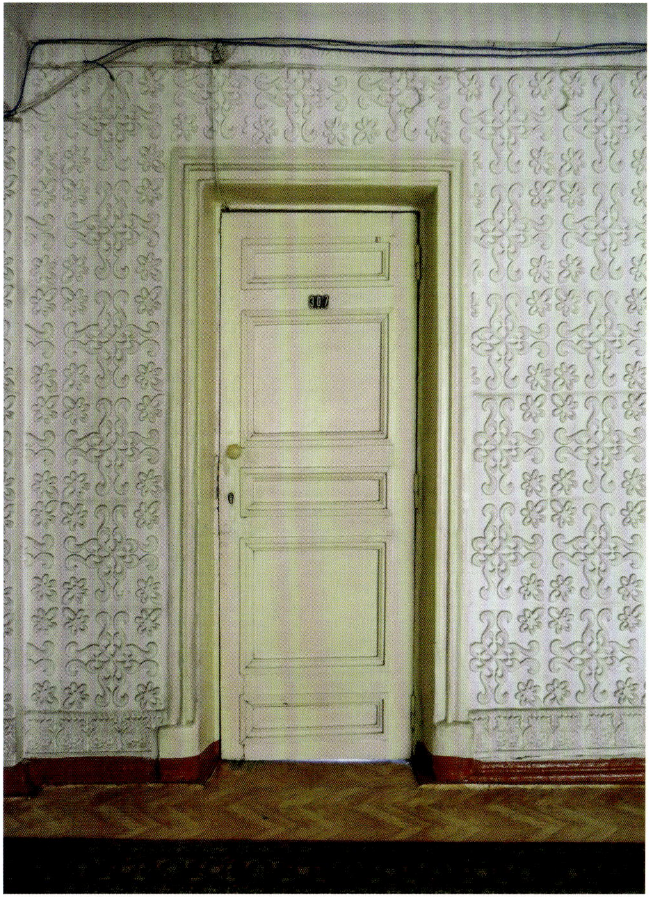

Hotel Vakhsh, Dushanbe, Tajikistan

on its date of construction it might, too, be grander-looking, with Stalinist-style prototypes and aesthetics such as an arched entrance, neo-classical columns or rusticated walls. Inside, there will likely be ruffled white net curtains, rug-lined corridors, and, almost certainly, spider plants in pots. Concrete balconies looking out like ever-watchful eyes are commonplace. The restaurant will be large and functional, canteen-like in spirit. The ballroom, usually used for receptions, might, in the evening, become a disco.

Depending on the country, creative flourishes and decorative motifs reflecting the surroundings may liven up the decor, such as a bas-relief or a mosaic, perhaps depicting Uzbek workers picking fruit or Armenians swilling the health-giving mineral water that the Caucasus is famous for. Overt quaintness, though, was avoided so as not to appear bourgeoise. Outside, on a patio, there will likely be benches sat next to fountains or tables set out for chess or backgammon. A shady area in which to sit and smoke or eat an ice-cream.

Whether the hotels could ever be classed collectively as welcoming – something we tend to prioritise nowadays – is debatable. Particularly in the past, these hotels were Potemkin-like, with image mattering more than the comfort of guests. Many are exceptionally large, with room enough for several hundred, meaning that they could only ever be imposing. Socialist buildings in general were designed to dominate, dwarfing guest and worker by their sheer architectural scale. Encouraging a feeling of irrelevance. Then there is the matter of surveillance. Hidden microphones and cameras often spread throughout, hiding amidst the interiors, in the lobby, in the restaurant and especially in the seemingly private space of the bedrooms. This is a topic I'll come back to later.

The name itself is usually telling, reflecting the vast geographic reach of the former Soviet Union, with its republics, and the wider Communist bloc. Hotels were sometimes named after important cities elsewhere, hundreds of miles away. Hotel Riga, featured in this book (p60), is not in Latvia as you might think but in the Bulgarian city of Ruse. And, as you'll see, there is a Hotel Moskva (p61) in Sofia, and predictably others elsewhere, gesturing to the Russian capital: Belgrade has a Hotel Moskva as does Budva in Montenegro and you'll find one too in Simferopol, the capital of Crimea. In Kyiv, the Hotel Moskva rebranded, changing its name in 2001 to Hotel Ukraina (p242), in order to mark the 10th anniversary of the country's independence.

Other clues are in the names, too. Take Dom Otdykha Neptun, featured in this book and located in Abkhazia (p18). The first two words tell us that it is a 'rest home', a place to revitalise, while Neptune, the god of water, hints at its location by the Black Sea.

Another common factor of the notable socialist hotel – state-owned, and therefore representing the country – will be its situation, which is usually central and superior.

Hotel Bulgaria (p50) is not, as its grand name suggests, in the capital Sofia, but in the Bulgarian Black Sea city of Burgas. A high-density tower block stretching skywards over 70 metres, it dominates the main tourist thoroughfare and has views across to the busy port. It has changed a lot since I first visited it, back in 2016, when it had a sickly yellow frontage and a red sign on the roof surrounded by satellite dishes and messy antennae. Today, very little of the original hotel – built in the mid-1970s – exists, as it has been through several major renovations. Last time I visited, as I began writing this introduction, it had been smartened up, a living example of a socialist hotel that is not only a survivor but a success story. It may look monolithic, heavy, confrontational even, but the room occupancy is healthy, its Sinatra piano bar lively and the staff helpful. The bedrooms, thoroughly modernised, are decked out in the sort of neutral vanilla-like tones associated with modern luxury. Rather than being slowly ruined by hubris, as has been the fate of so many old hotels, Hotel Bulgaria, robust and remade and remade again, continues to evolve and carry on. No 'concrete monstrosity,' it is instead recognised locally, at least, as something of an icon.

Surely conservation is possible, and preferable to dilapidation and destruction? And with the distance of time, surely it is possible, too, to build appreciation while not being blind to complex histories or mythologising troubled legacies. The Hotel Bulgaria certainly suggests it is feasible.

While a prominent site was key for many of the planners and architects of these hotels, location has not always proved defence enough against changing times. Take the trapezoid-shaped Hotel Pelegrin (p71), star of what was once known as the Yugoslav Riviera with its unbeatable views over the Adriatic Sea and a crescent-shaped beach. Once popular with the military elite, nowadays it sits in a terrible state of repair and is dismissed, along with its neighbours, as part of 'the bay of abandoned hotels'. As regimes change the desires of citizens change too. What once would have been considered a prestigious setting for a holiday is now a reflection of past authoritarian leadership and historical decline. Unlike the Hotel Bulgaria, the Hotel Pelegrin has been laid to waste.

Seaside, or more rural, settings revealed the health aspect of socialist hotels, pairing the Marxist concept of leisure (as an opportunity for the full development of the individual) with a Scandinavian-style emphasis on physical fitness. Away from the cities, they were somewhere to relax, restore health and spend time meaningfully. Sun-bathing was encouraged during a stay and there might be evening classes to attend, or a dance or facilities for badminton. Suitable activities for the working man and his family. Never having the same international pull on sun seekers as say the Mediterranean, the Black Sea – strategically important then and now – remains popular with holidaymakers from the countries that share

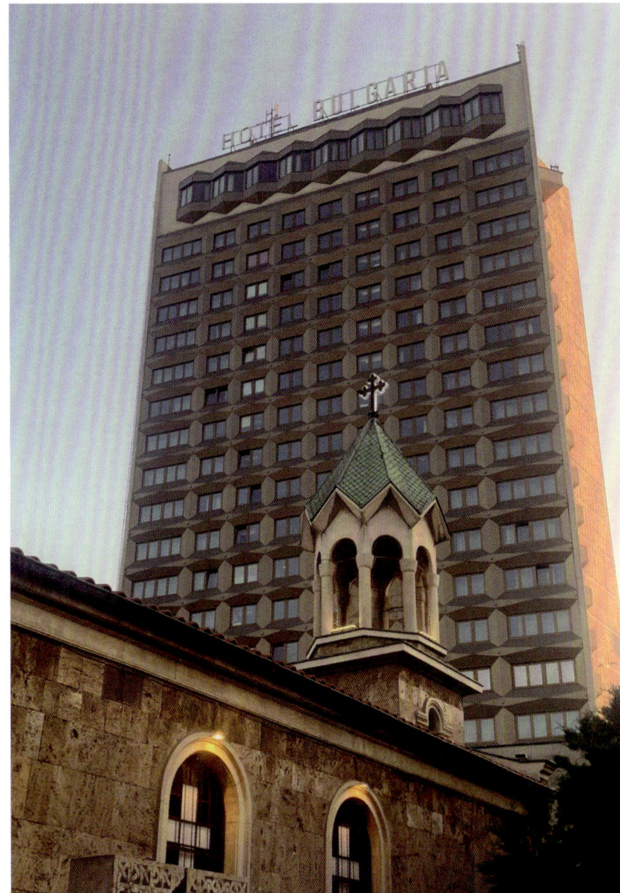

Hotel Bulgaria, Burgas, Bulgaria

its borders: Ukraine, Romania, Bulgaria, Turkey, Georgia and Russia. The coast boasts many visually striking formerly state-run hotels, such as the futuristic spaceship-like Hotel Druzhba ('Friendship') in Crimea overlooking the Black Sea (p69). A prime example of Soviet-era Brutalist architecture, built by Igor Vasilevsky, it looks at once like a UFO and a military institution, raised above the ground by huge concrete columns, while fulfilling its role as a health spa and hotel.

Professions sometimes inspired the odd hotel. Hotel Journalist (p56) near Varna, Bulgaria, has a façade that calls to mind the keys of typewriters, then there is the Writers' House on Lake Sevan in Armenia, an architectural masterpiece, with part of it shaped like a giant snowshoe, balanced on a single thick concrete leg, jutting out from a rock face. Jean-Paul Sartre and Simone Beauvoir stayed once, arriving by car from neighbouring Georgia. Later, de Beauvoir described the landscape surrounding Sevan as 'a pinkish, chaotic desert with a bright blue lake in the middle of it'.

When I got to the Writers' House, on a hot summer afternoon, I wasn't sure what to expect or if I'd be able to stay the night (all telephone calls had gone unanswered). But on arrival I was immediately met by a tall bald blue-eyed man who spread his arms wide to welcome me with the words 'Soviet modernism', in English, before confirming that yes, there was space, and here was a key for 'room number one'. It was an actual key, heavy and reassuring in the hand, so much more satisfying to use than a modern, plastic credit card-style one. I was the only guest but dinner would be served, 'not to worry', he added.

On the wall, by the dining room, there were photographs of the original architectural sketches for the snowshoe building, completed in the 1960s. An older building, nearby and known as the residence hall, was opened in the mid-1930s, with characteristic semicircle balconies. That is still where the guest rooms are today.

The lake had captivated the poet Osip Mandelstam, who had visited Armenia for several inspiring months in 1930 before he was targeted by Soviet authorities and sent into the vast network of Gulags. On Lake Sevan, he looked out and saw a tantalising, long-gone, spectacle: 'Daily at five o'clock on the dot, the lake, which teems with trout, would boil up as though a huge pinch of soda had been thrown into it.' Such numbers of trout have gone today but that night, white drapes billowing in the dining room, I was served some of the pudgy little fish for dinner. Tables had been laid with cloths of a pomegranate design, and from a serving hatch came the fried fish along with plates of fresh herbs and paper-thin lavash bread, backbone of Armenian cuisine. Armenian Ararat brandy was served as it got dark, along with

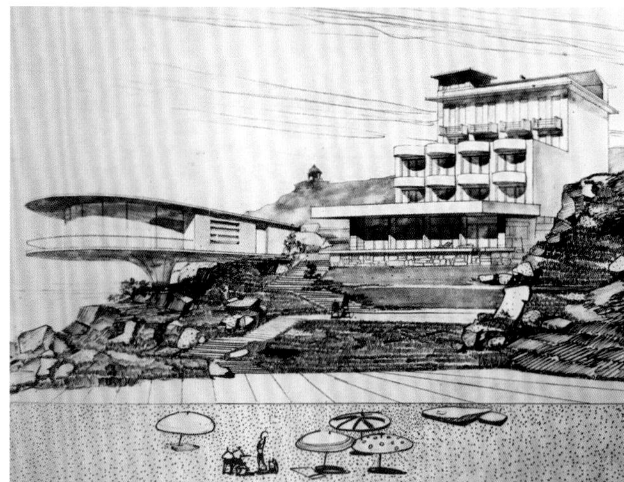

Sevan Writers' House, Sevan, Armenia

glasses of refreshing Jermuk sparkling water. I couldn't help but feel sad that the resort was so quiet as it was such an atmospheric meal and experience. After independence in 1991, the Writers' Union kept the Sevan resort operating for its original purpose, though anyone, not only writers, can stay today.

But who does book a room in a socialist hotel nowadays? The bedroom at the Writers' House, spectacularly located as it was, felt sparse and smelled musty, and had clearly not been renovated in many years. Such problems are typical. The bedrooms in particular tend to be poorly fitted out which results in low occupancy. Subsequently, the hotel doesn't generate the money needed to renovate the building.

The evening meal at the Writers' House was exceptional and quite different to typical socialist hotel restaurant experiences. Usually, the dining rooms are far more utilitarian and are distinctly retro in taste. What comes to the table depends on the location, a bit like with the architectural flourishes found in a mosaic or bas-relief, and commonly there will be a melding of wider socialist-style tastes with national ingredients and flavours.

In Uzbekistan – a country, that along with Ukraine, Armenia and Georgia, has always been celebrated for its food throughout the former Soviet Union – meals will likely arrive on classic Uzbek navy and white china, rimmed with gold paint. This crockery is collectively known as *pakhtagul*, meaning cotton flower, a reflection of Uzbekistan's cotton industry, the foundation of its Soviet-era economy. Teapots,

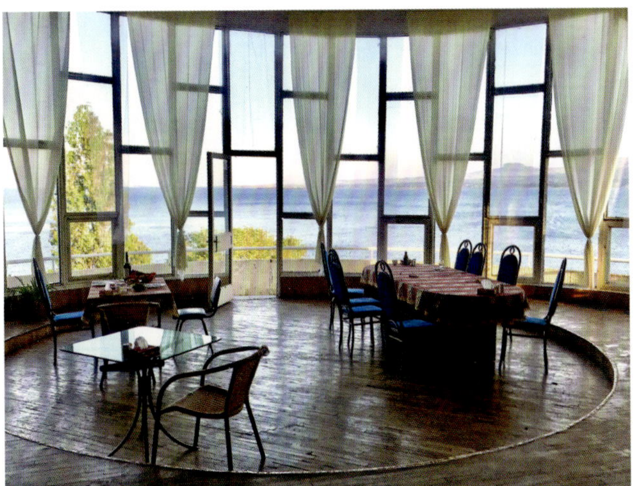

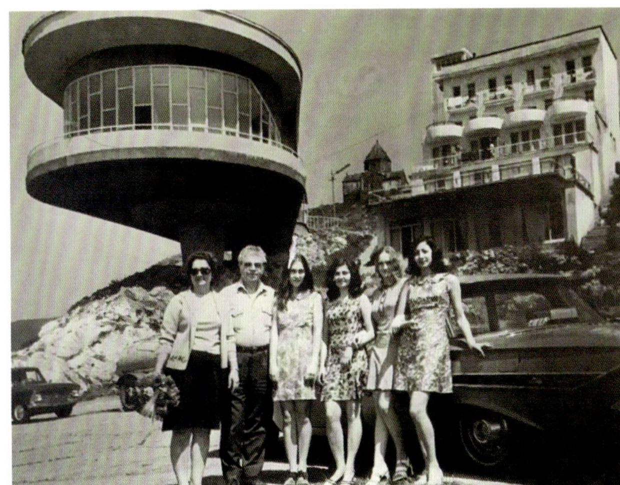

in the same design, brimming with green tea, will be placed down, too, followed by baskets of bread and, usually, side plates of refreshing tomato and purple basil salad, all partners for the platter of plov (the rich layered rice dish served across Central Asia) which will likely be piled high as a sandcastle.

Elsewhere, there will almost always be soup on offer, usually borscht, and always salads, quite often psychedelic-looking variations of shredded orange carrots and ruby-red beetroot, rich in antioxidants and vitamins but often slathered in mayonnaise and neon with dill. For breakfast, it will inevitably be bright pink frankfurters, fried eggs and pancakes with sour cream.

In Kazakhstan, in the heavily industrial city of Karaganda, a menu lives on at the Hotel Chaika little changed in decades. Offering a smorgasbord of different tastes, there is *forshmak*, a pâté of herring and apple popular with Jewish communities in Russia and Ukraine, Georgian-style spatchcocked chicken known as *tabaka* and Russian Olivier salad. To drink, the choice is simple: tea, juice or vodka. But then the Hotel Chaika trades on its past, and understandably so.

At the front desk hangs a diploma from the Federation of Cosmonauts of the USSR, acknowledging the hotel's role as part of the Soviet space programme. Dozens of cosmonauts stayed here, having launched from the Baikonur Cosmodrome in the south of Kazakhstan, a spaceport set in miles of semi-desert. Valentina Tereshkova, who made history by becoming the first woman in space, not only checked in but inspired the name of the hotel. *Chaika*, meaning seagull in Russian, was her codename. Plaques remembering the space men and women cover the exterior wall, while inside, by white ruffled net curtains, are dozens of mounted portraits. More museum than hotel. I didn't stay at the Chaika, opting instead for the Hotel Cosmonaut, a ten-minute drive away. Little of the original 1972 construction remains, but this hotel too was built specially for the return of cosmonauts. Nowadays, Hotel Cosmonaut is often a base for mining experts, many working for ArcelorMittal, the world's leading steel and mining company who operate eight mines in the Karaganda region. I kept a box of Hotel Cosmonaut matches as a souvenir.

It is in the dining rooms, especially at breakfast, when the tables are usually at their busiest, that you can survey your fellow guests. More than once, I have met groups of touring sports teams queuing for coffee or hovering at the omelette station. They are instantly recognisable in their matching tracksuits, with flags and the names of their countries emblazoned. Perhaps it is the state-run history and nature of the hotels, or their nationalistic character, that makes them

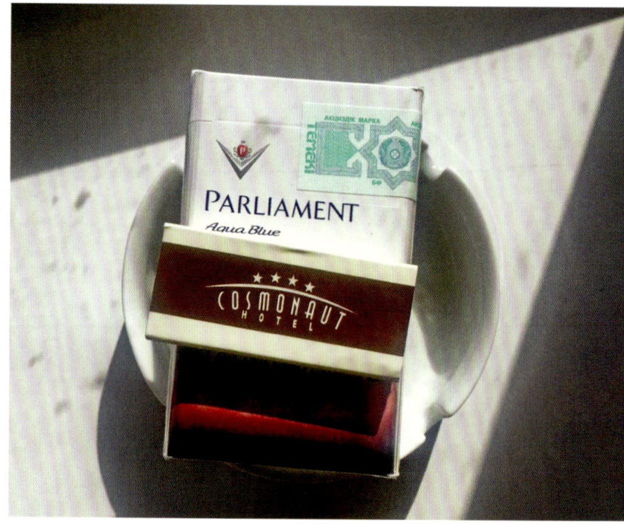

Matches from Hotel Cosmonaut, Karaganda, Kazakhstan

a fitting place to stay for those representing their country at wrestling or fencing. I recall such a troupe in the lobby of Hotel Uzbekistan (p246), Tashkent's giant 17-storey landmark. Dynamic in appearance, it boasts a strong vertical presence and sits right on Amir Temur Square, at the very centre of the city. The linear geometric latticework of its façade, giving the appearance of honeycomb, is both kaleidoscopic and fantastic on the eyes. As a result, the hotel is much photographed. Huge and significant as it is, the hotel recalls Tashkent's past, as the capital not only of the country but of Soviet Central Asia, and it is, in a way, also a reminder of the fact that many who were in power then remain in power today, despite reforms. Its lobby, a buffer zone offering interconnectedness with the interior and external world, is still a popular meeting point for the city's residents.

In 2016, I was unexpectedly upgraded and thus spent a night in Hotel Uzbekistan's presidential suite. I remember two things clearly about that stay: that there was a single smashed wine glass under the giant bed and that the running machine, facing the window and balcony, offered the very best view of the city.

Across Eastern Europe, the Baltics, the Caucasus and Central Asia, huge urban changes are taking place, with architects reimagining, recycling and sometimes 'restroying' (refurbishing in theory but destroying in reality) in the process. Uzbekistan, in particular, is in the midst of a nationwide rebrand and general beautification project which is running in tandem with its large-scale tourism drive. It is keen shake off its communist past.

Samarkand, once a city of tilting minarets, crumbling ribbed domes and collapsing mosques – some of their original brickwork was made from mortar mixed with camel's milk and egg yolk – is being reconstructed again, long after the Soviets aggressively restored some of the older monuments. It was no surprise, therefore, that Samarkand's 11-storey Intourist hotel was demolished in 2017, having sat empty for over a decade, no doubt seen as another dated and ugly high-rise. Fifty years ago, in very different times, the hotel's design was deemed worthy of a postage stamp. Intourist, the main travel agency for foreign tourists in the Soviet Union, had under its umbrella tour packages, gift shops and hotels spread throughout the USSR. Well positioned, its hotel in Samarkand was close to the Gur-e-Amir, the mausoleum of empire builder and nomadic warlord Tamerlane. This hotel had some of the classic attributes of a socialist hotel, blending brutalist hulk with local flair: it was quite plain but on it façade there was a circular emblem of Samarkand's city seal which depicts a legendary winged snow leopard known as Aq Bars.

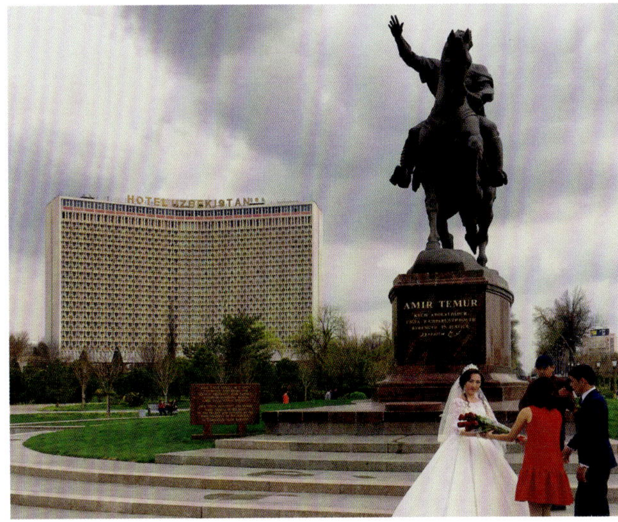

Hotel Uzbekistan, Tashkent, Uzbekistan

Drawn to it, I photographed the hotel just before it was flattened (p13).

Next for the wrecking ball might be another former Intourist favourite, Hotel Național (p138) in Chișinău. With an unbeatably central position in the Moldovan capital, it was once described by the *New York Times* as 'a giant and graceless gem of socialist modernist architecture cherished by aficionados of concrete...' Today, the Hotel Național sits empty and slowly decaying, its red signage still announcing it in a bygone font. But while it lacks guests it does not lack interest. It is something of an unlikely star on social media as a quick internet search will attest. The hotel ties in with the urban exploration movement, or 'urbex', where photographers, and the merely curious (technically, trespassers), driven by a fascination with decaying aesthetics, visit and often film the locations.

Intourist hotels, being places that foreigners gathered, were also hotbeds of surveillance, sometimes to an almost laughable degree. The doorman? Likely KGB. Your room? Certainly bugged. Your bedside phone? Tapped. The table you've been pushed towards sitting at for dinner? Most likely to contain a hidden microphone somewhere. The floor ladies were, of course, effective monitors or informants. In the Estonian capital Tallinn, even the sauna was bugged at the Hotel Viru (p90). Completed in 1972, as the city's first skyscraper, the hotel had over 400 rooms and 23 floors but the lift only went as far as the 22nd. That's because the 23rd floor was entirely given over to a KGB listening centre, a surveillance hub with a direct line to Moscow, that was used to spy on guests who were not only foreign tourists but also business people, journalists and diplomats. In the summer of 1991, as the Soviet Union collapsed, the hotel's KGB agents fled, leaving behind a mass of papers and listening devices. These lay undiscovered until 1994 when the hotel was sold and renovated. Today, anyone can travel up to the 23rd floor, which now operates as a museum telling the story of the hotel's KGB past. The other open secret was that many of the hotels aimed at foreigners would attract the more elite local prostitutes who had arrangements with security and staff allowing them to pass through the lobby and into the dimly lit bar, a place where various black market deals would take place.

It comes as no surprise that the days of the very last existing floor ladies are numbered. In 1986, the *Washington Post*, ran a colourful feature called *'Nyet to Matrons of Morality'* in which it was reported that Moscow's iconic Hotel Moskva had plans to save tens of thousands of rubles a year by eliminating 130 floor ladies, or as they referred to them, 'hotel housemothers'. The article read: 'Their elimination in hotels in the Russian republics is a move toward efficiency in an industry known for a low level of service and excessive number of personnel.' The Kremlin's drive against inefficiency in the workplace was bolstered by a campaign led by the *Literaturnaya Gazeta* (*Literary Gazette*), the weekly newspaper of the writers' union, which campaigned for years to end the custom and rule of the key ladies.

Today, there are no more floor ladies at Dushanbe's Hotel Vakhsh, even though the management there held onto them far longer than most. Nobody is asked for jewellery as a deposit on arrival either. In fact, no one arrives at all. While I was writing this introduction news came that the Hotel Vakhsh had been pulled down.

I know it'll tear at my heart to see it gone, for selfish reasons if nothing else. I remember, so clearly, a slightly nervous, younger me, checking in alone, late at night, at the start of a great adventure. Demolition by neglect, as is the destiny for so many old buildings filled with history and secrets. What was once a vast atlas of socialist hotels, is fast becoming an archive.

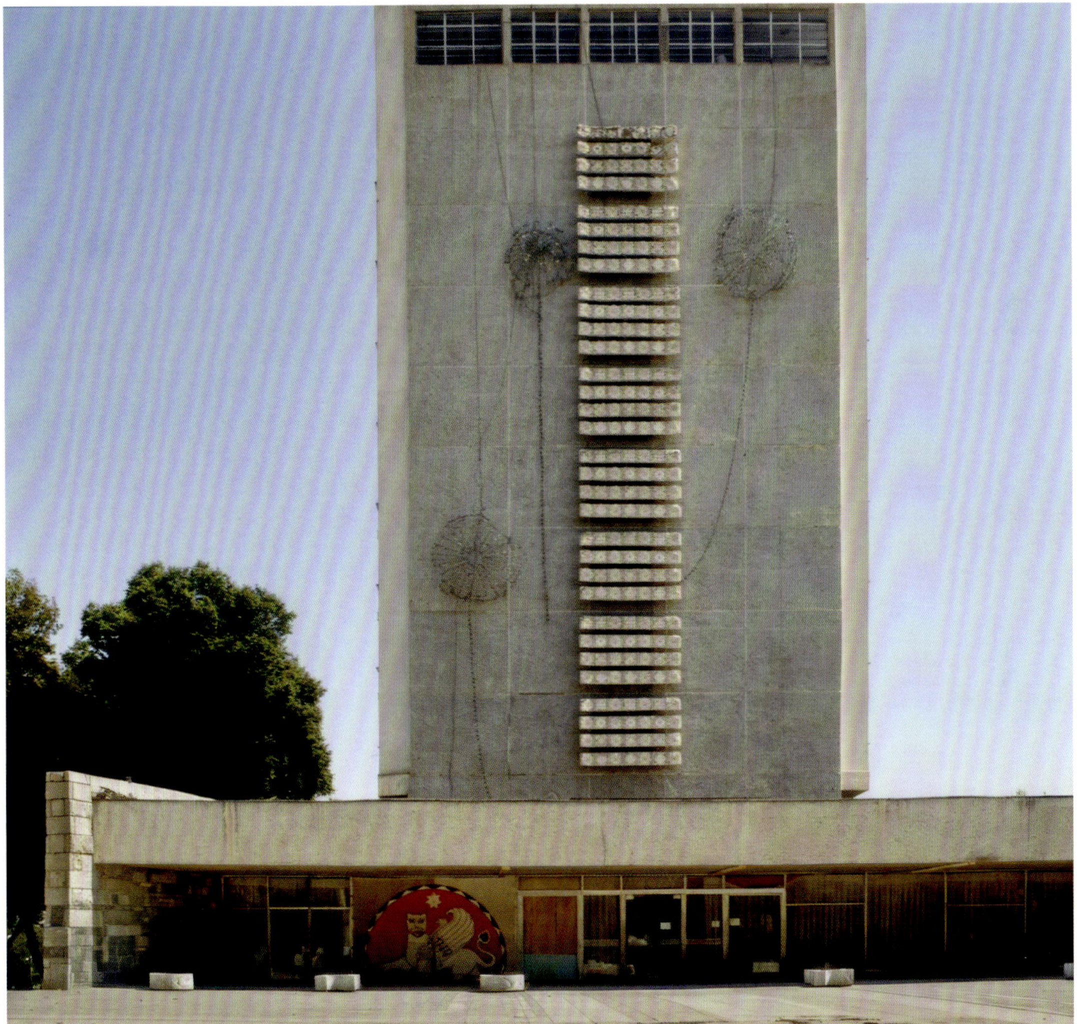

Hotel Intourist, Samarkand, Uzbekistan (demolished in 2017)

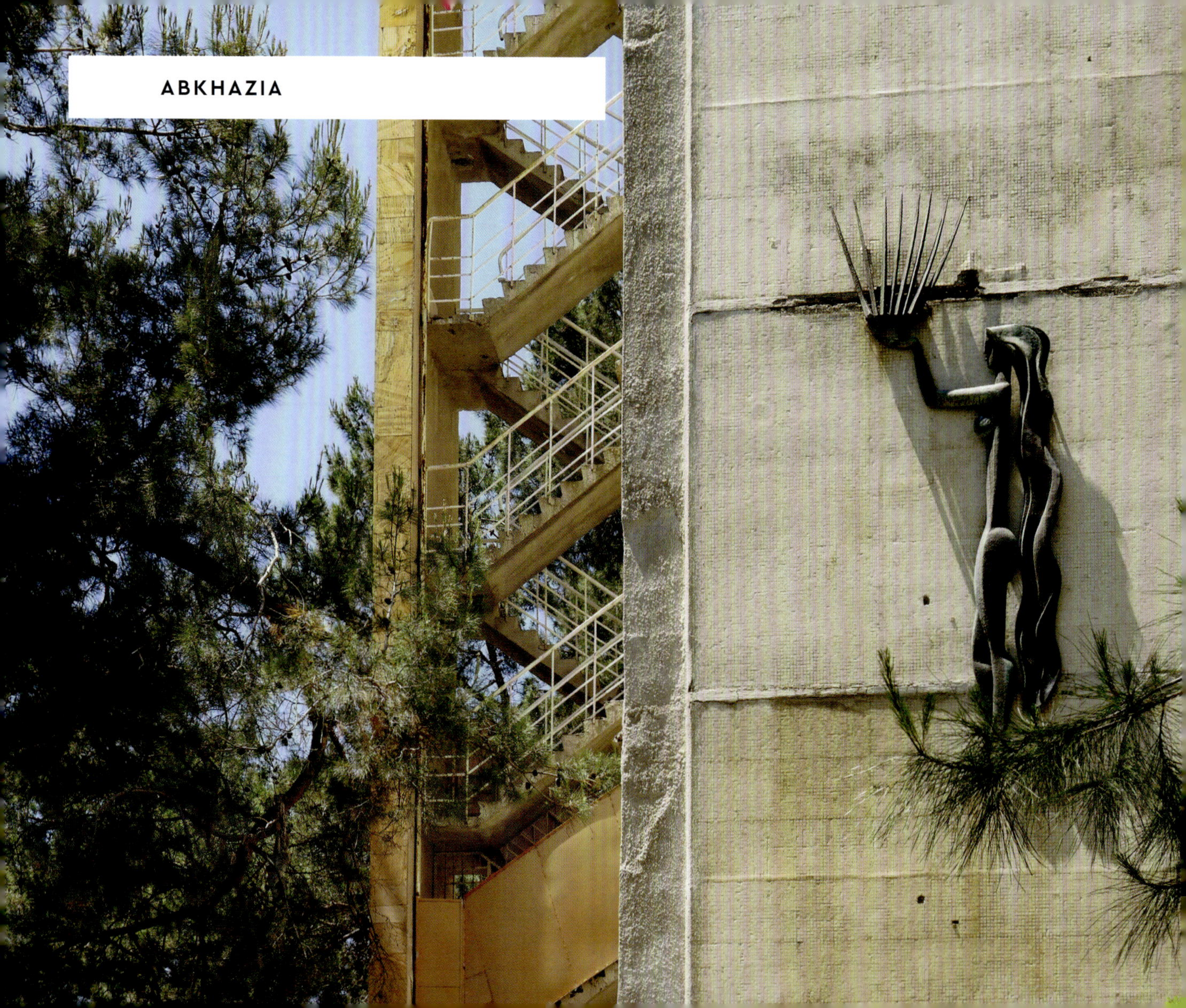

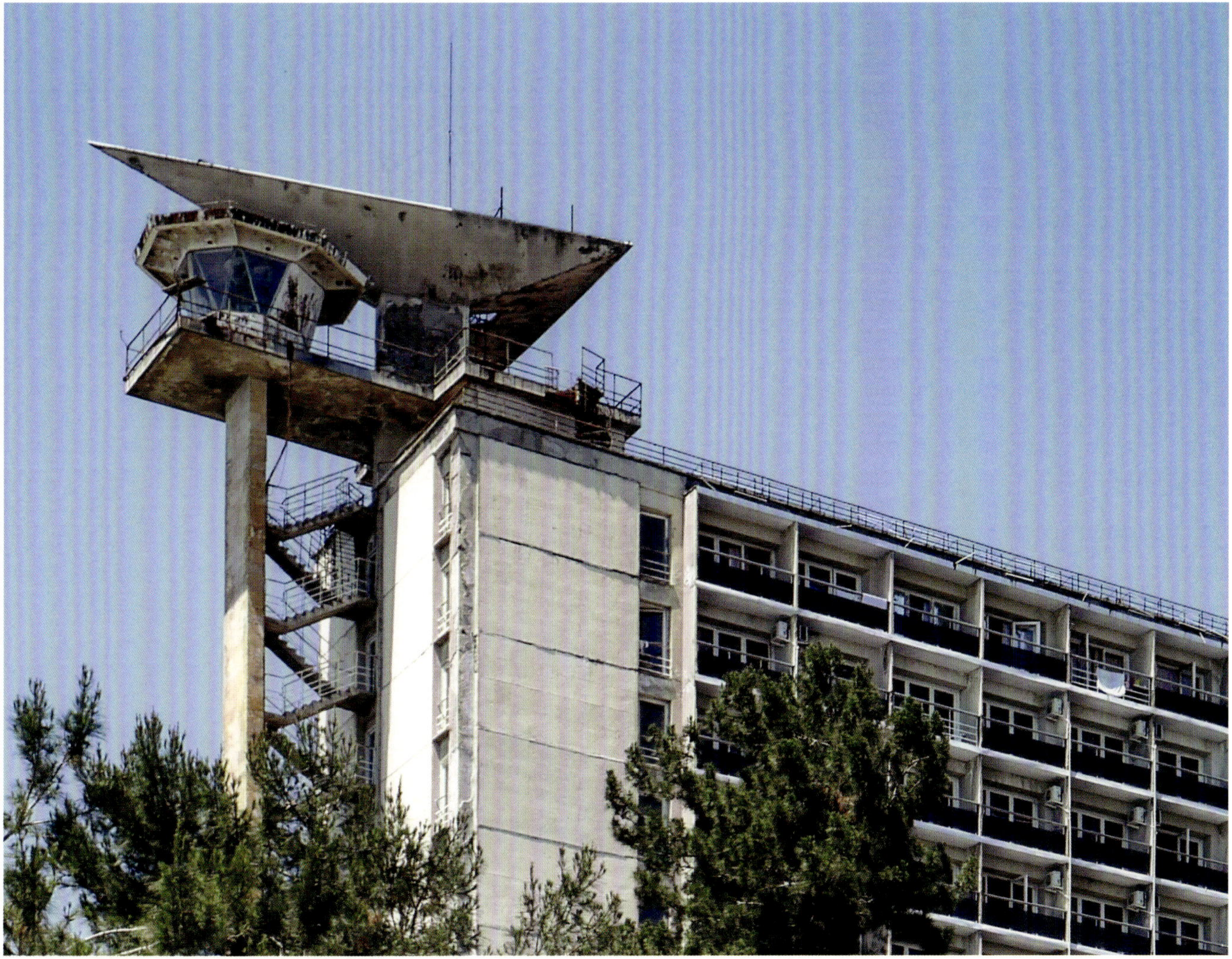

Pansionat Mayak, Pitsunda, Abkhazia

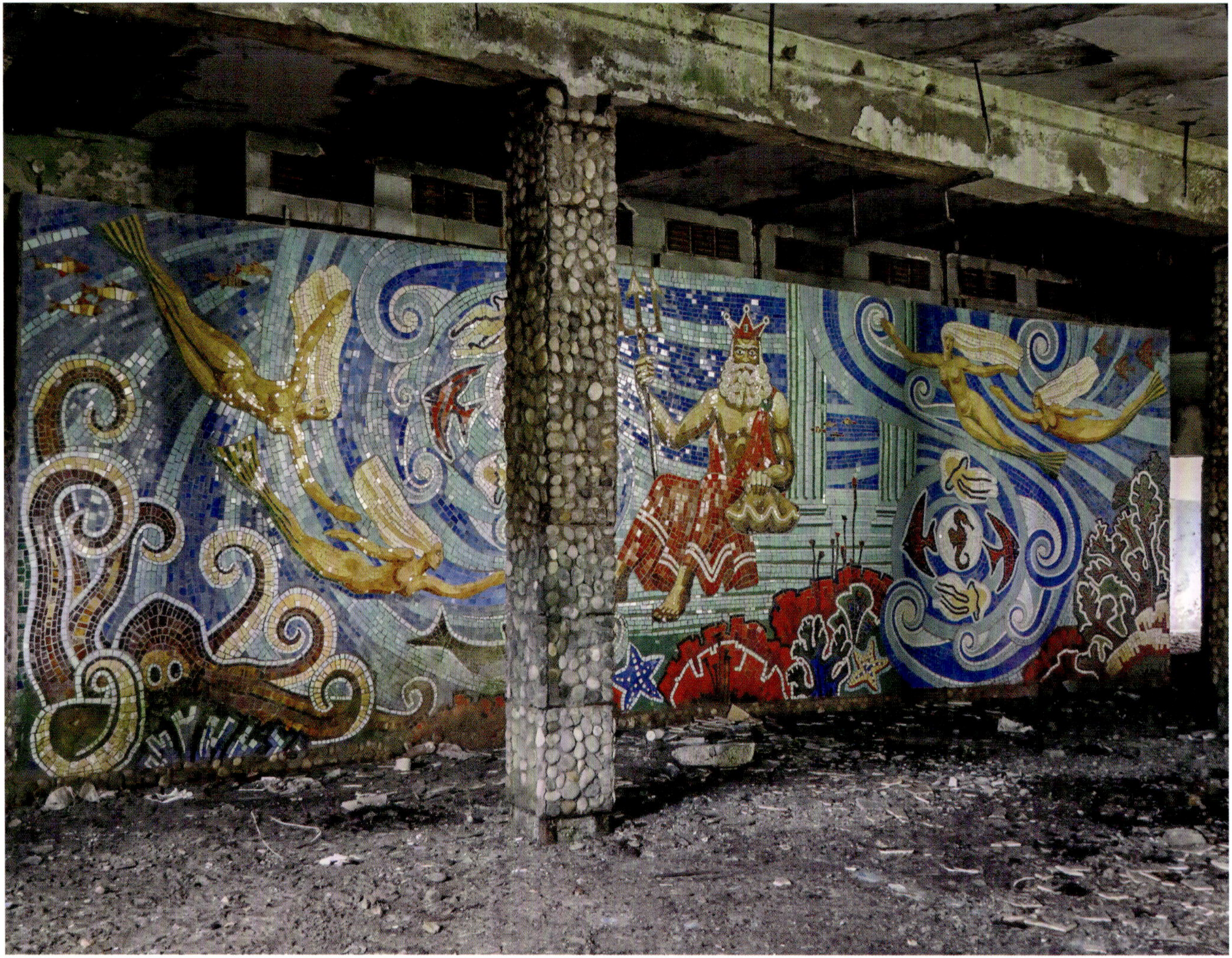

Dom Otdykha Neptun, Mugudzirkhva, Abkhazia

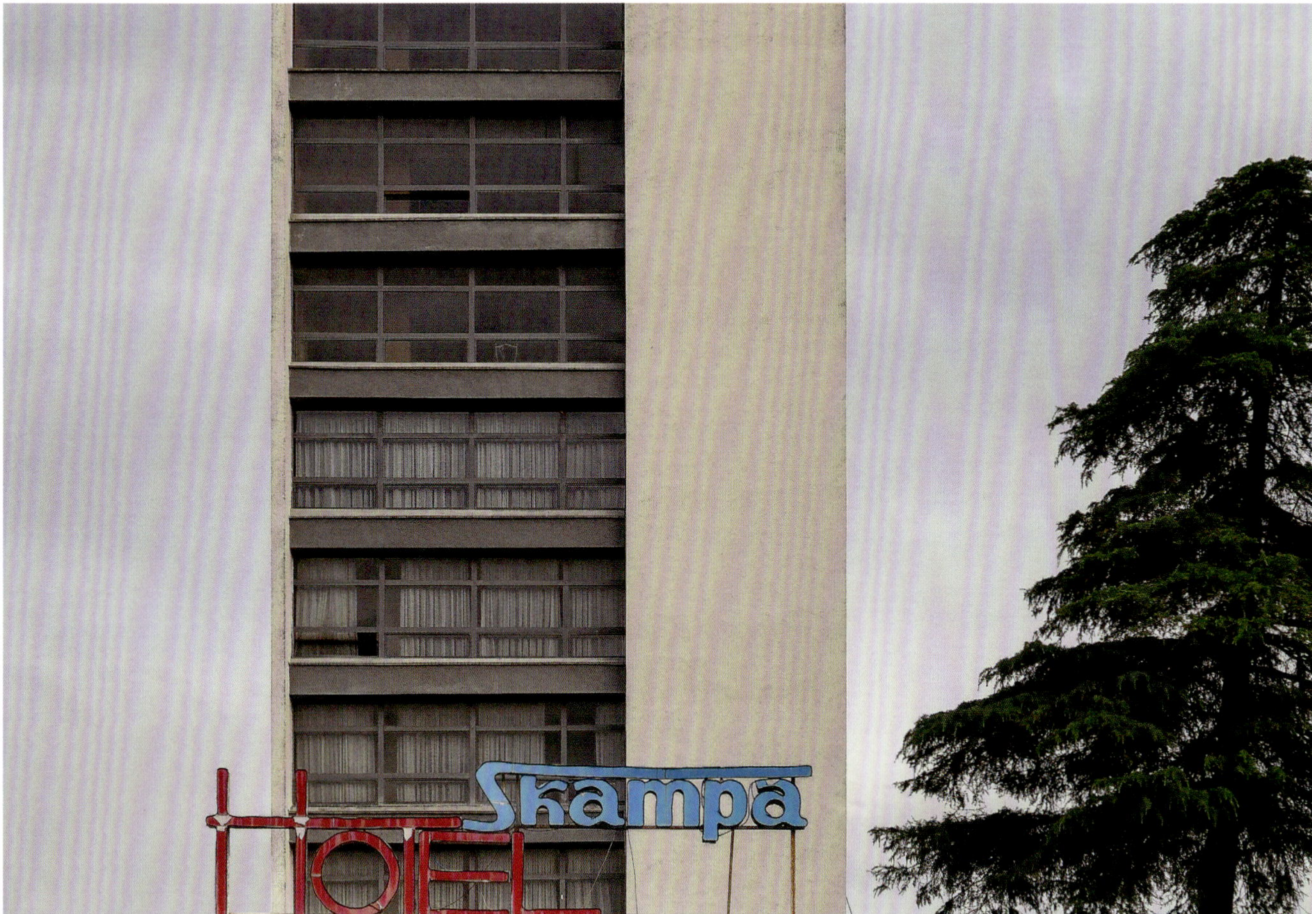

Hotel Skampa, Elbasan, Albania

ARMENIA

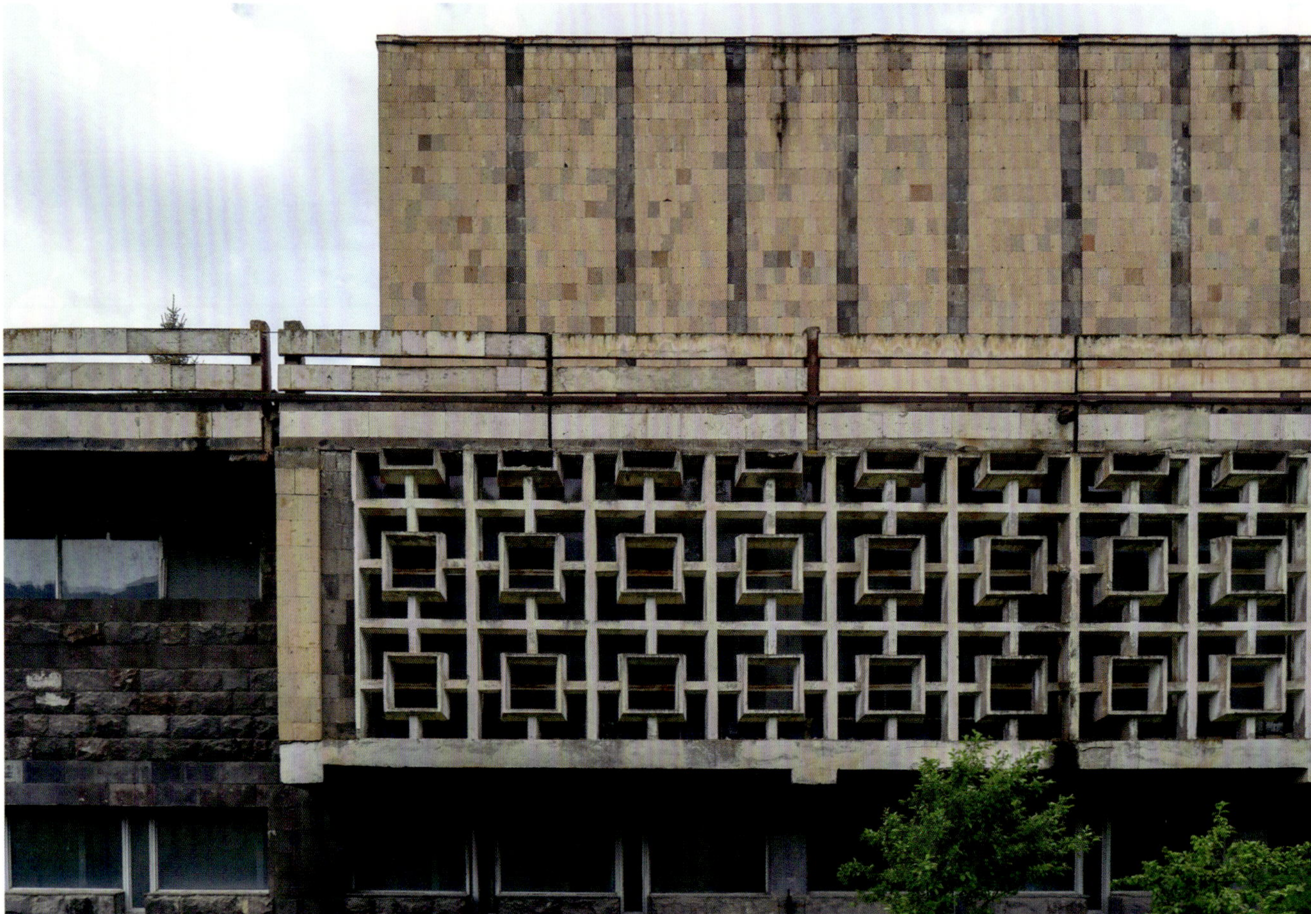

 Sanatorium Khotordzhur, Hankavan, Armenia

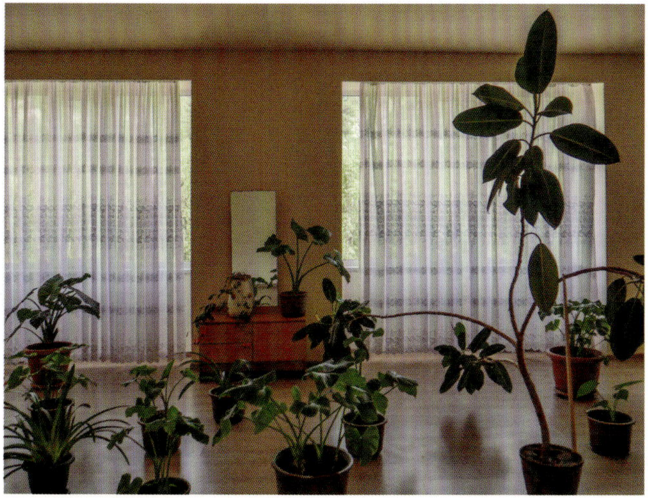

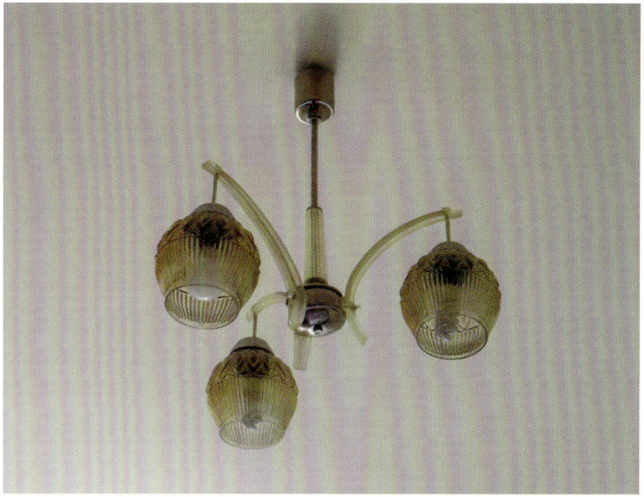

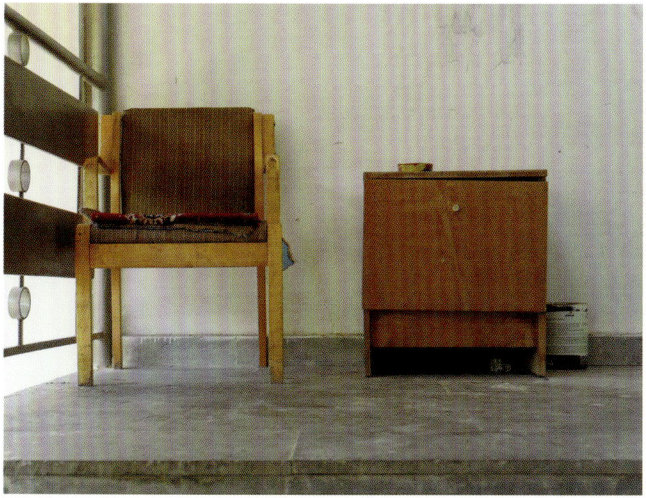

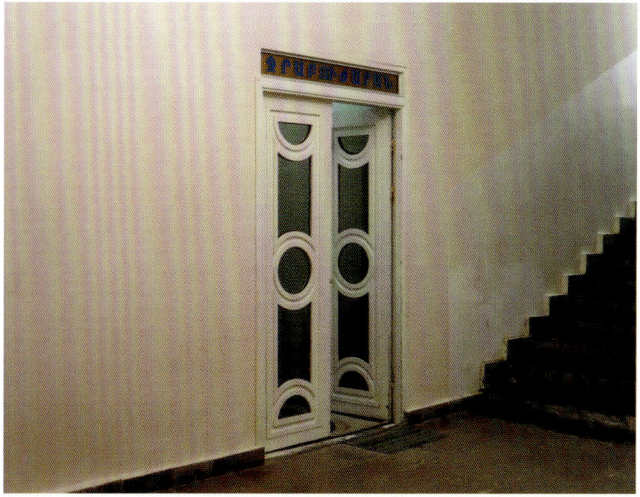

Ararat Health Spa (former Sanatorium Ararat), Jermuk, Armenia

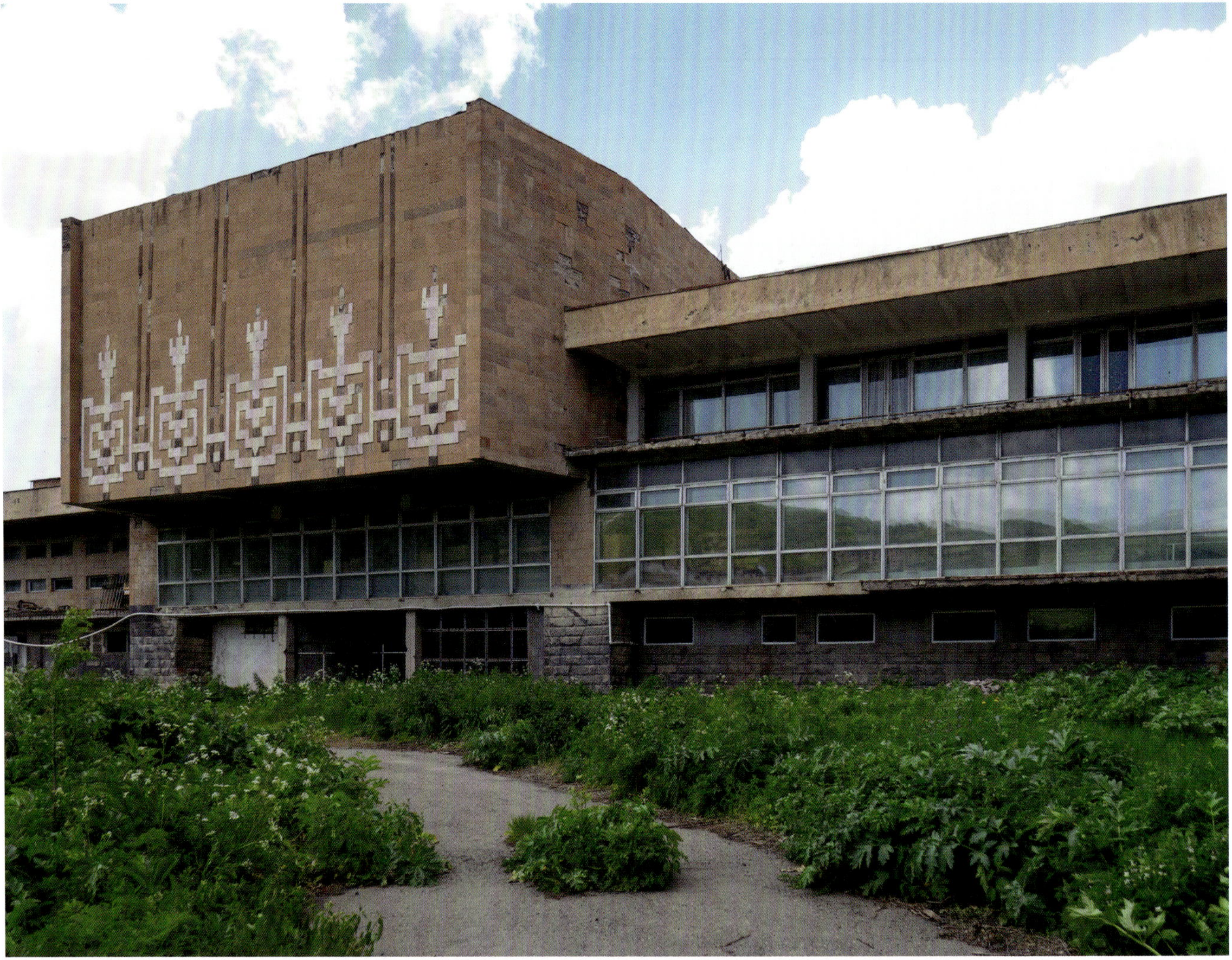

Sanatorium Gladzor, Jermuk, Armenia

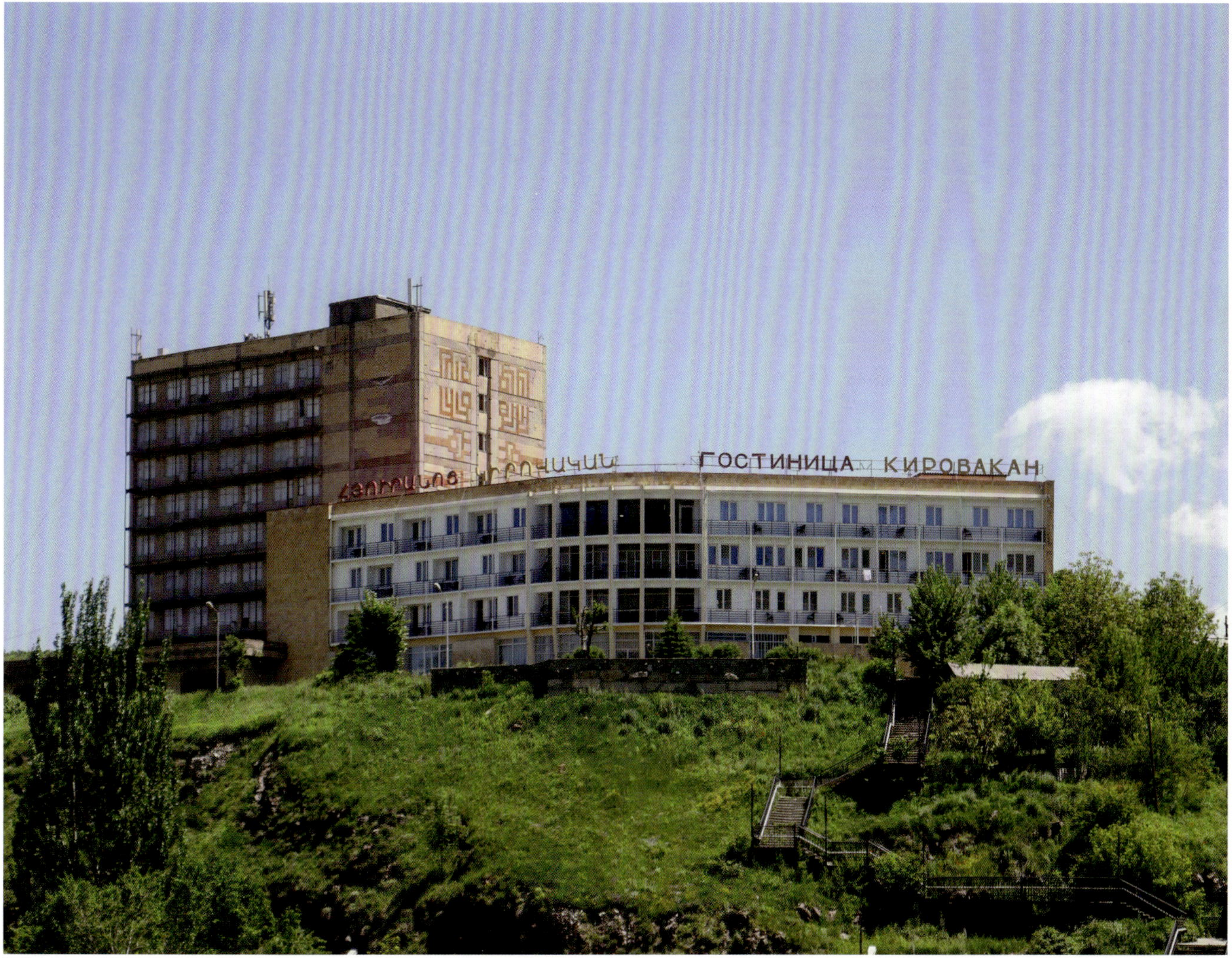

Hotel Kirovakan, Vanadzor, Armenia

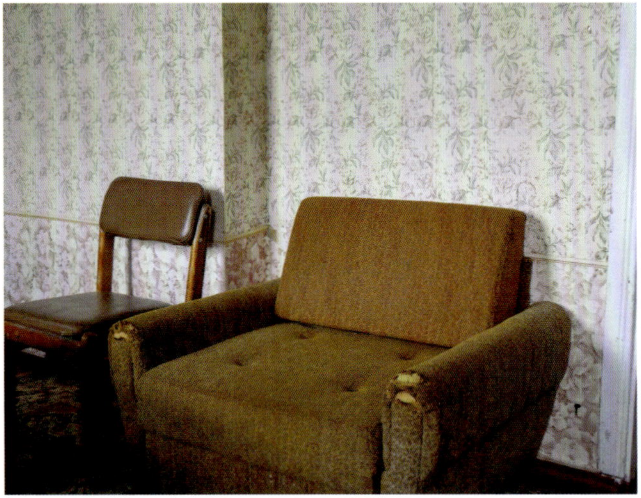
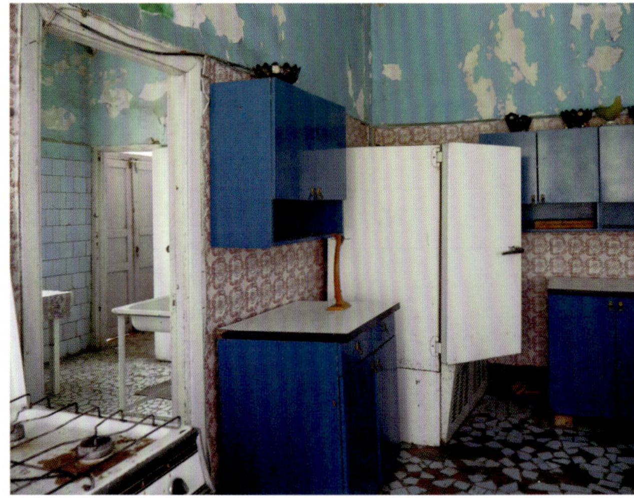
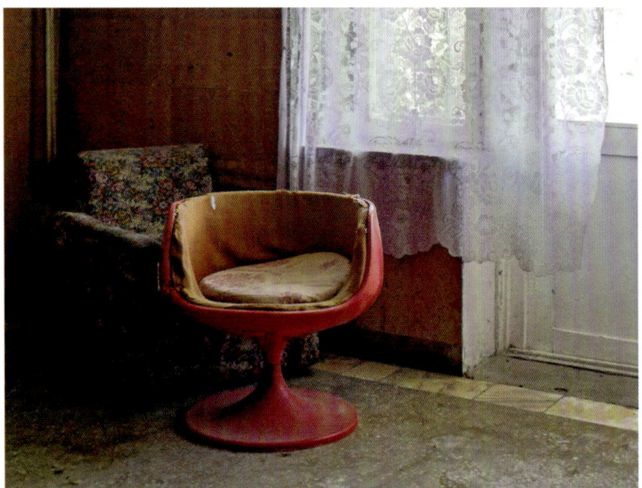
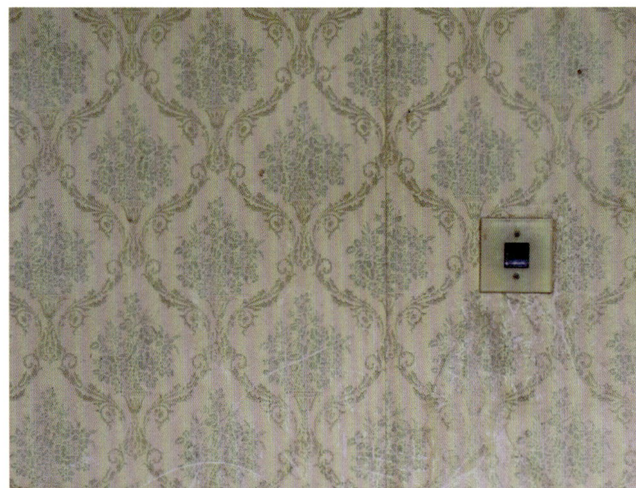

Hotel Karap, Marmarik, Armenia

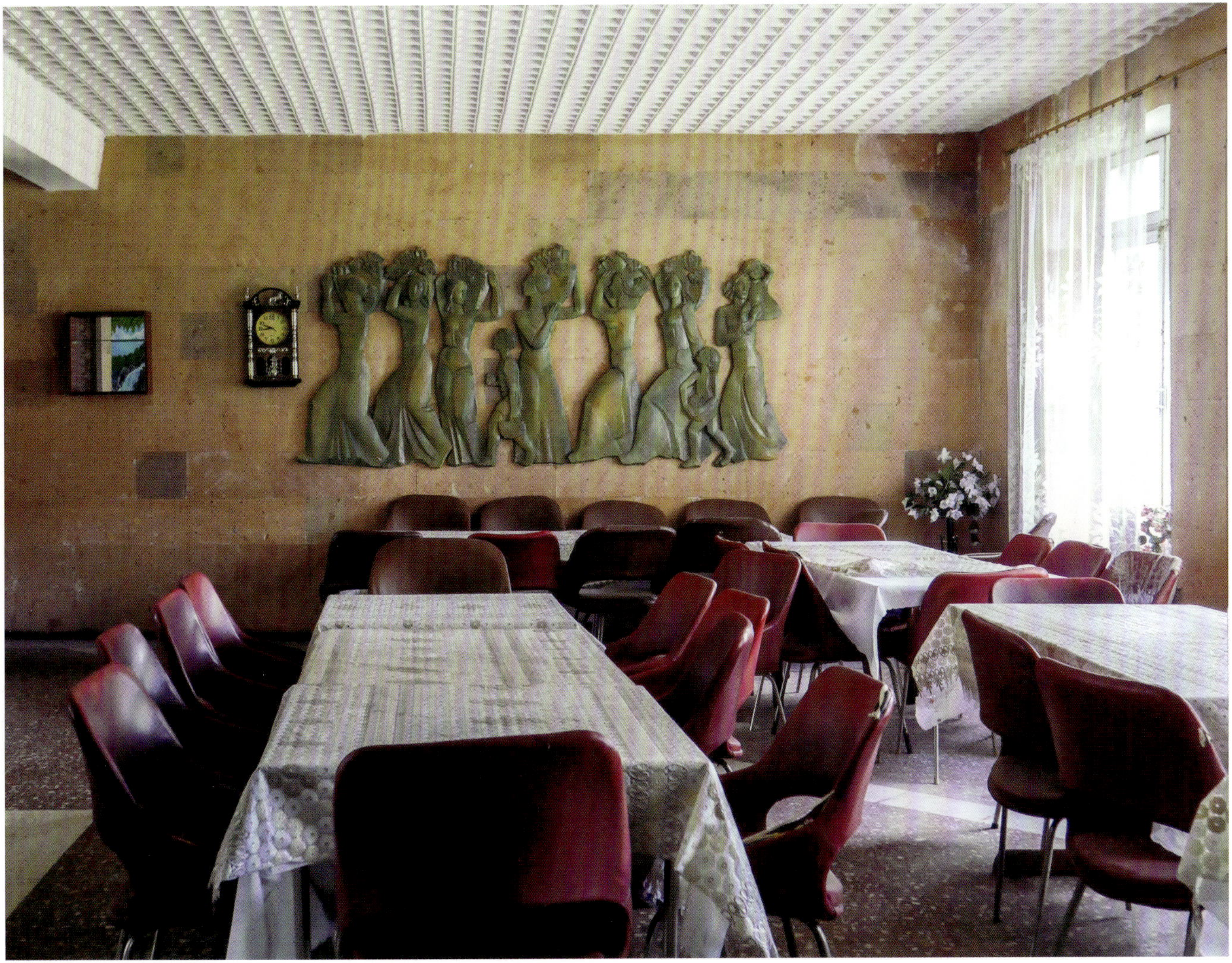

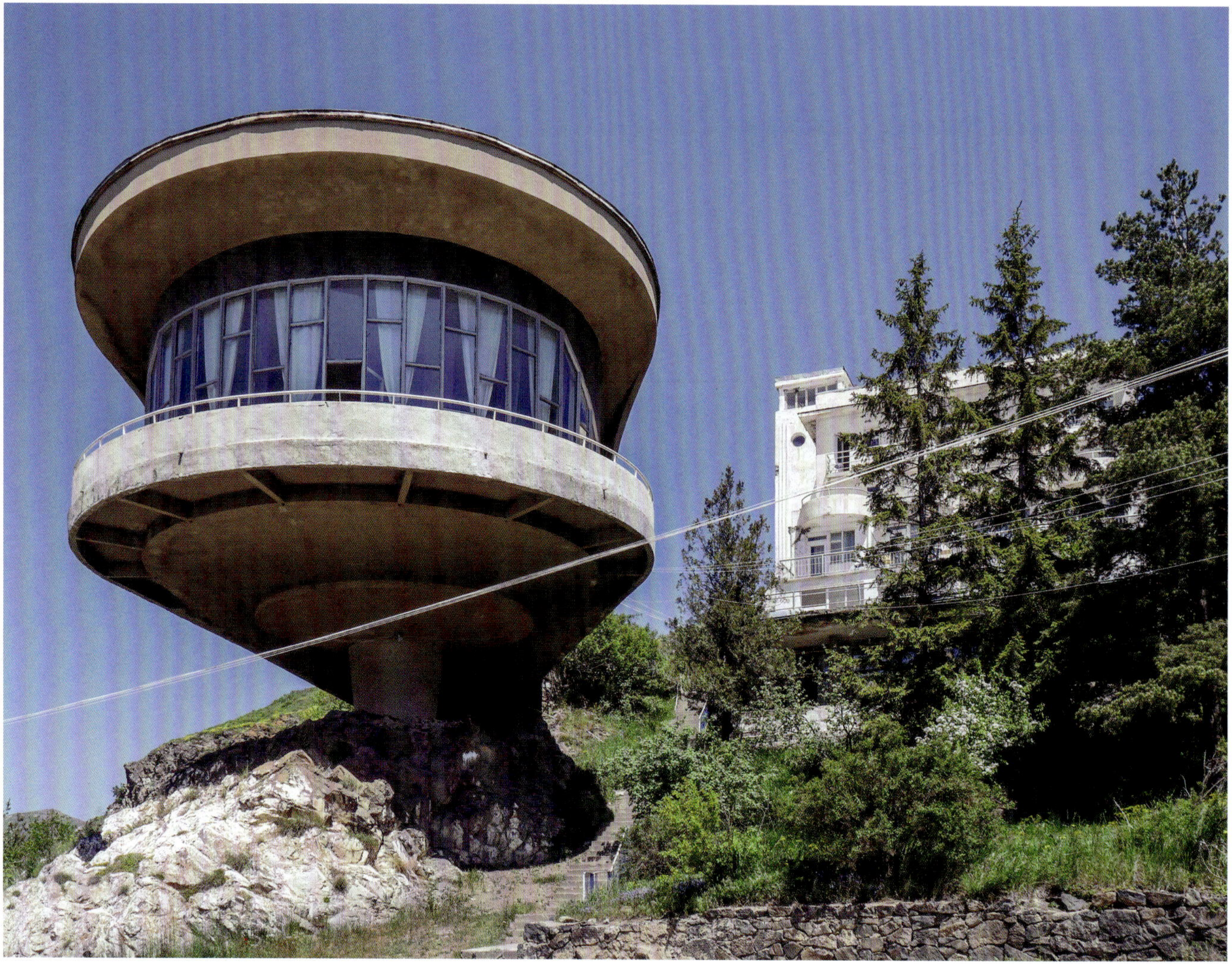

Sevan Writers' House, Sevan, Armenia

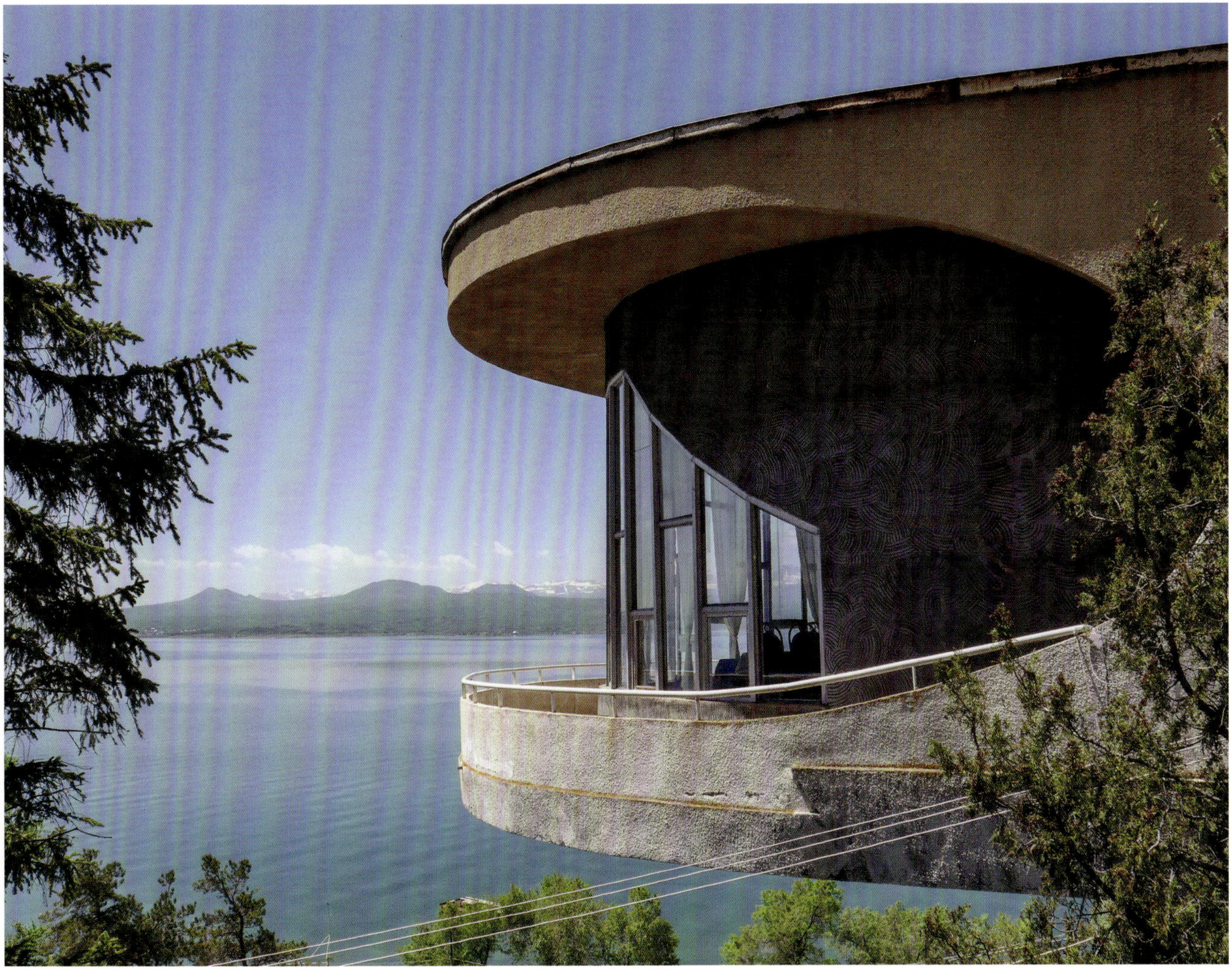

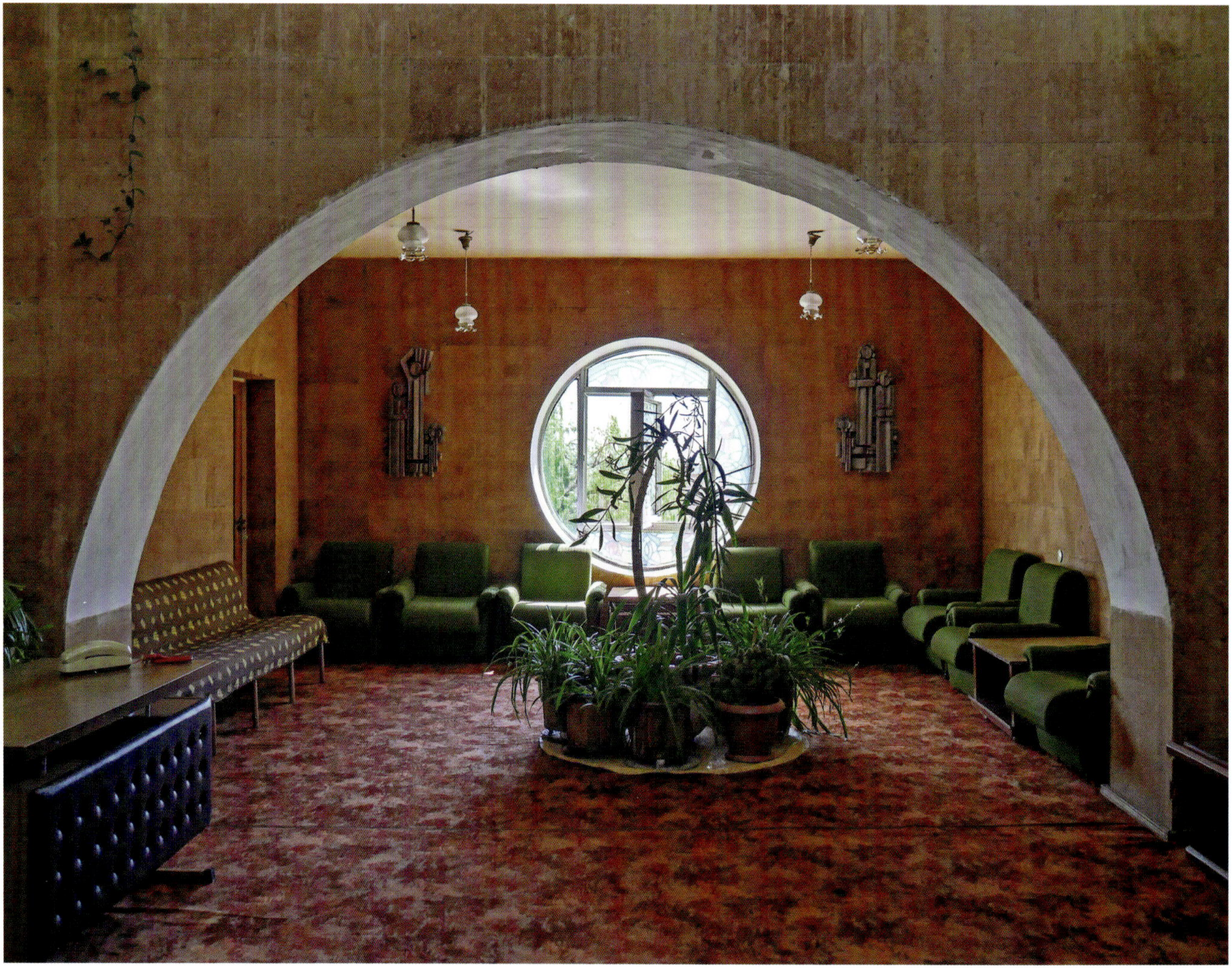

 Writers' House, Tsaghkadzor, Armenia

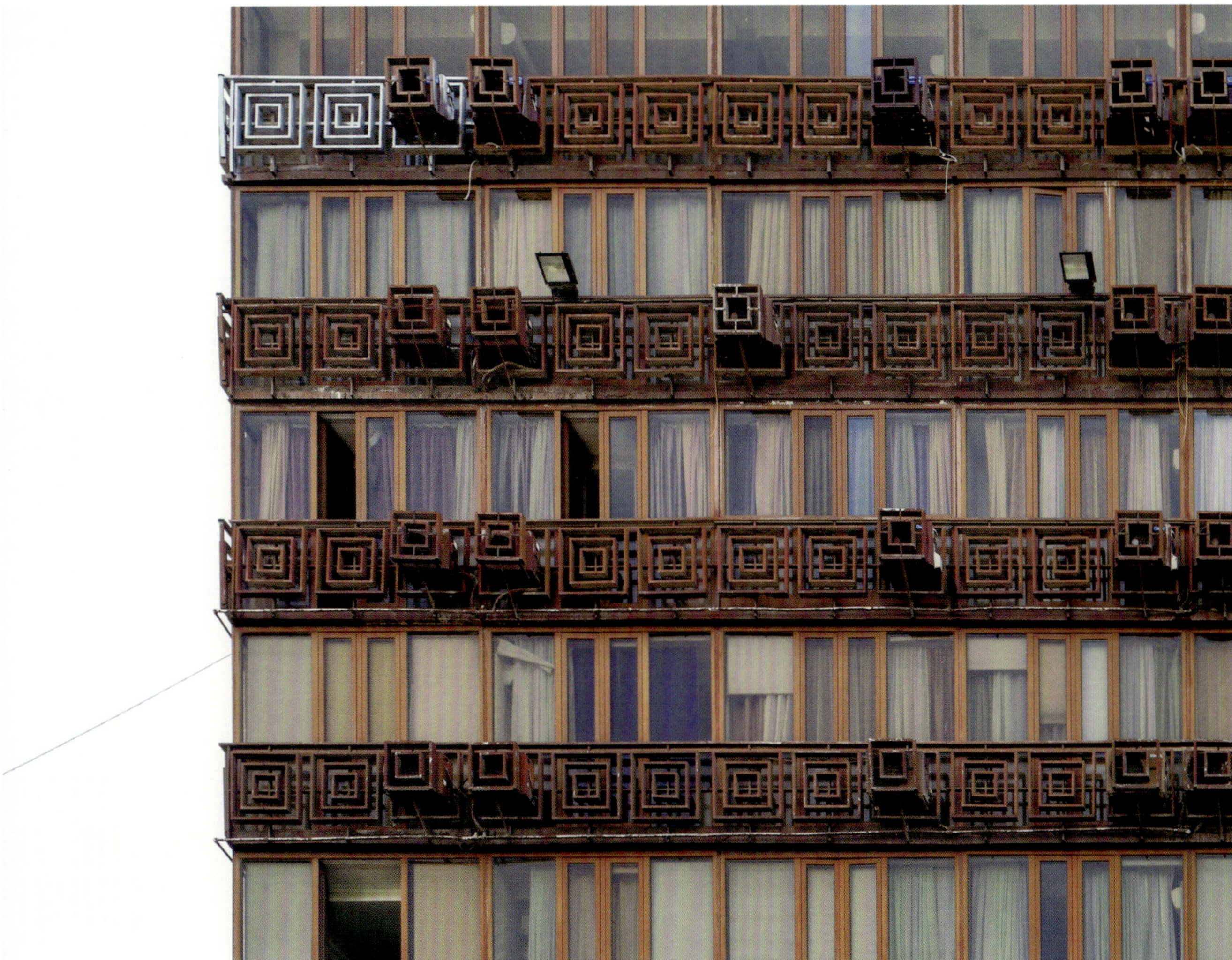

Hotel Shirak, Erevan, Armenia

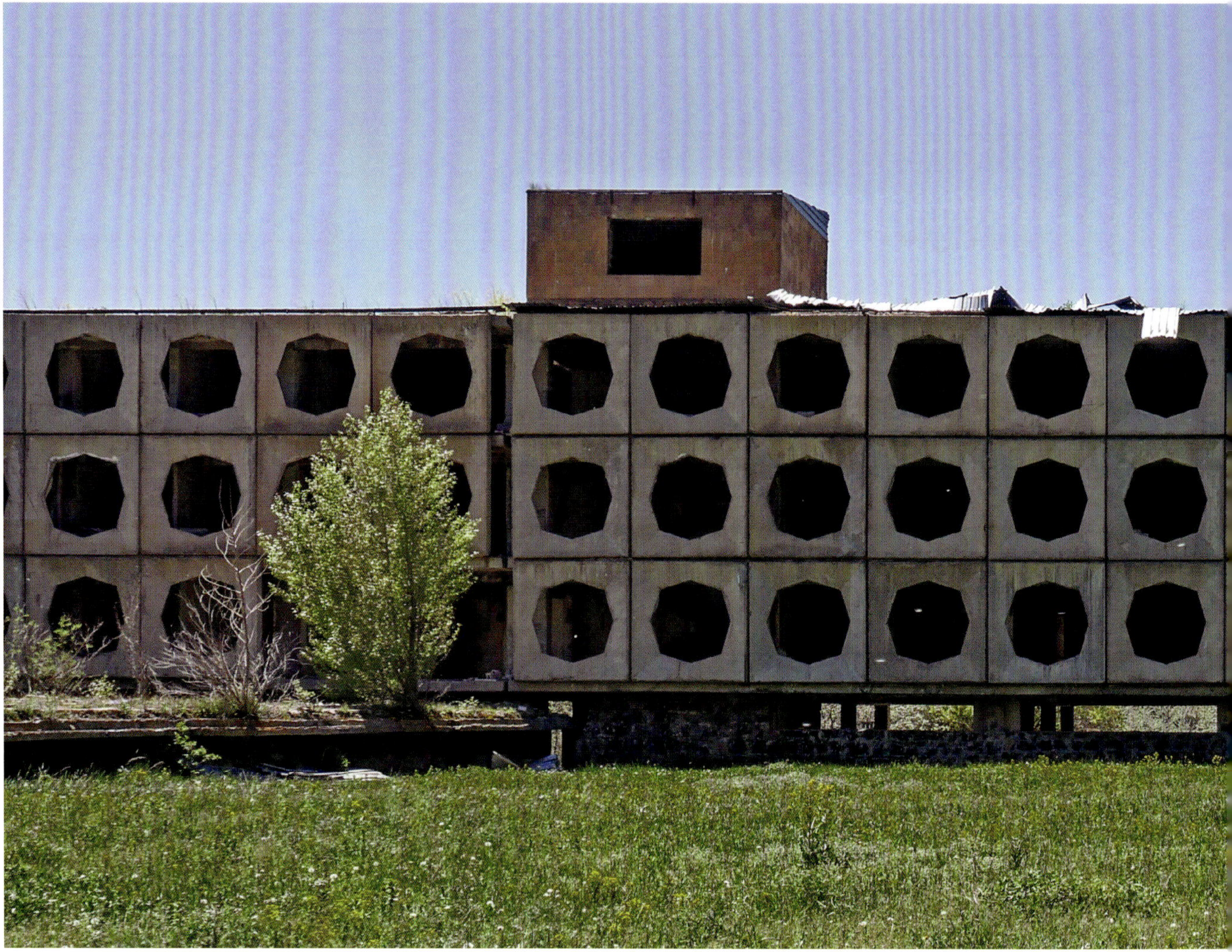

Hotel Avantgard (unfinished), Tsovagyugh, Armenia

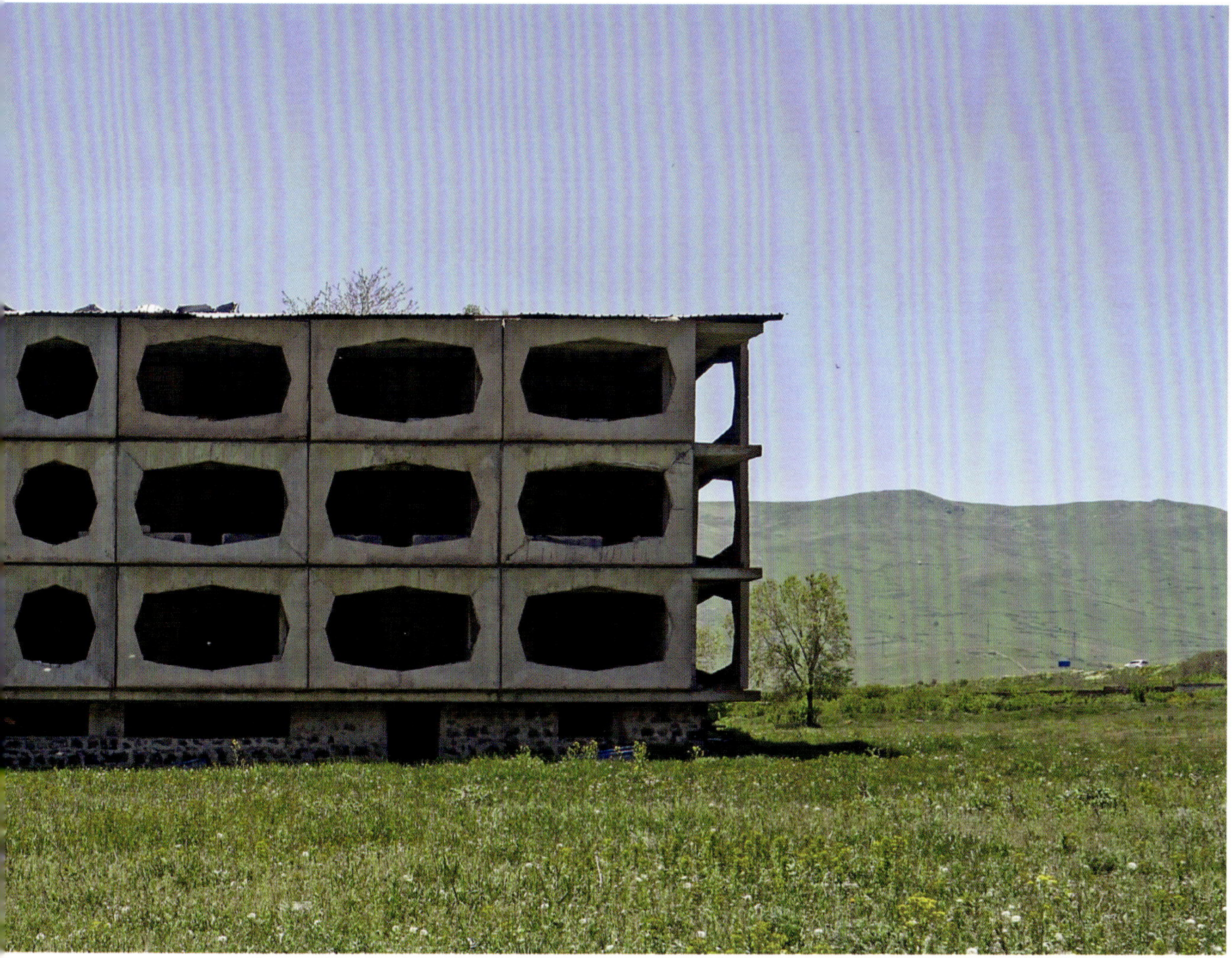

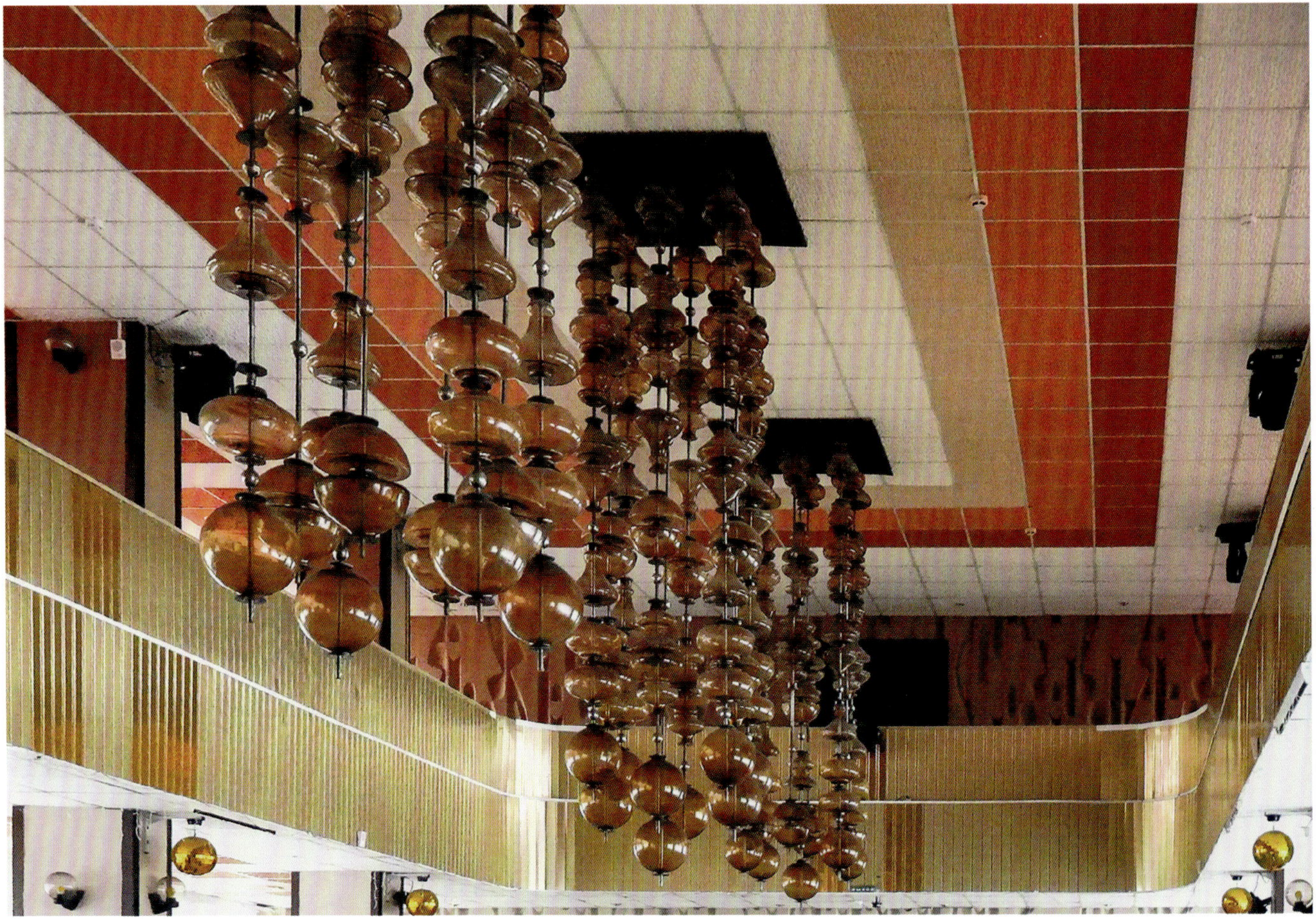

 Hotel Yubileynaya, Babruysk, Belarus

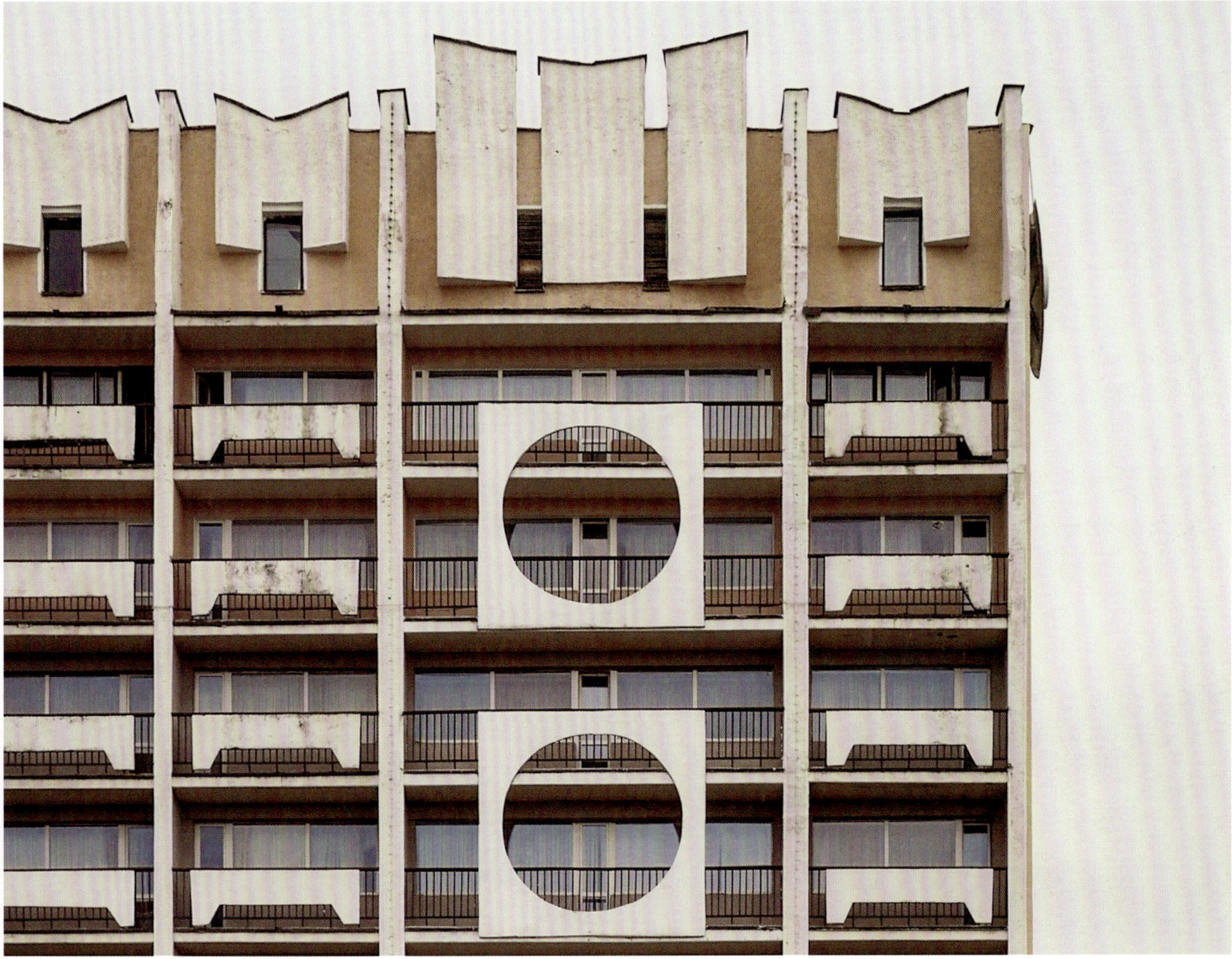

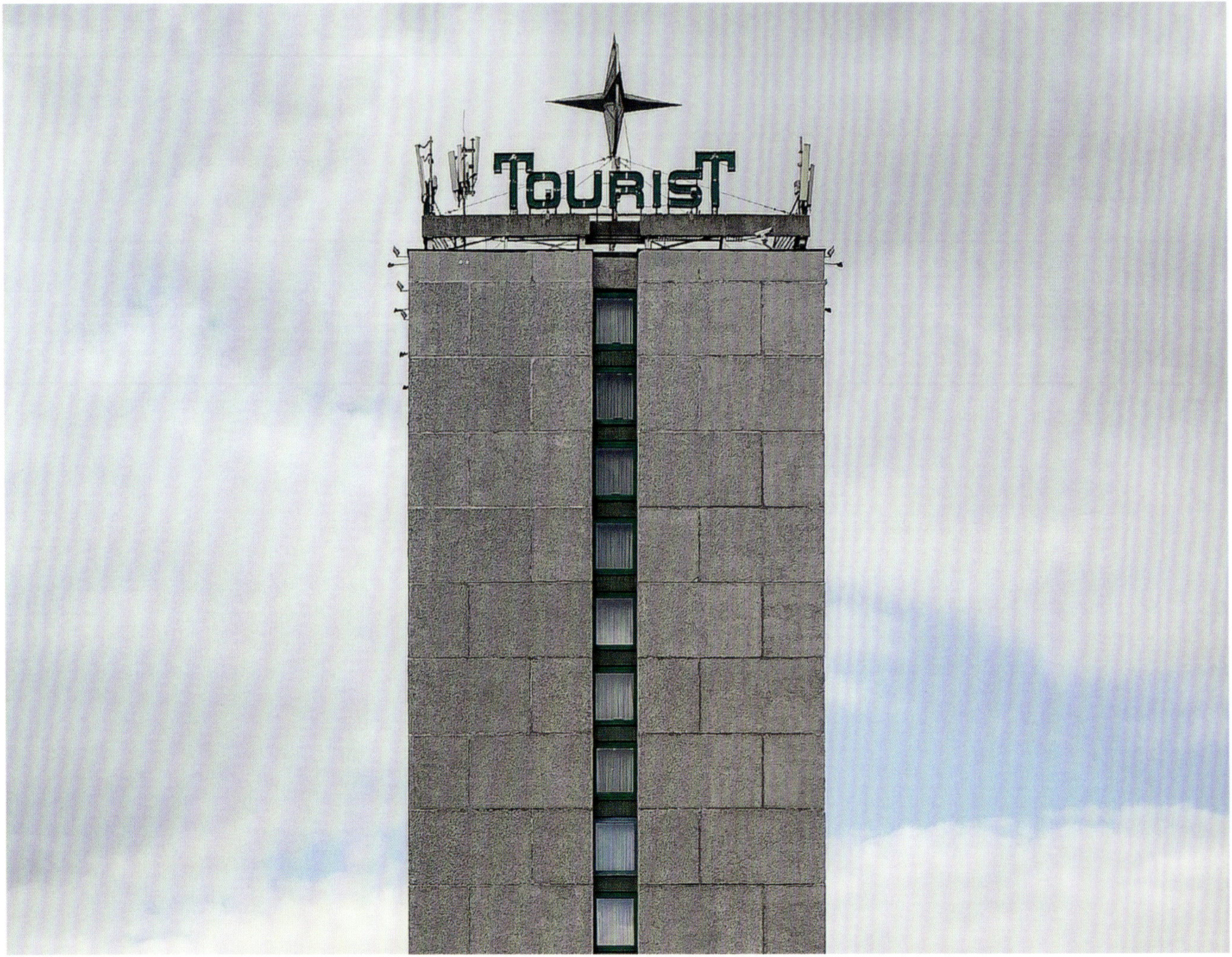

 Hotel Tourist, Minsk, Belarus

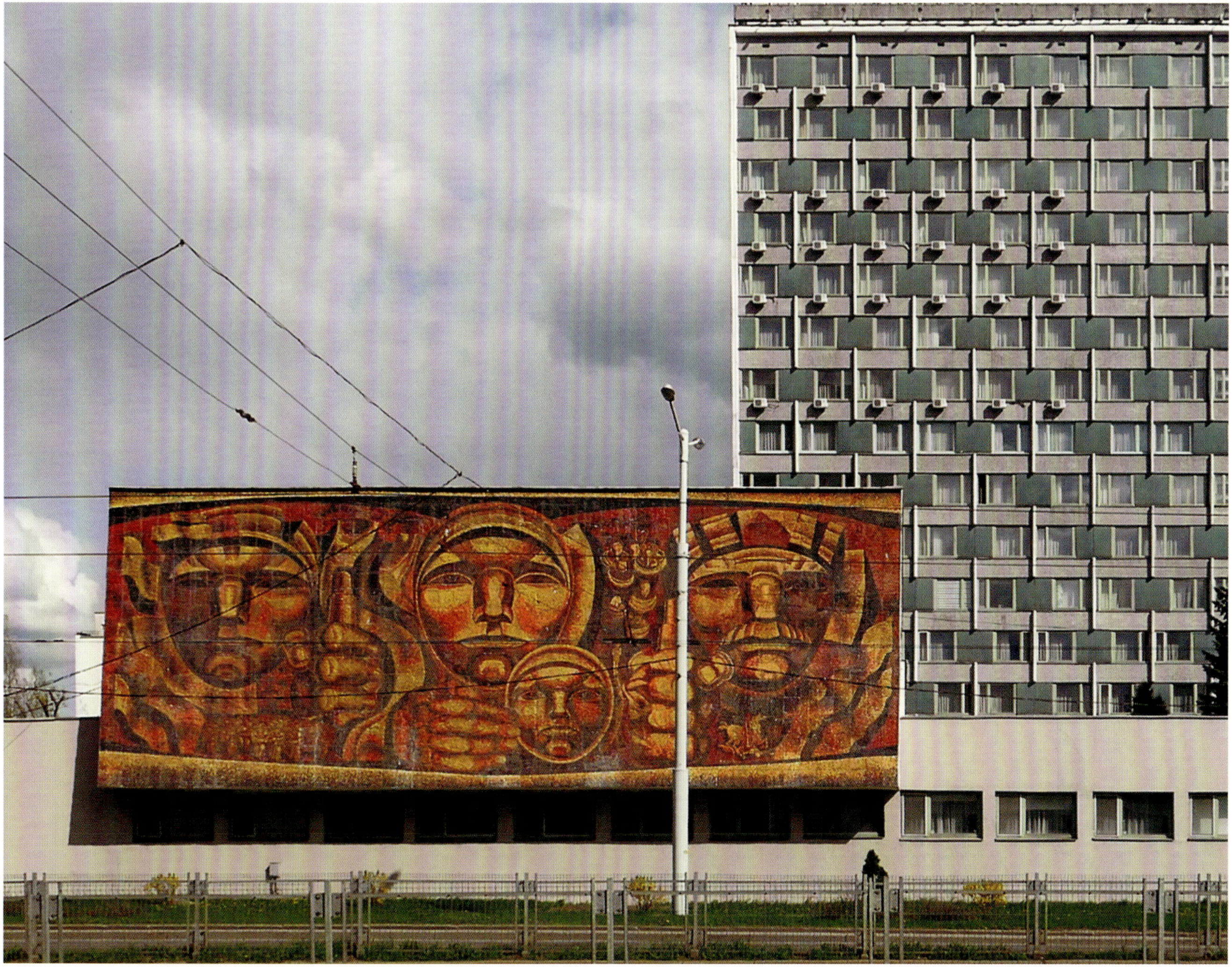

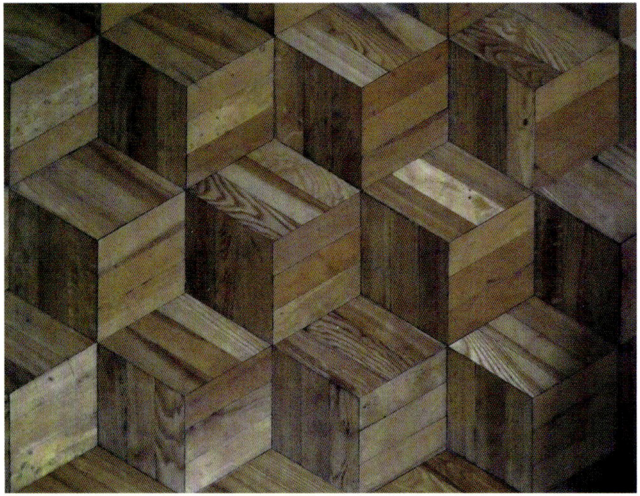

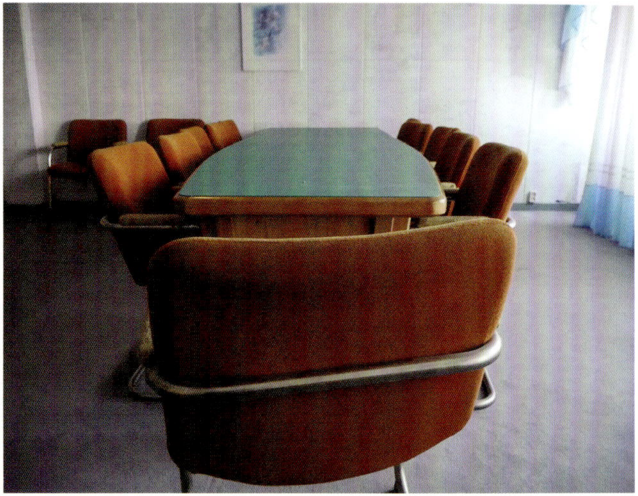

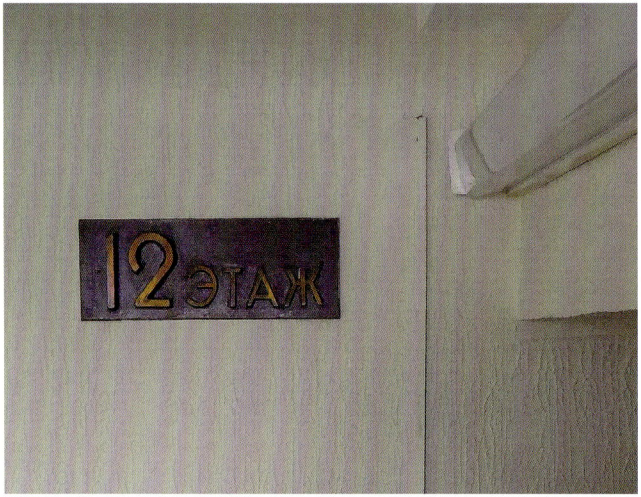

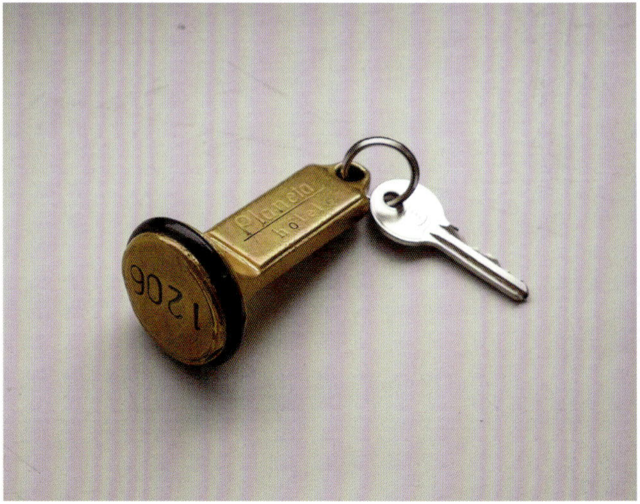

 Hotel Planeta, Minsk, Belarus

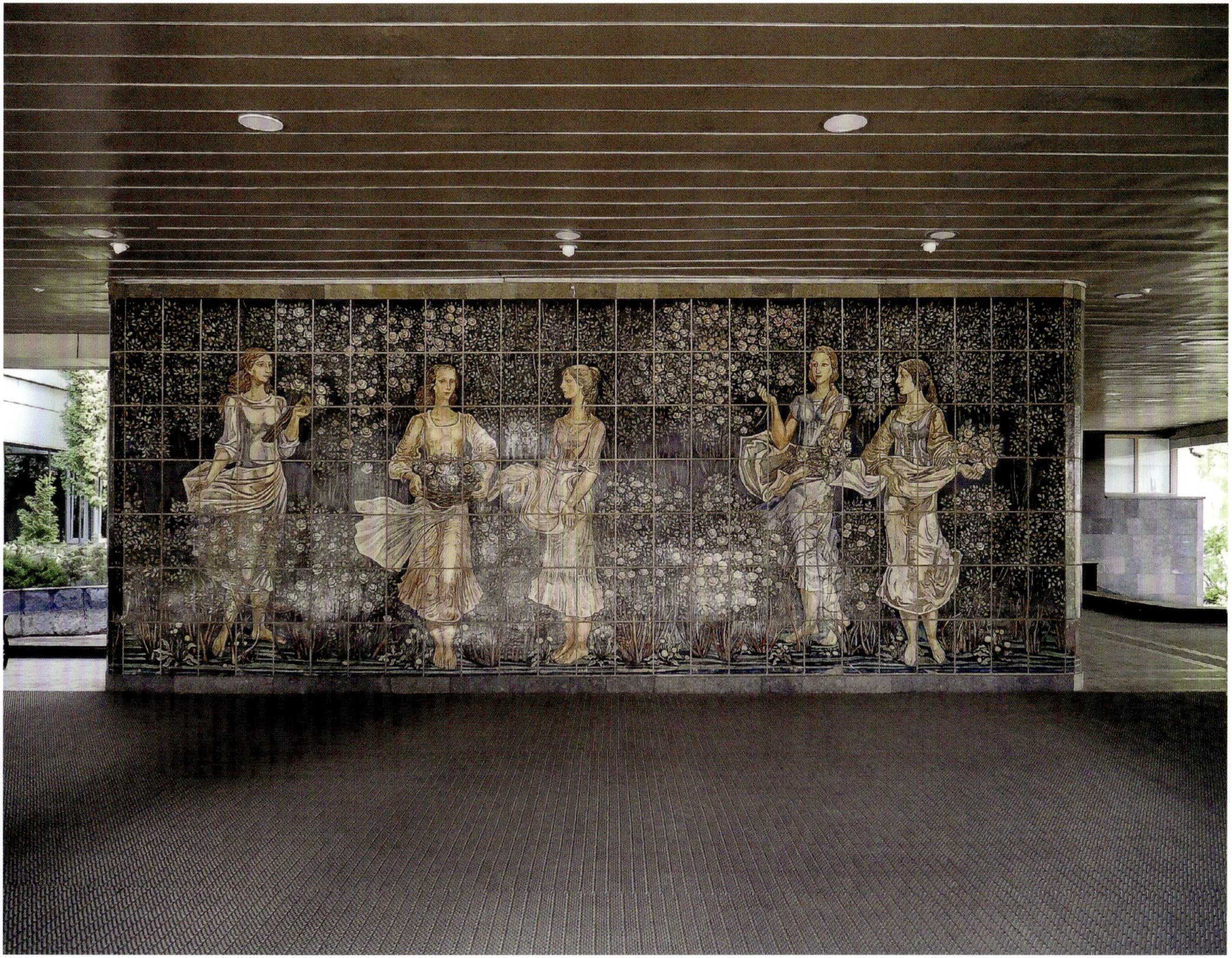

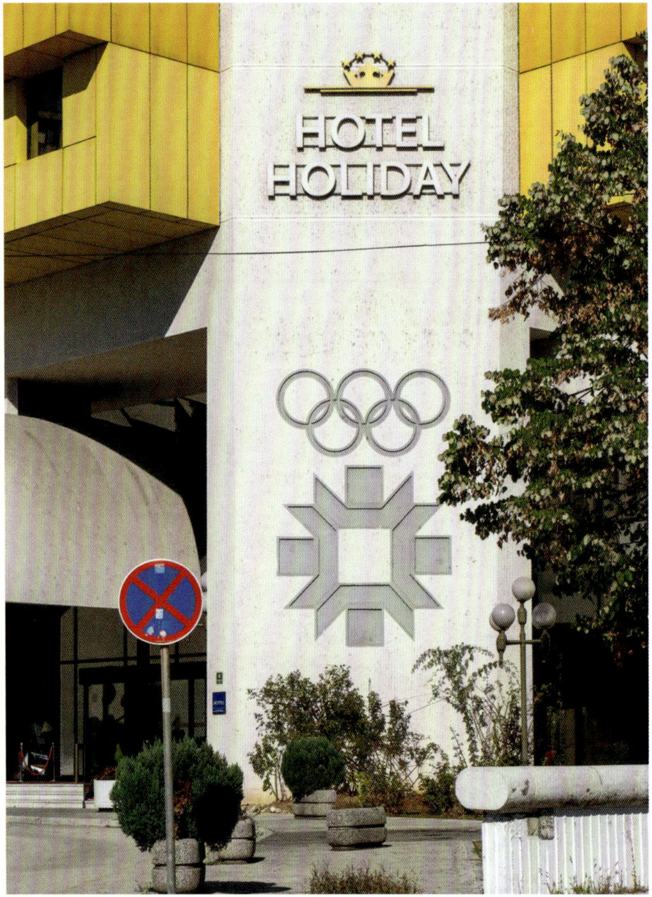

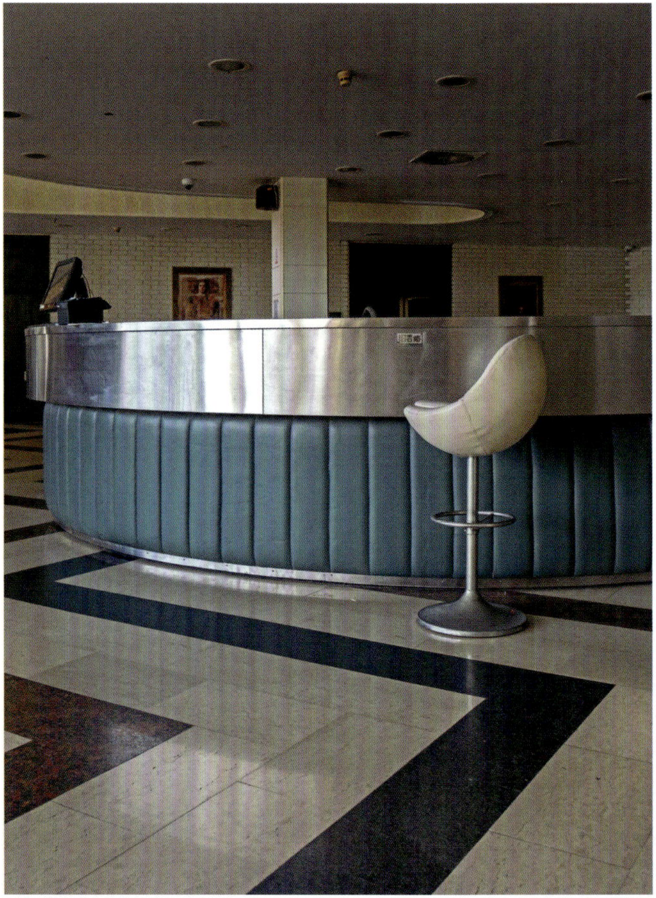

 Hotel Holiday (former Holiday Inn), Sarajevo, Bosnia and Herzegovina

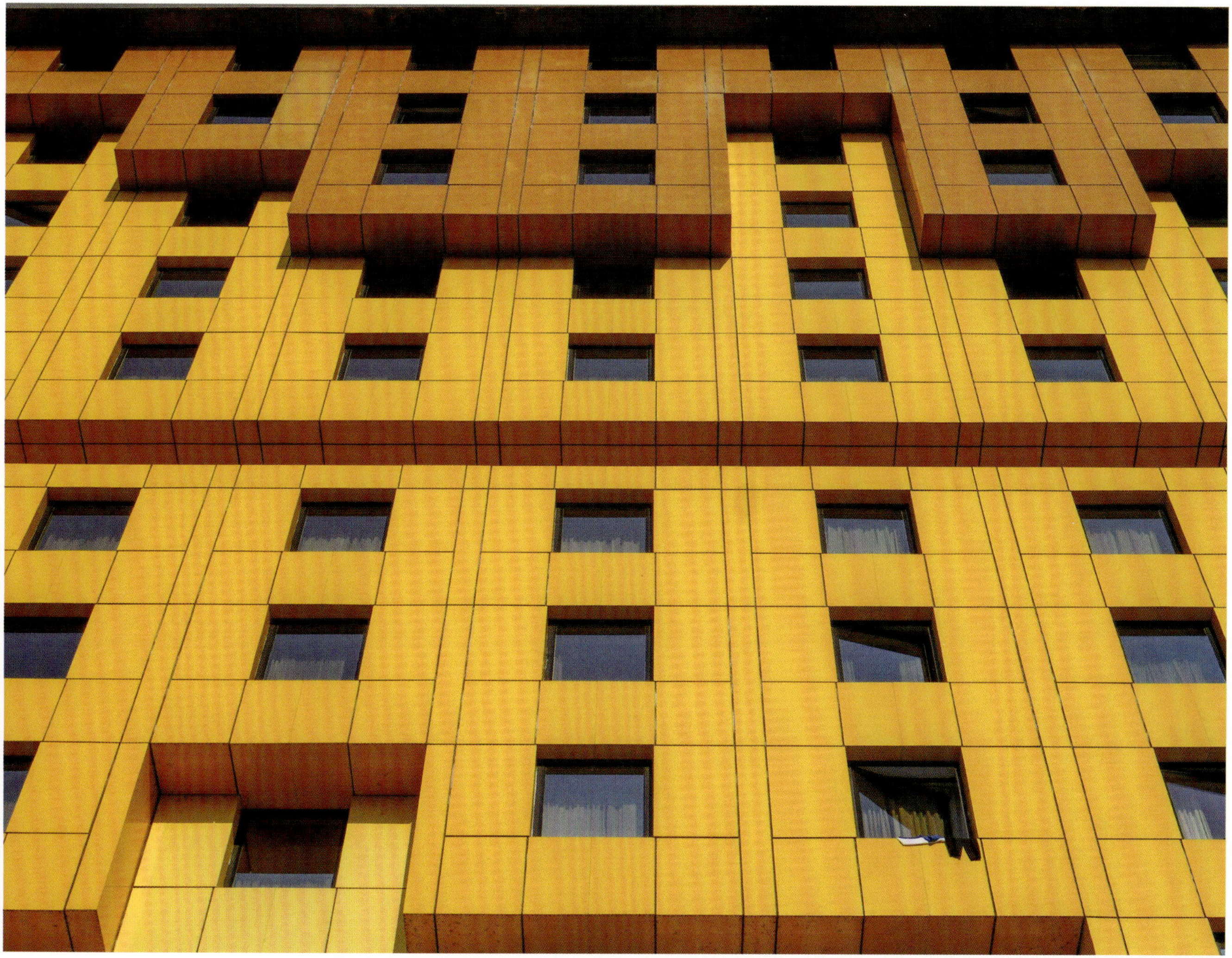

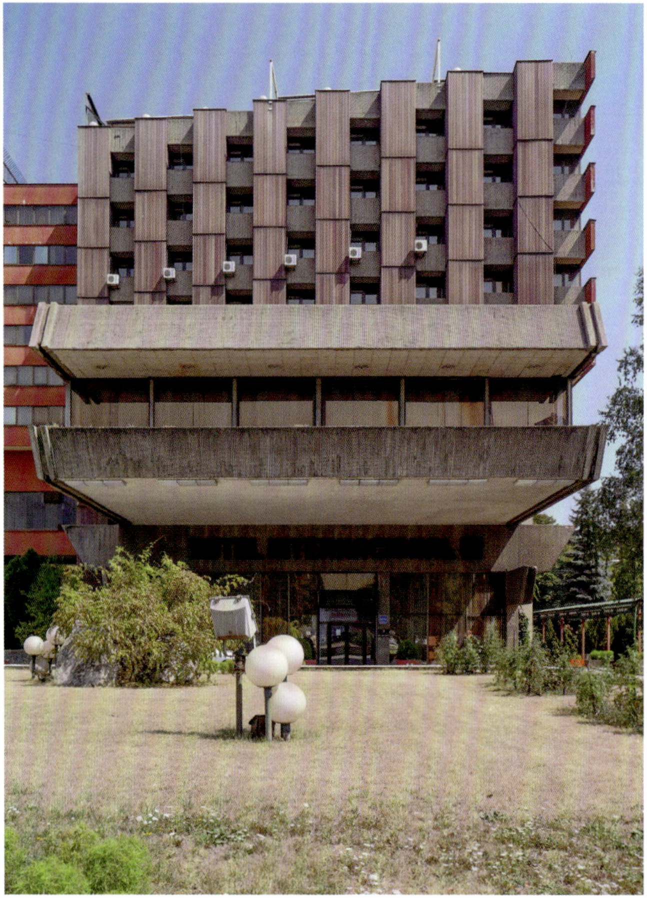

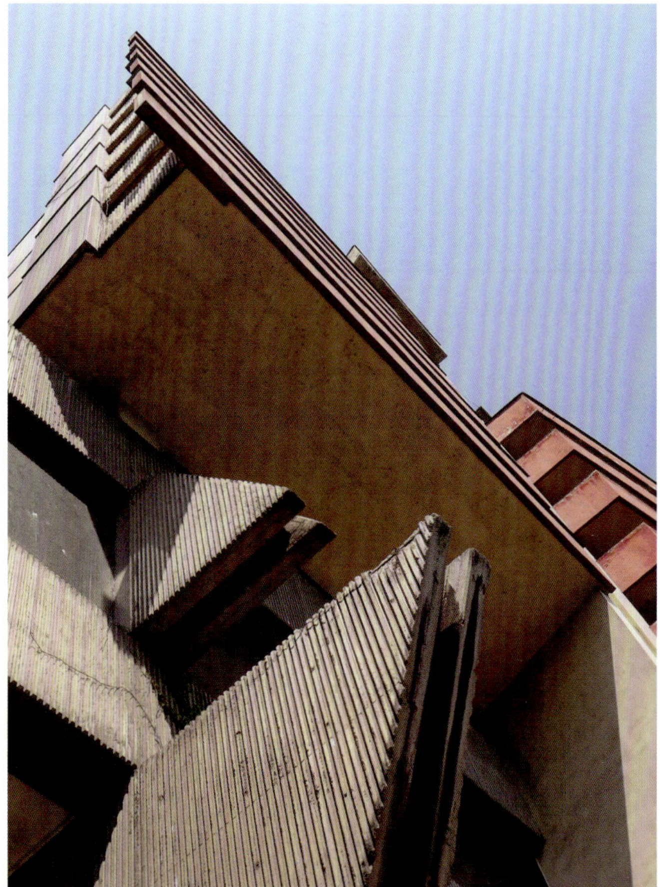

 Hotel Internacional, Zenica, Bosnia and Herzegovina

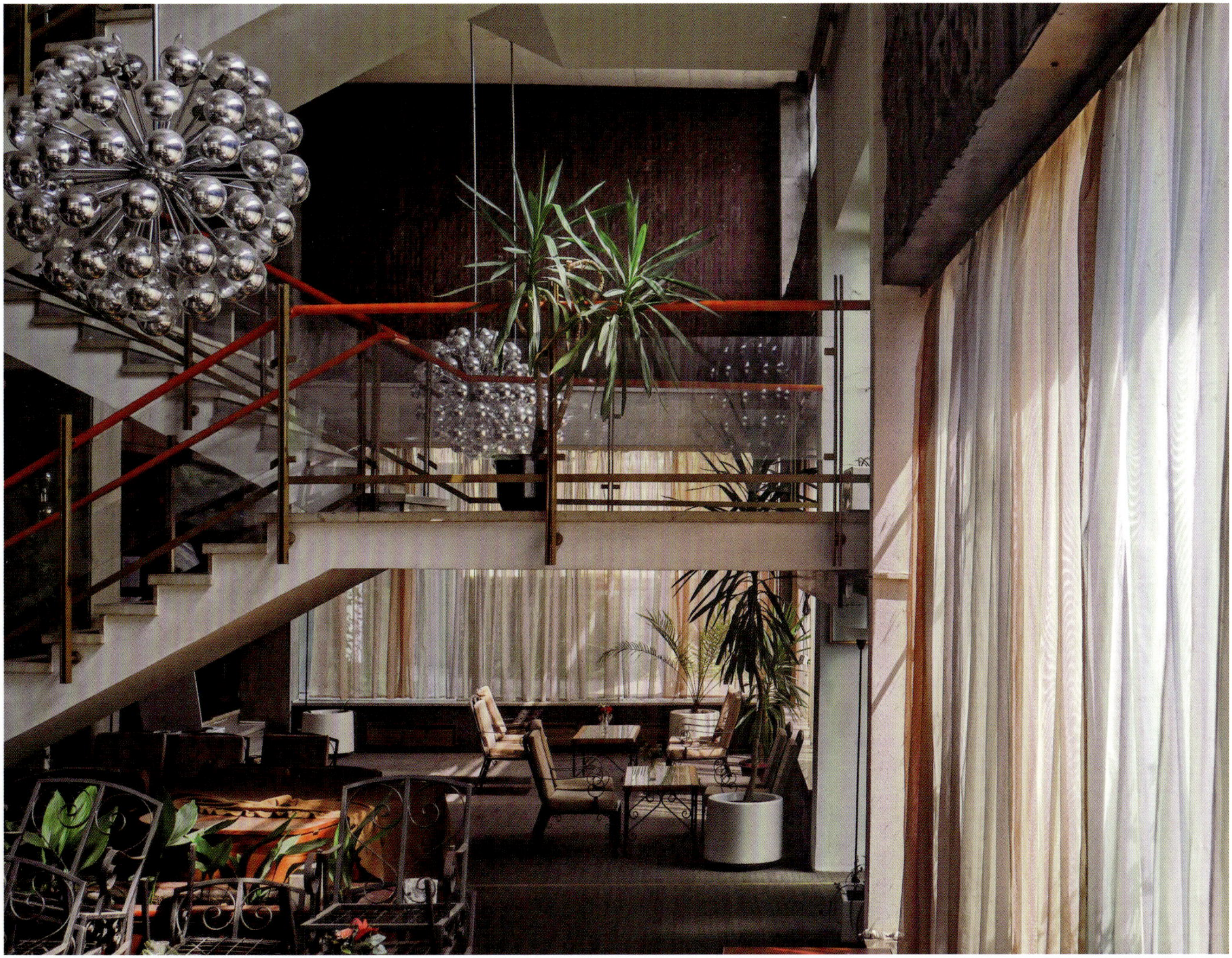

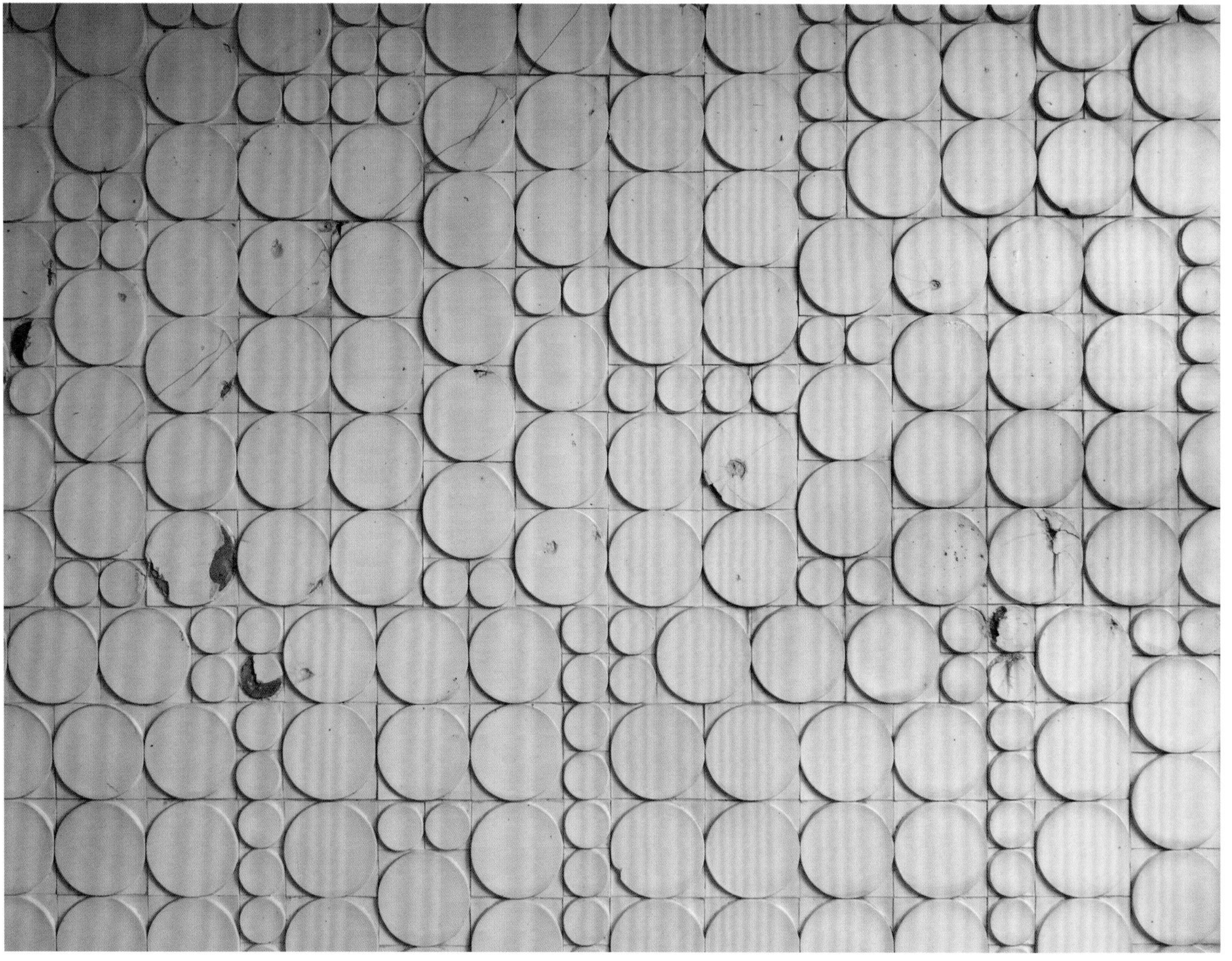

 Hotel Jajce, Jajce, Bosnia and Herzegovina

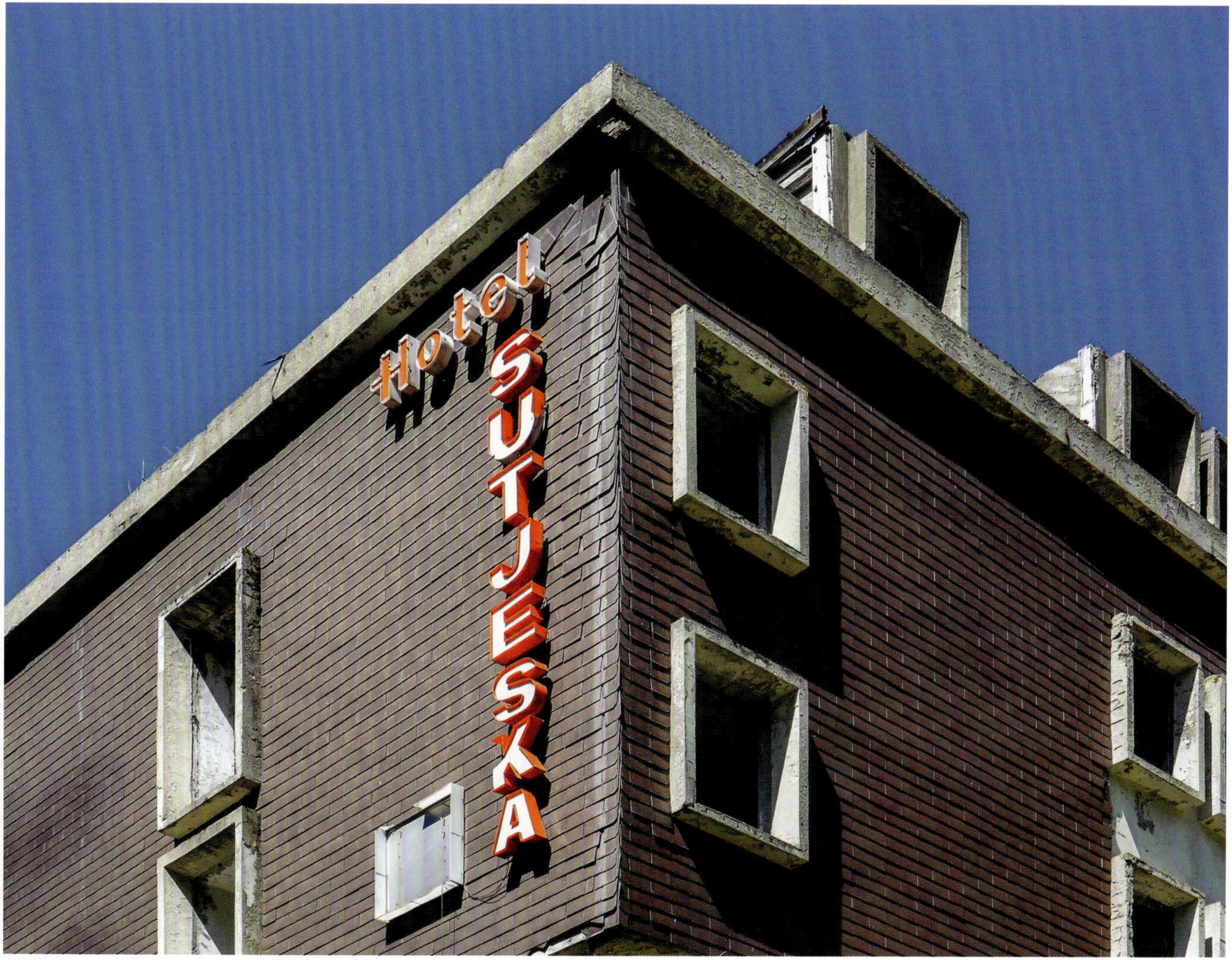

Hotel Sutjeska, Tjentište, Bosnia and Herzegovina

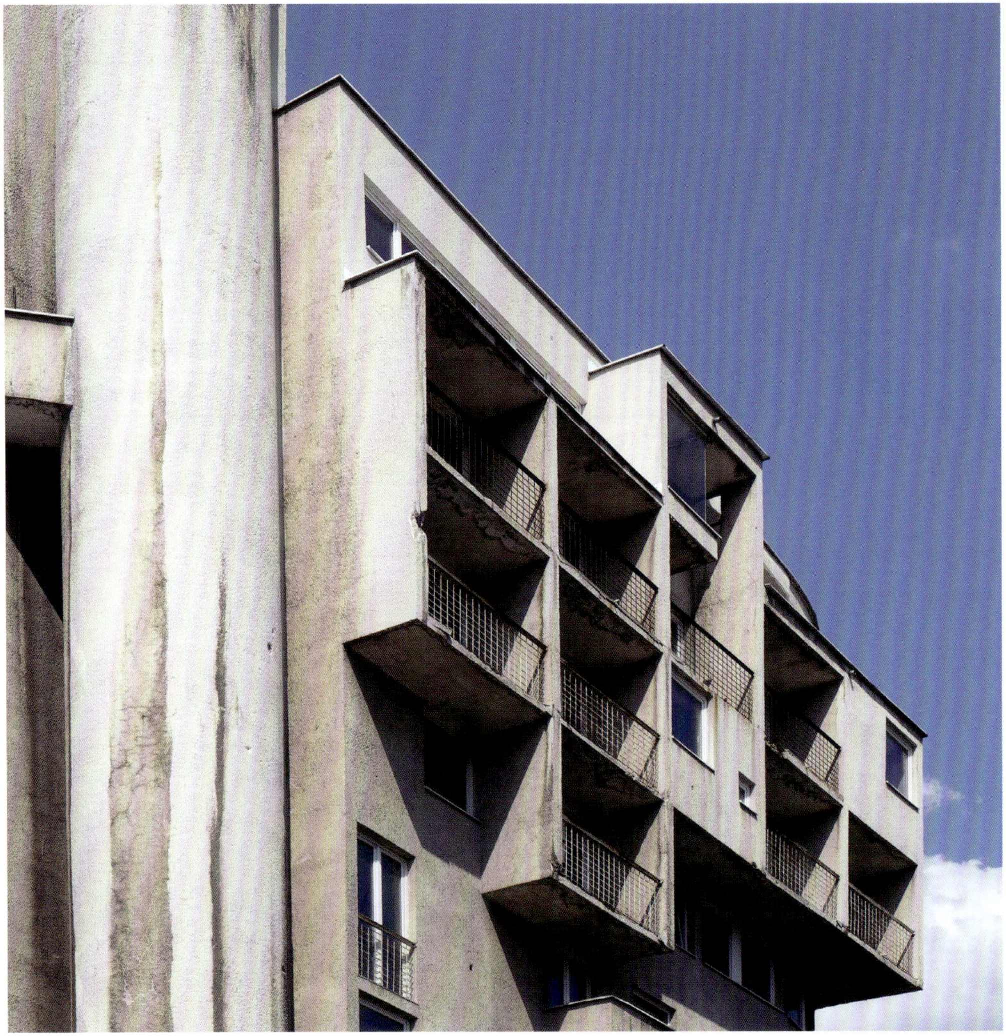

 Hotel Visoko, Visoko, Bosnia and Herzegovina

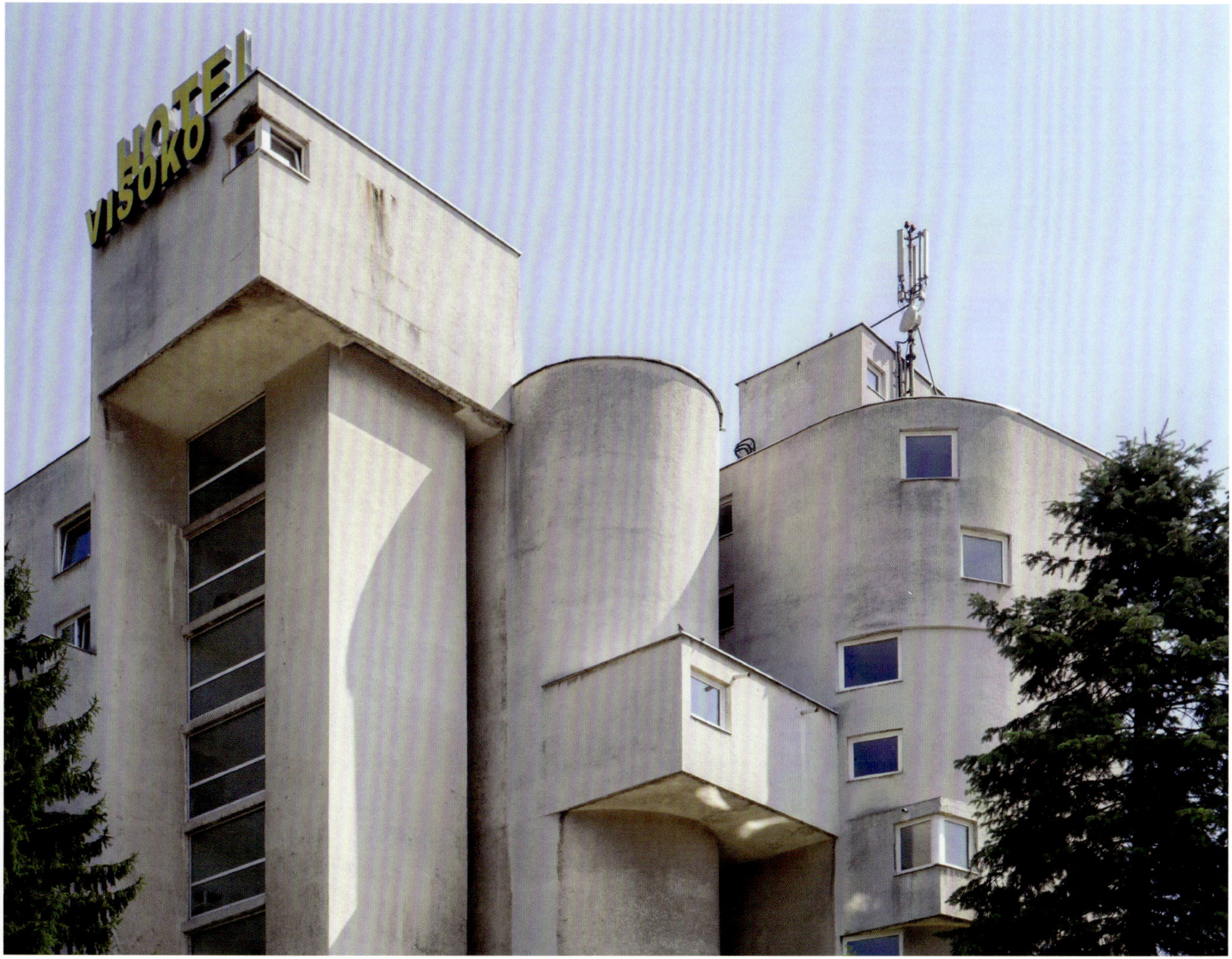
HOTEL
VISOKO

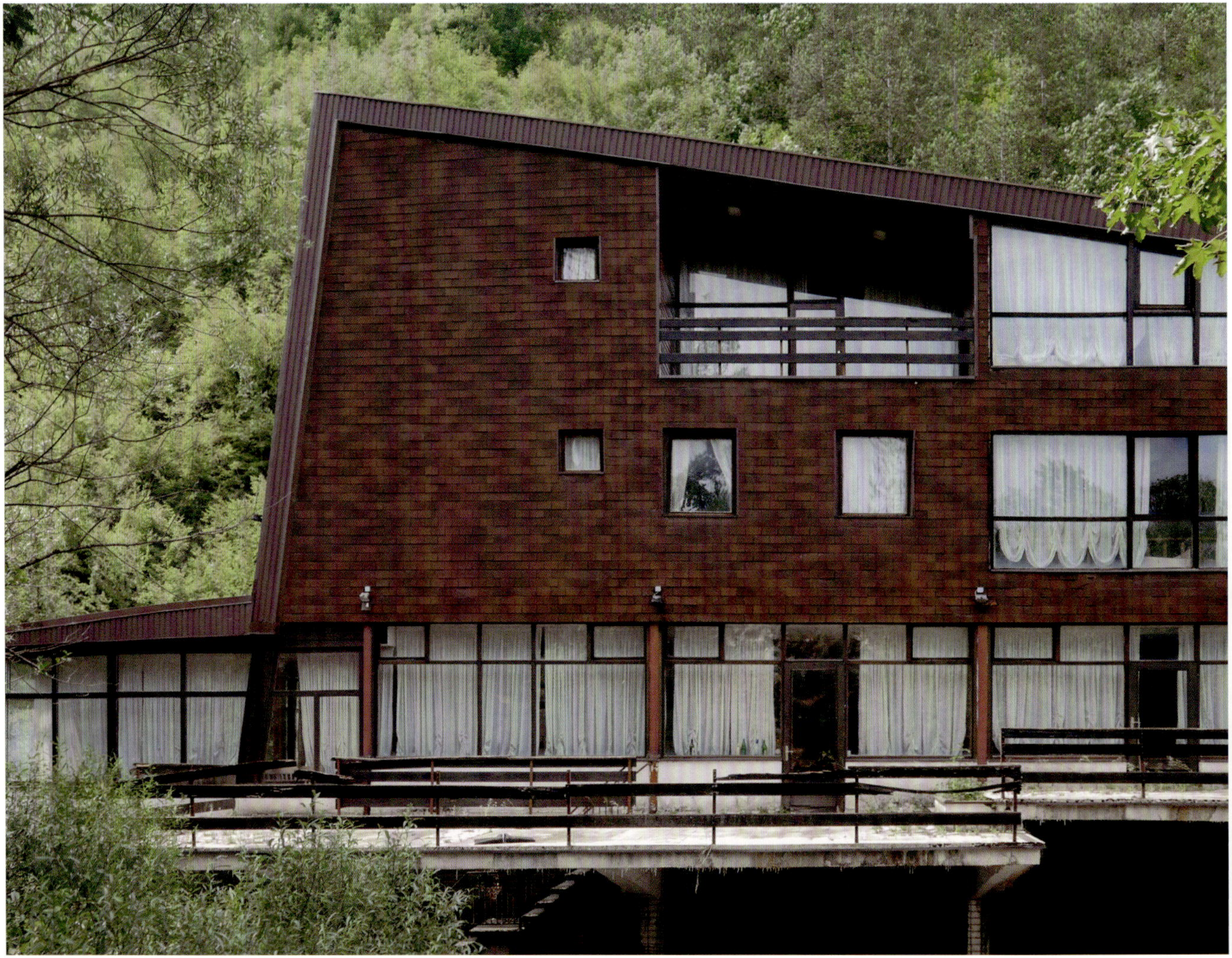

 Hotel Bastasi (former Motel Bastašica), Bastasi, Bosnia and Herzegovina

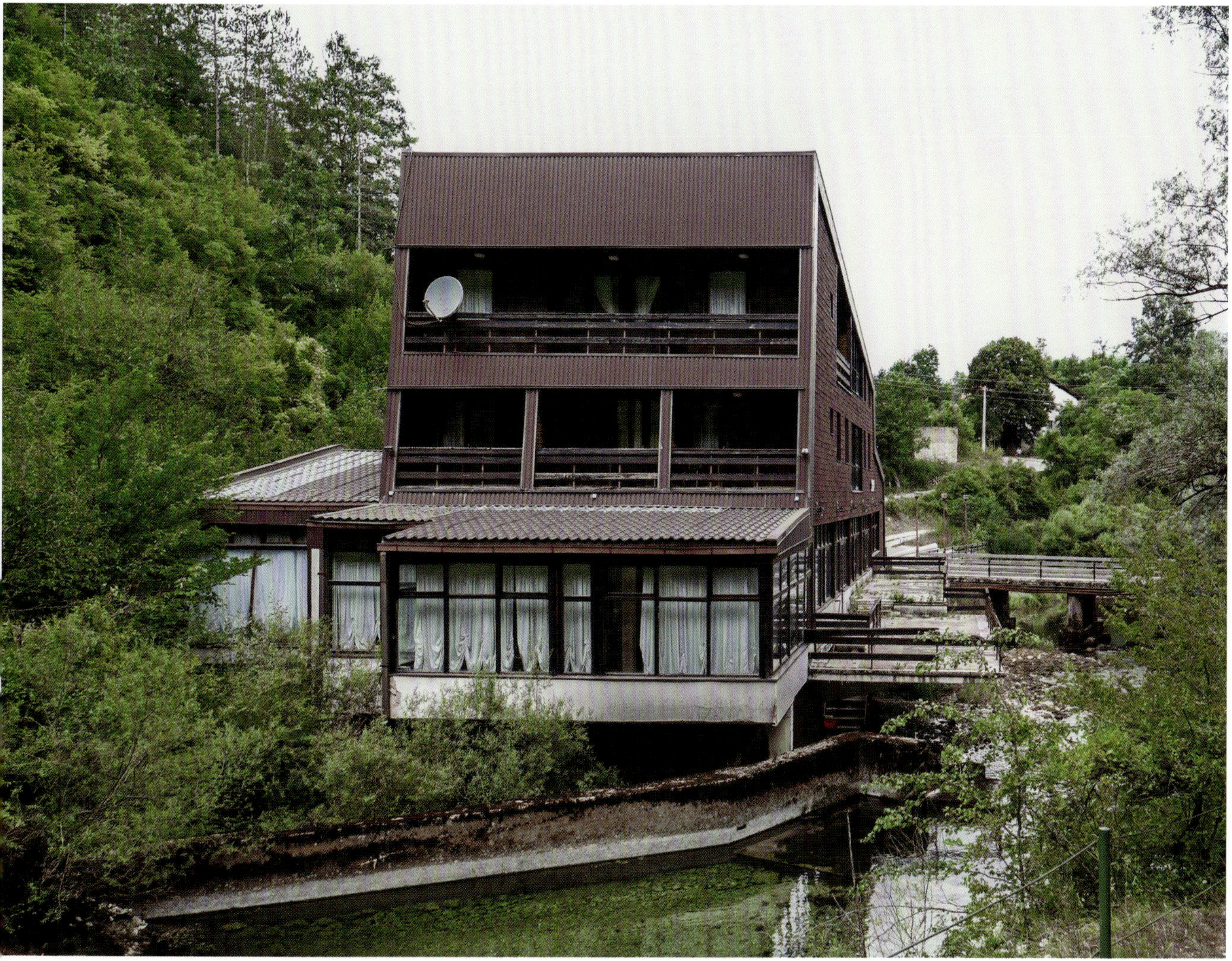

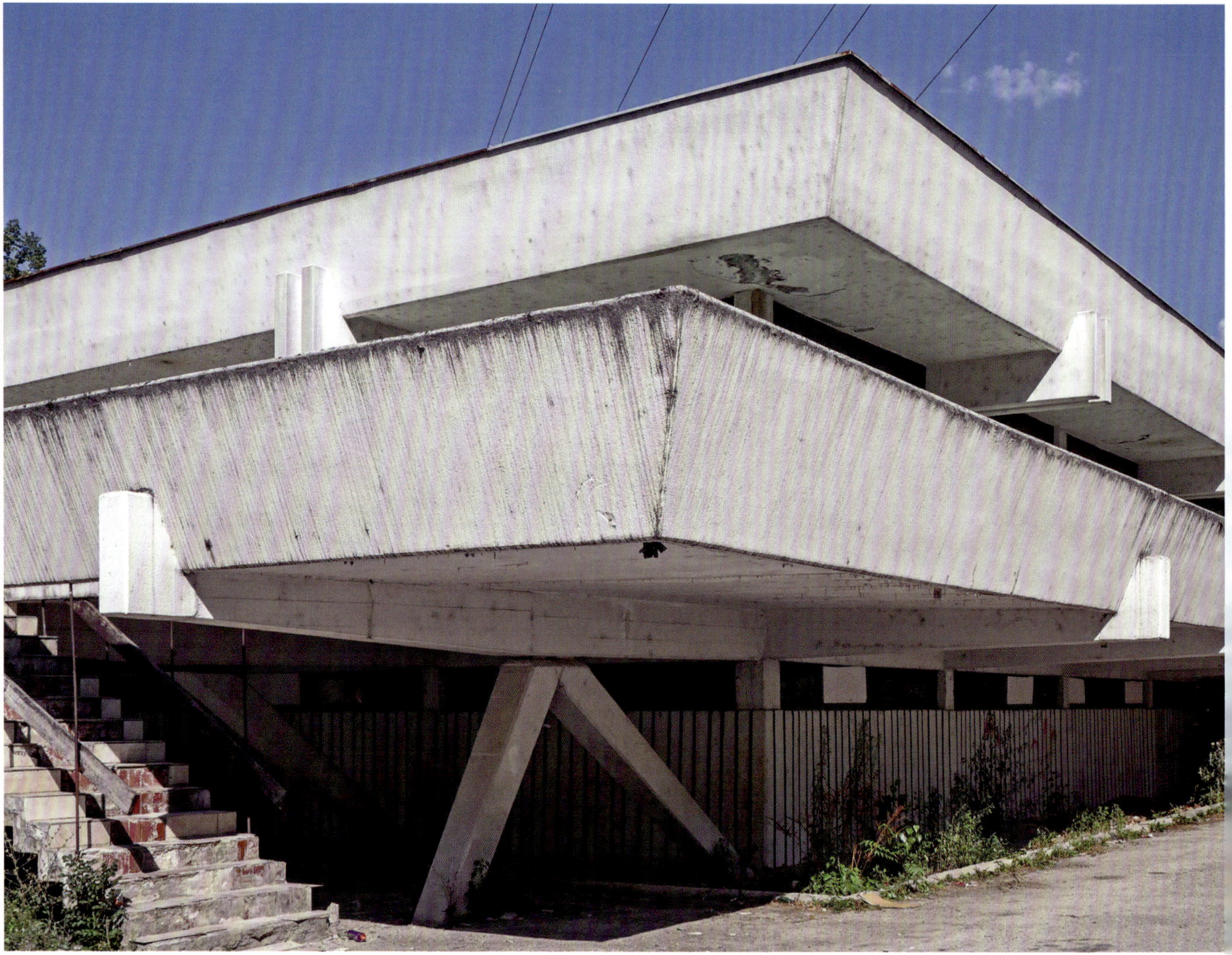

 Motel Konjic, Konjic, Bosnia and Herzegovina

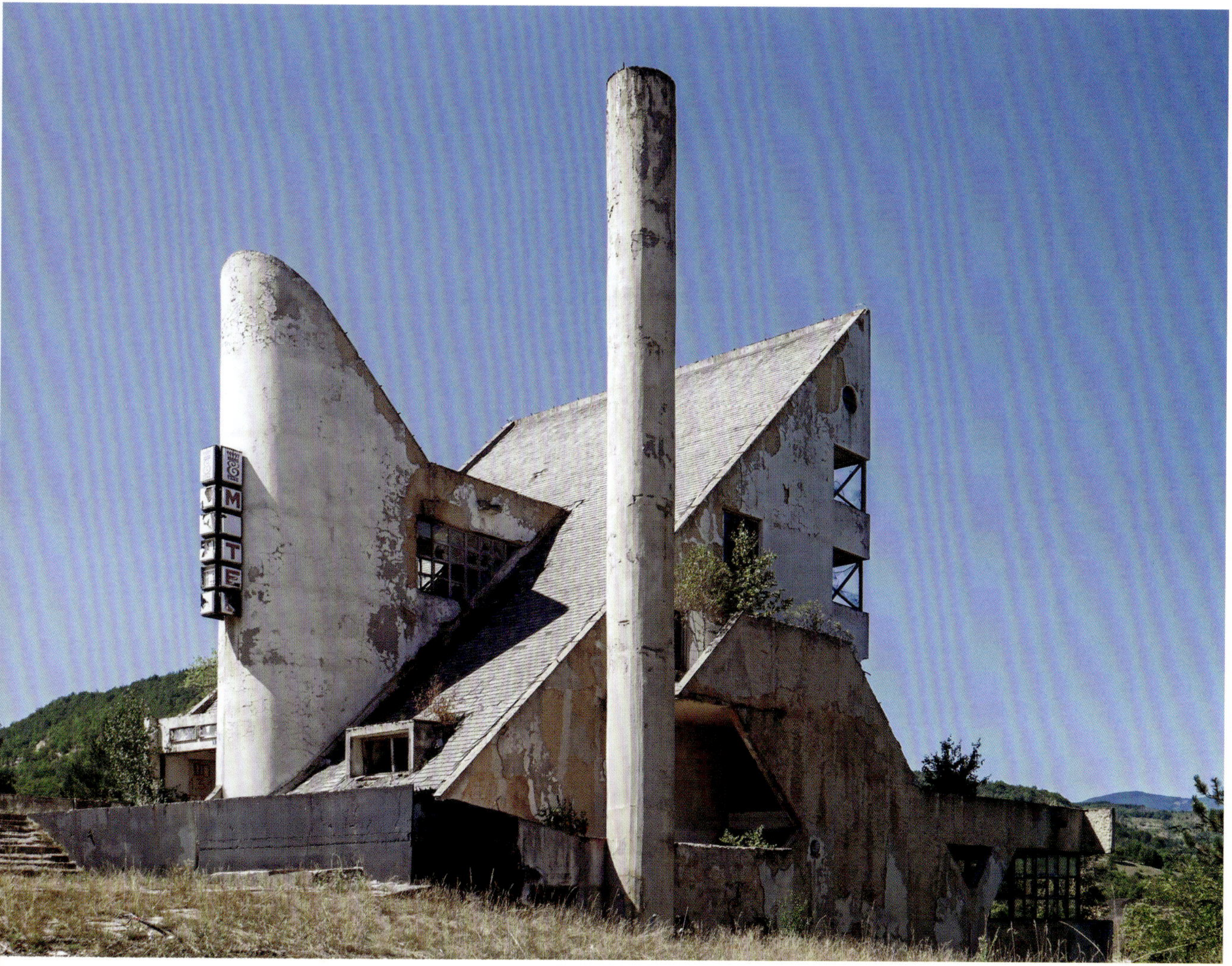

Motel Miljevina, Miljevina, Bosnia and Herzegovina

BULGARIA

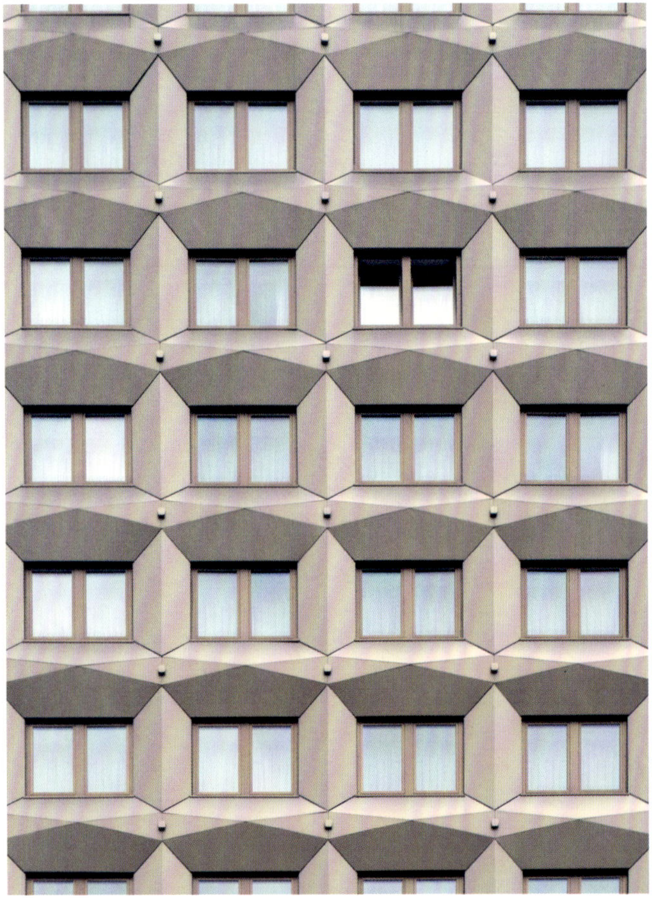

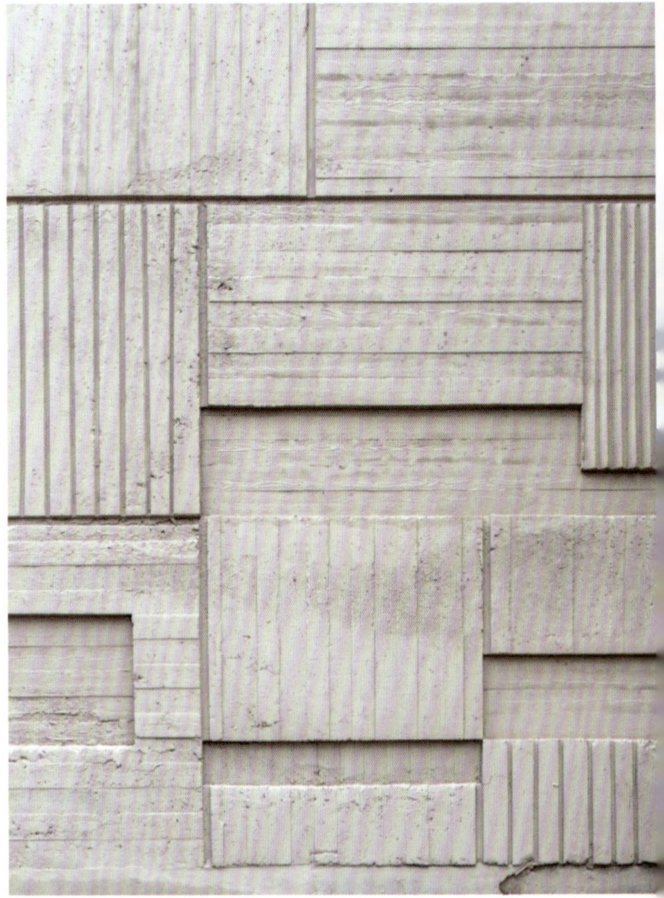

Hotel Bulgaria, Burgas, Bulgaria

right: Grand Hotel Plovdiv (former Novotel Plovdiv), Plovdiv, Bulgaria

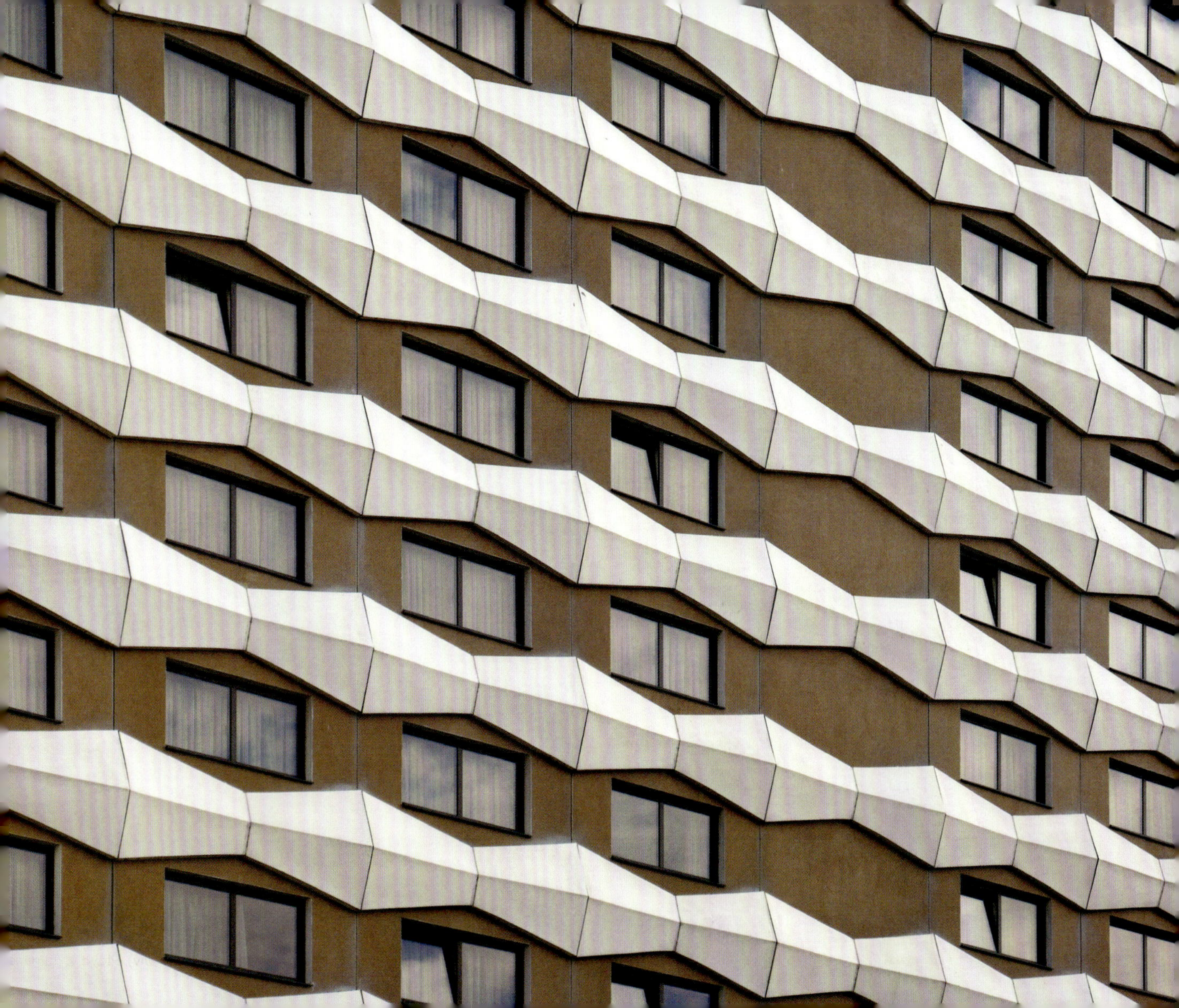

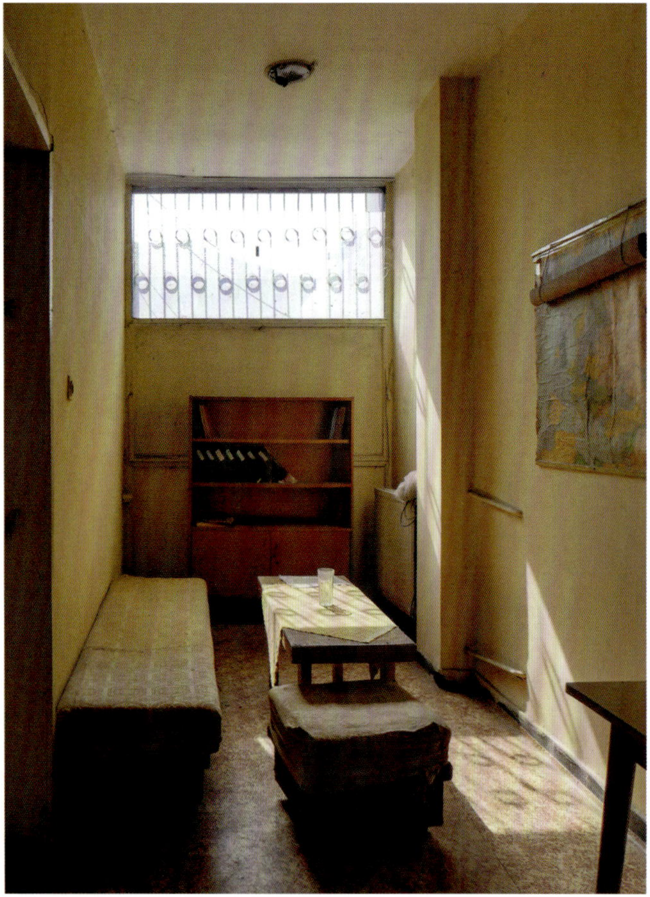

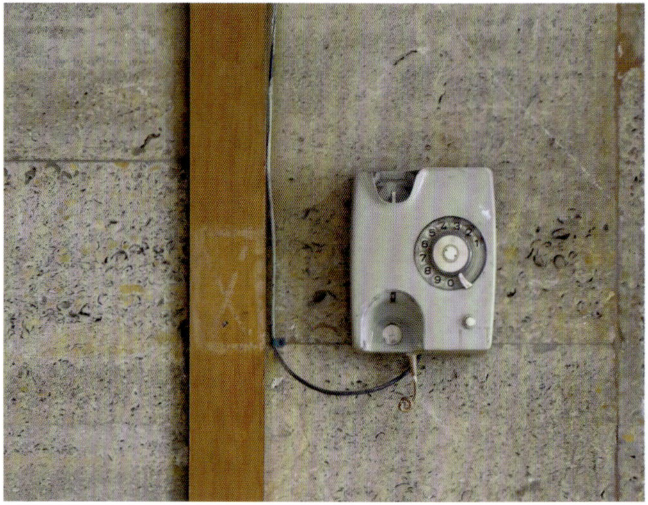

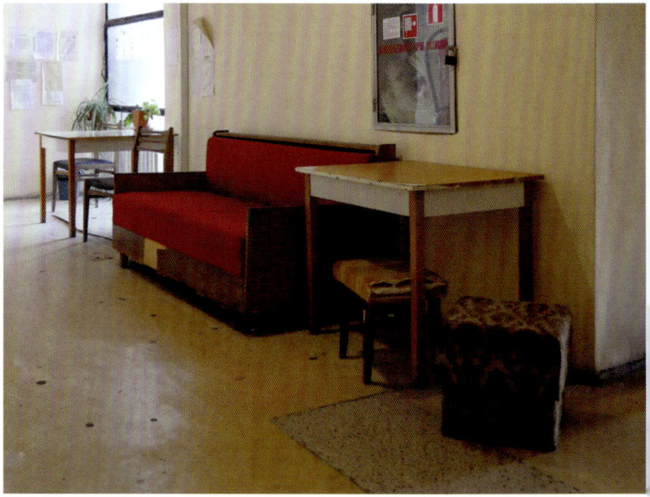

 Hotel Dunav, Plovdiv, Bulgaria

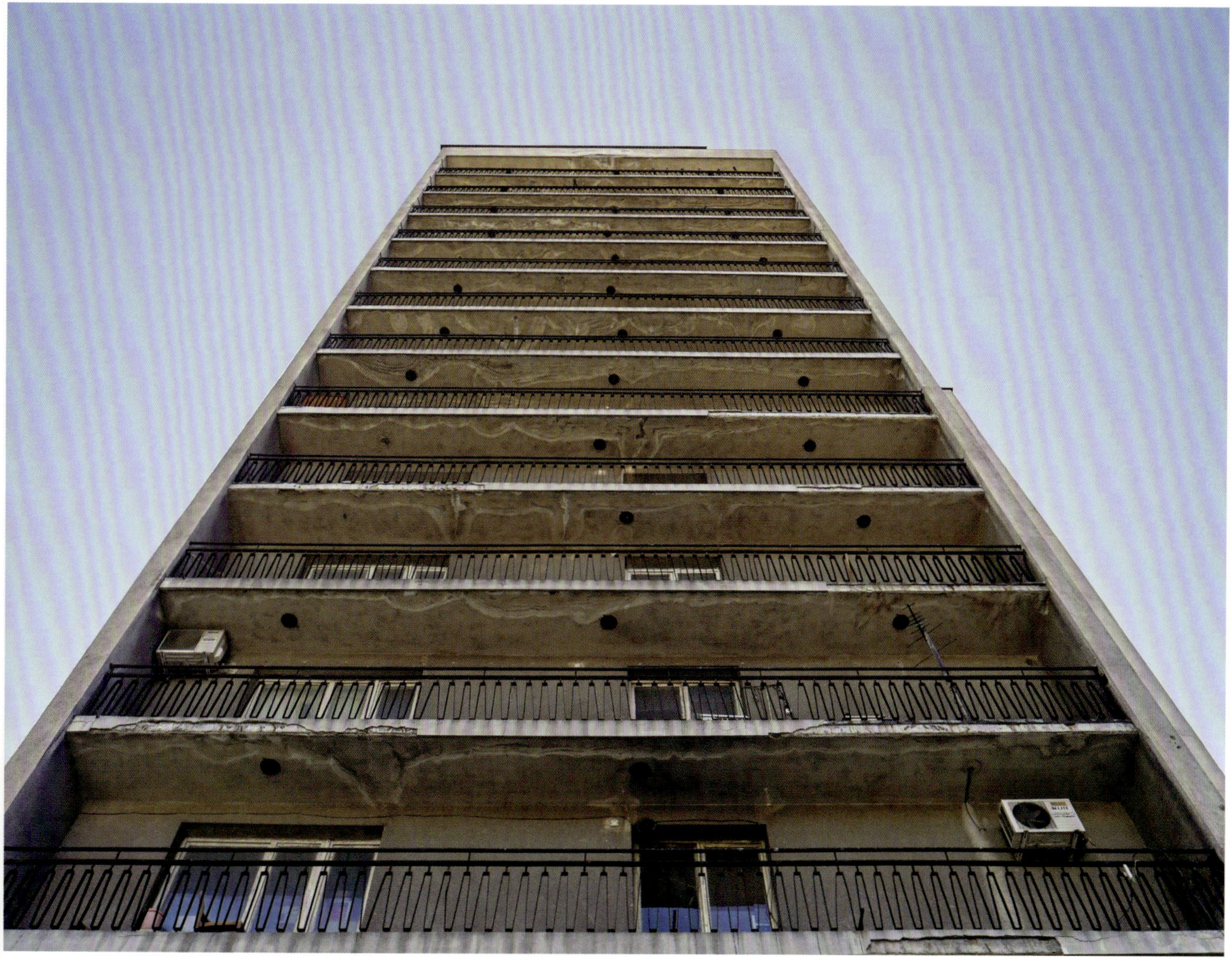

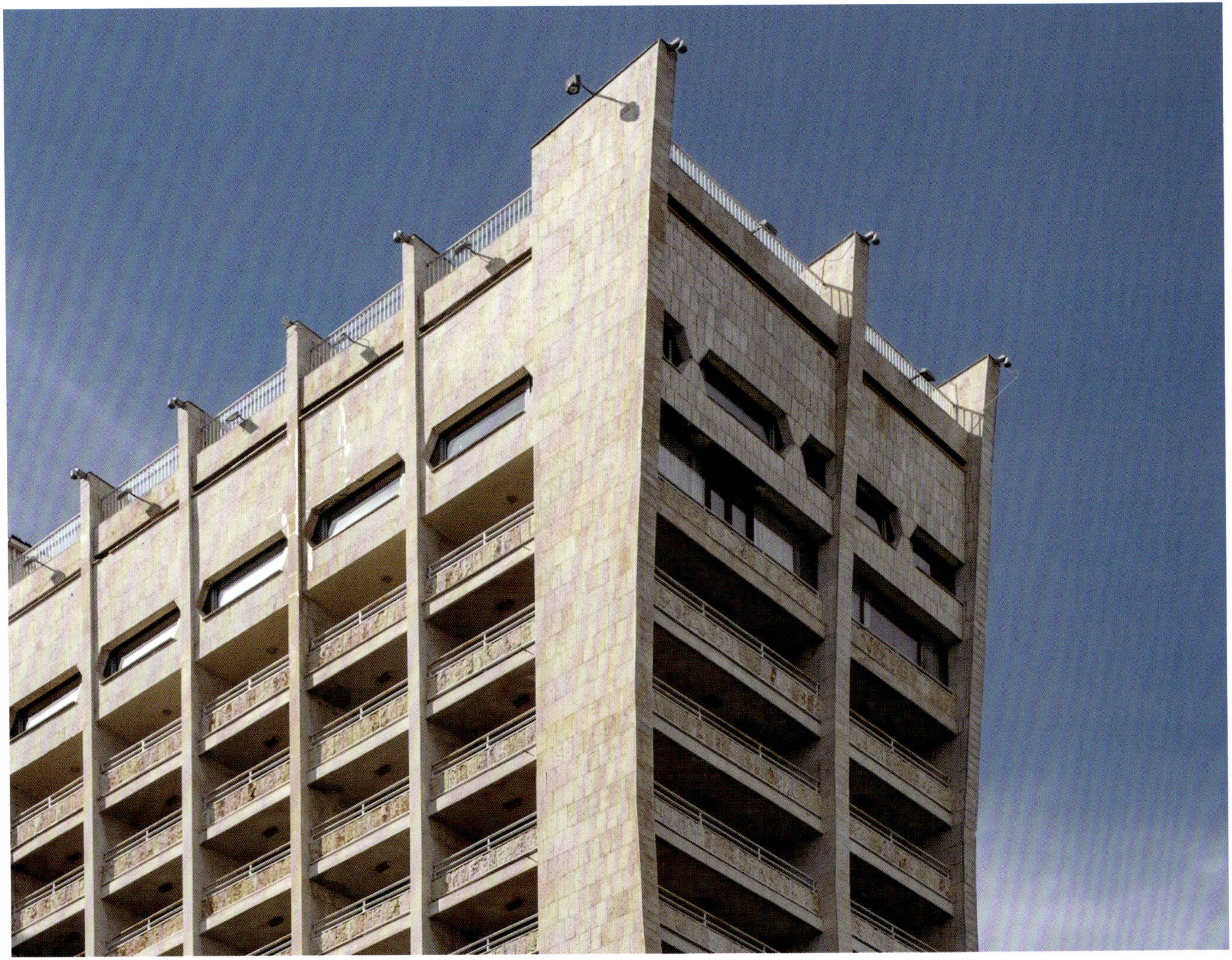

 Hotel Dobrudzha, Albena, Bulgaria

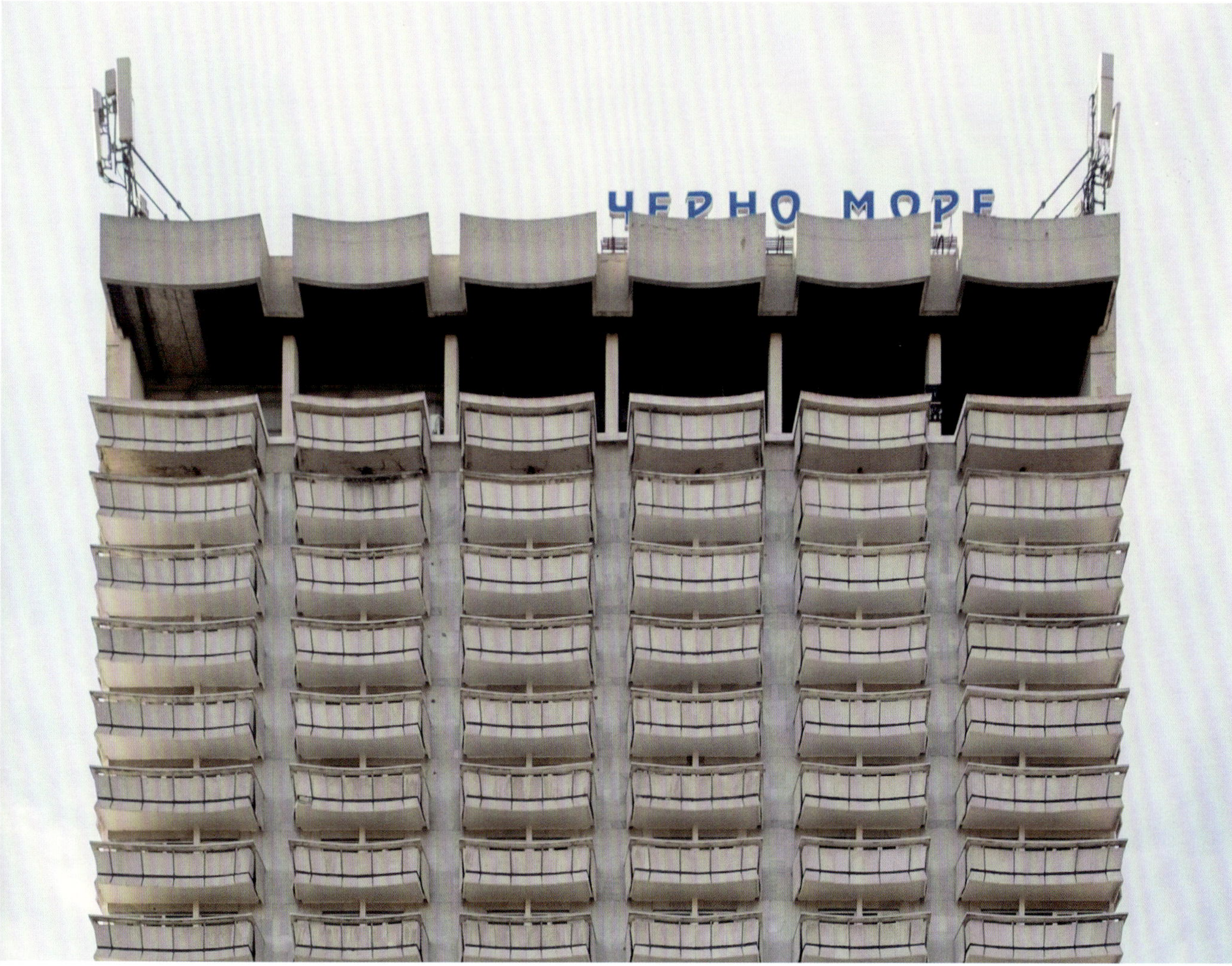

Hotel Cherno More, Varna, Bulgaria

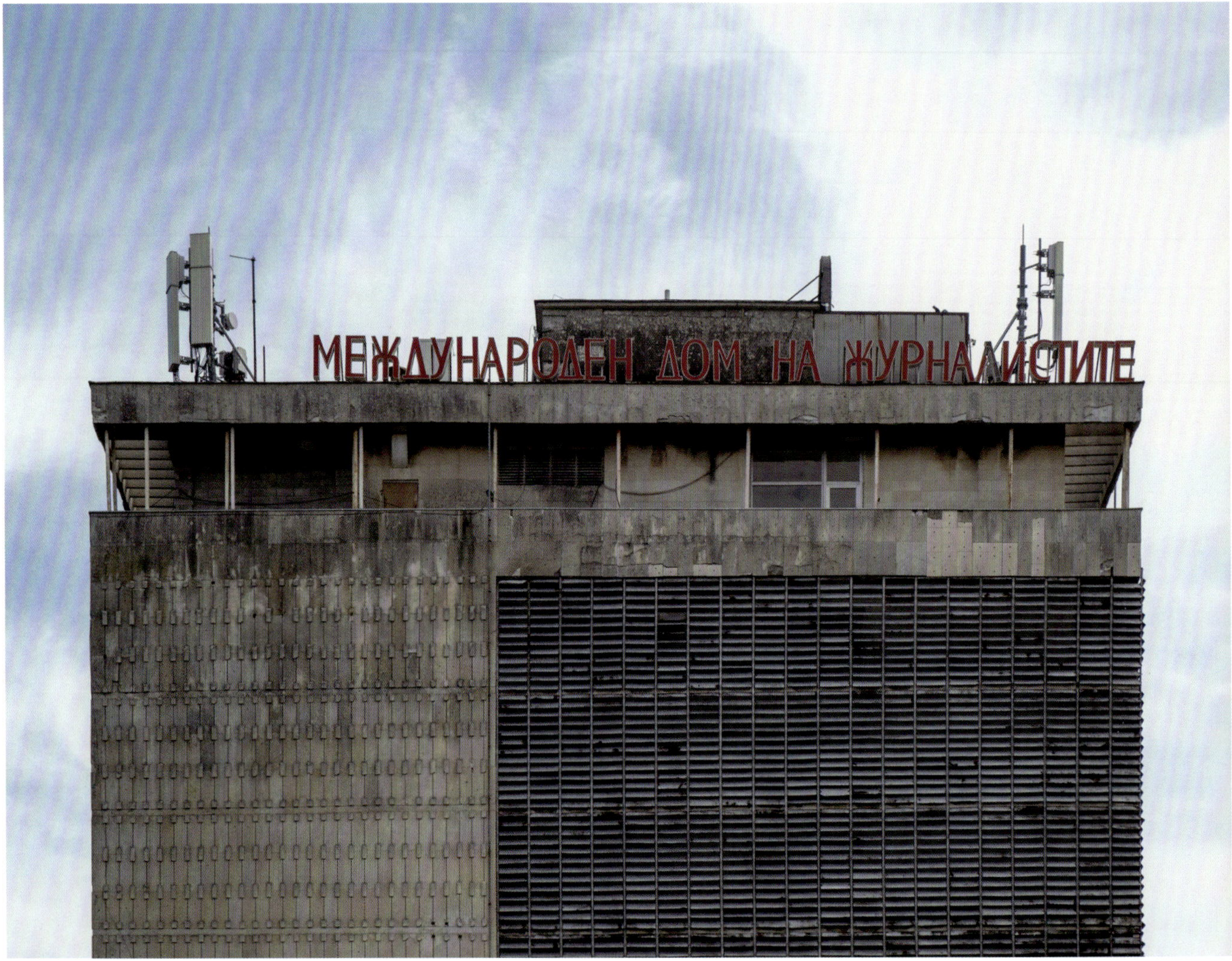

 Hotel Journalist, Chayka, Bulgaria

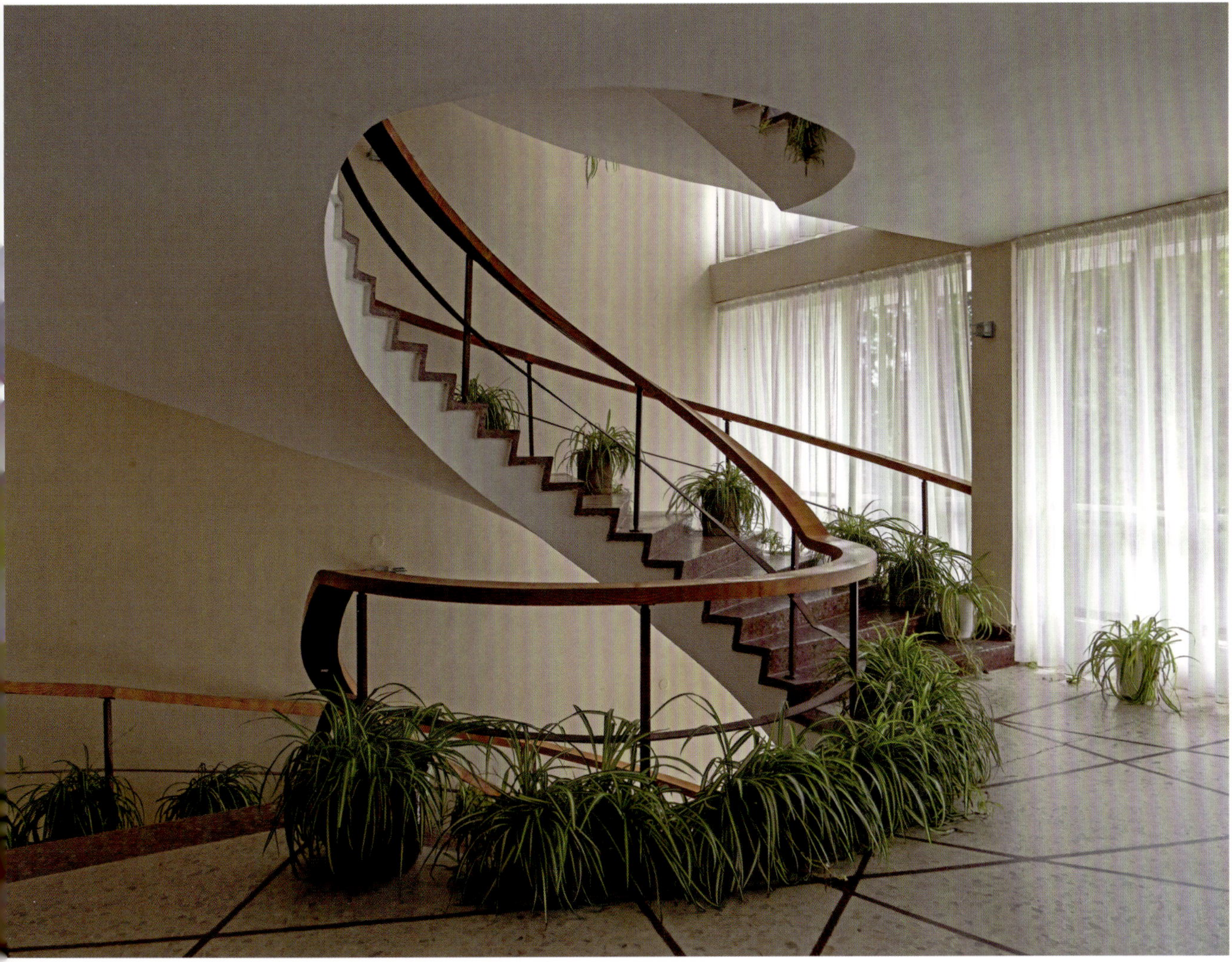

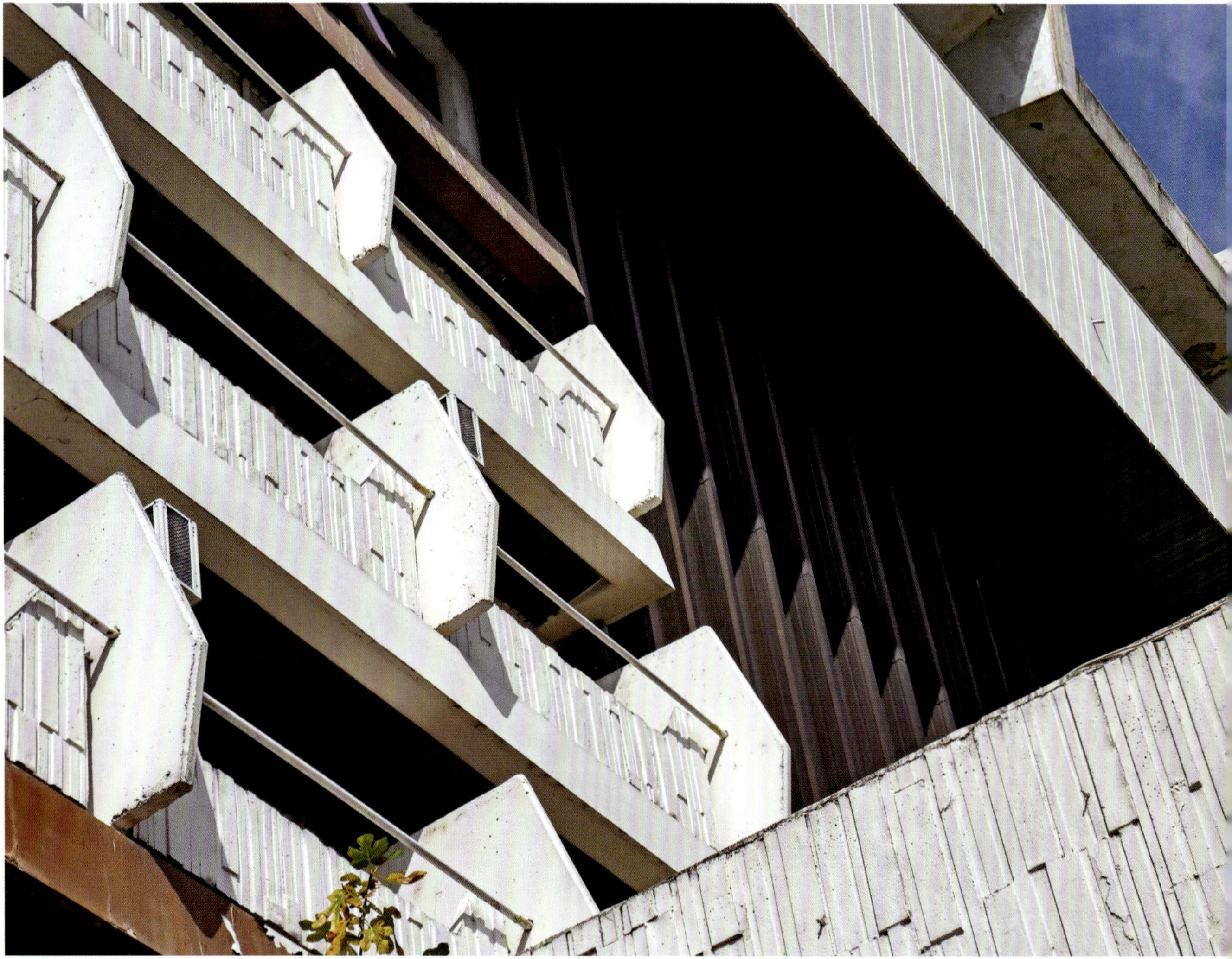

 Hotel Kazanlak, Kazanlak, Bulgaria

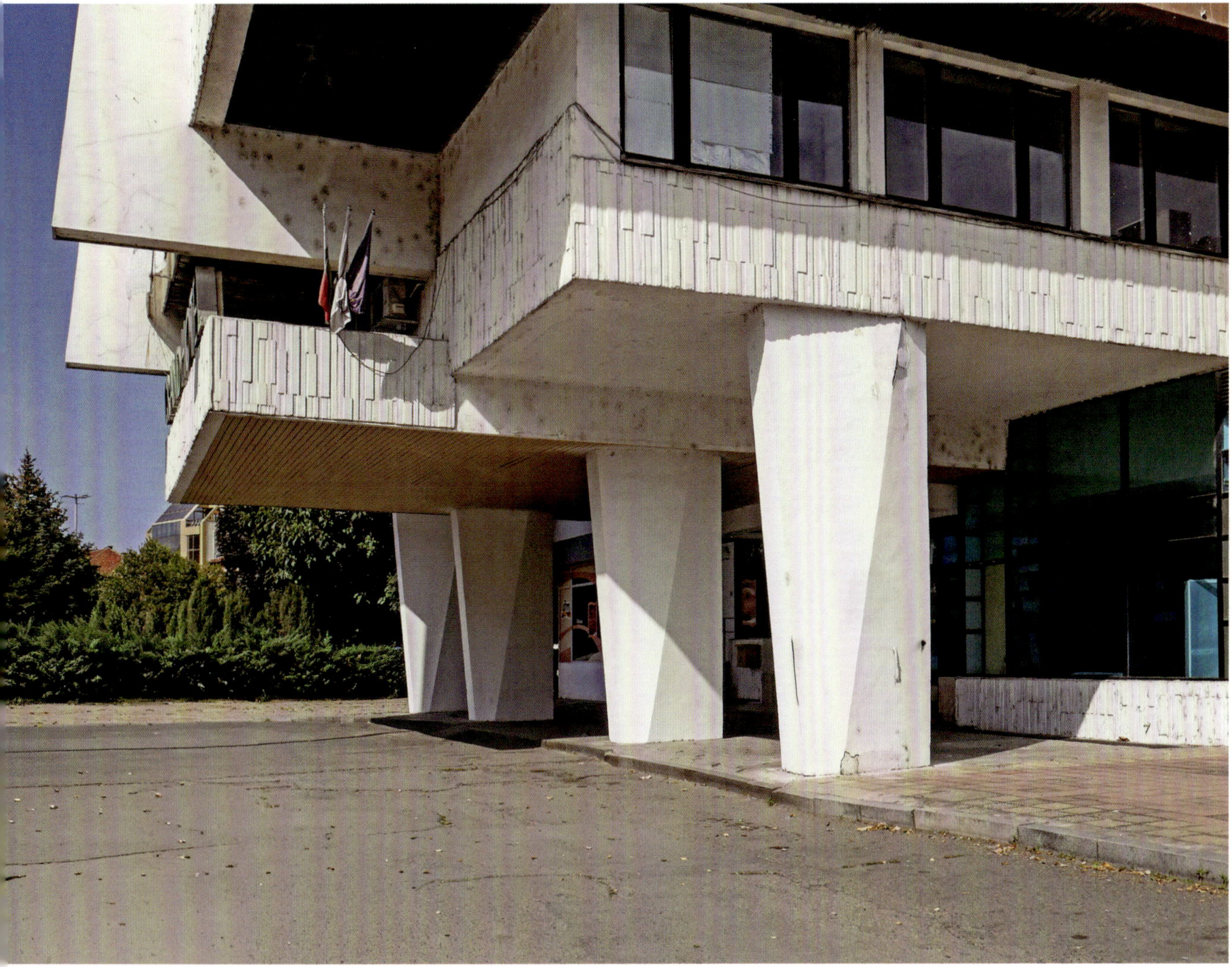

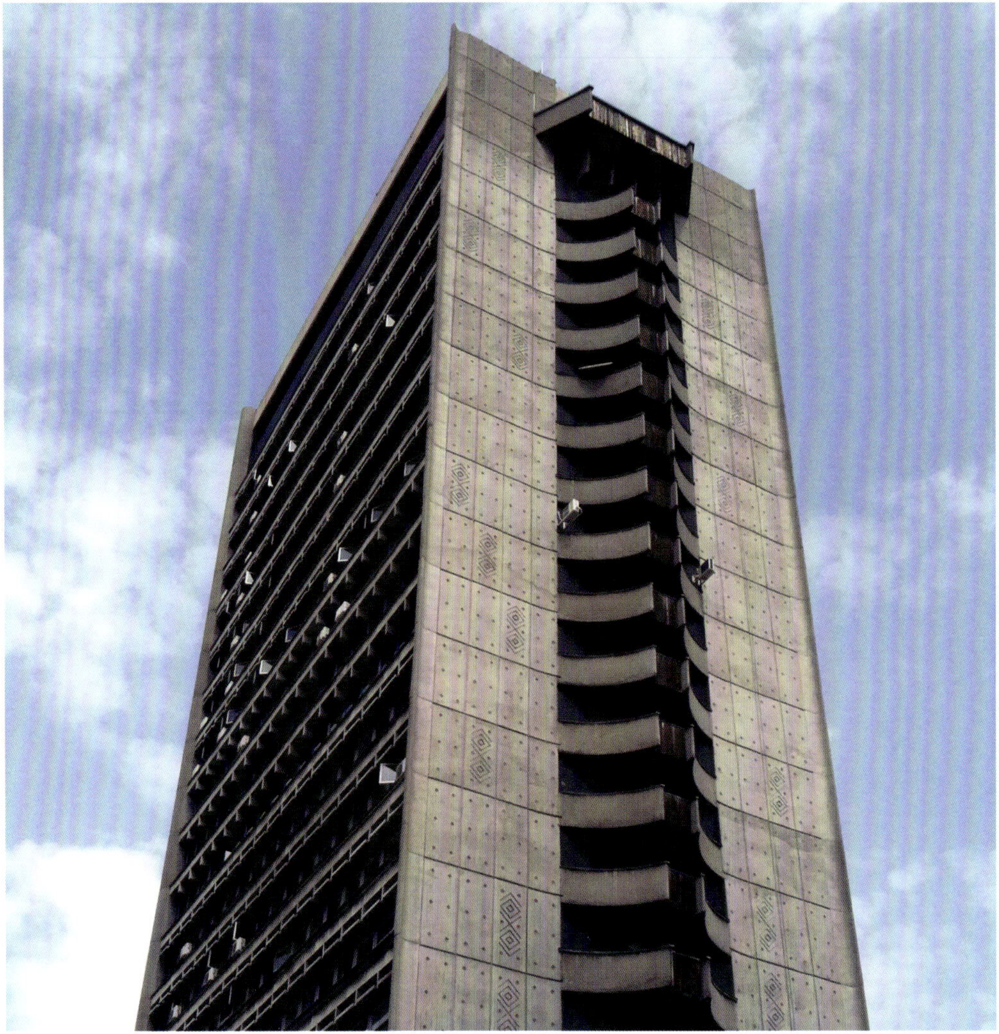

 Hotel Riga, Ruse, Bulgaria

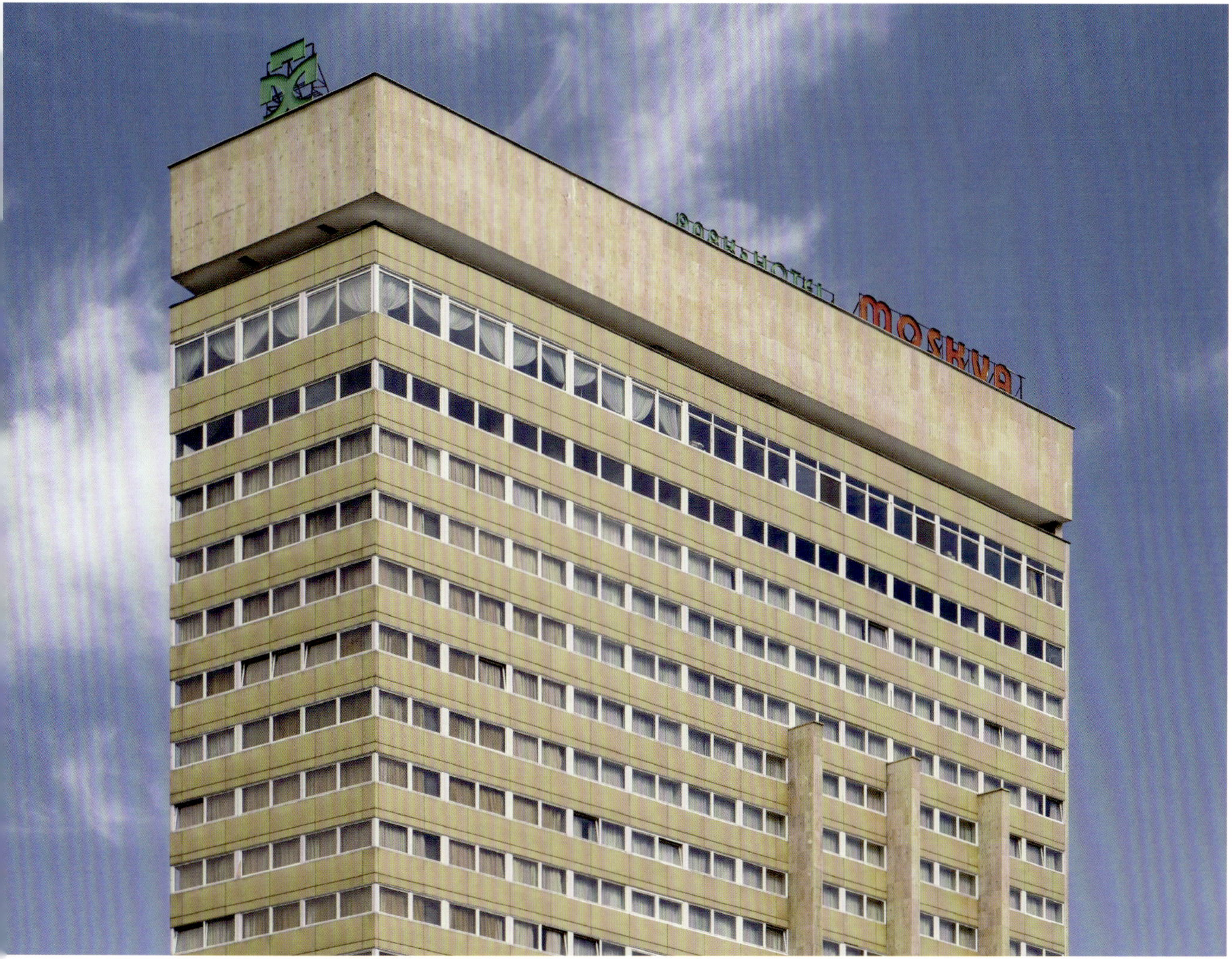

Park Hotel Moskva (former Hotel Moskva), Sofia, Bulgaria

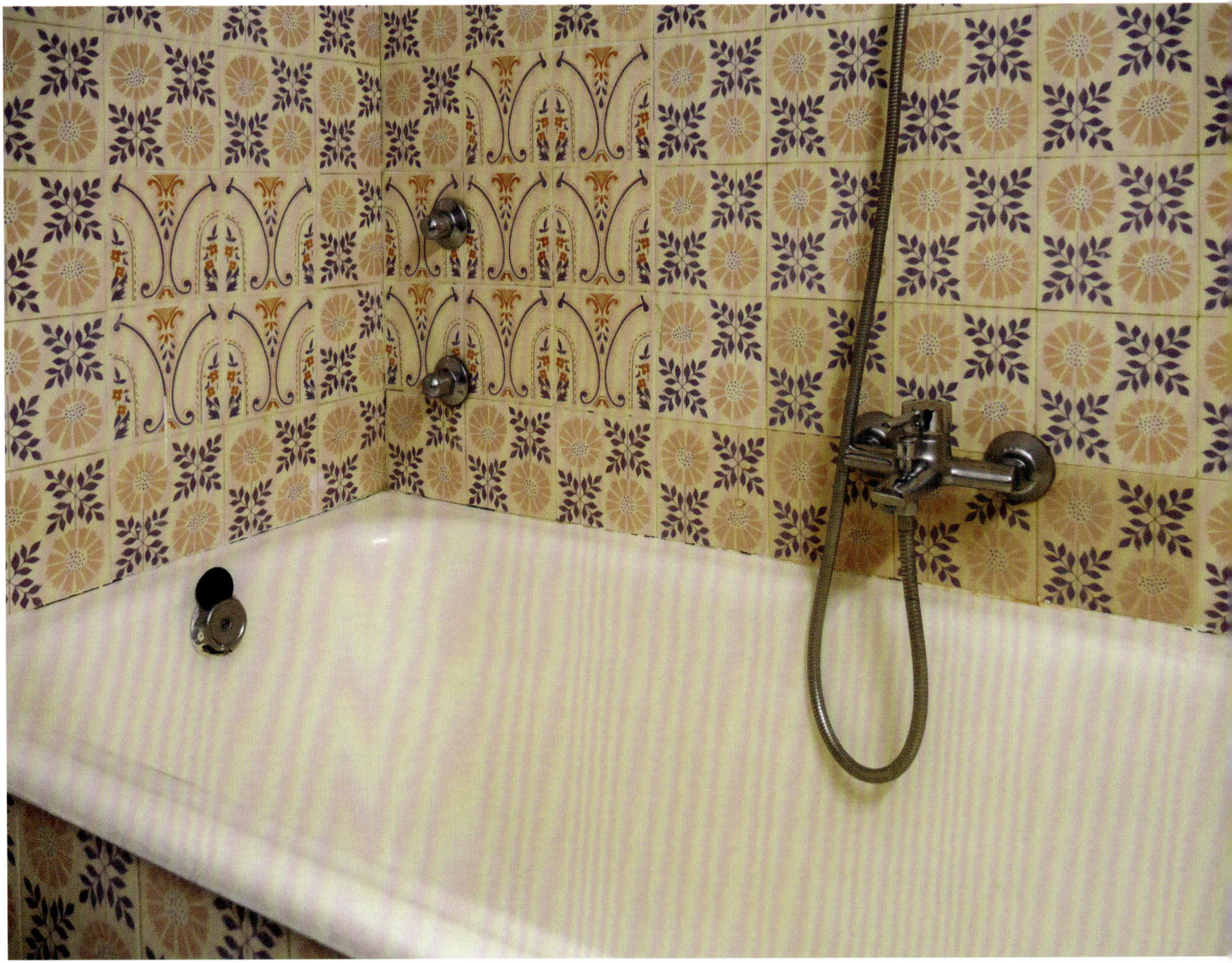

 Hotel Rila, Sofia, Bulgaria

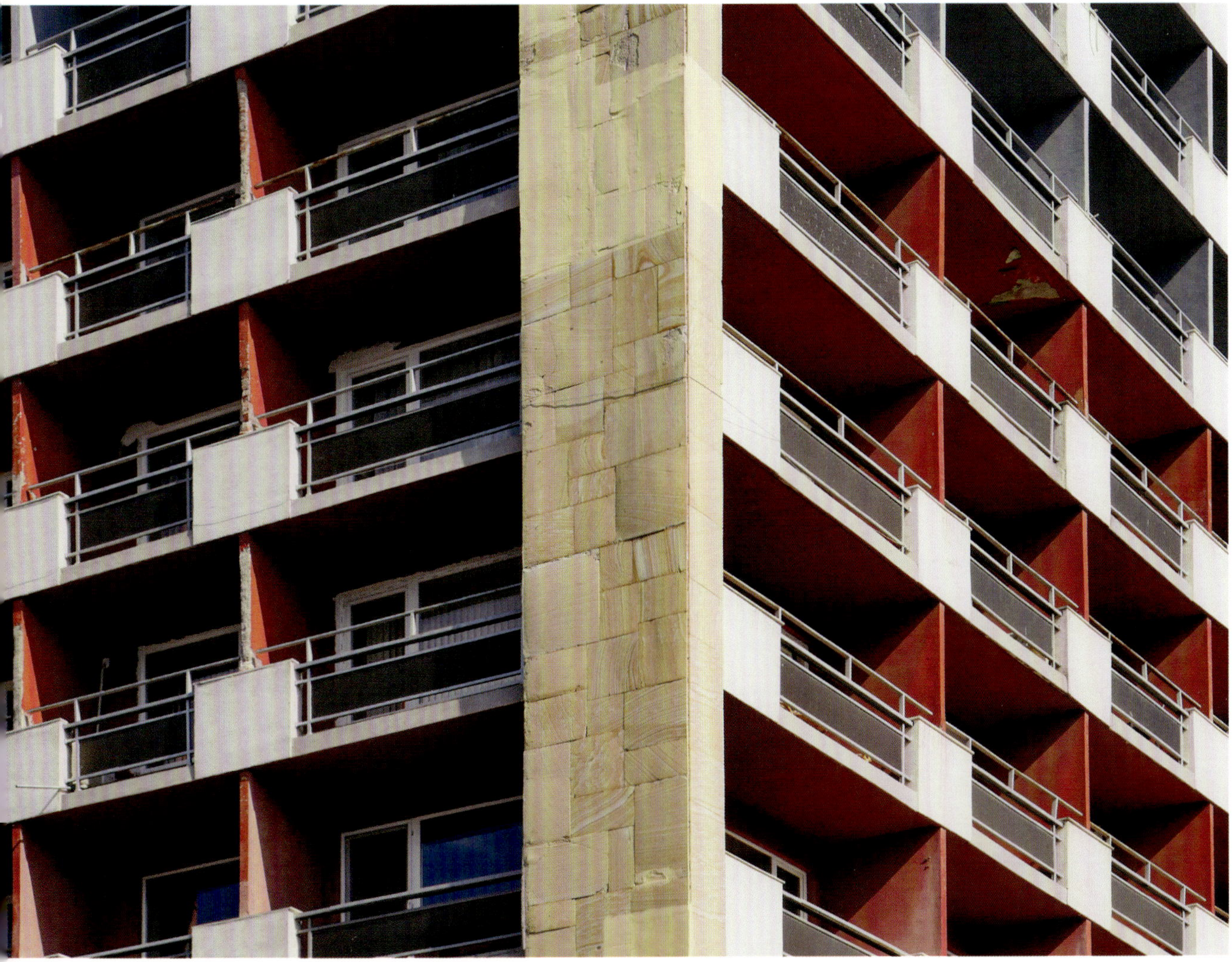

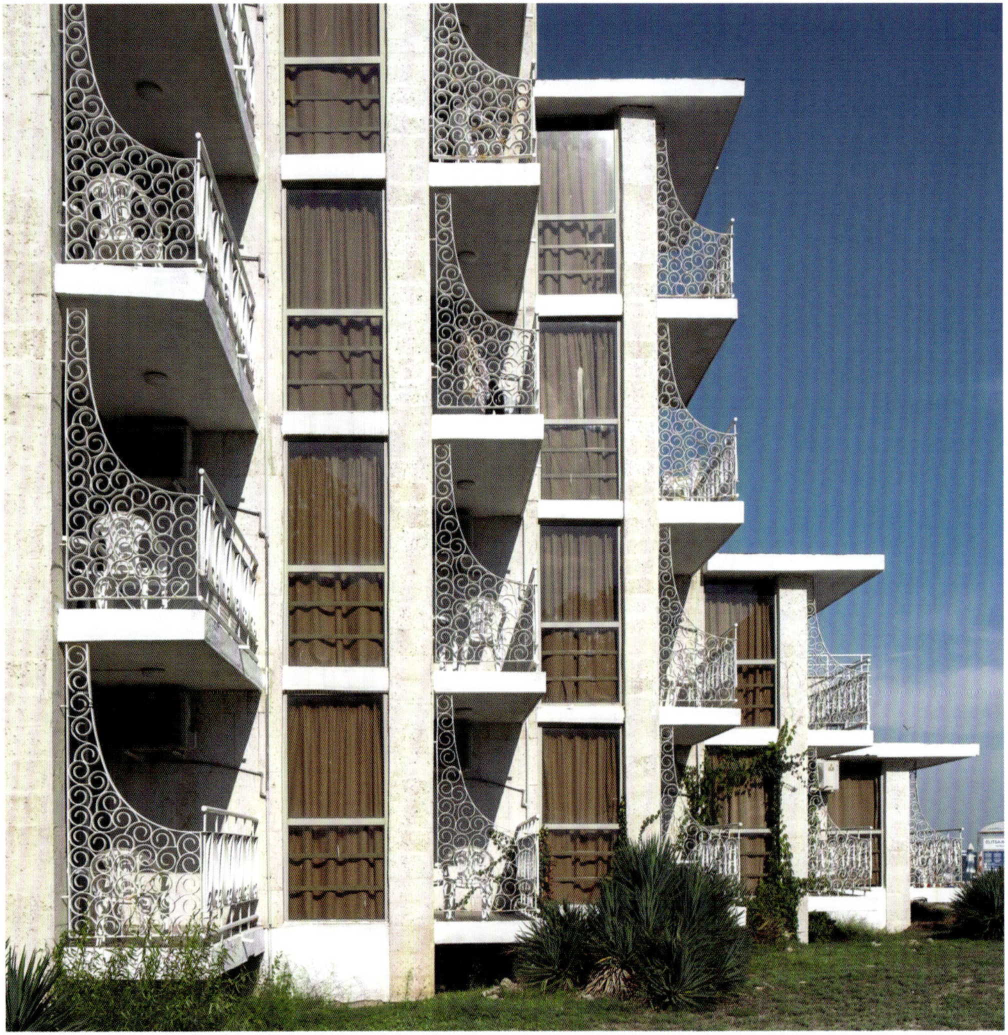

 Hotel Nona, Albena, Bulgaria

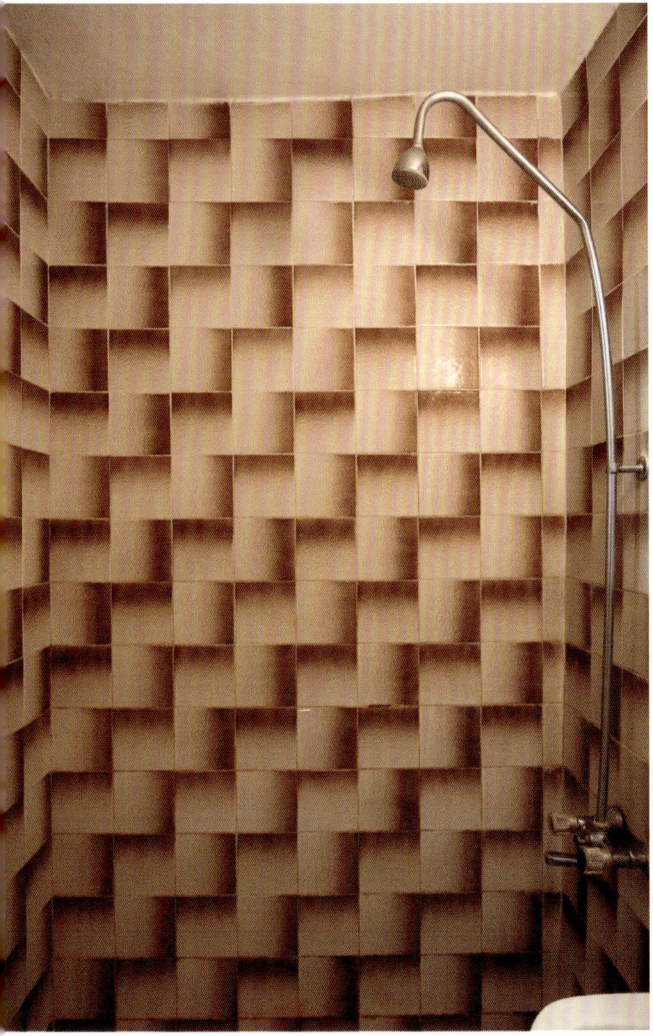

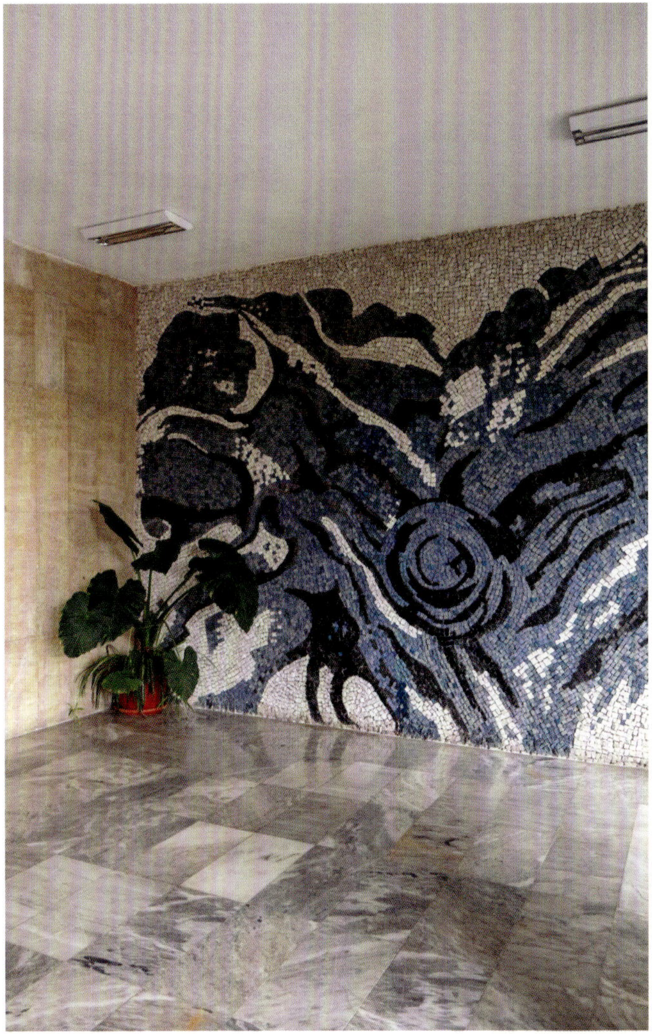

Hotel Park, Burgas, Bulgaria

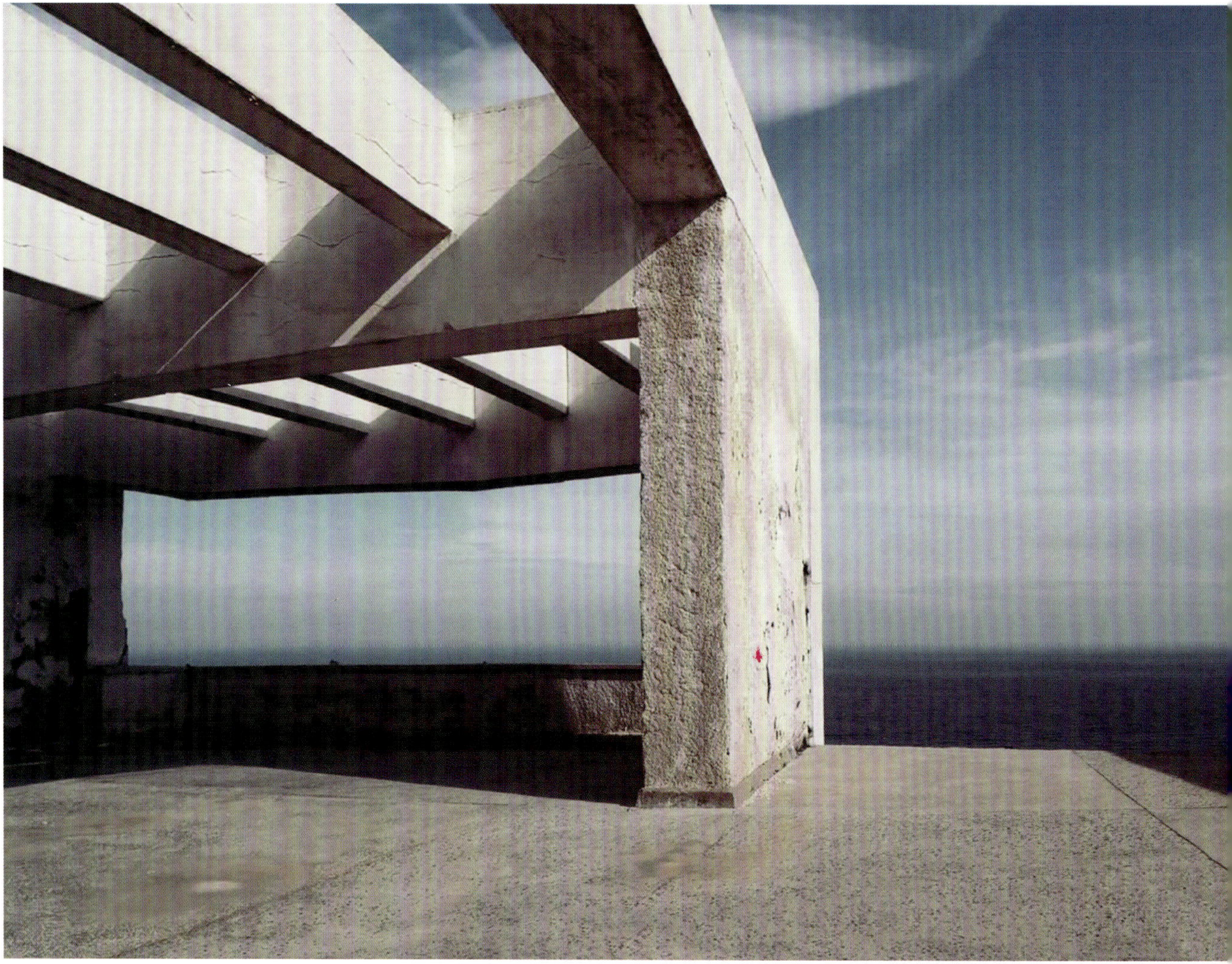

Hotel Delfin, Zlatni Pyasatsi, Bulgaria

right: Hotel Pomorie, Pomorie, Bulgaria

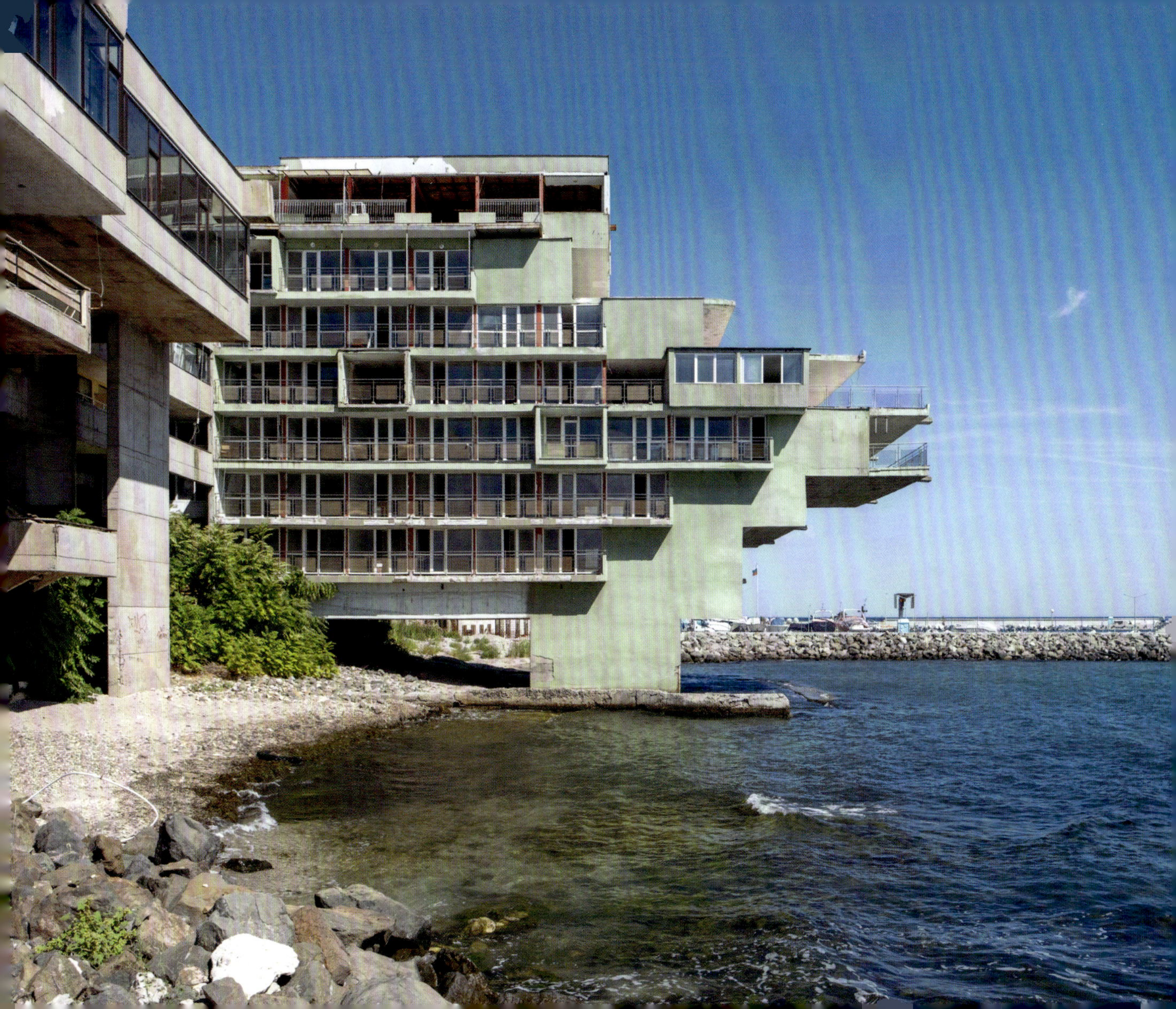

CRIMEA

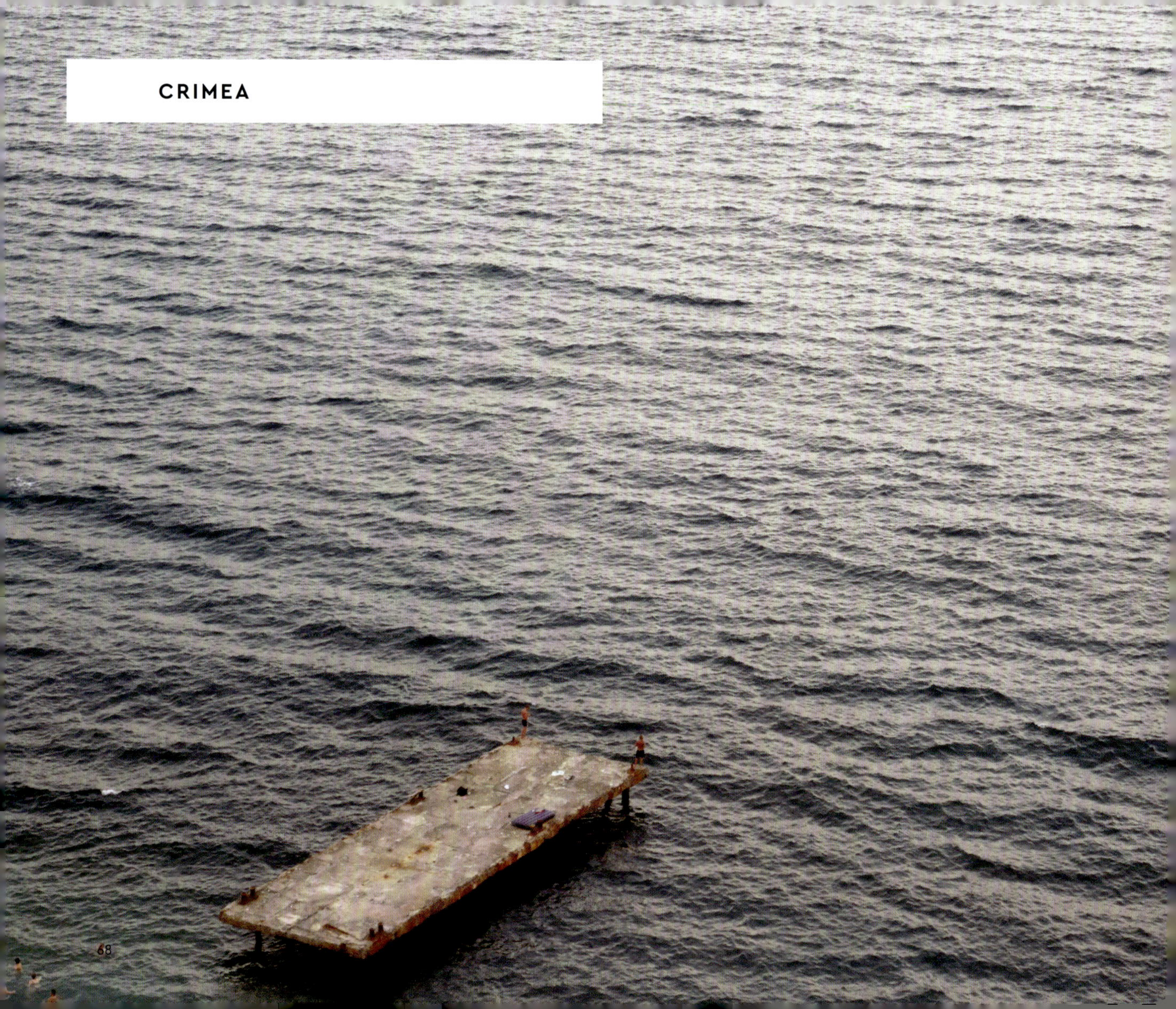

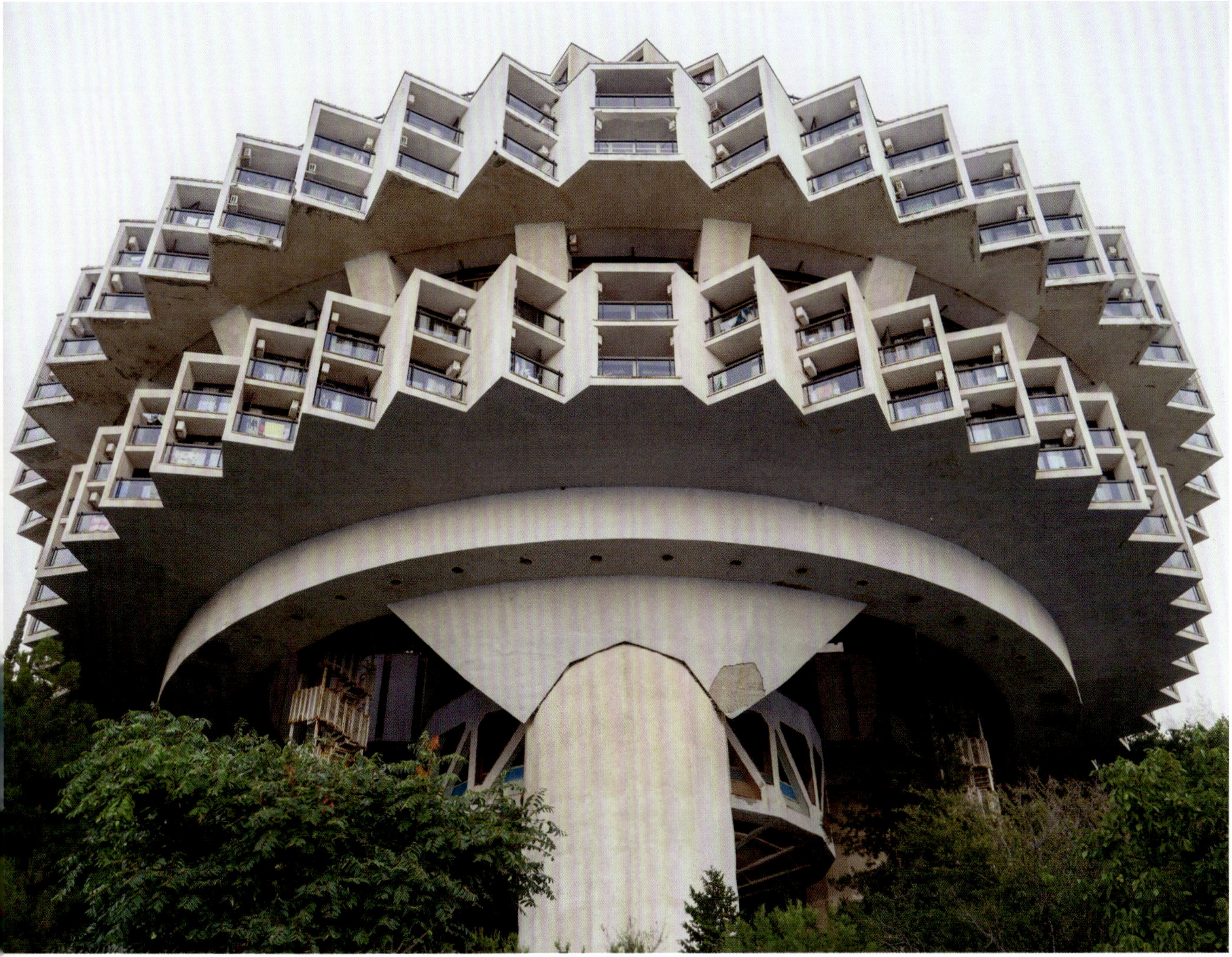

Hotel Druzhba, Kurpaty, Crimea

CROATIA

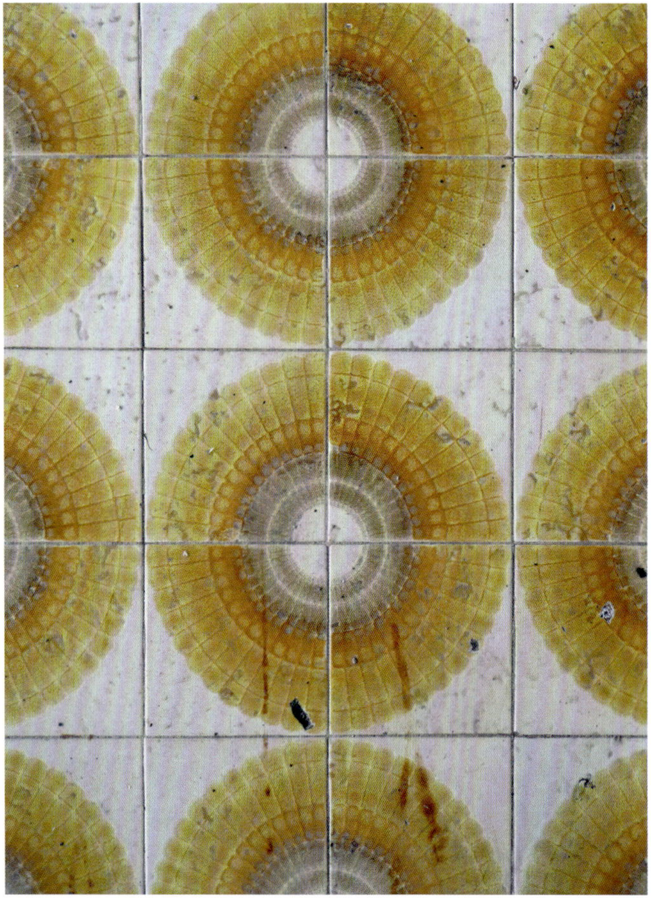

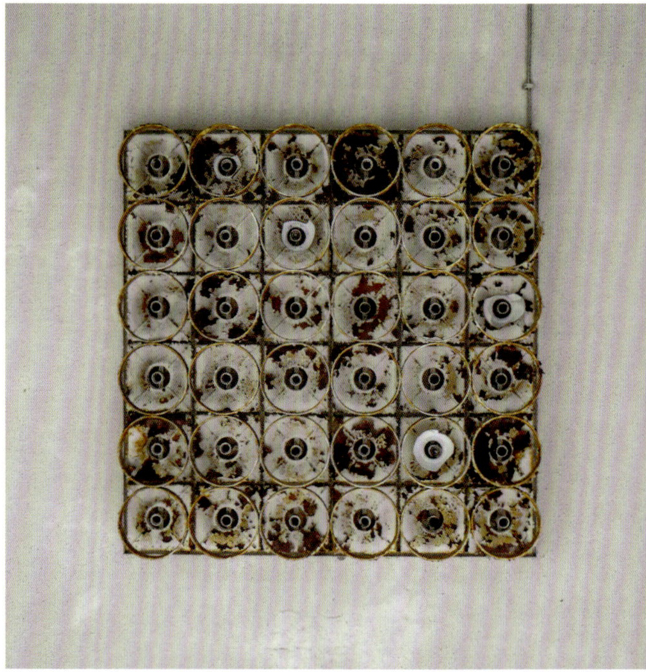

Haludovo Palace Hotel, Malinska, Croatia

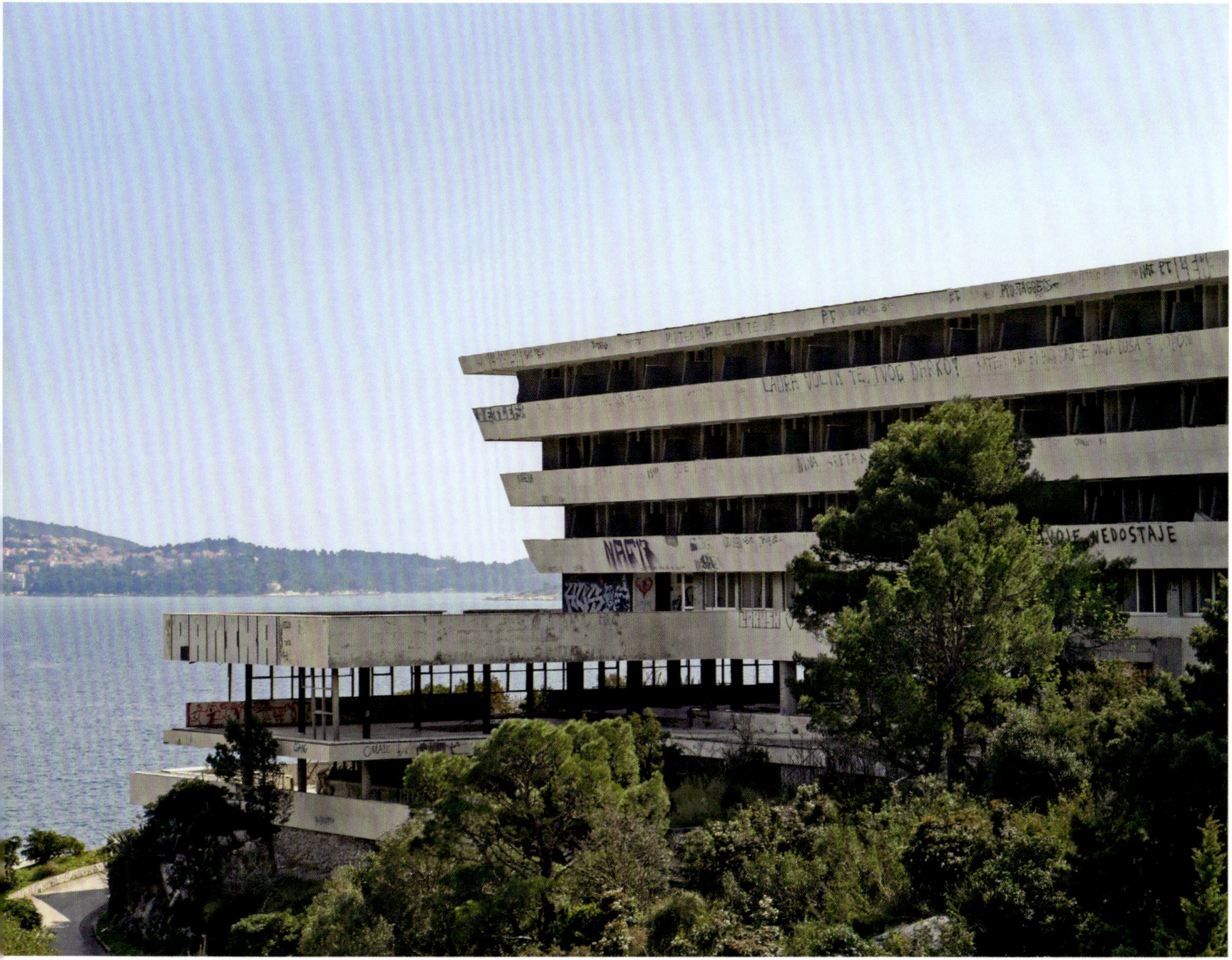

Hotel Pelegrin, Kupari Bay, Croatia

CZECH REPUBLIC

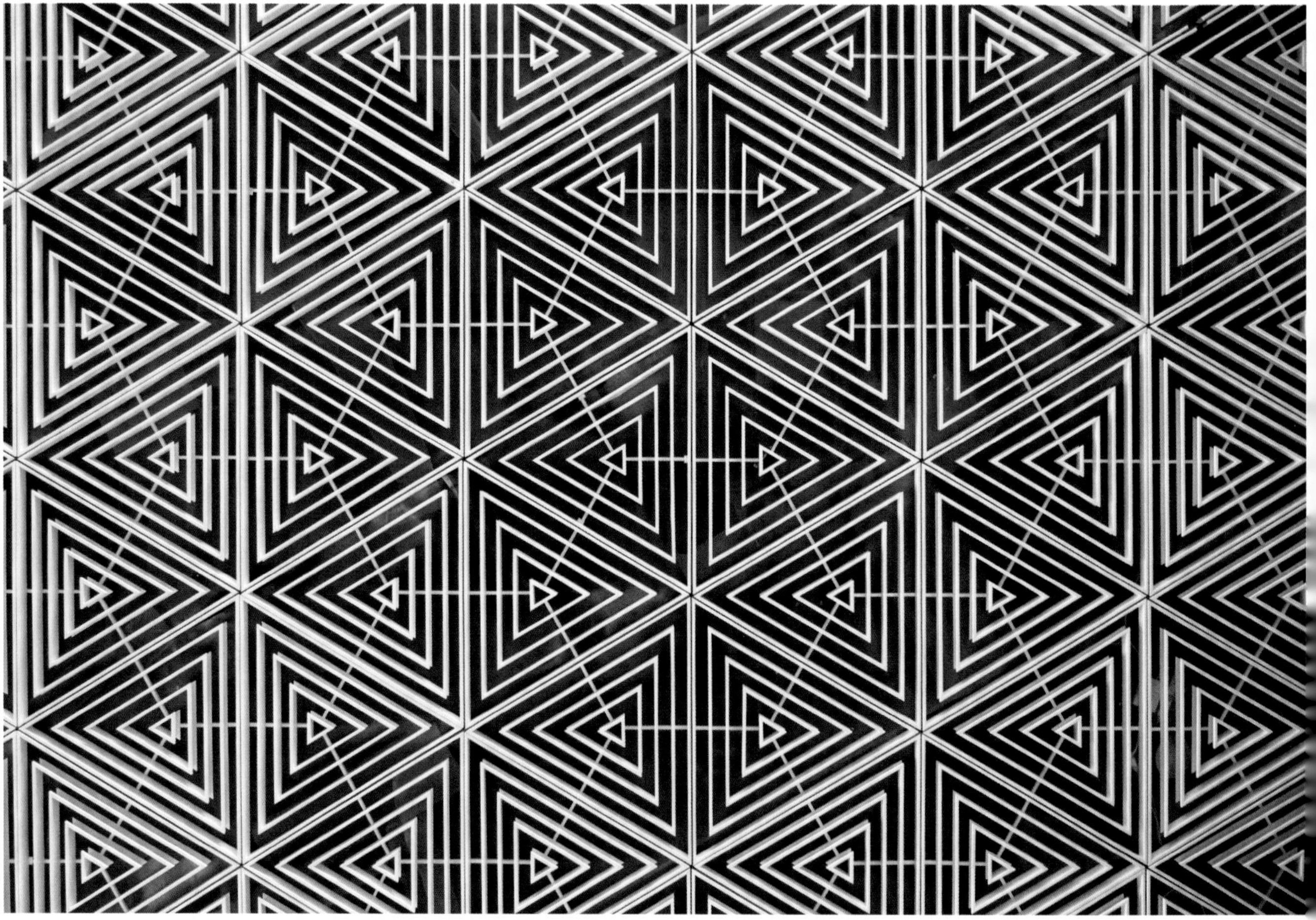

 Hotel Continental, Brno, Czech Republic

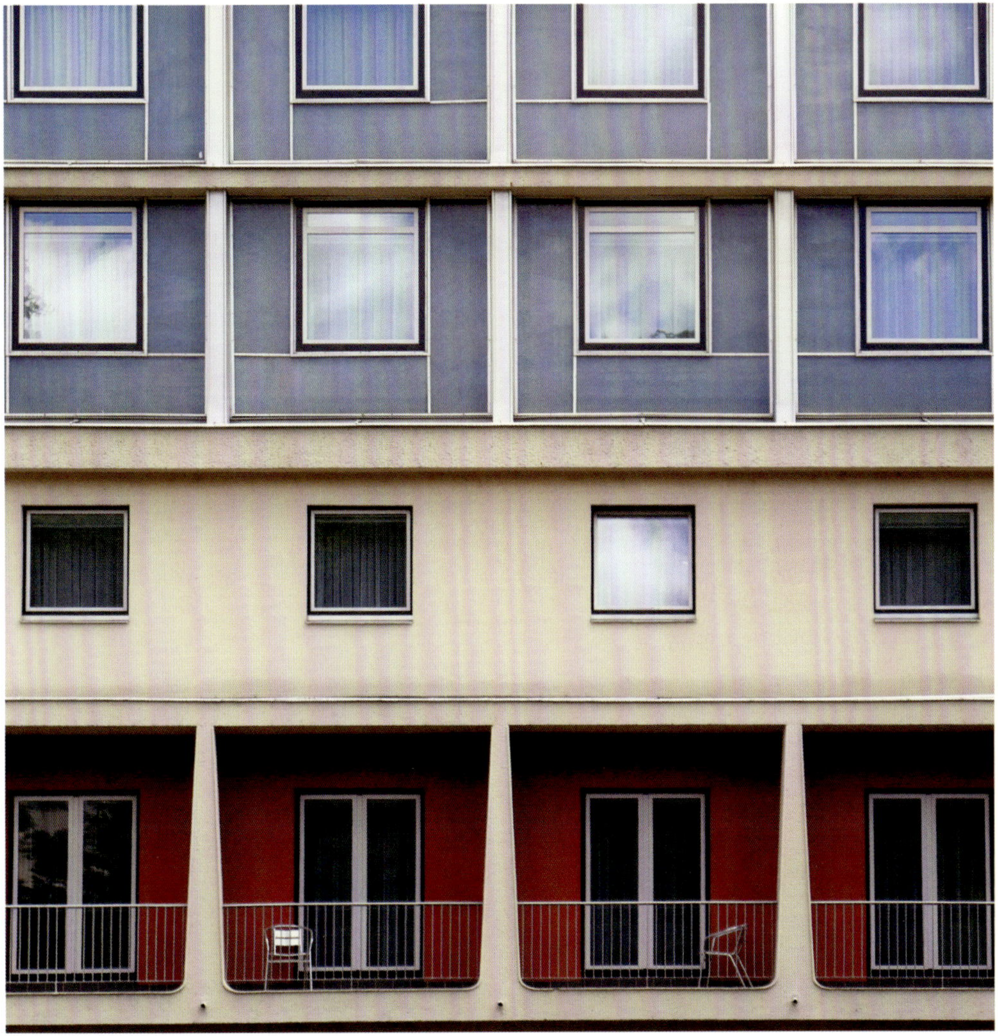

Hotel International, Brno, Czech Republic

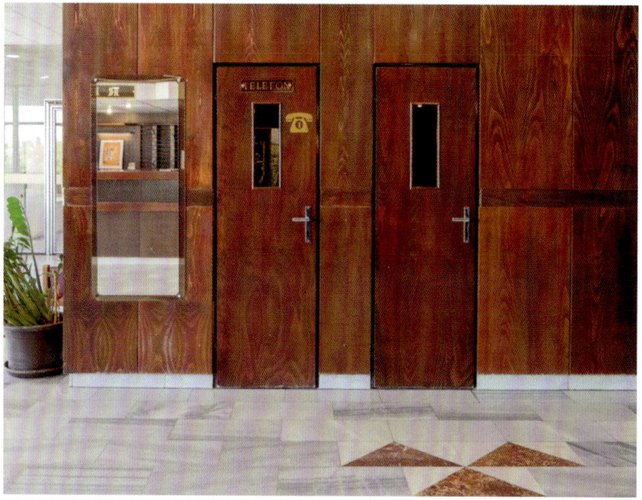

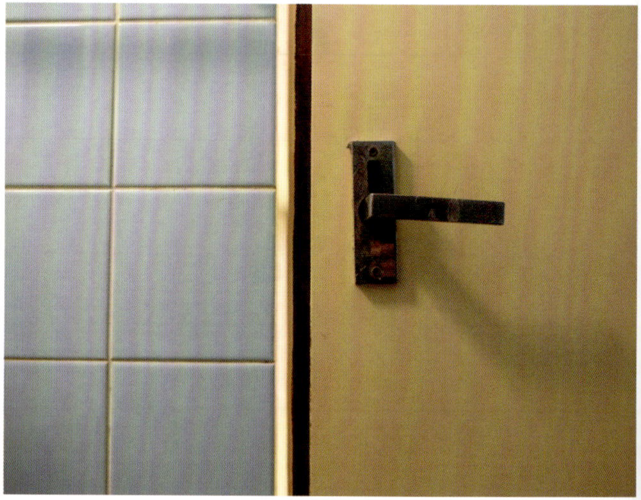

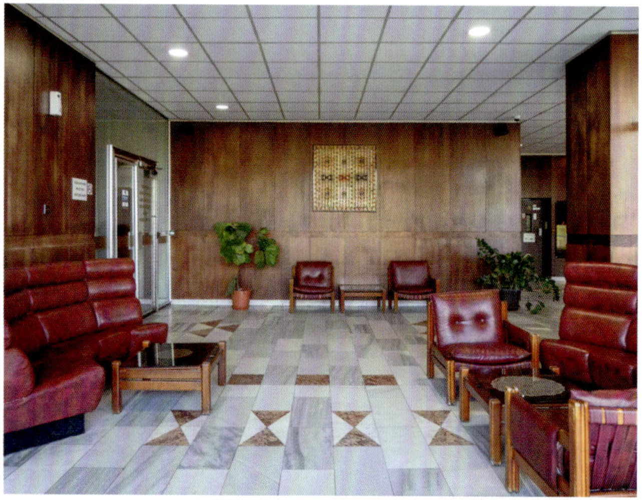

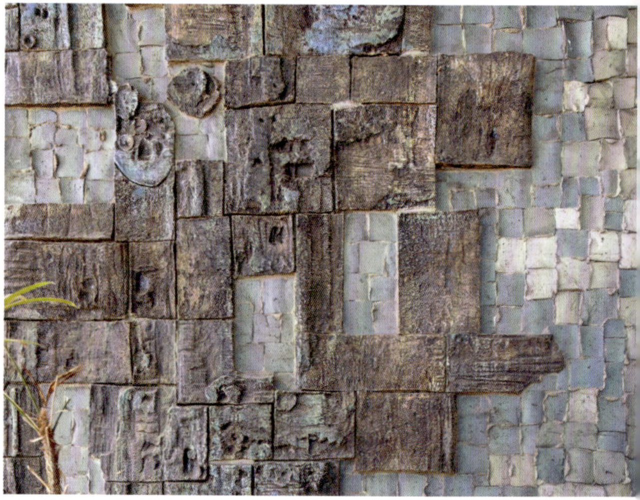

Hotel Kladno, Kladno, Czech Republic

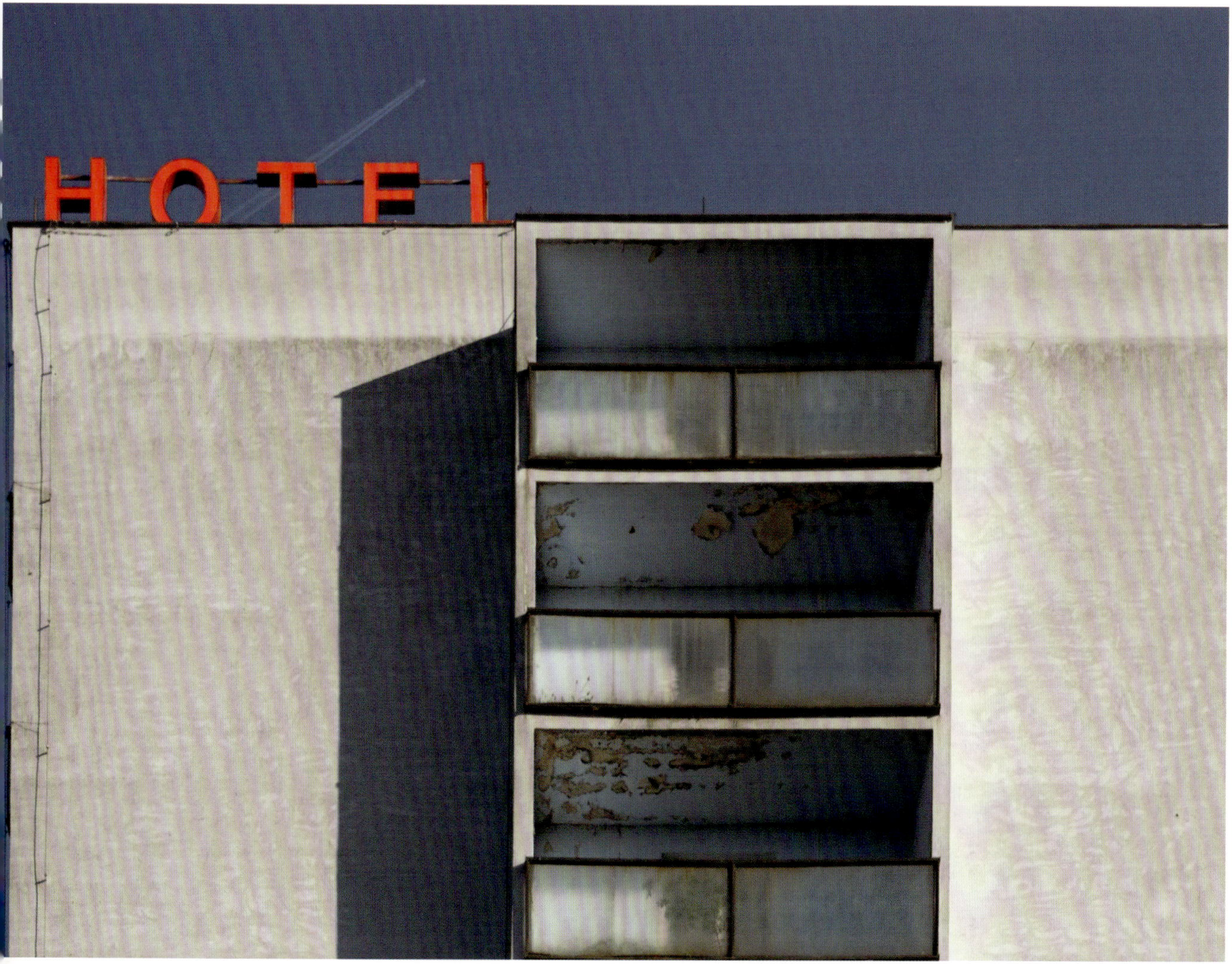
HOTEL

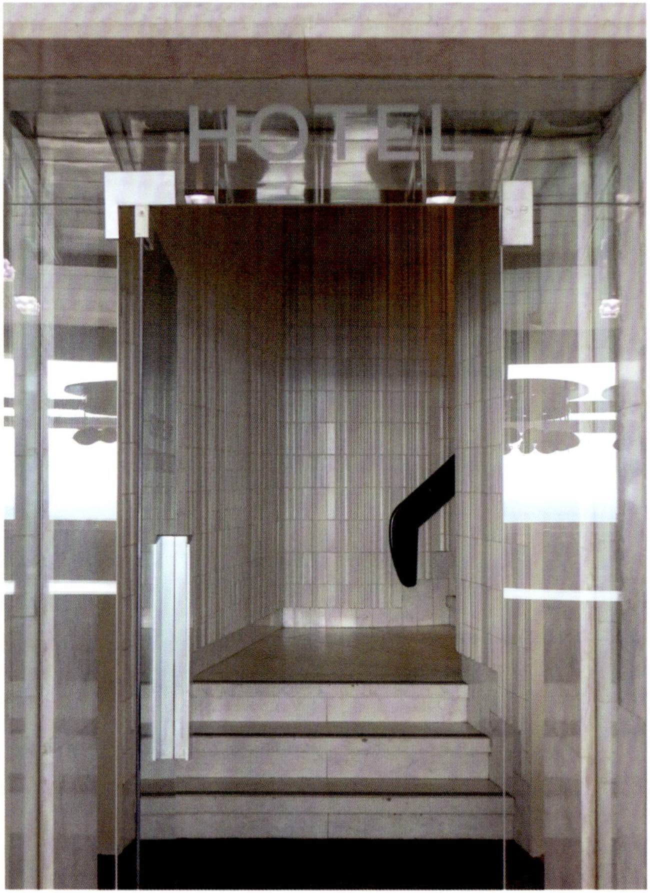

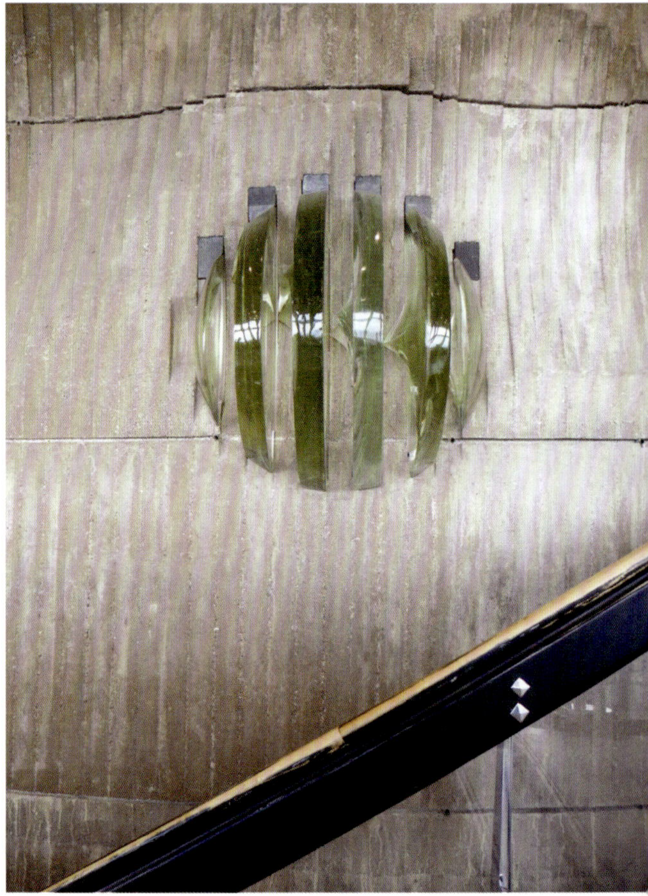

 Hotel Ještěd, Liberec, Czech Republic

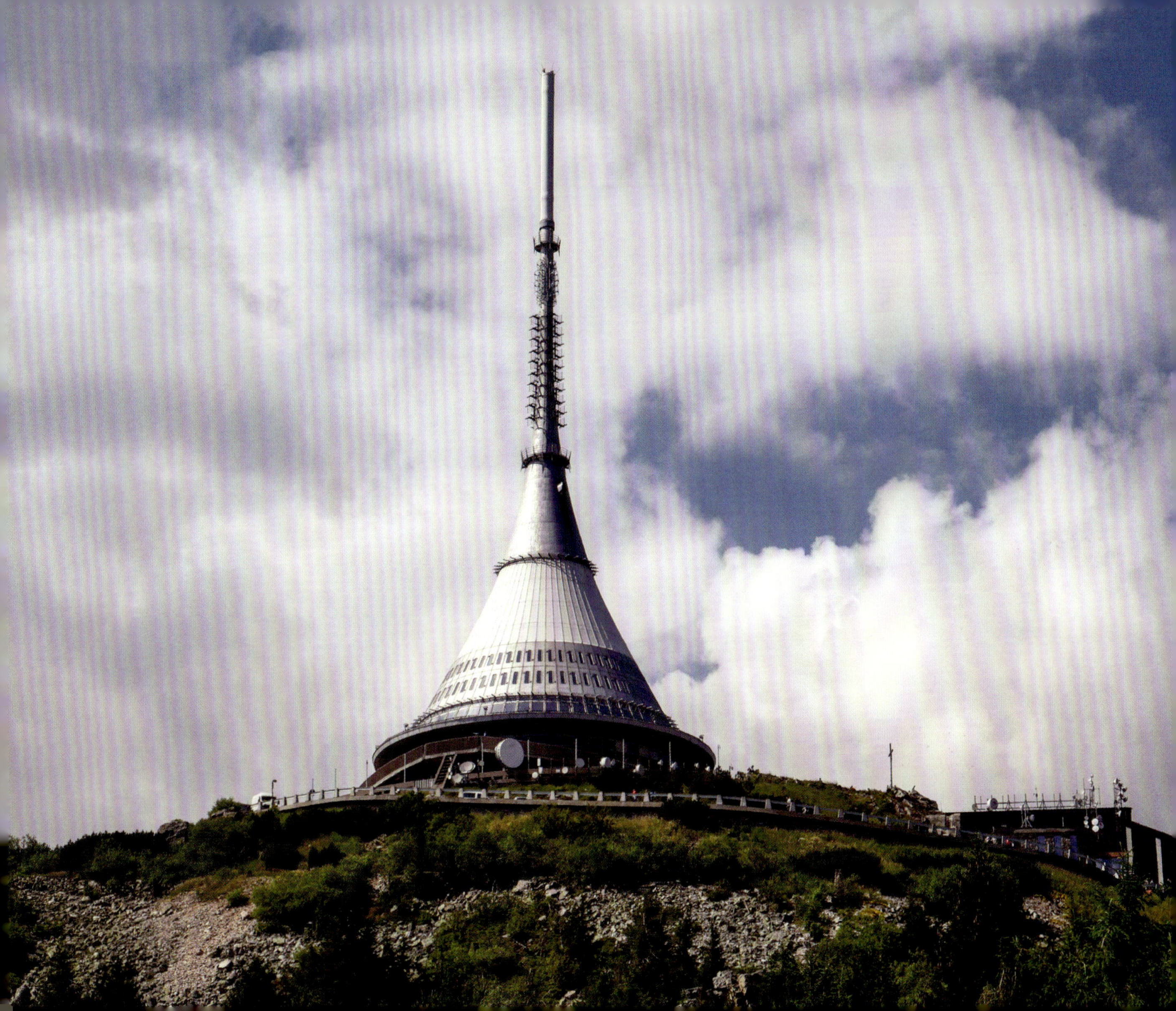

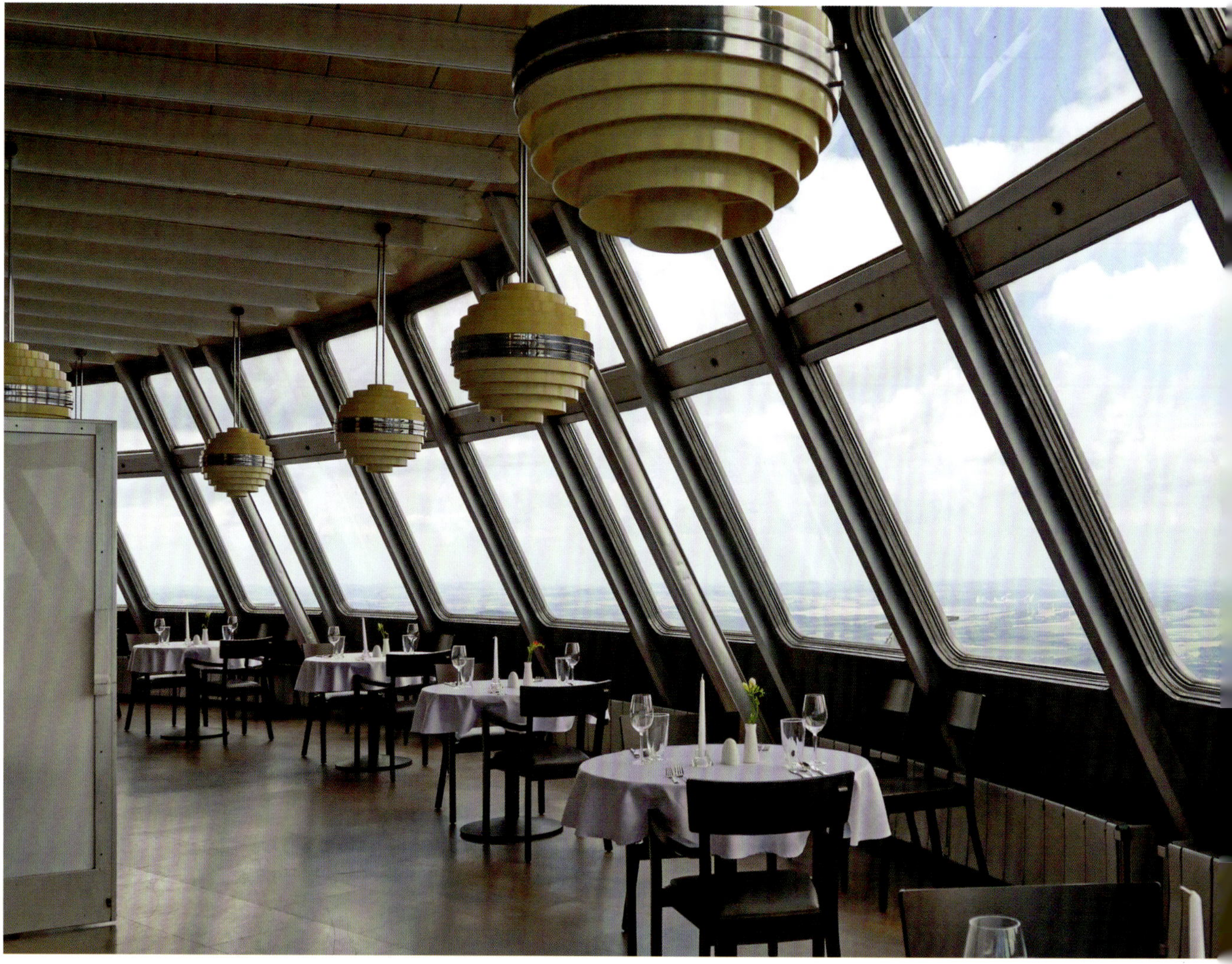

 Hotel Ještěd, Liberec, Czech Republic

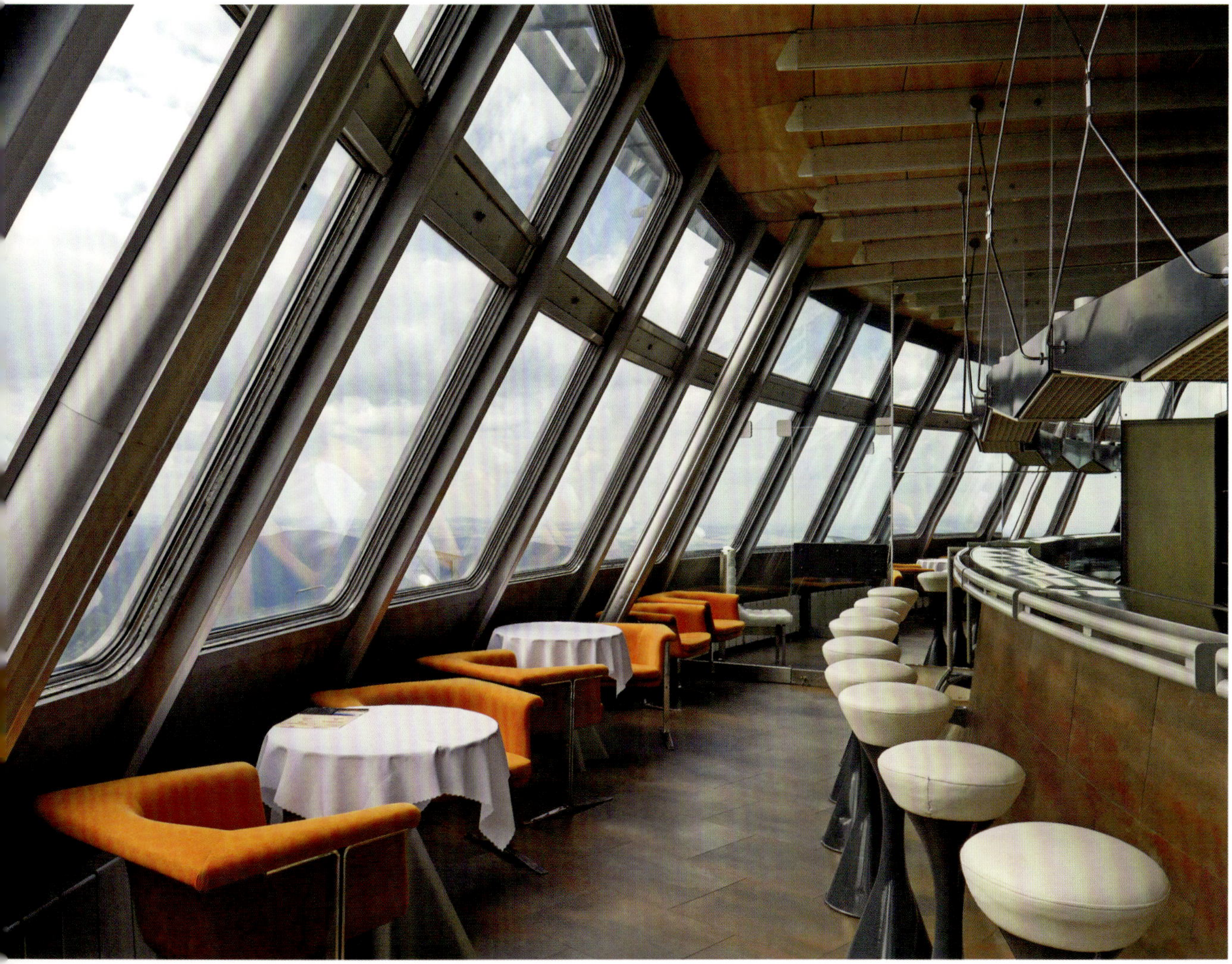

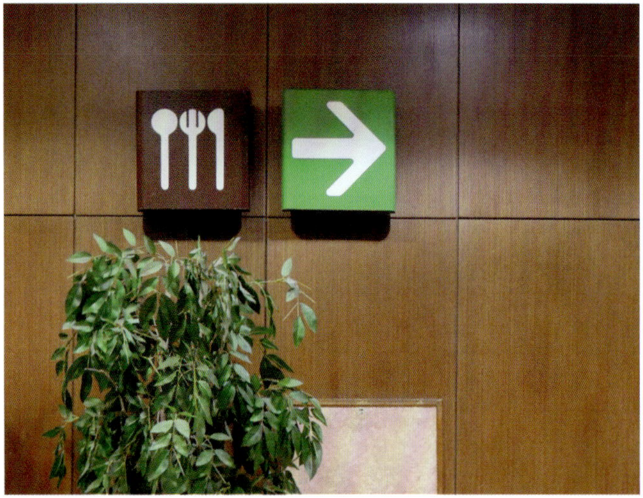

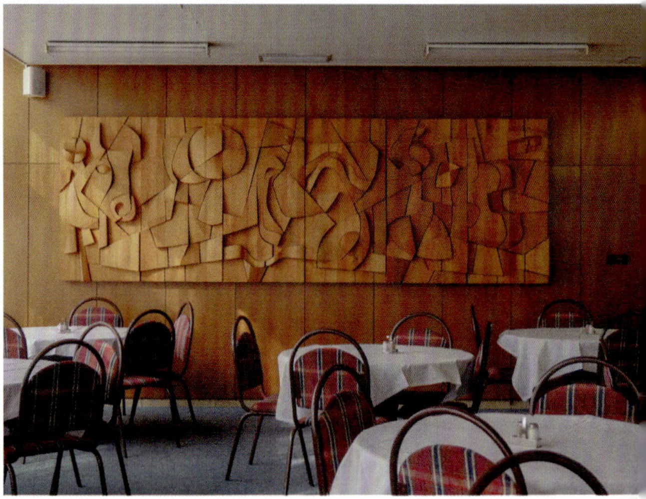

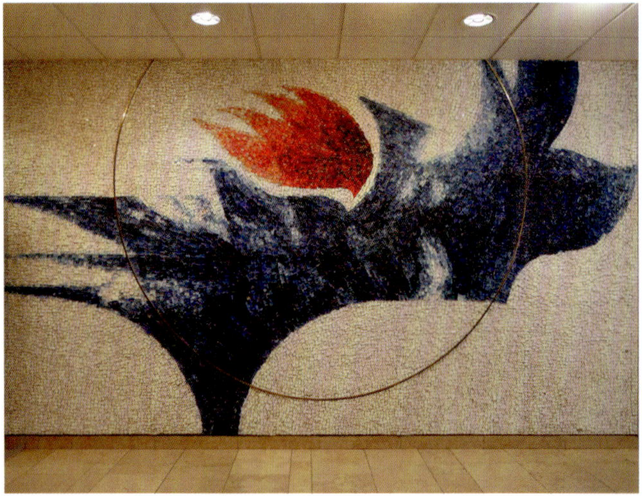

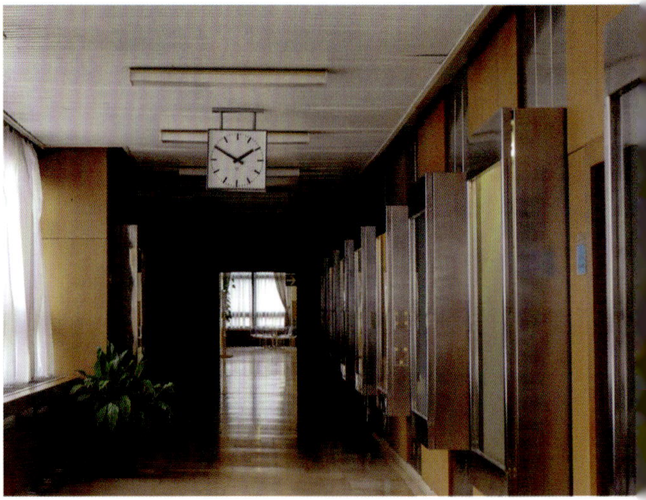

Hotel Krystal, Prague, Czech Republic

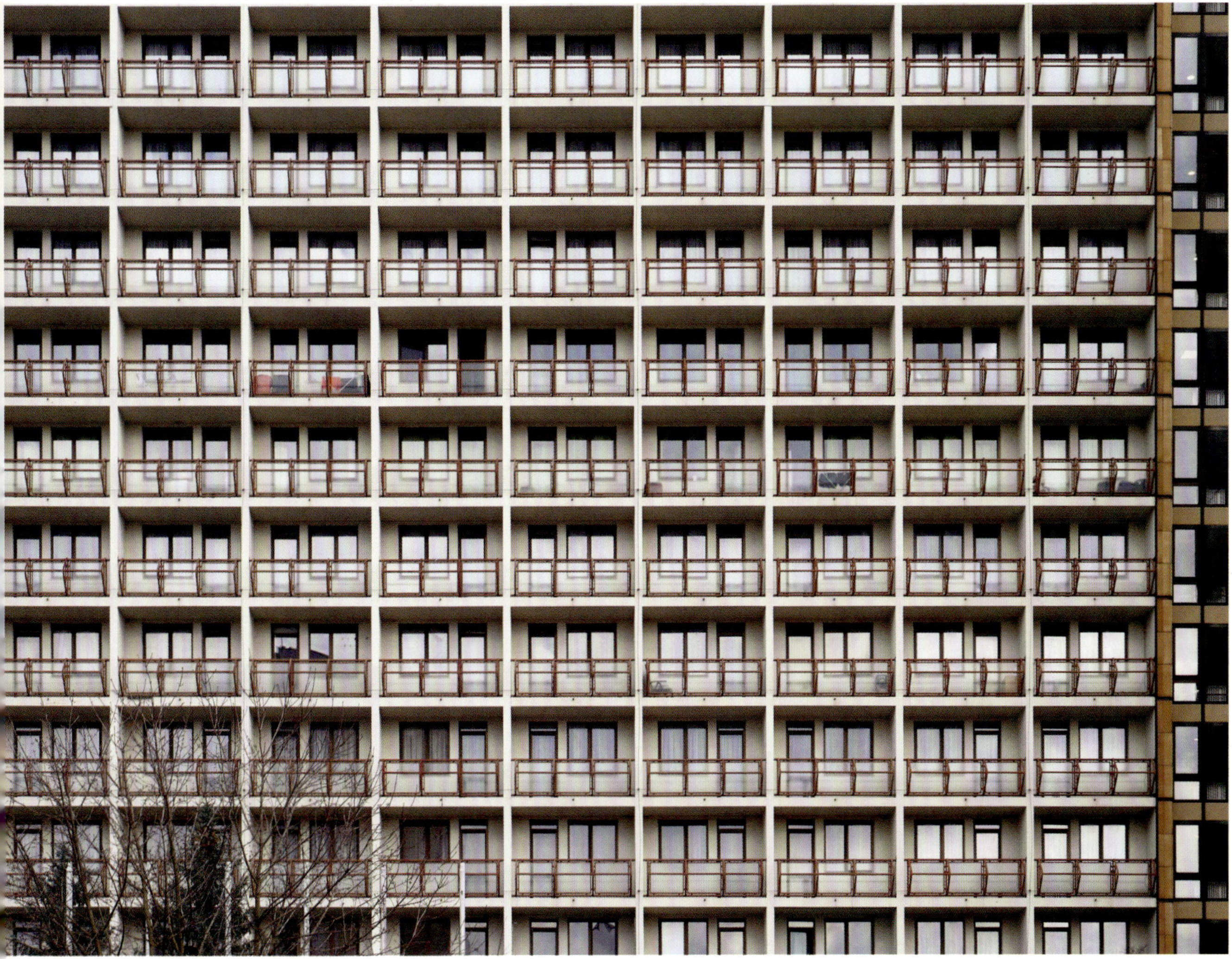

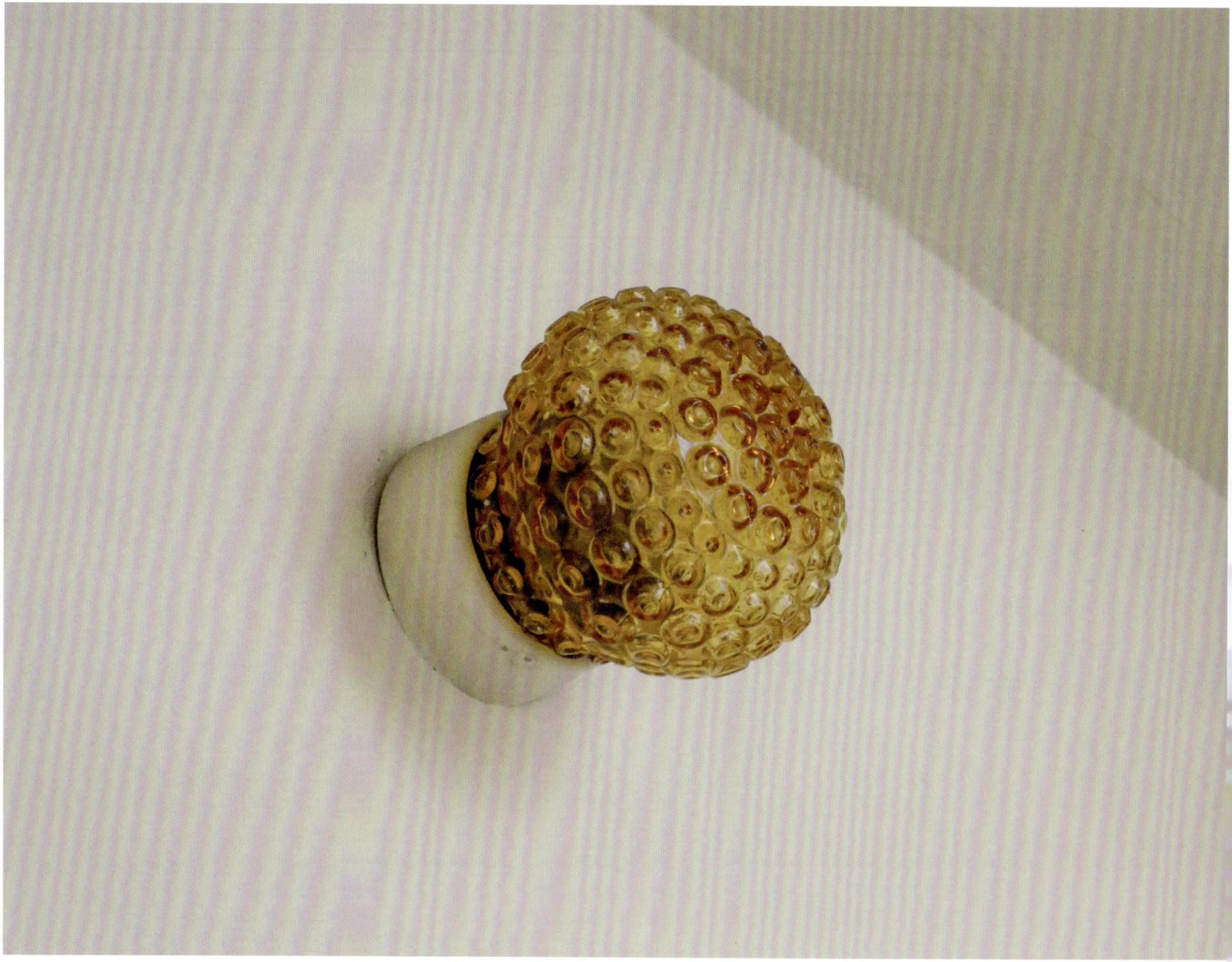

 Hotel Cascade (former Hotel Murom), Most, Czech Republic

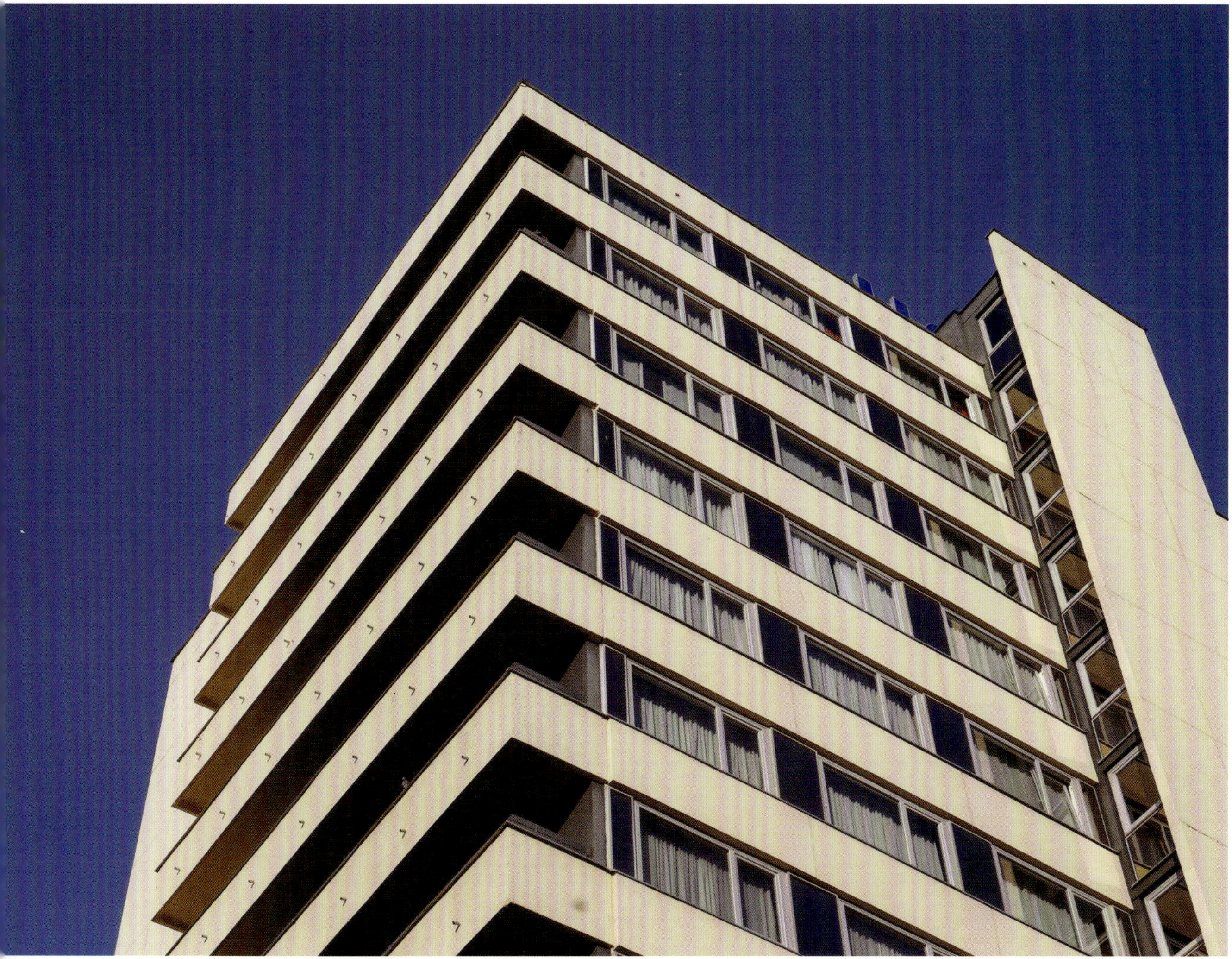

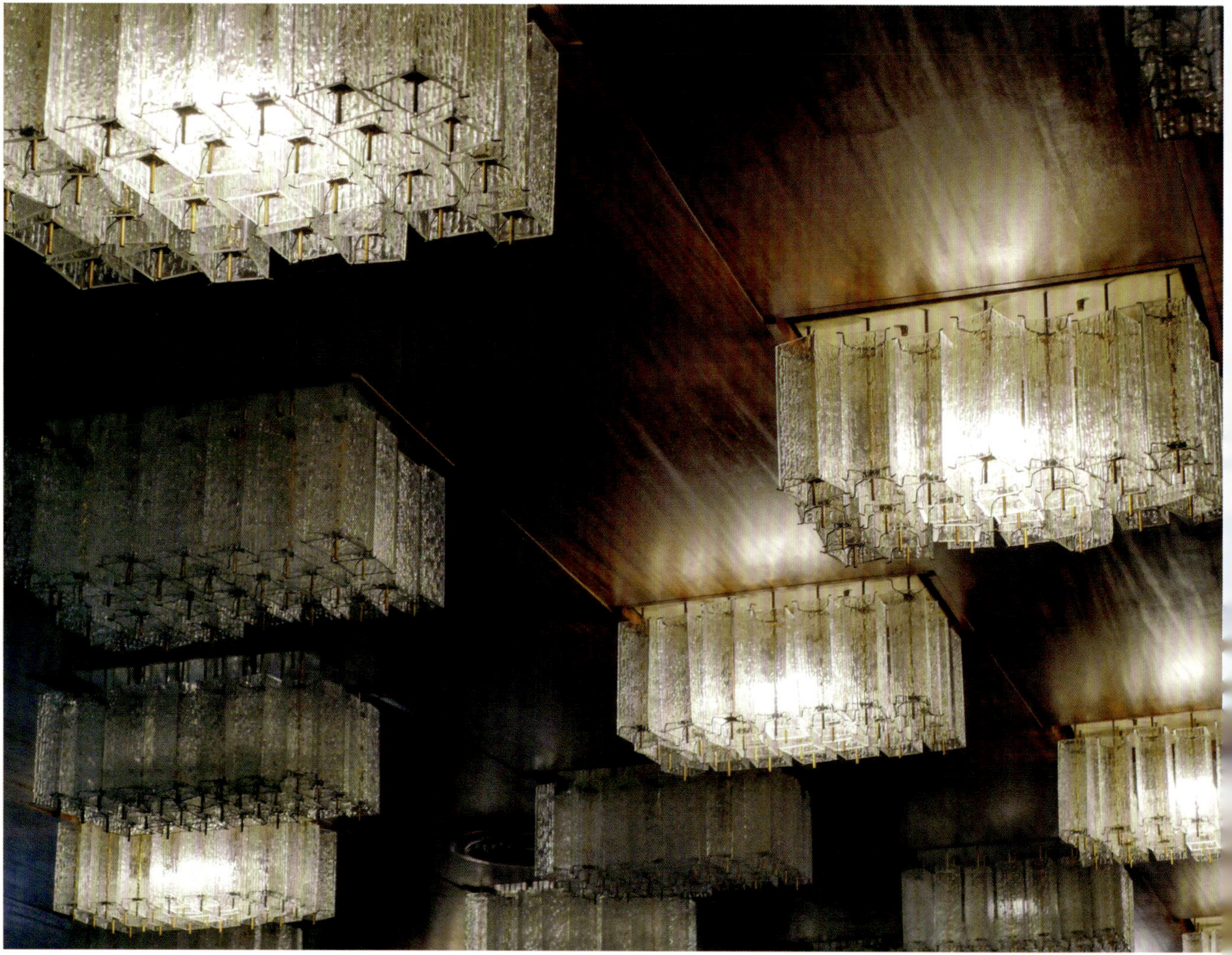

 Hotel Cascade (former Hotel Murom), Most, Czech Republic

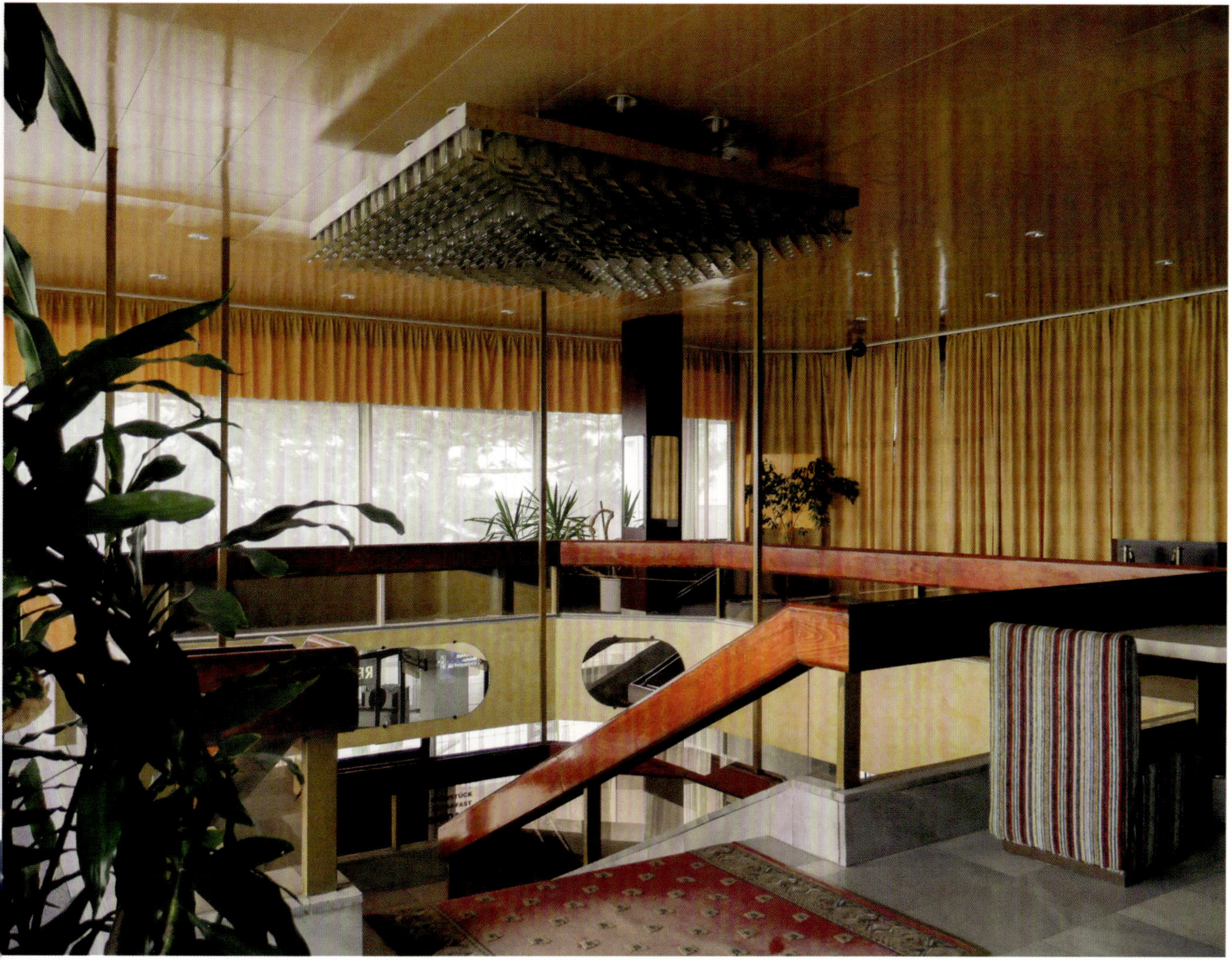

Hotel Labe, Pardubice, Czech Republic

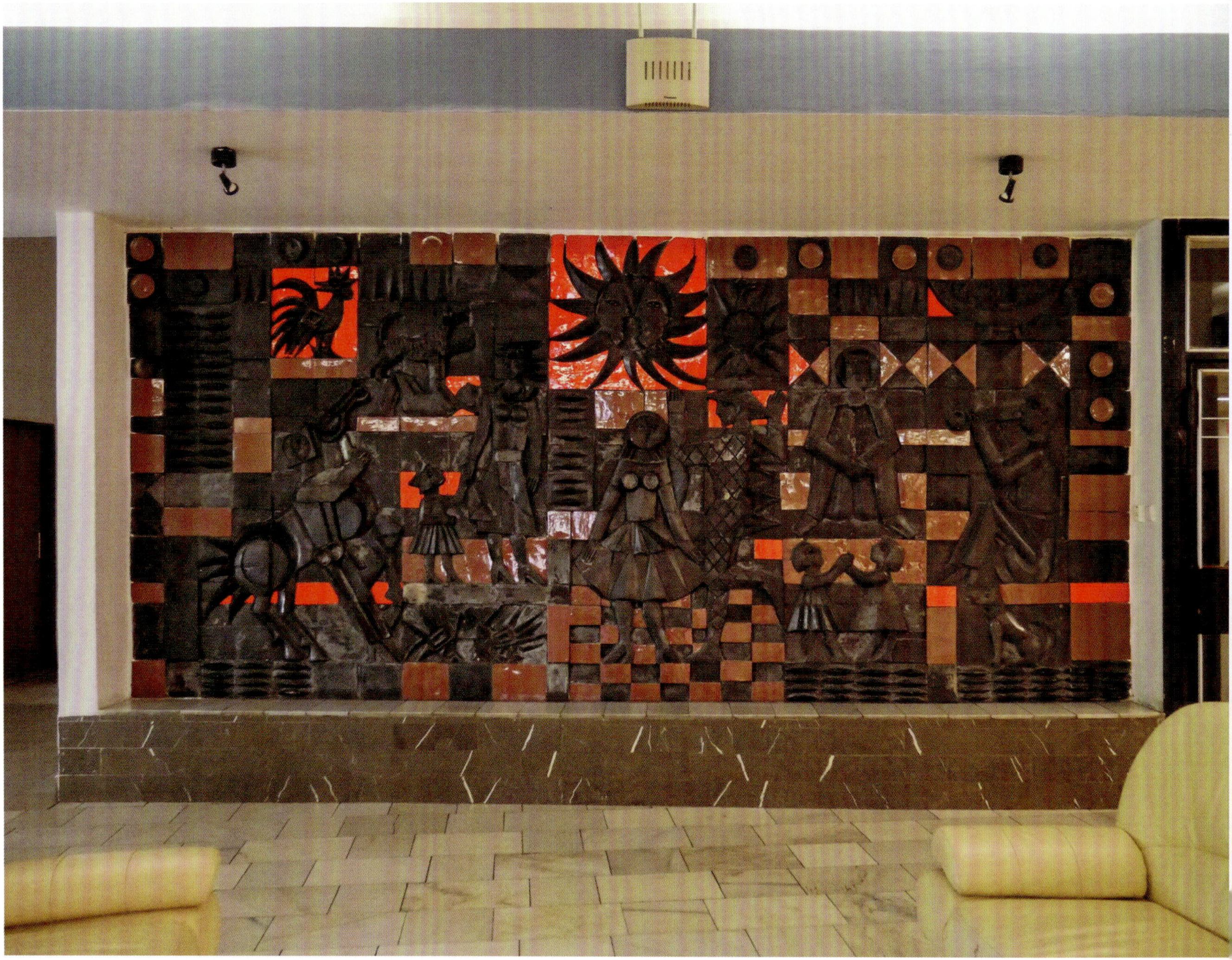

Hotel Relax, Rožnov pod Radhoštěm, Czech Republic

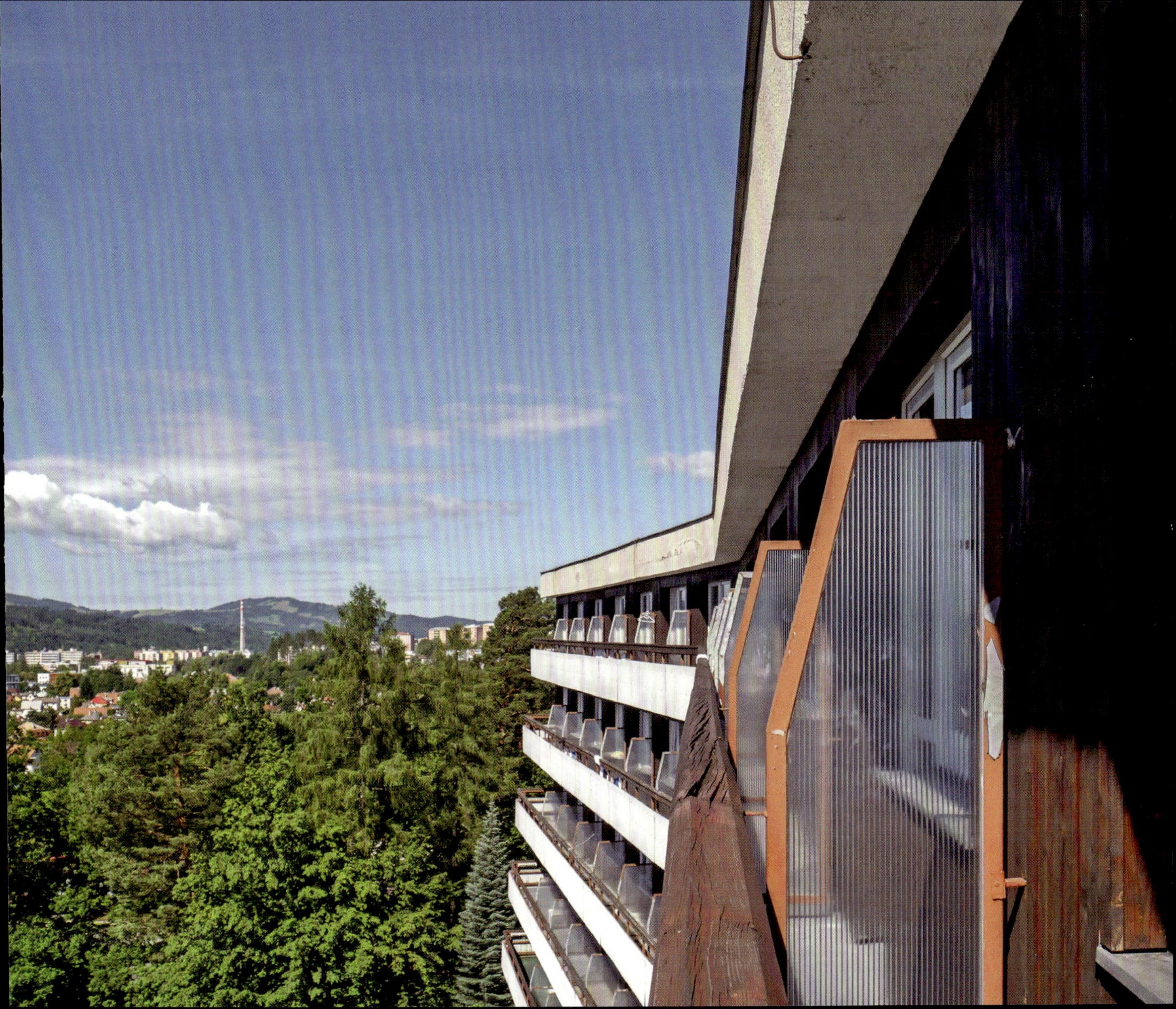

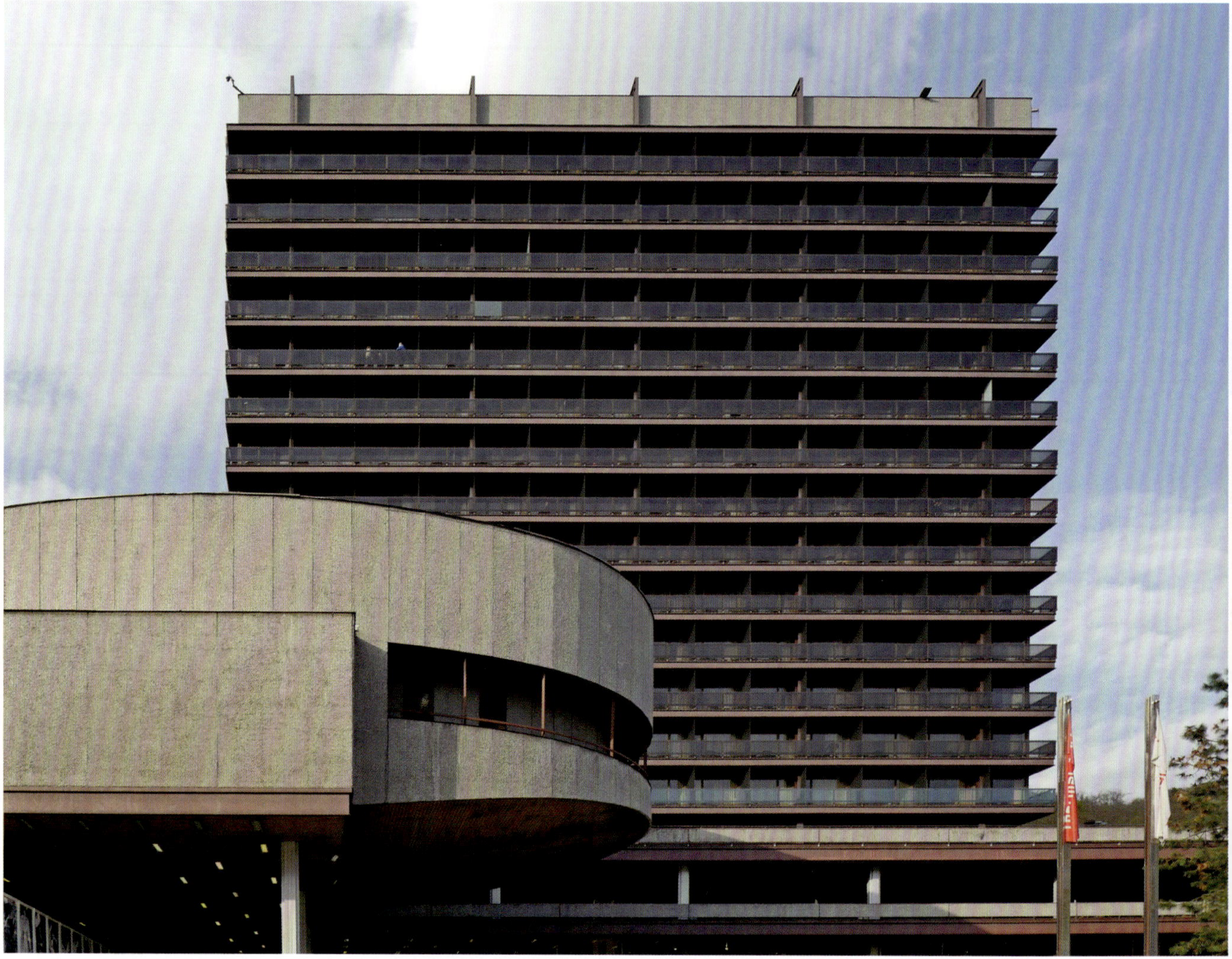

Hotel Thermal, Karlovy Vary, Czech Republic

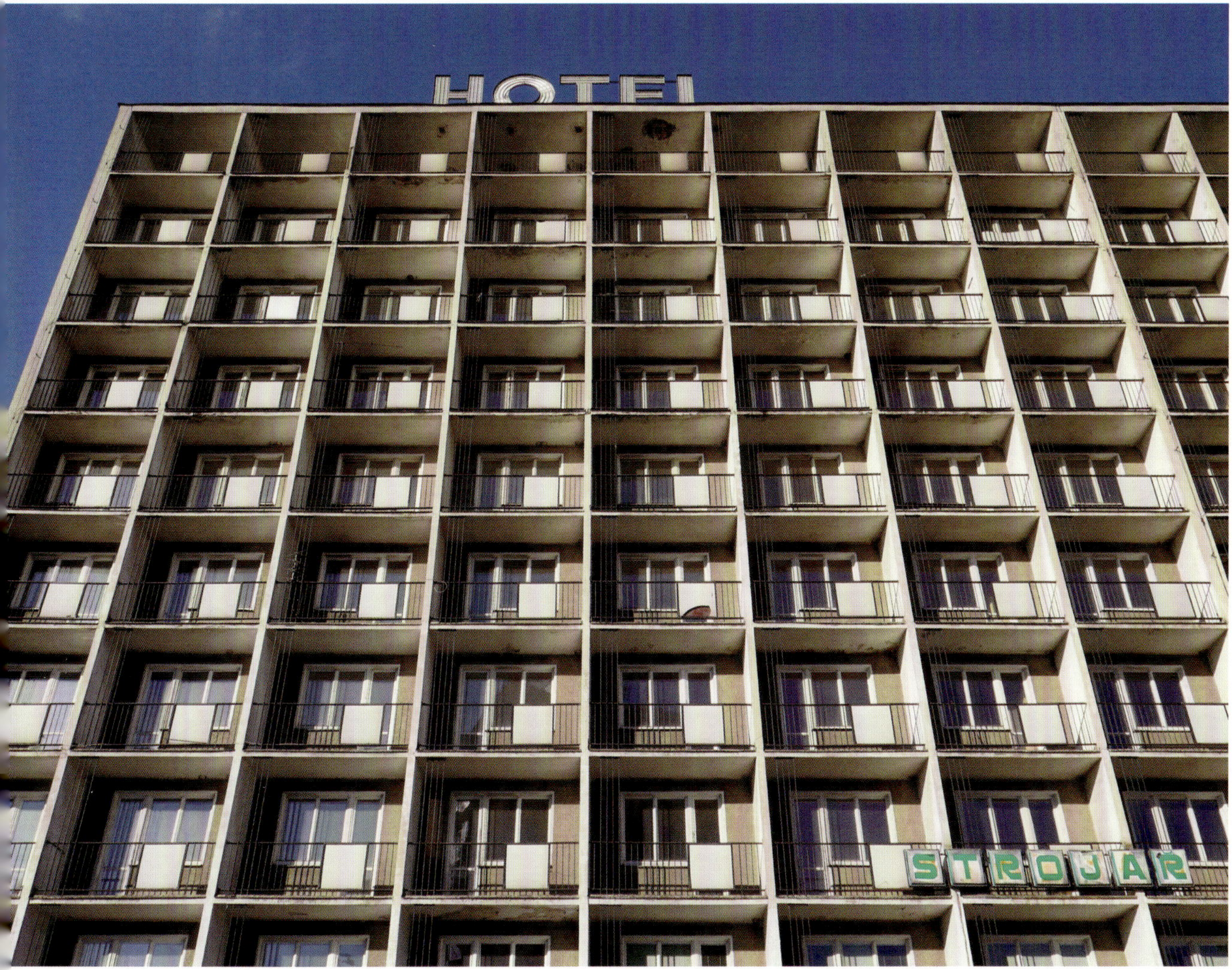

Hotel Strojař, Přerov, Czech Republic

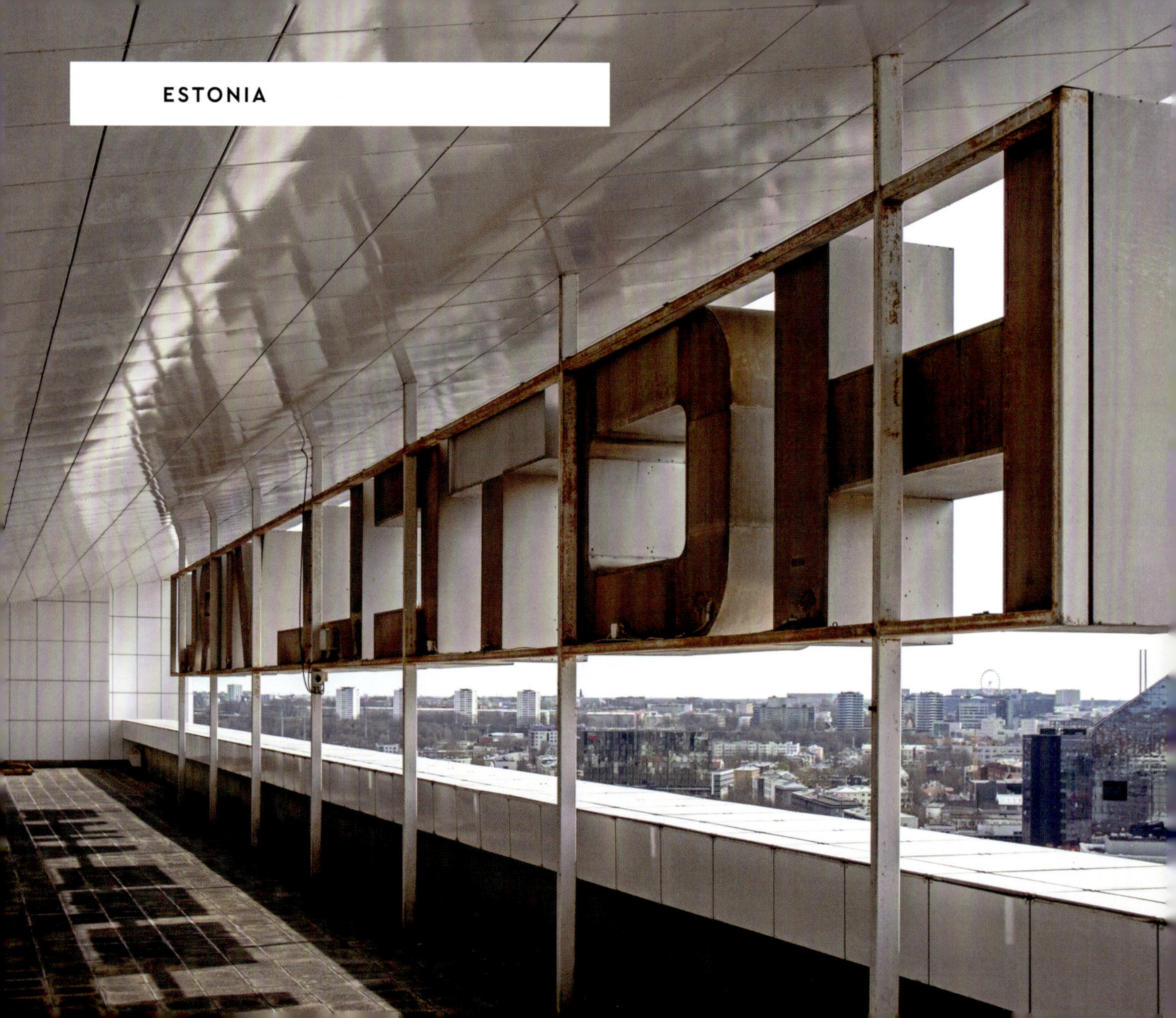

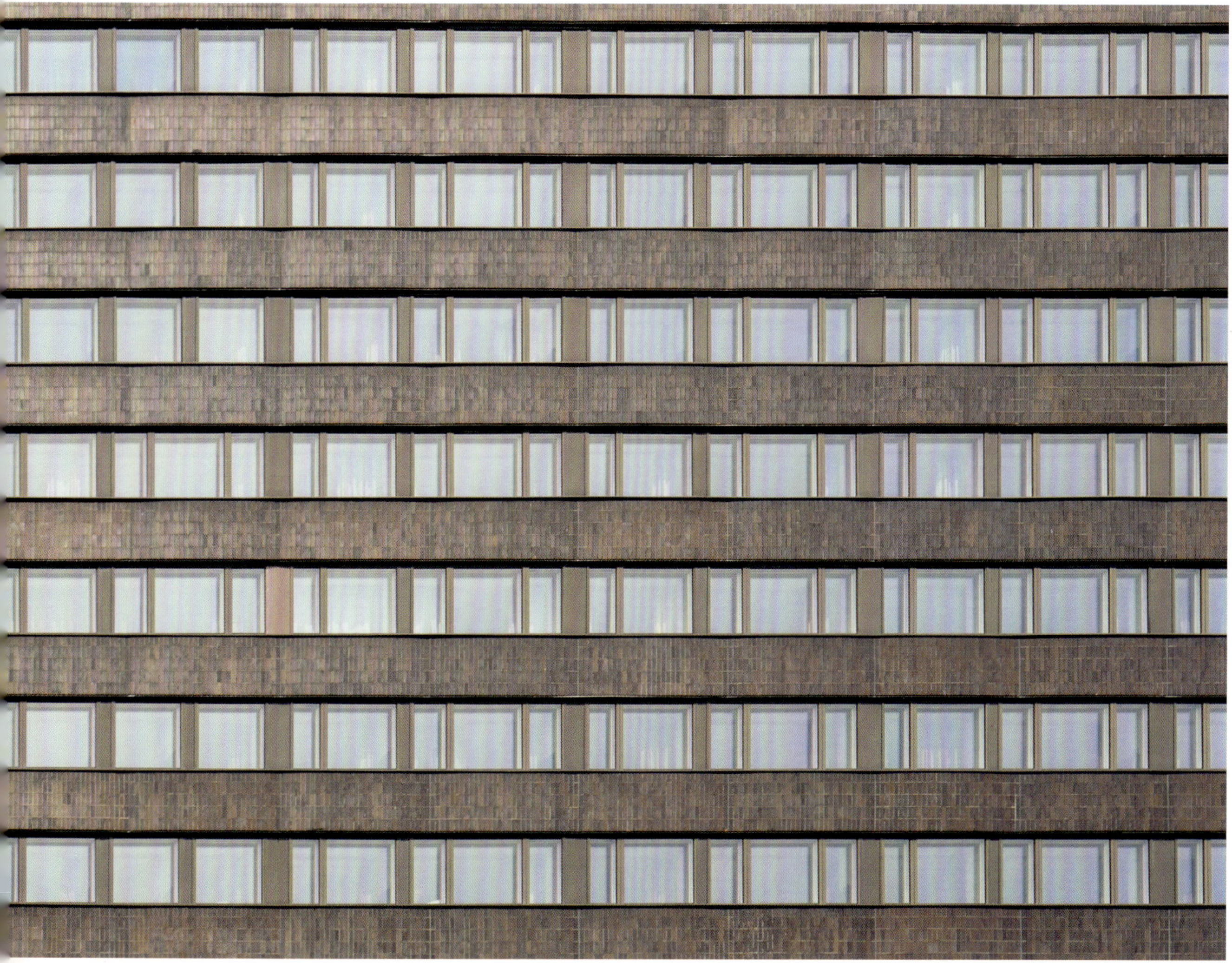

Hotel Viru, Tallinn, Estonia

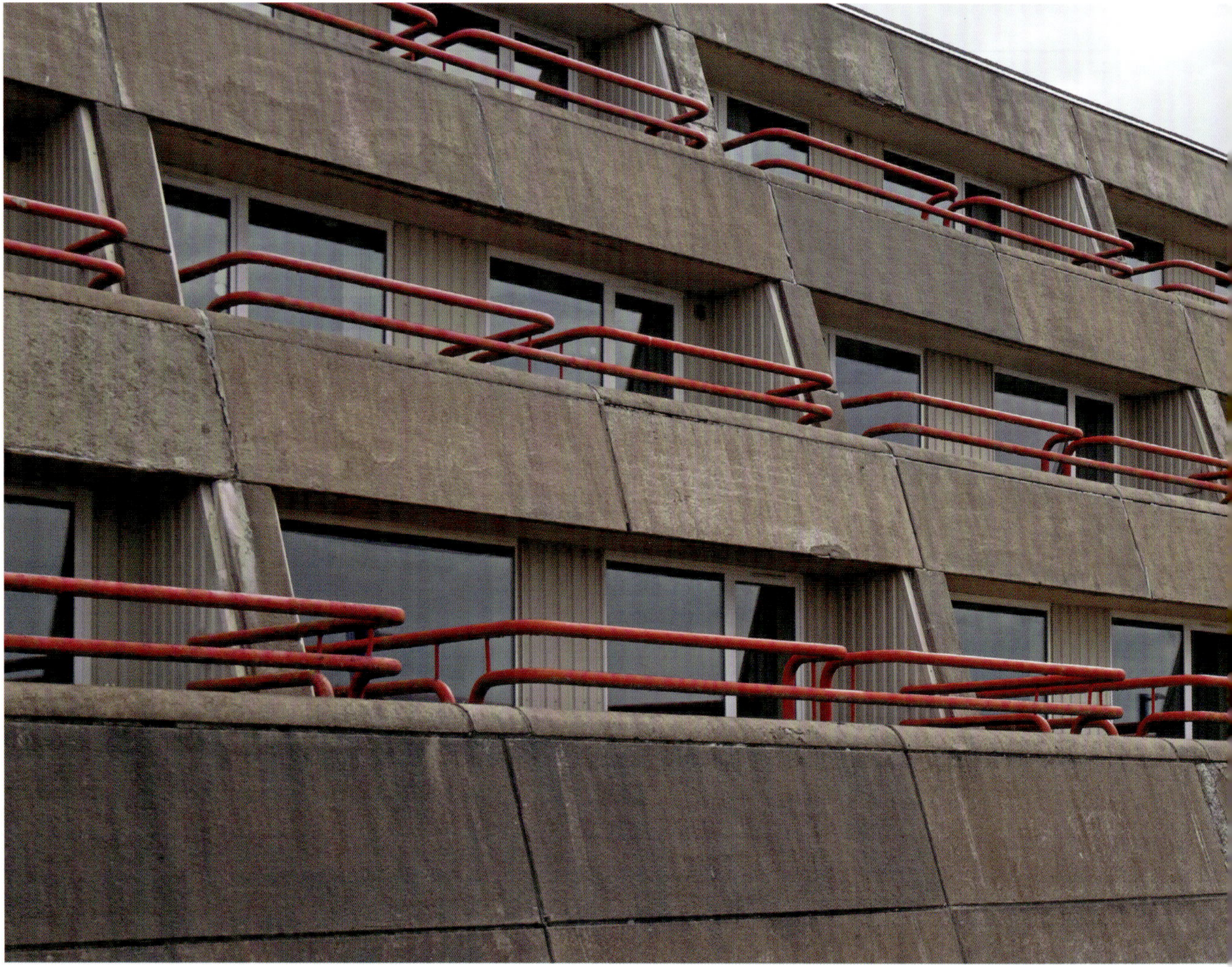

 Hotel Pirita Marina (former Hotel Sport), Tallinn, Estonia

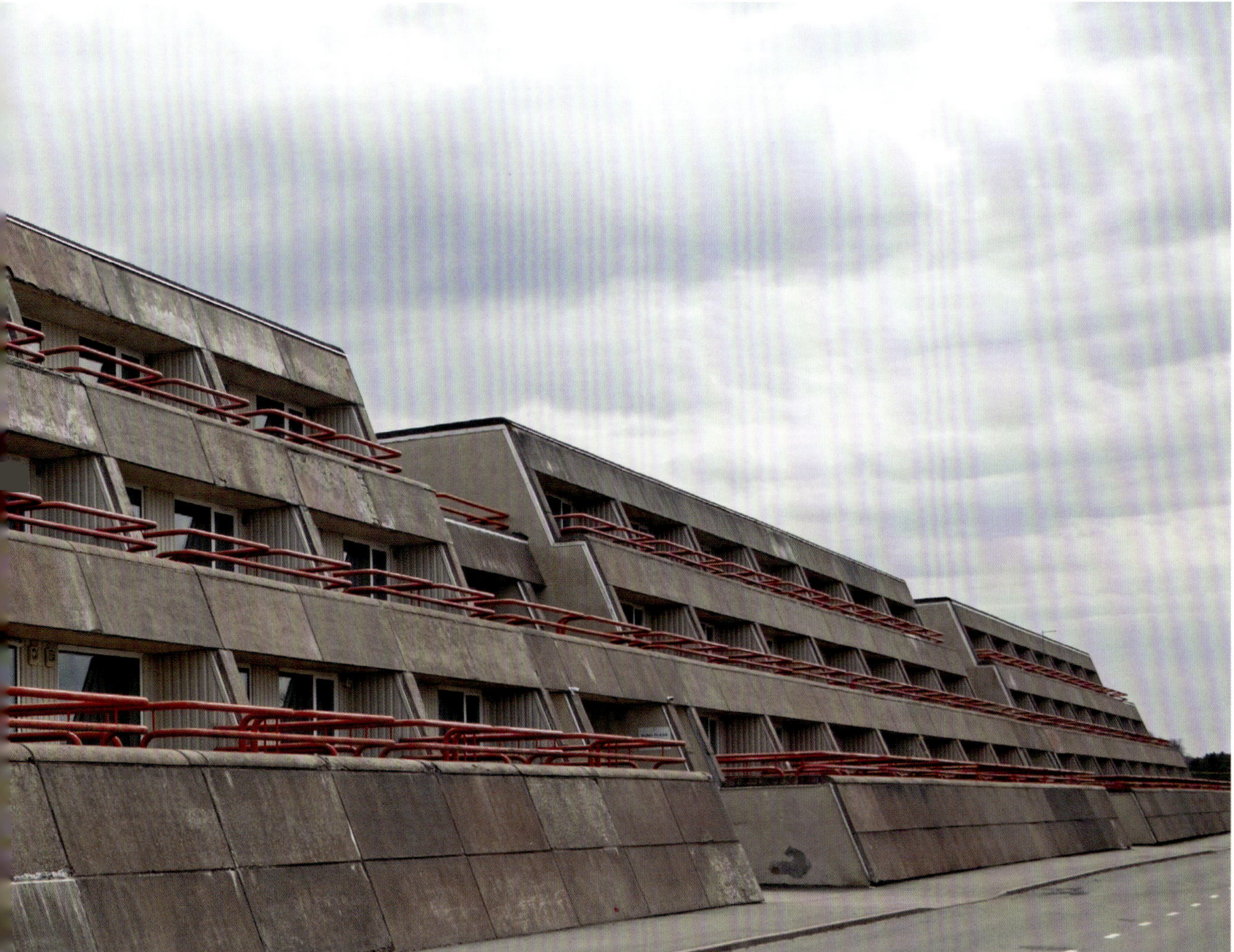

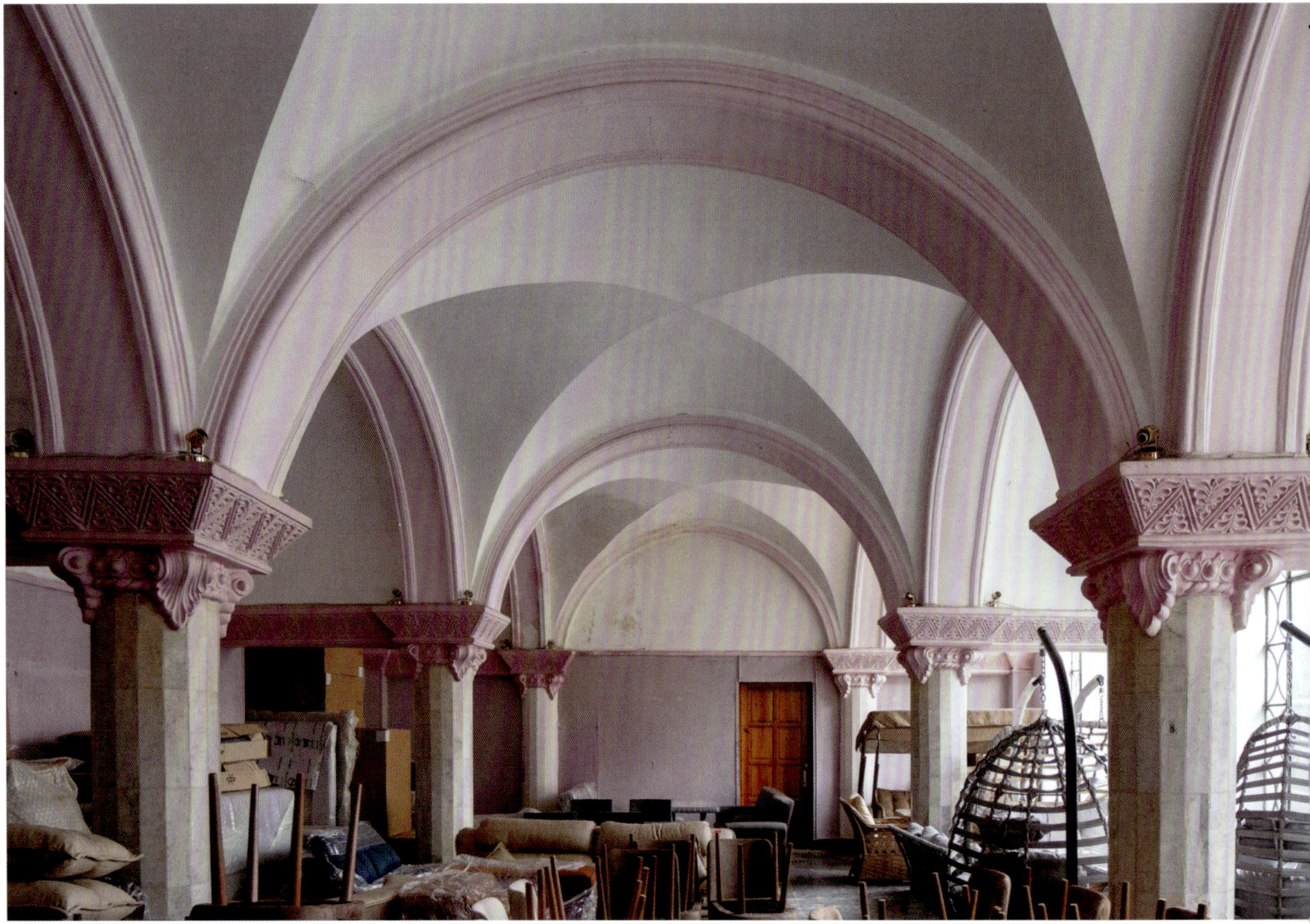

 Hotel Intourist, Gori, Georgia

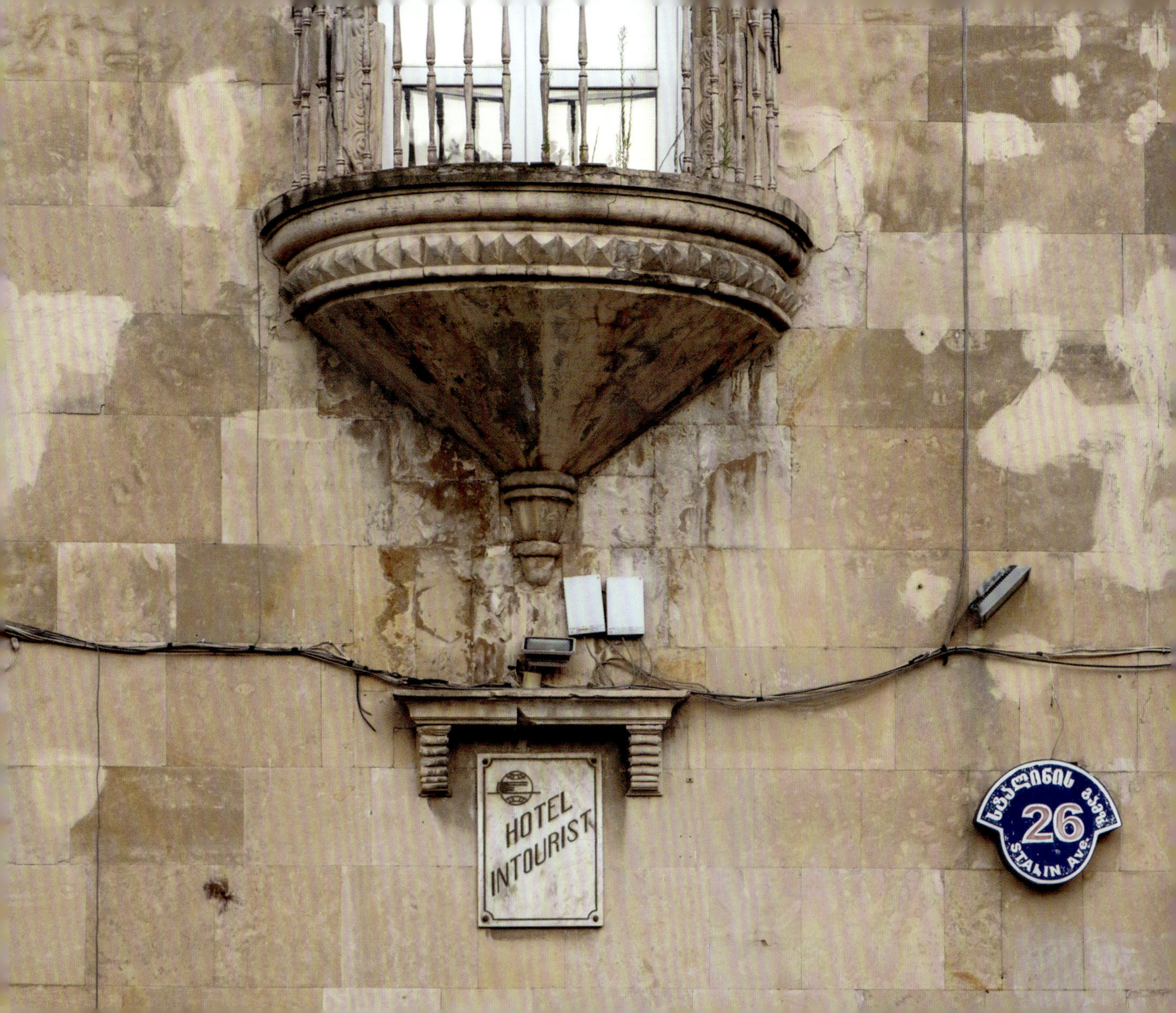
HOTEL
INTOURIST
სტალინის გამზ.
26
STALIN AVE.

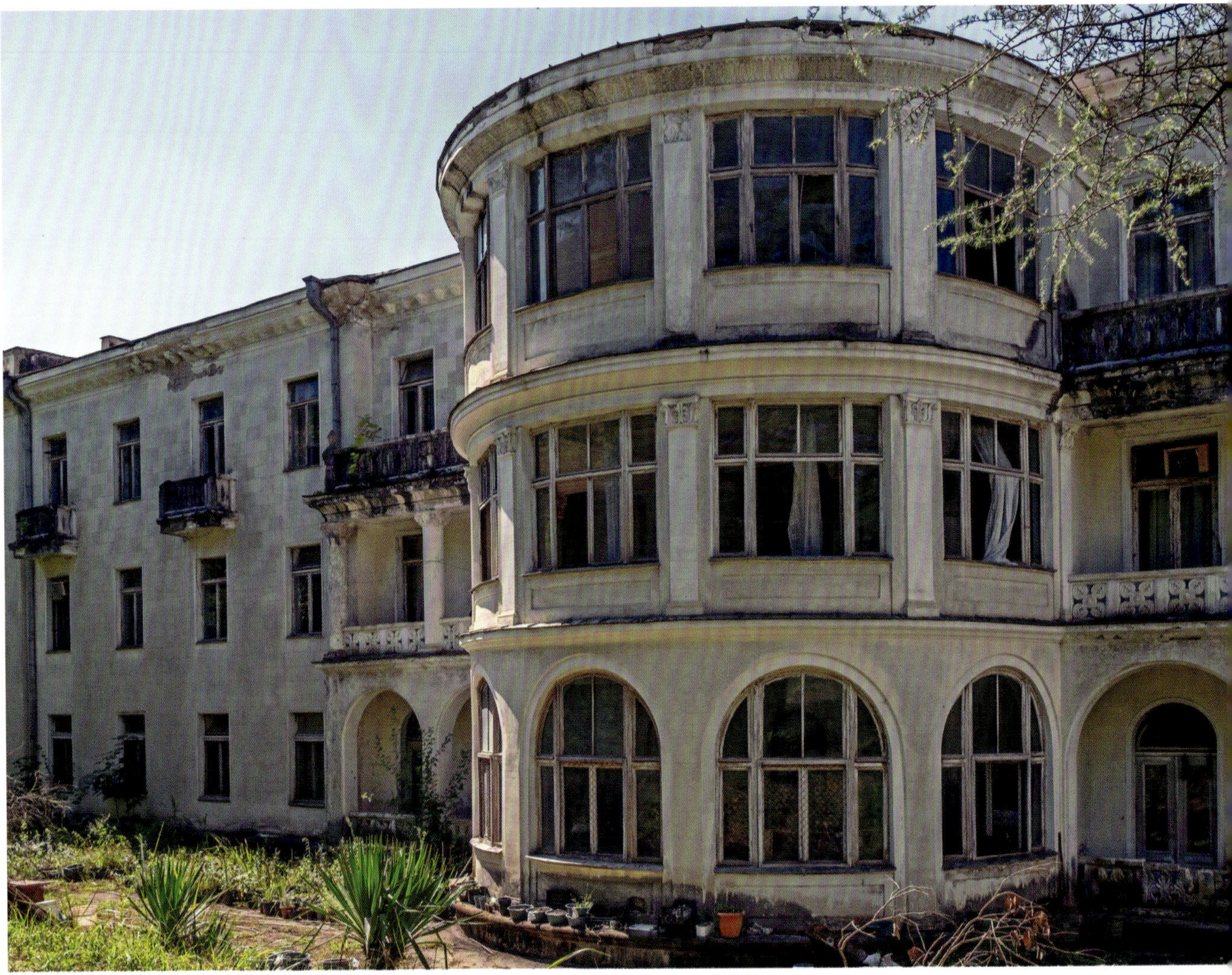

Legends Tskaltubo Spa Resort (former Ministry of Defence Sanatorium), Tskaltubo, Georgia

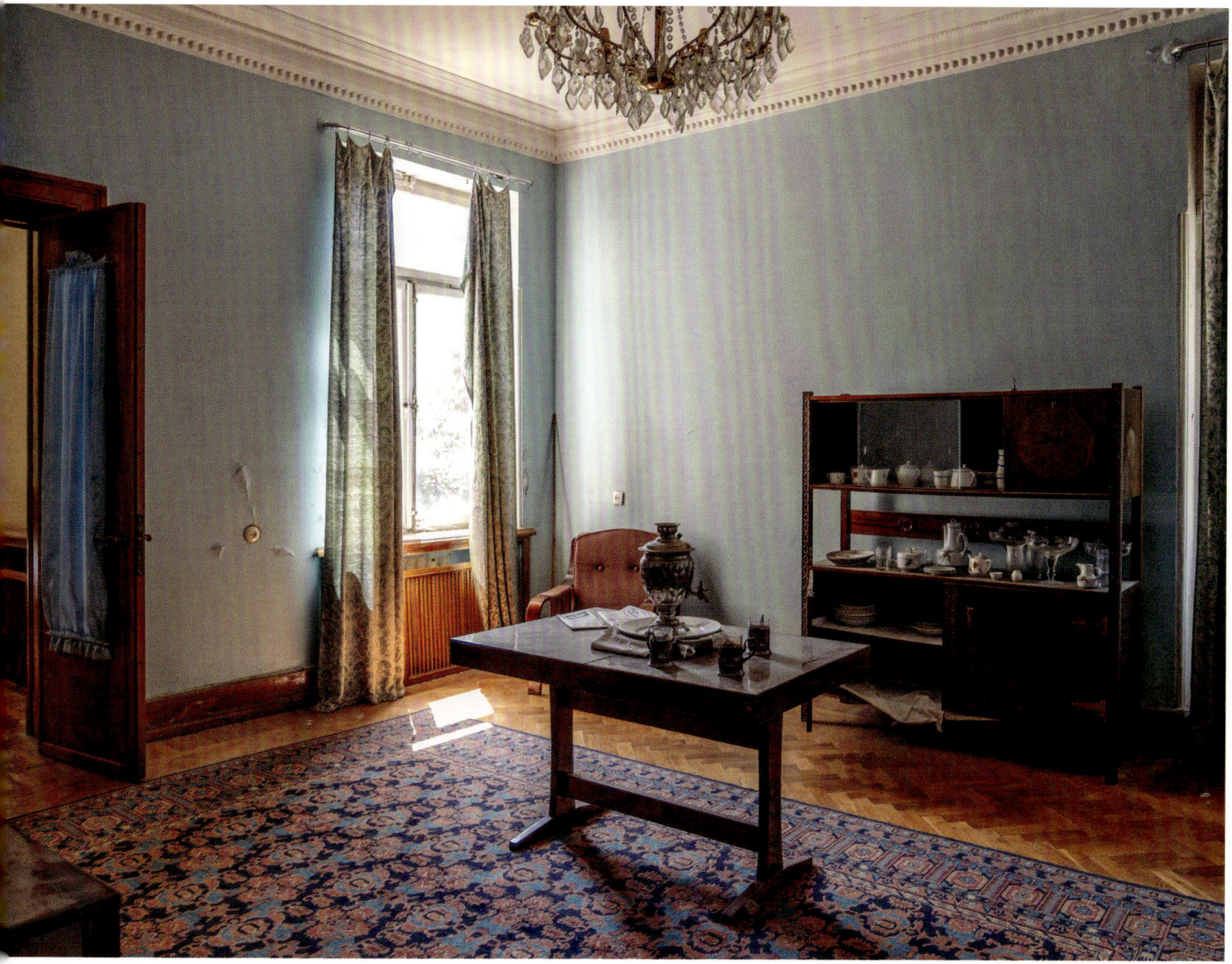

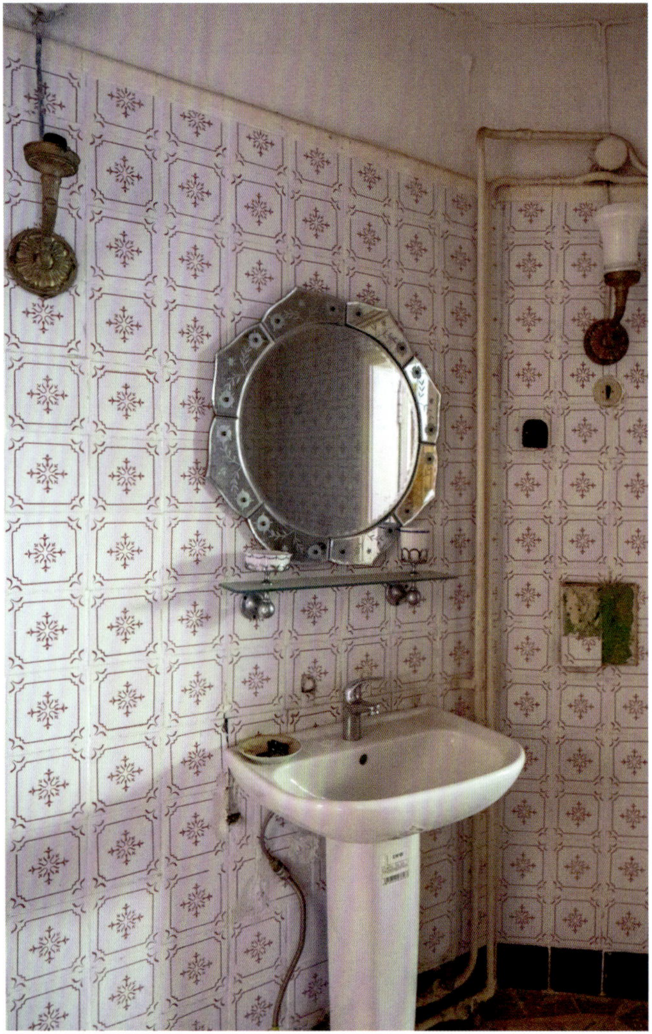

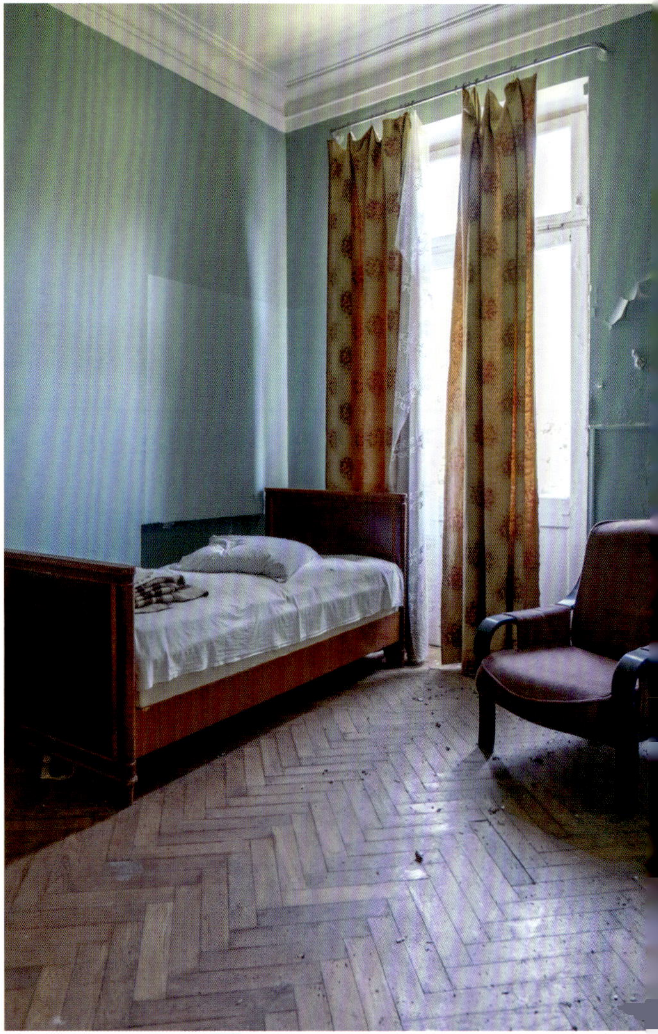

 Legends Tskaltubo Spa Resort (former Ministry of Defence Sanatorium), Tskaltubo, Georgia

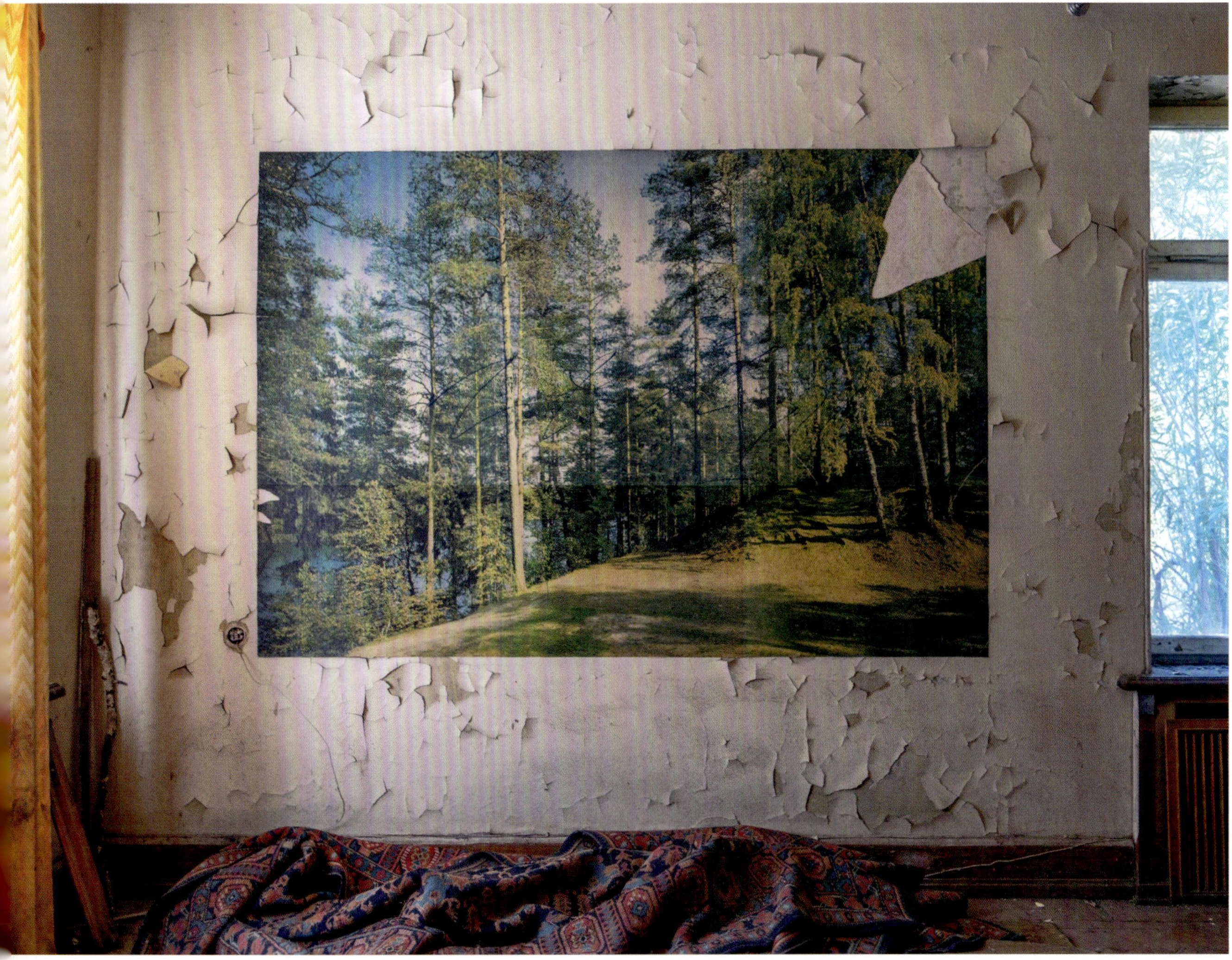

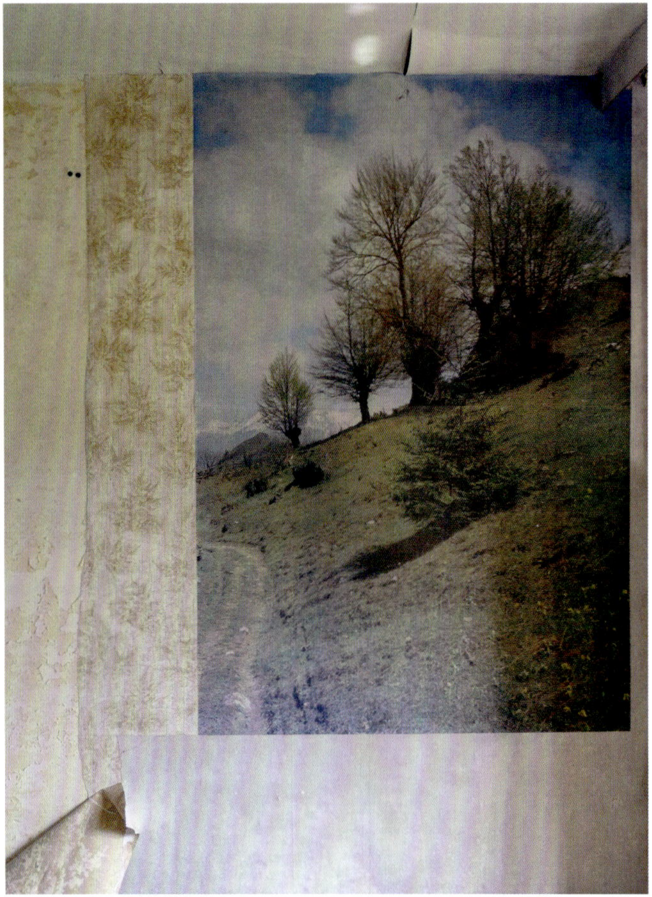

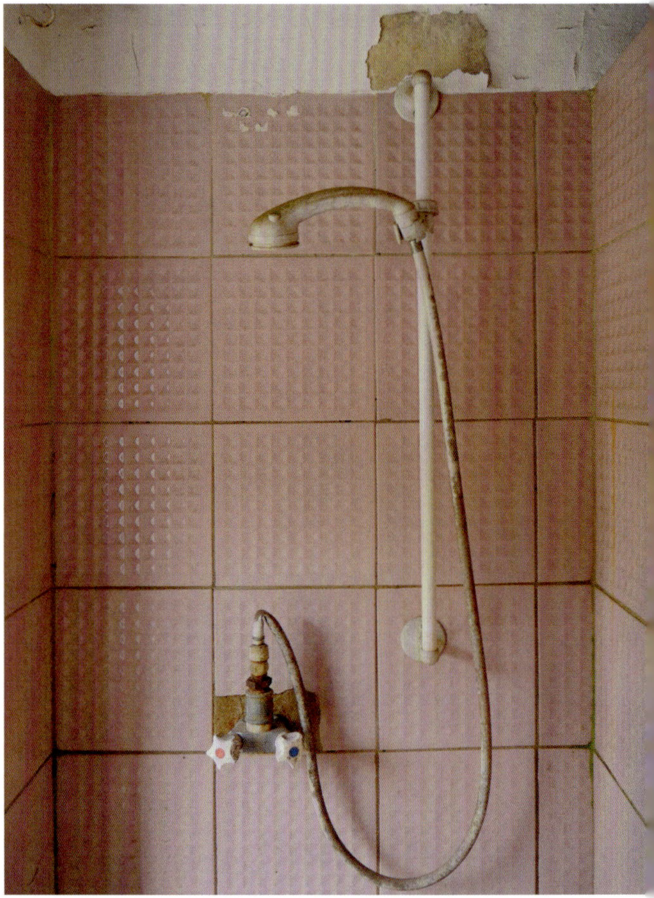

 Hotel Buschhaus, Mühlleithen, GDR

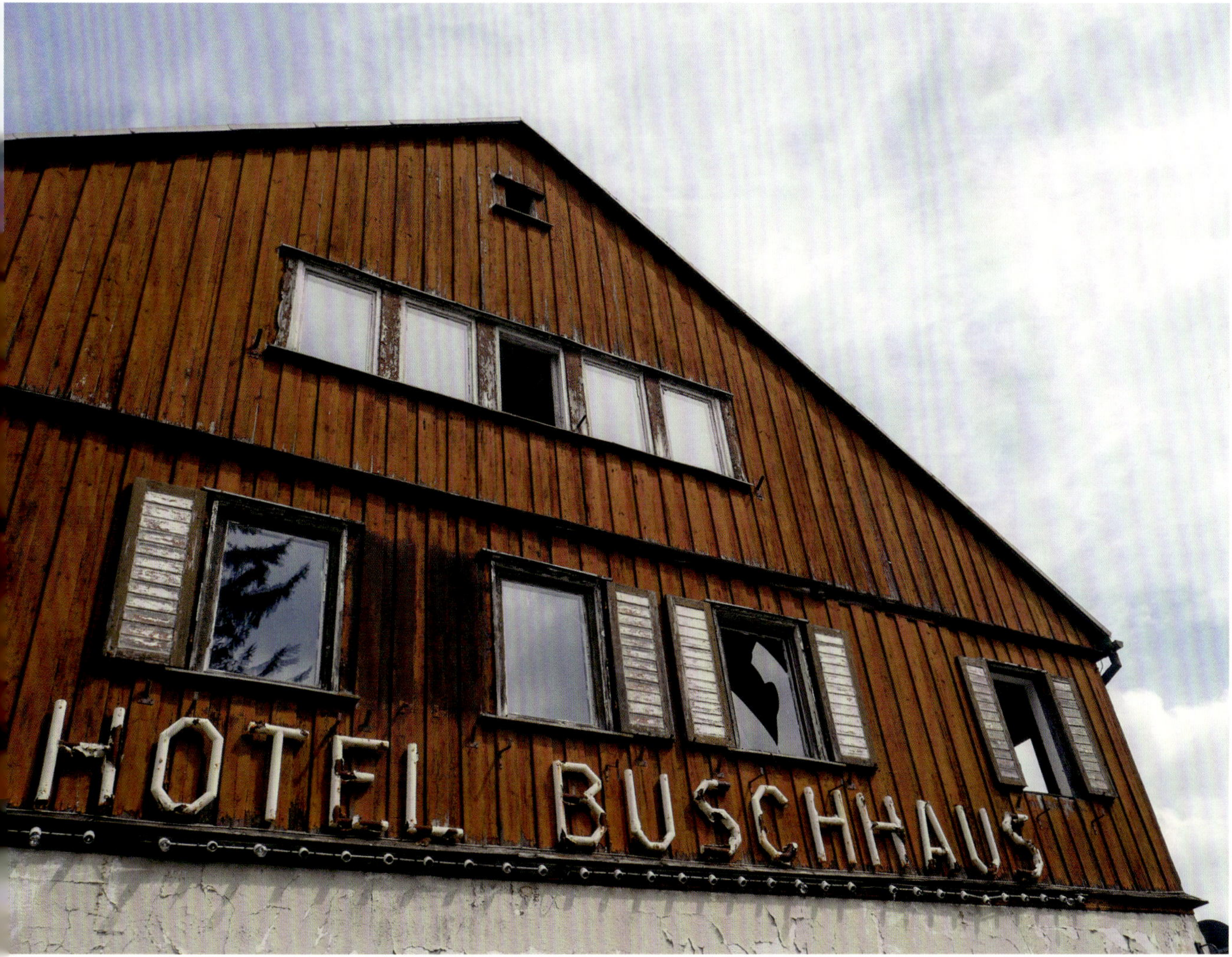
HOTEL BUSCHHAUS

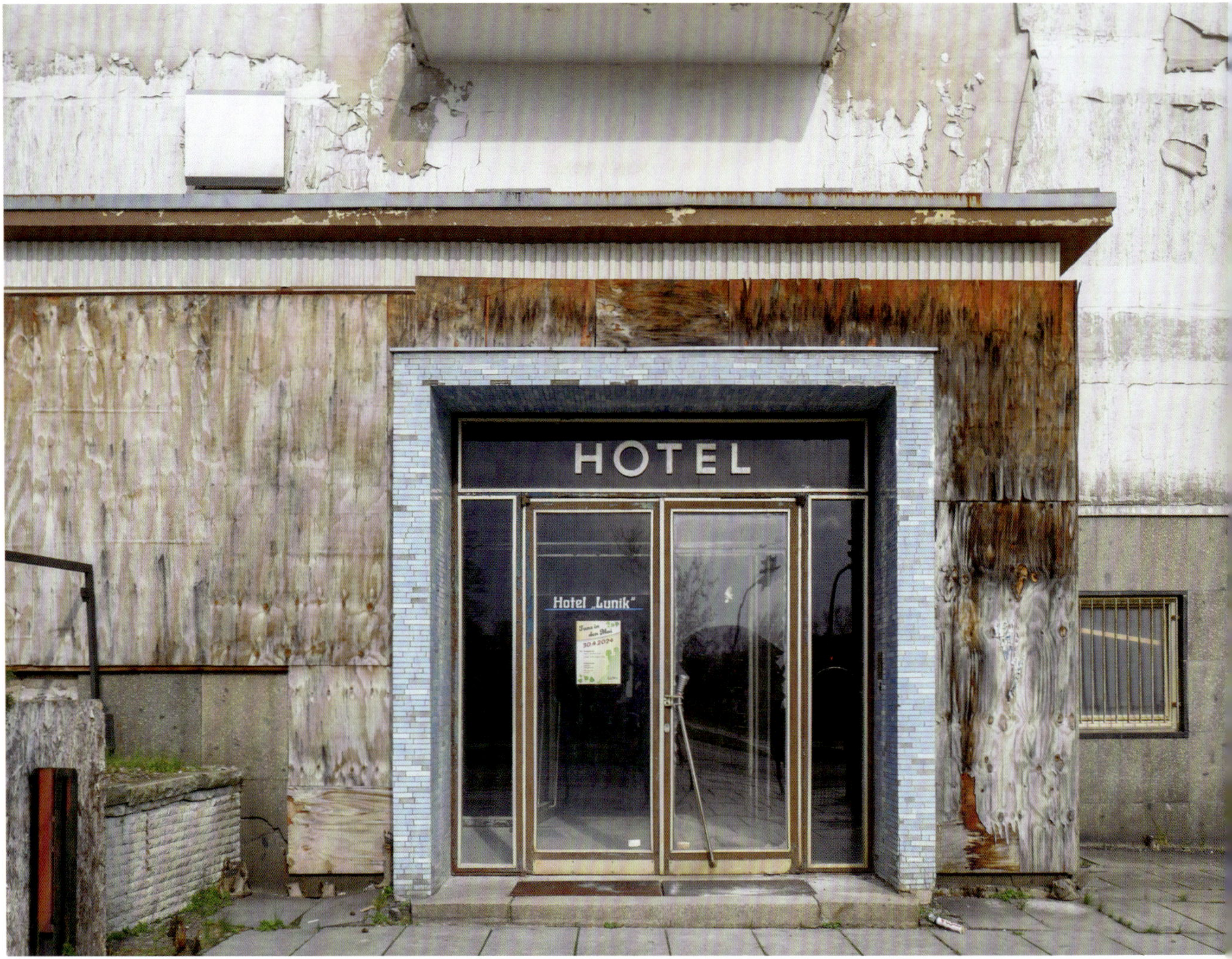

 Hotel Lunik, Eisenhüttenstadt, GDR

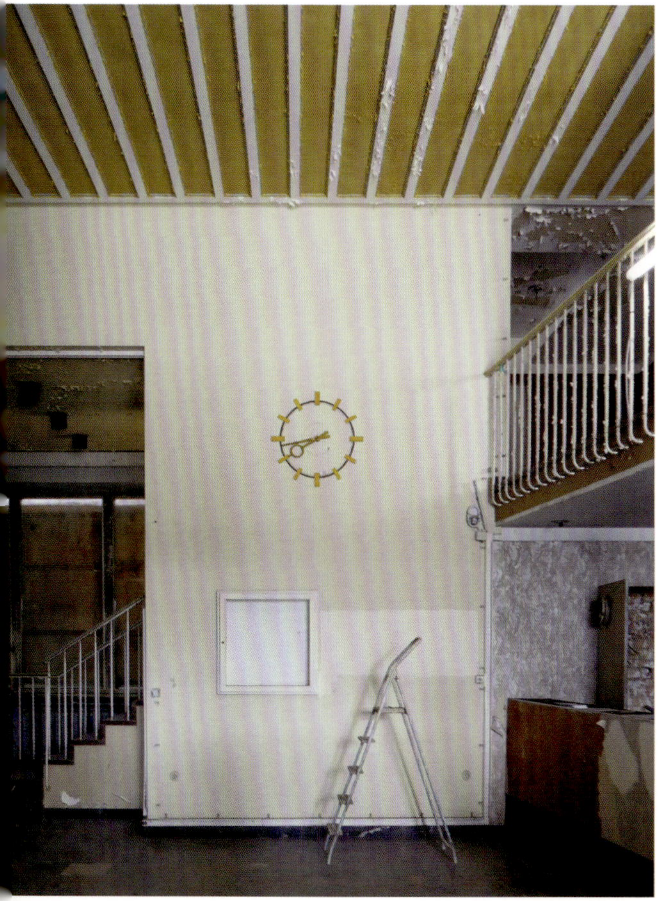

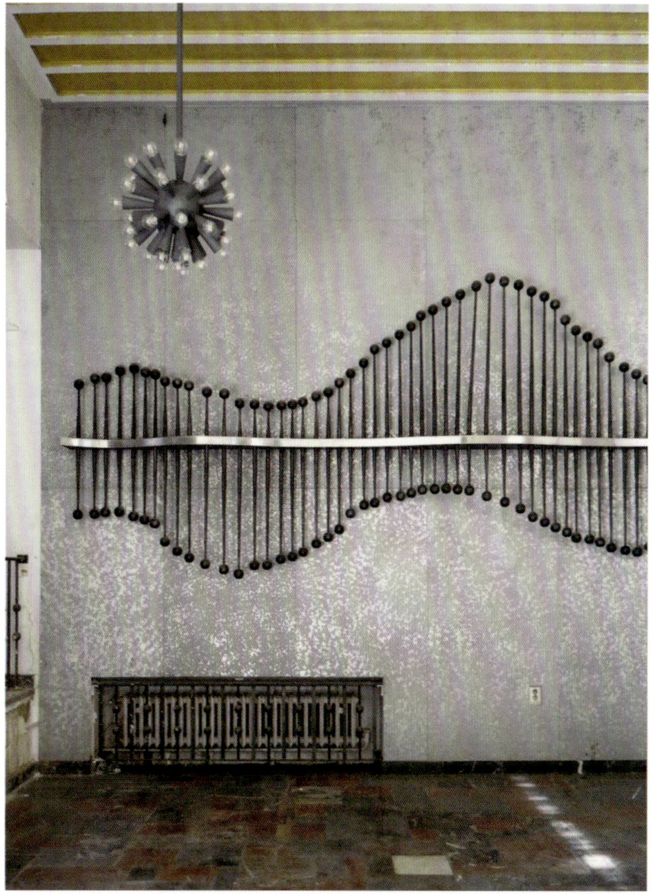

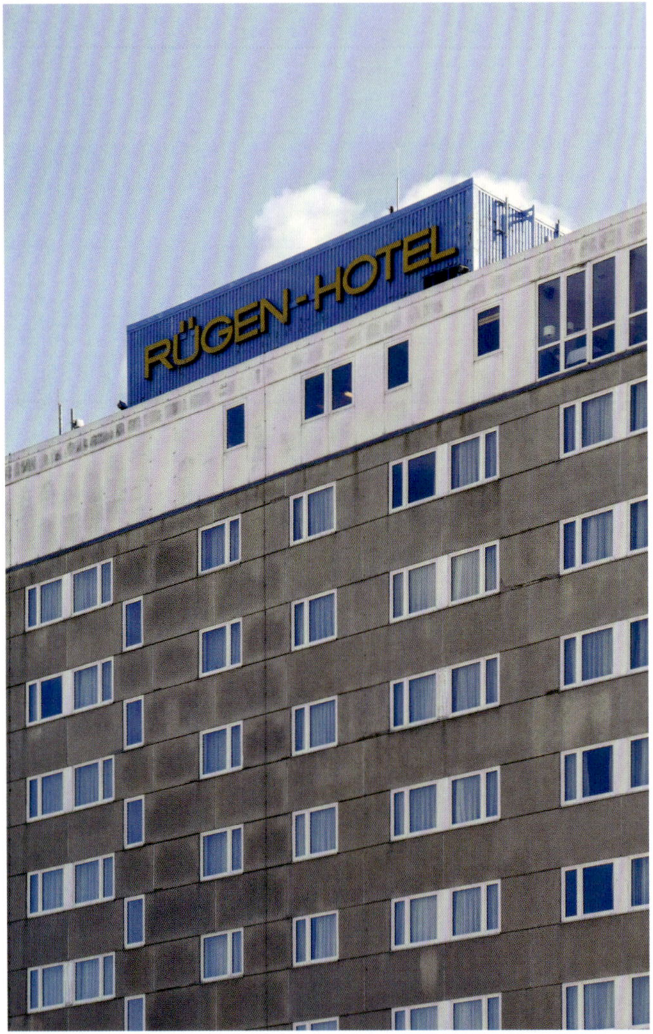

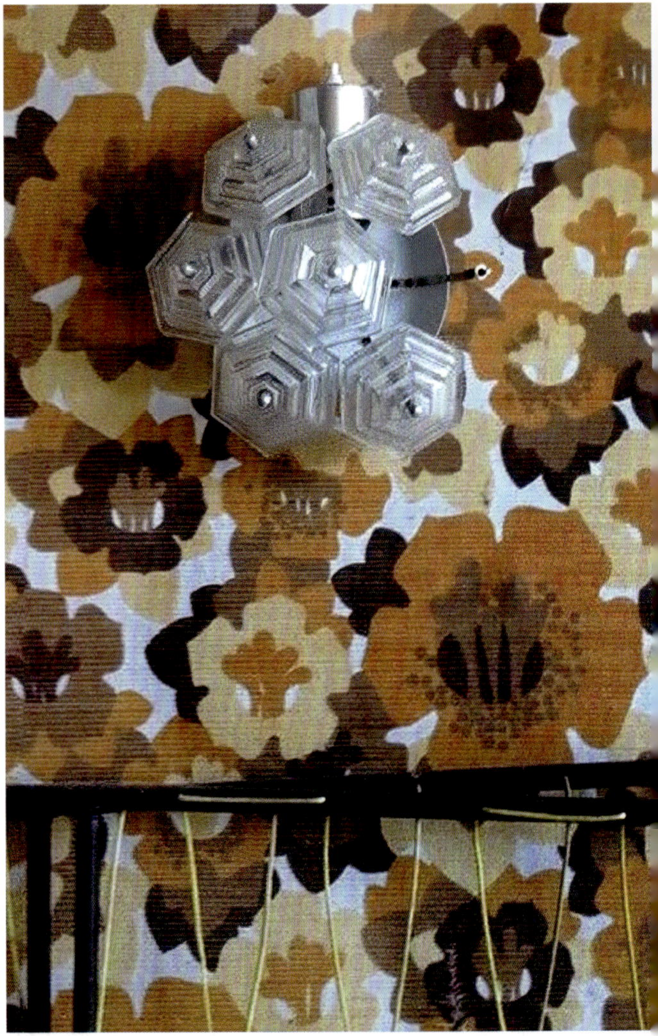

 Rügen-Hotel, Sassnitz, GDR

FDGB Holiday Home, Jasmund National Park, Rügen, GDR

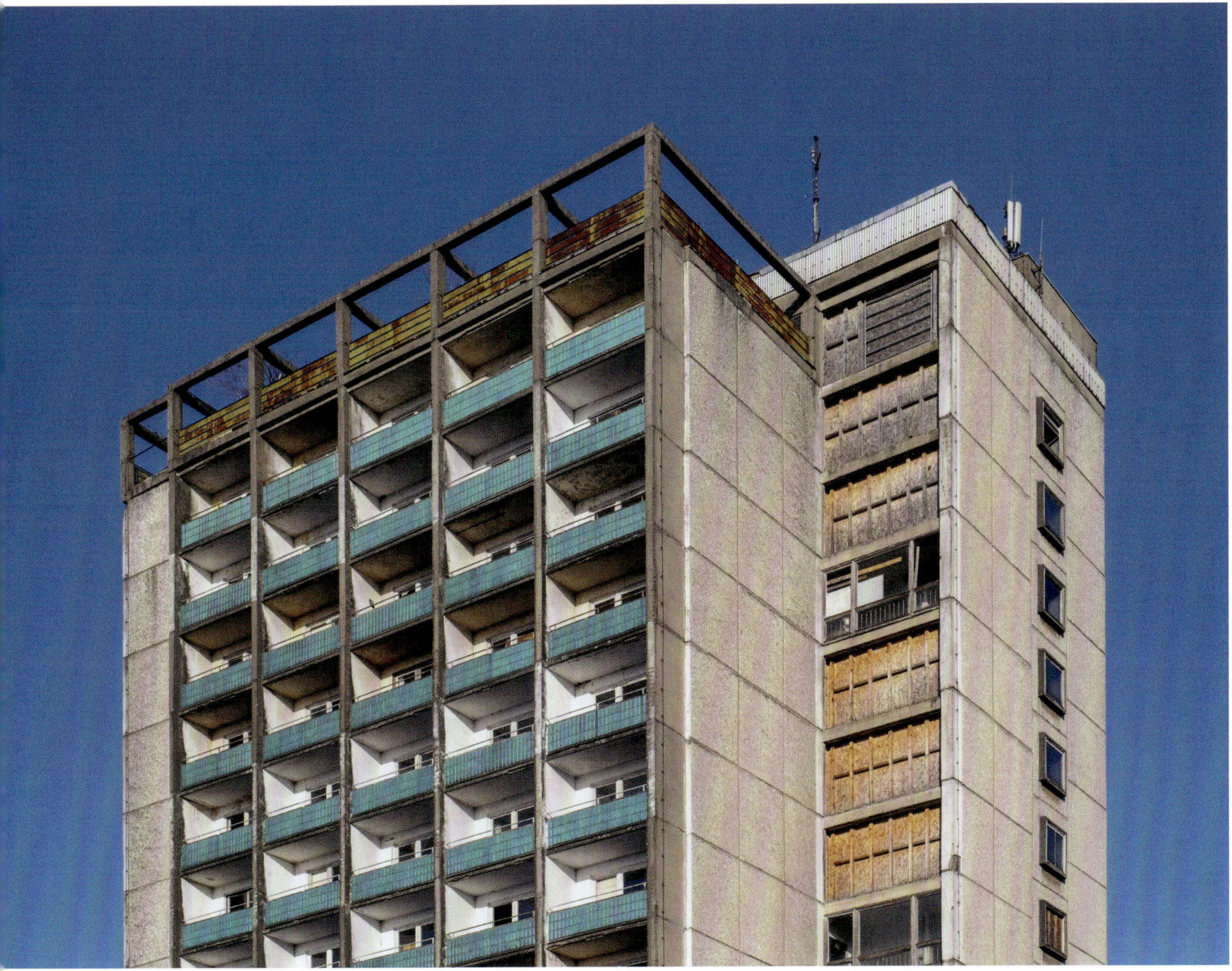

Hotel Panorama (former Hochhaus), Guben, GDR

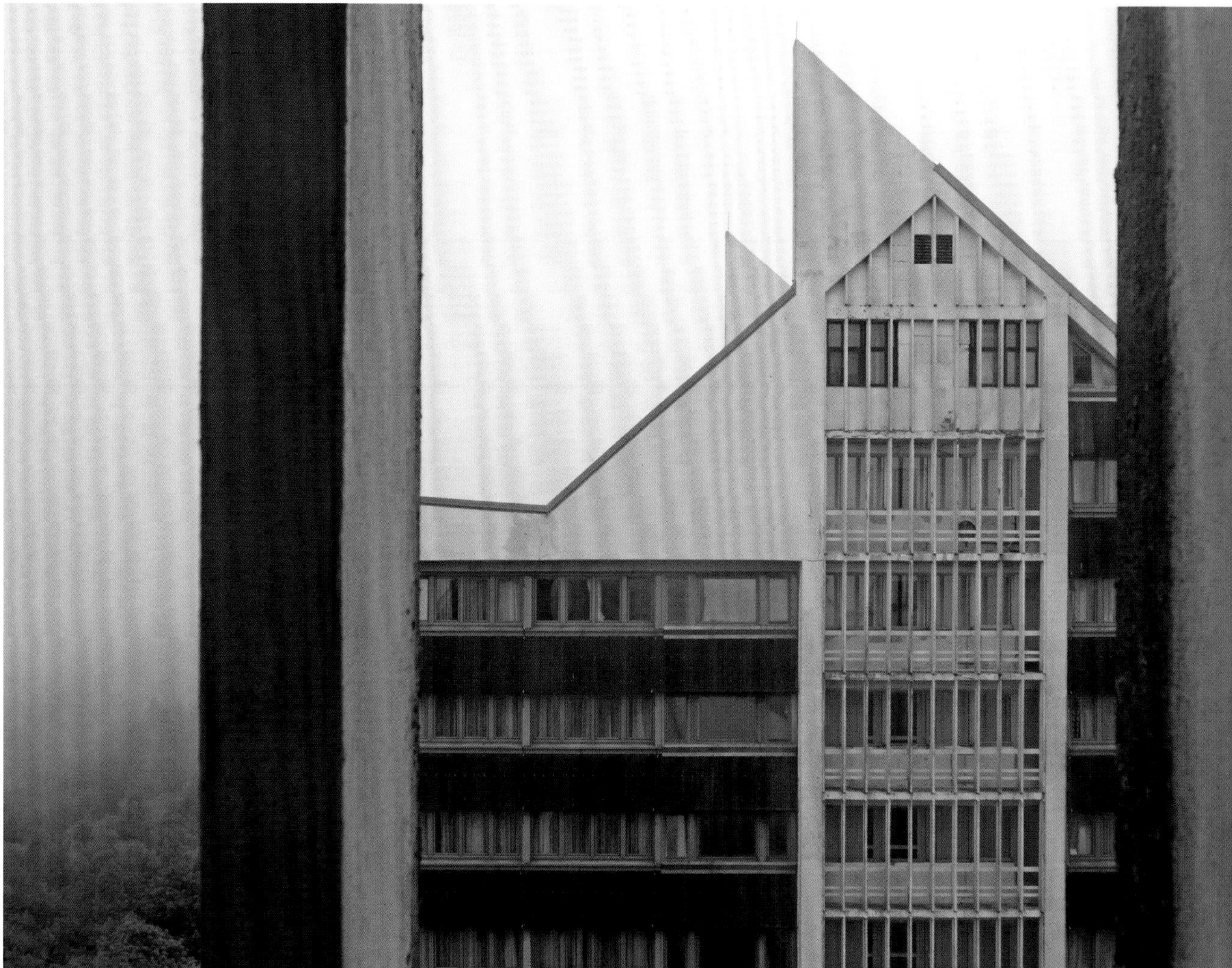

 Hotel Panorama, Oberhof, GDR

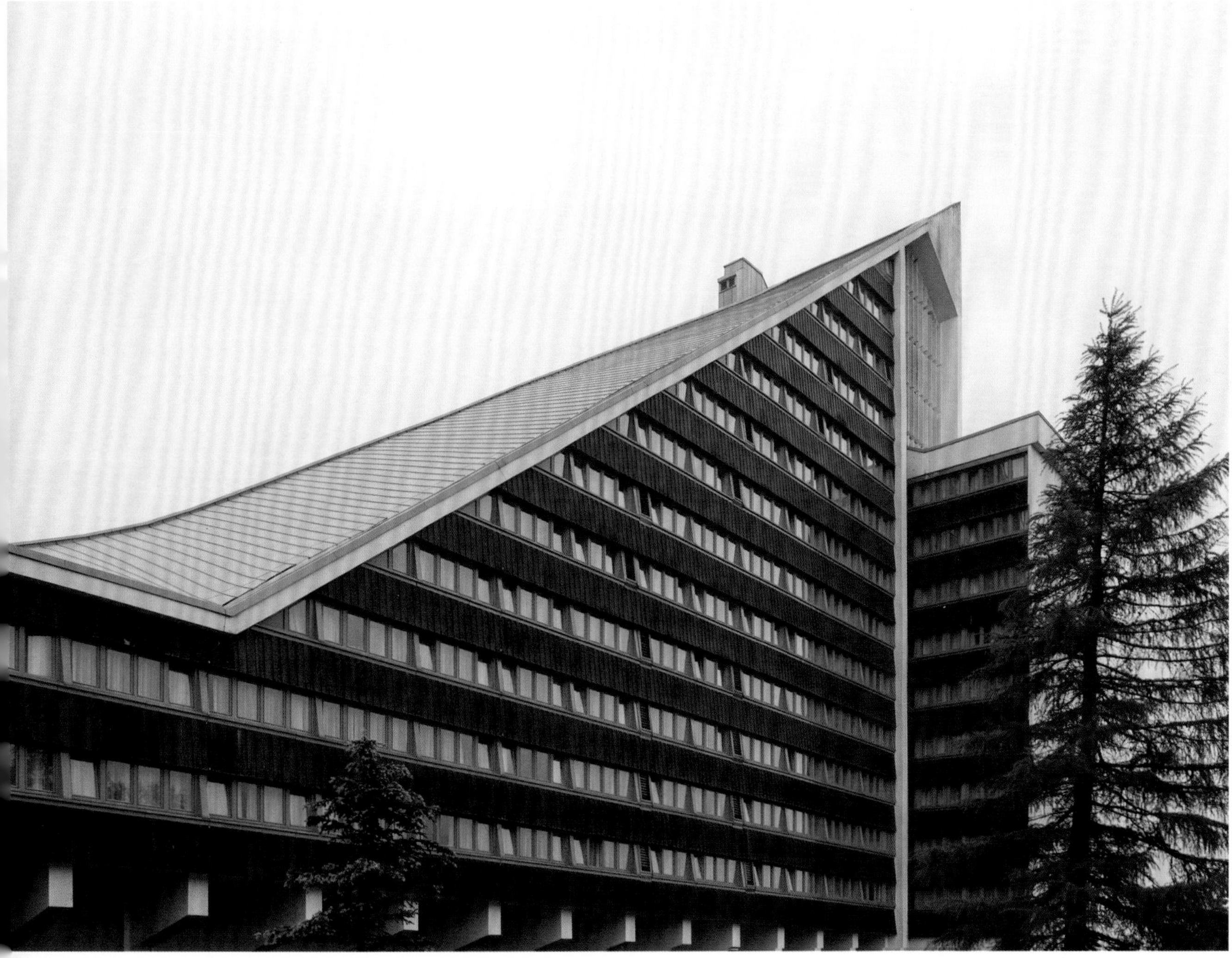

HUNGARY

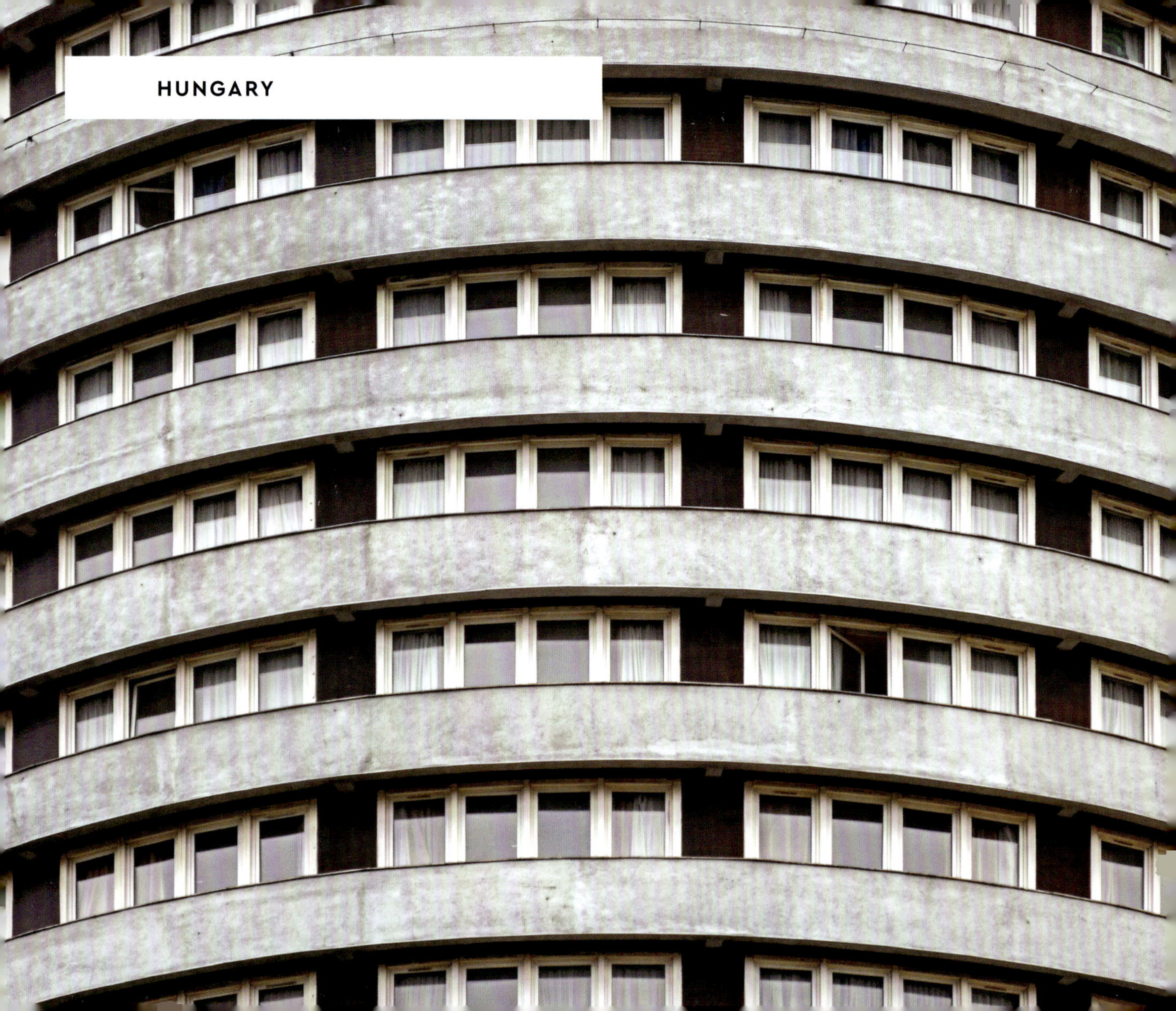

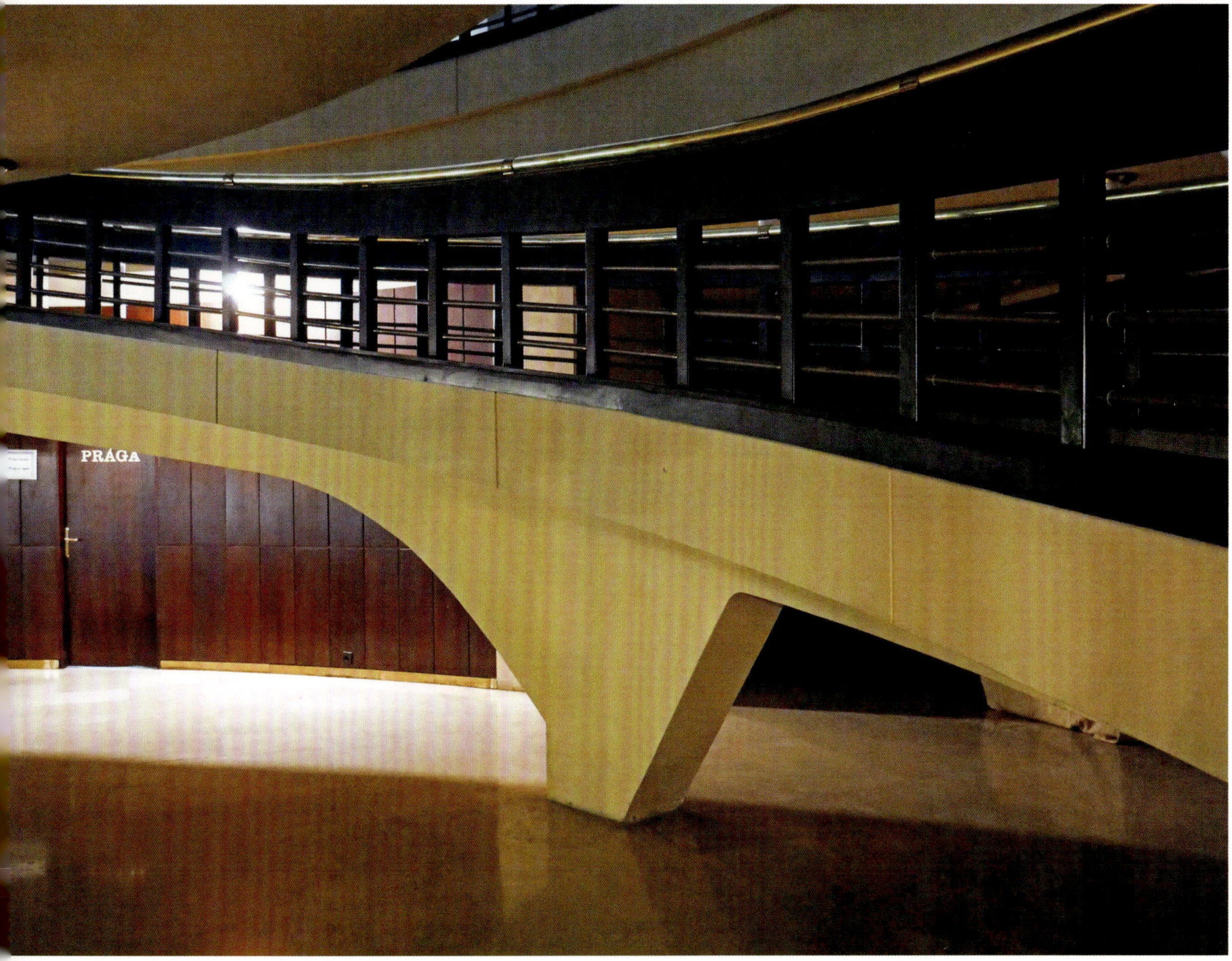

Hotel Budapest, Budapest, Hungary

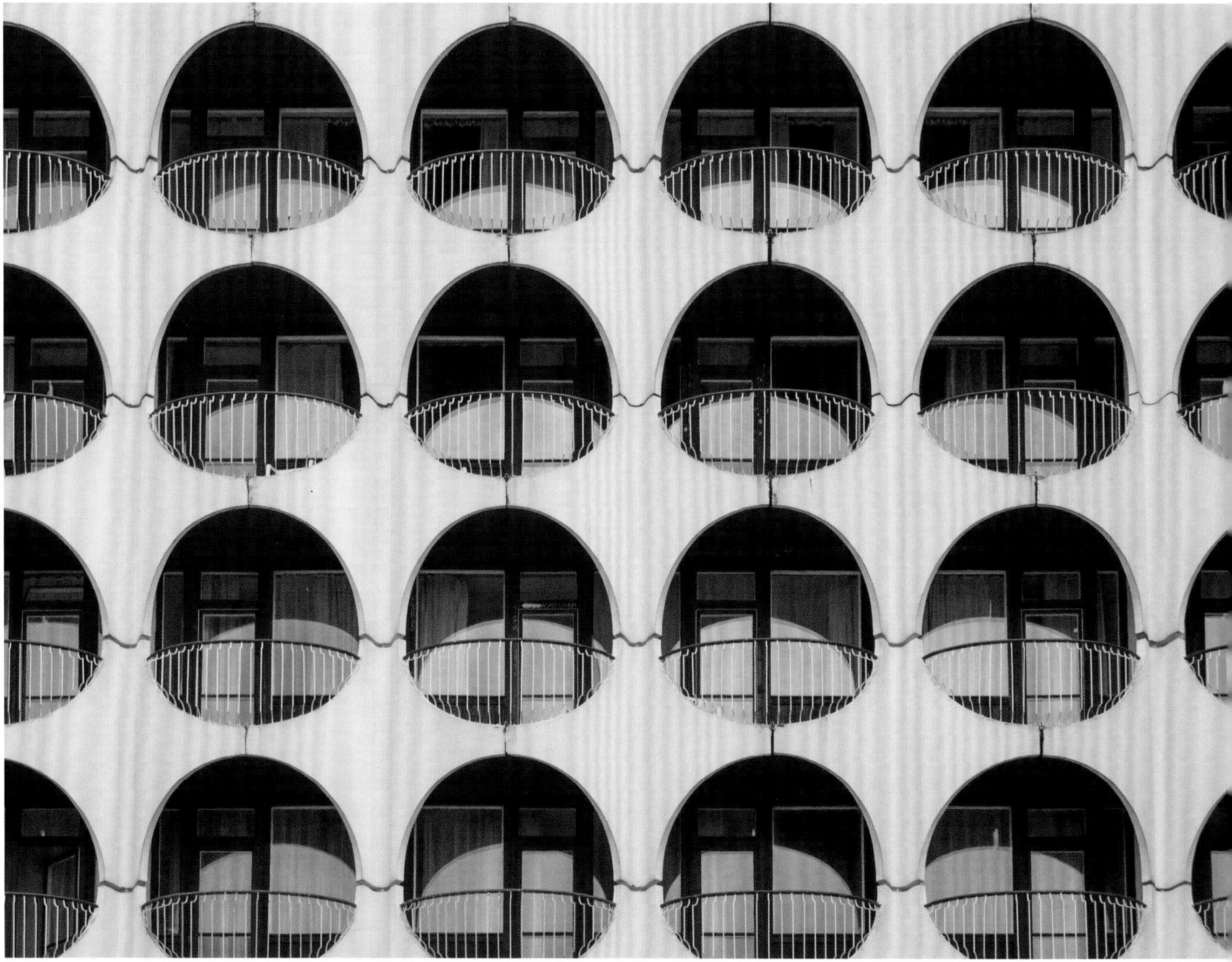

 Hotel Ezüstpart, Siófok, Hungary

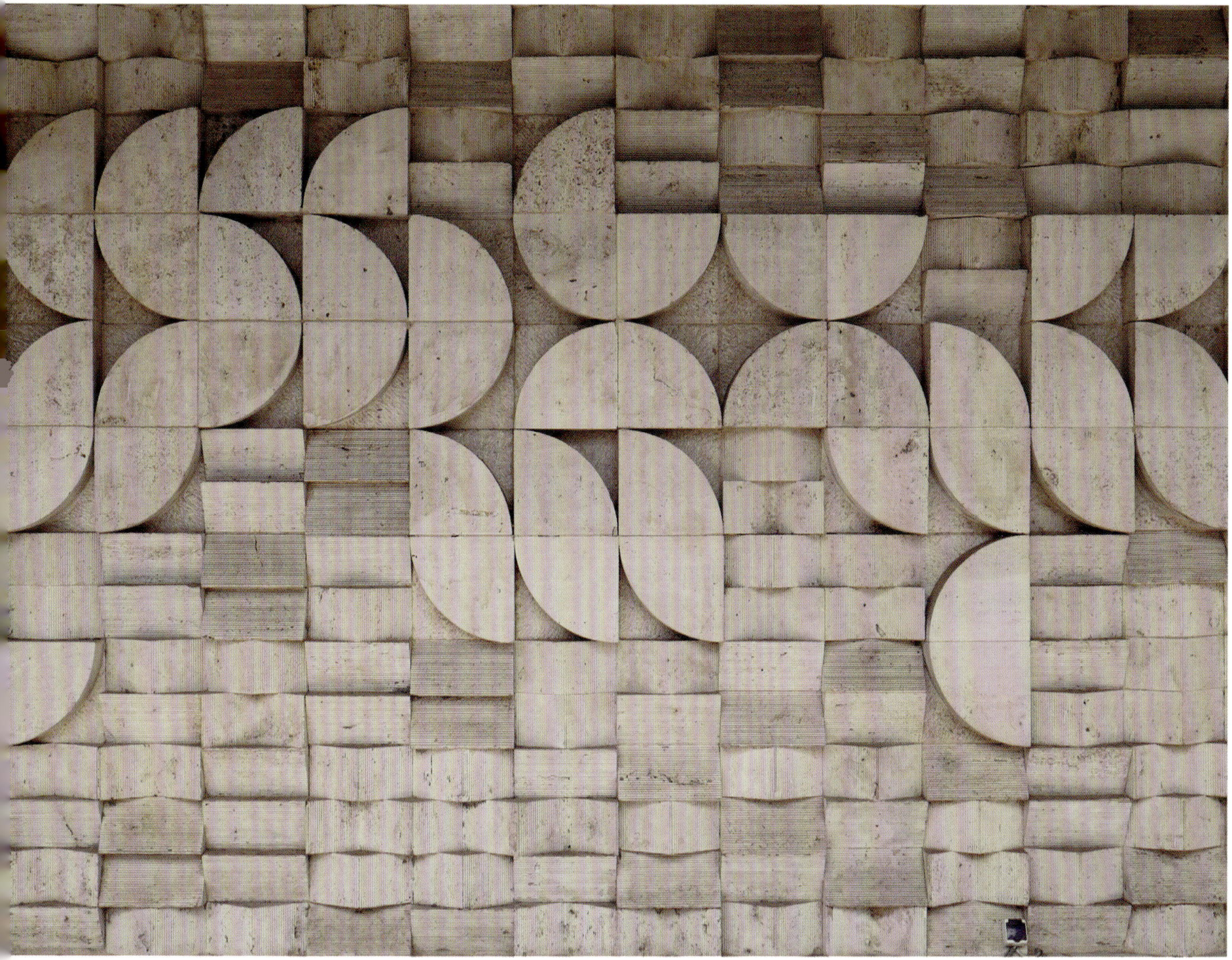

Hotel Marriott (former Hotel Duna InterContinental), Budapest, Hungary

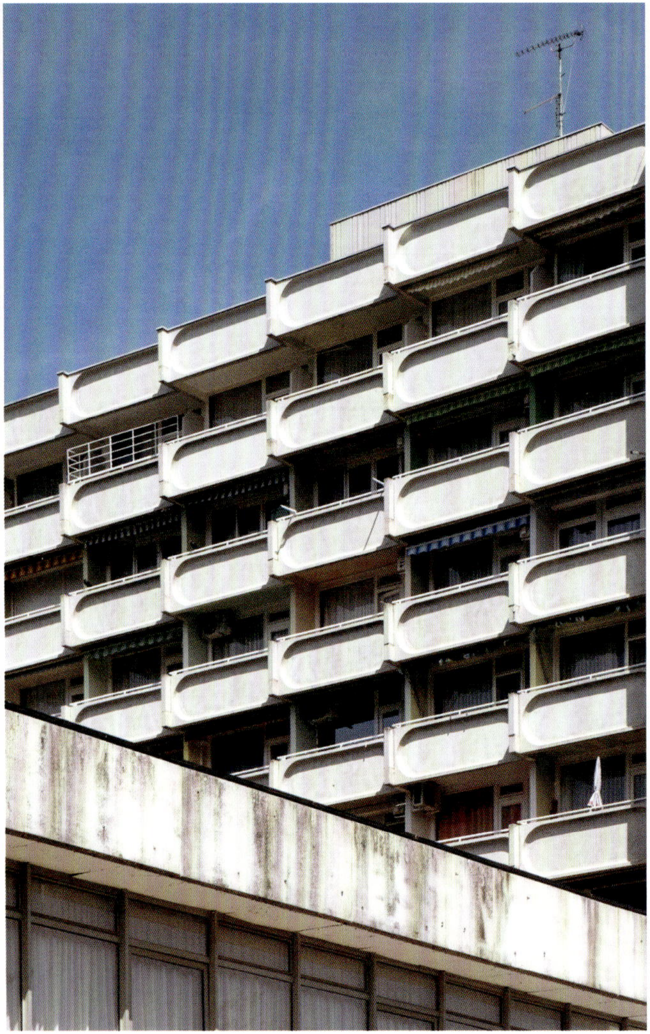

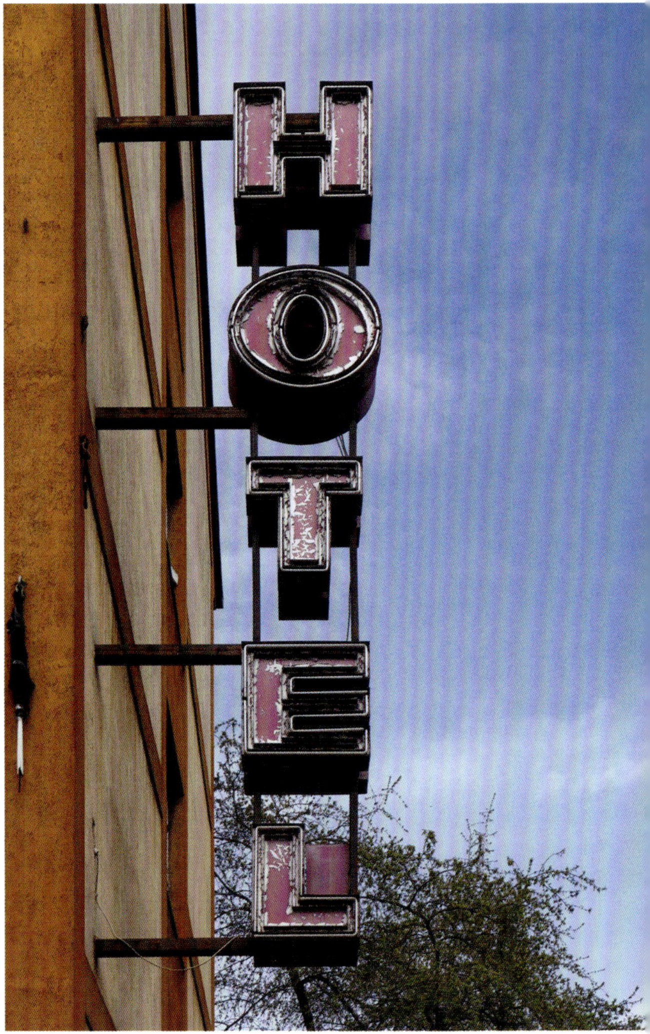

 Hotel Festival, Balatonföldvár, Hungary

Hotel Platánus, Budapest, Hungary

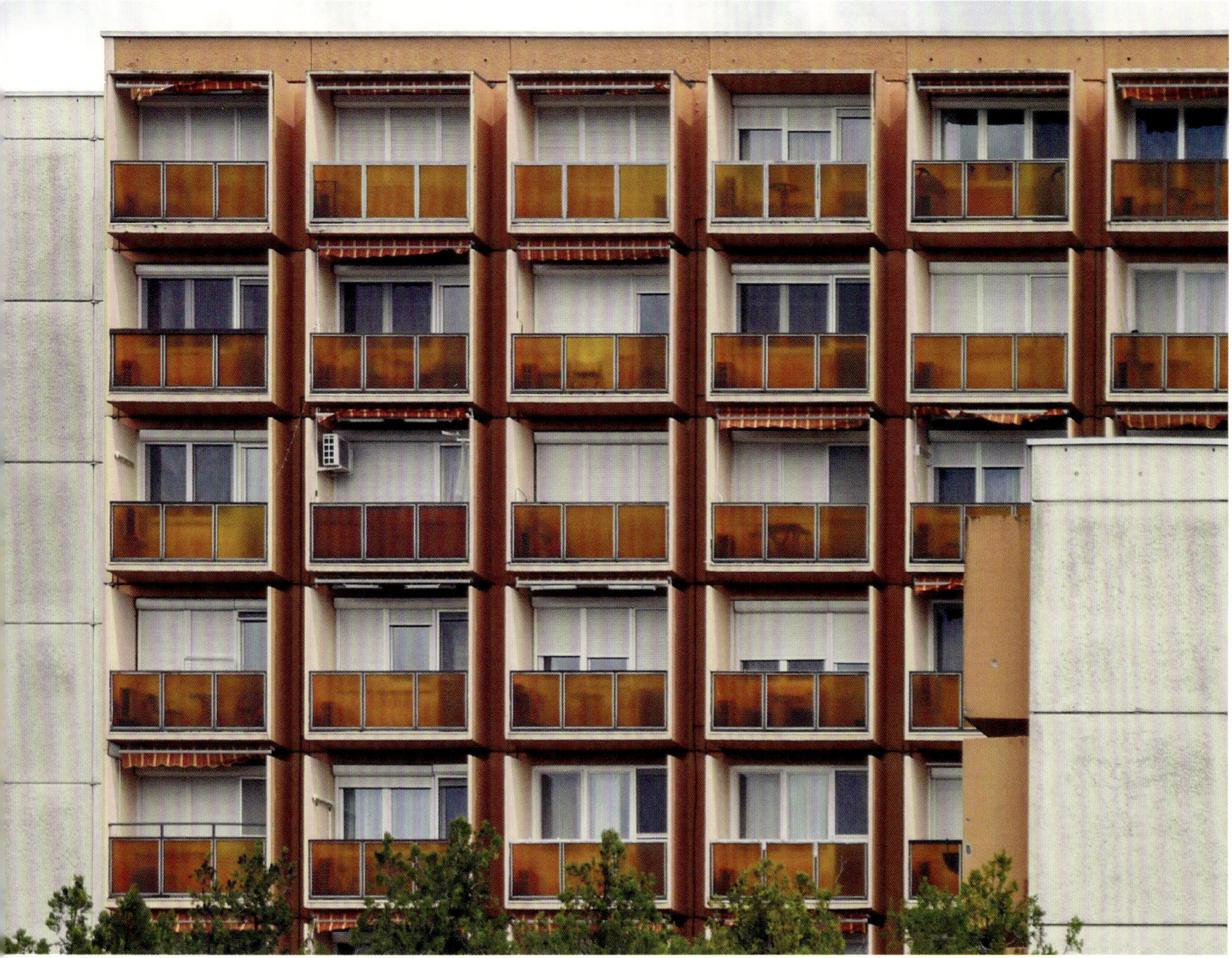

Hotel Aranyhíd, Siófok, Hungary

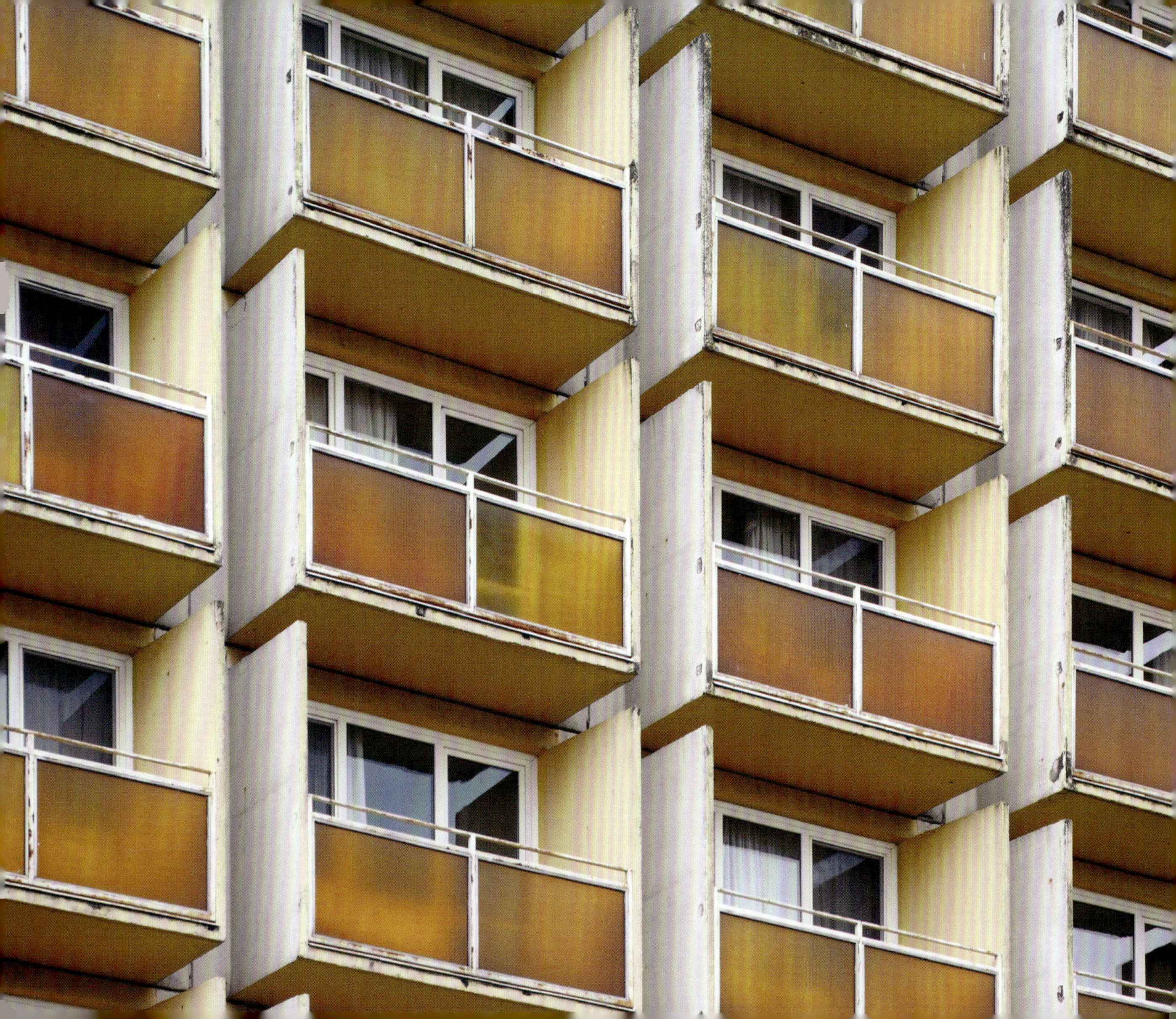

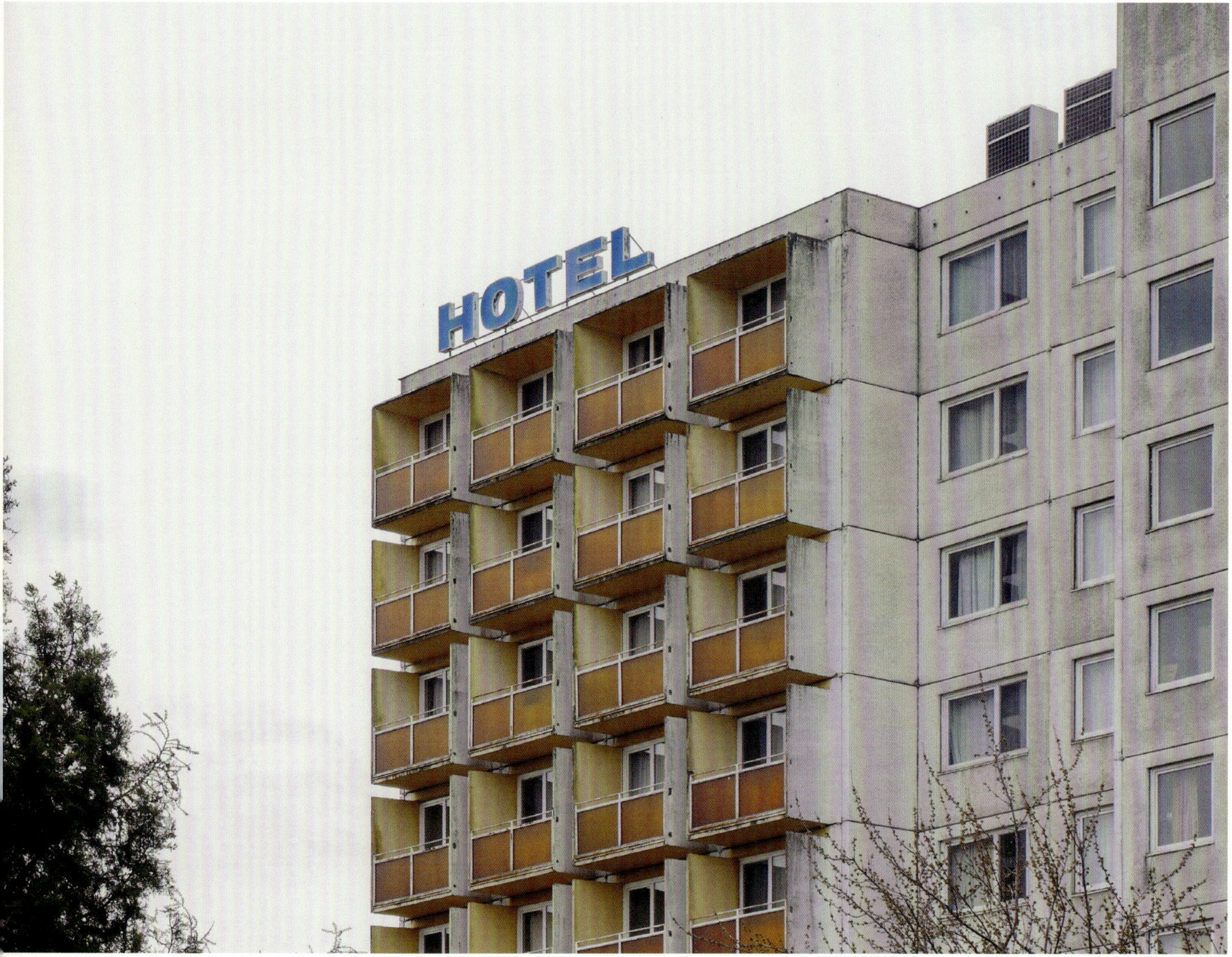

Hotel Aranypart (former Ministry of the Interior BM Holiday Resort), Siófok, Hungary

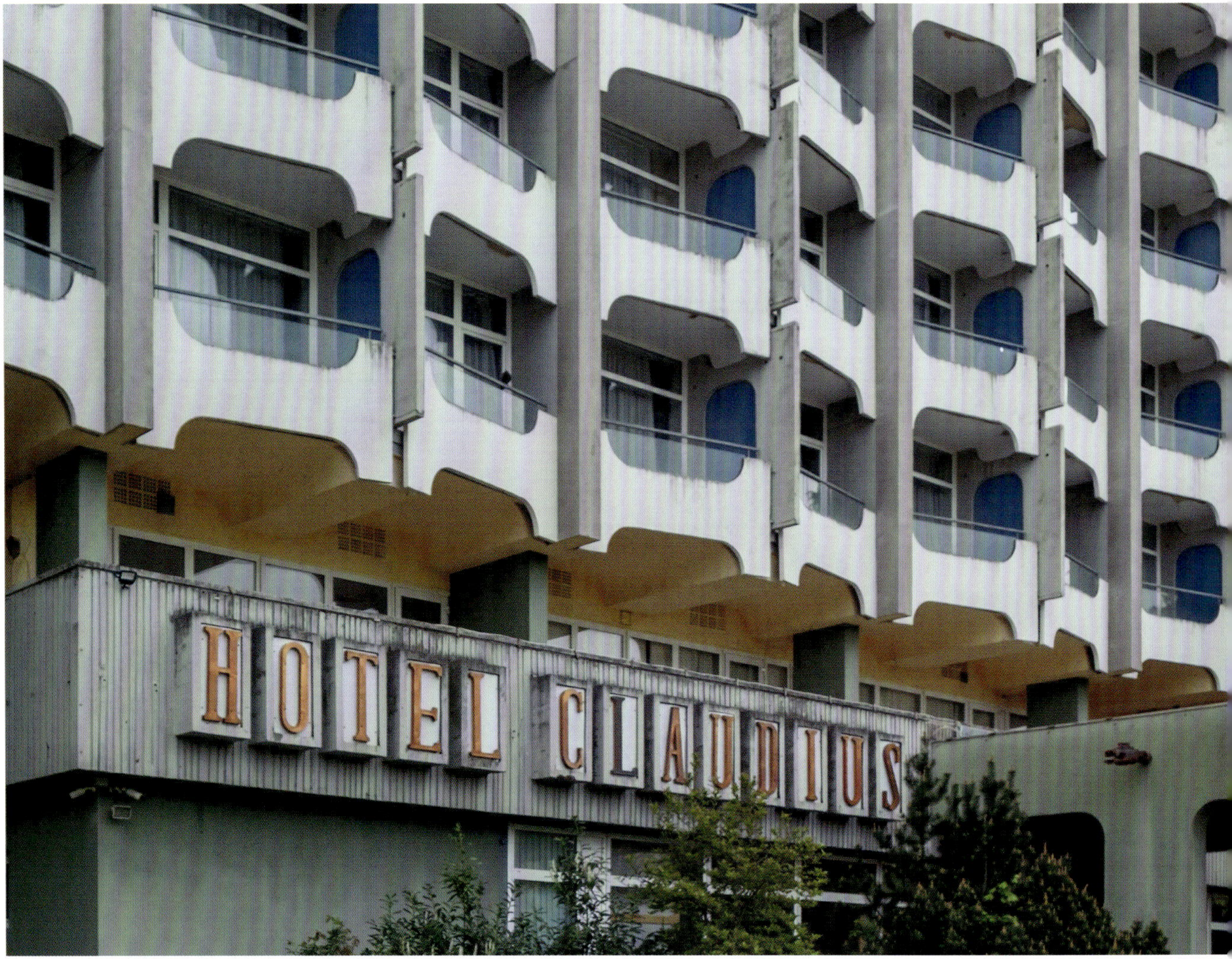

 Hotel Claudius, Szombathely, Hungary

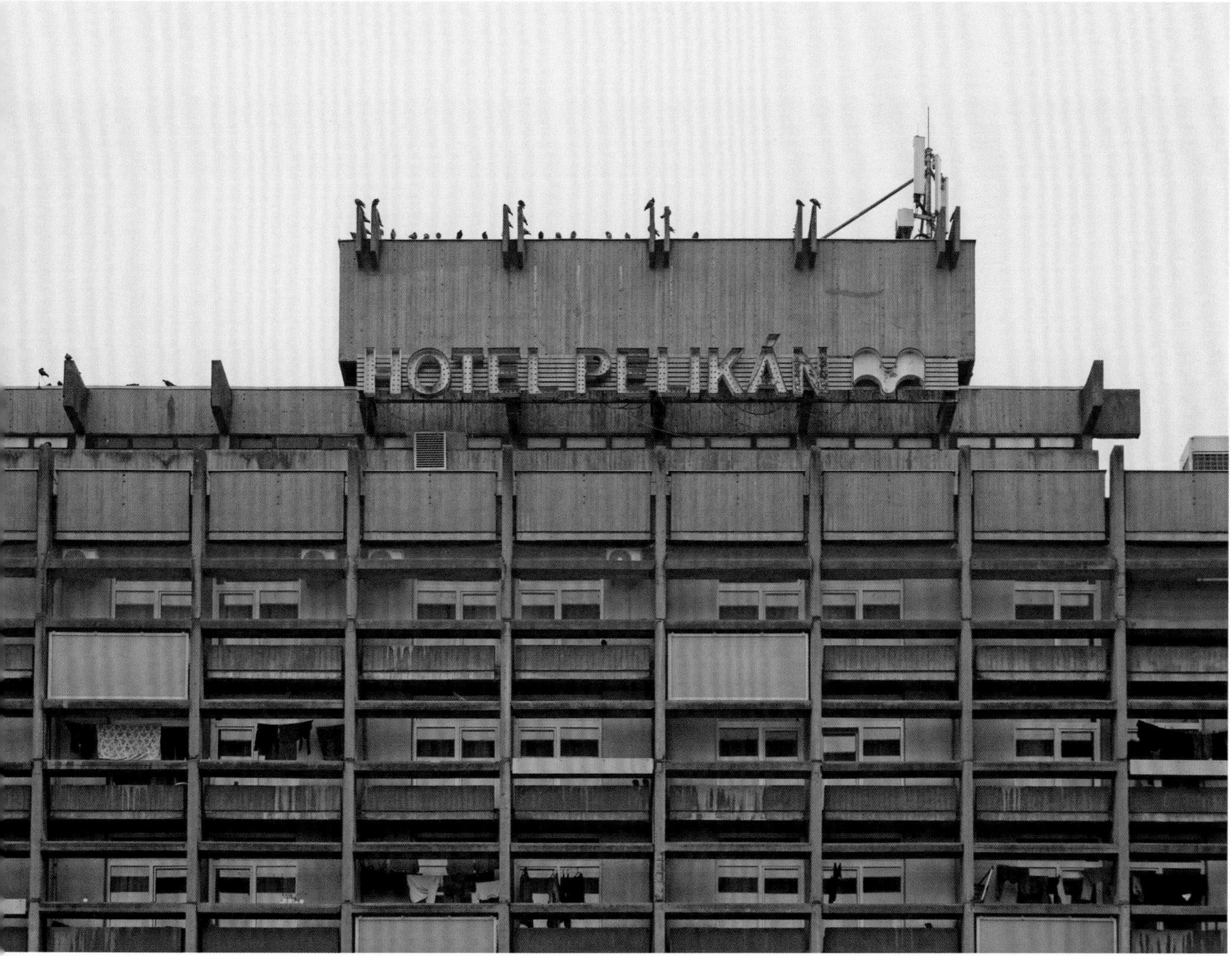

Hotel Pelikán, Szolnok, Hungary

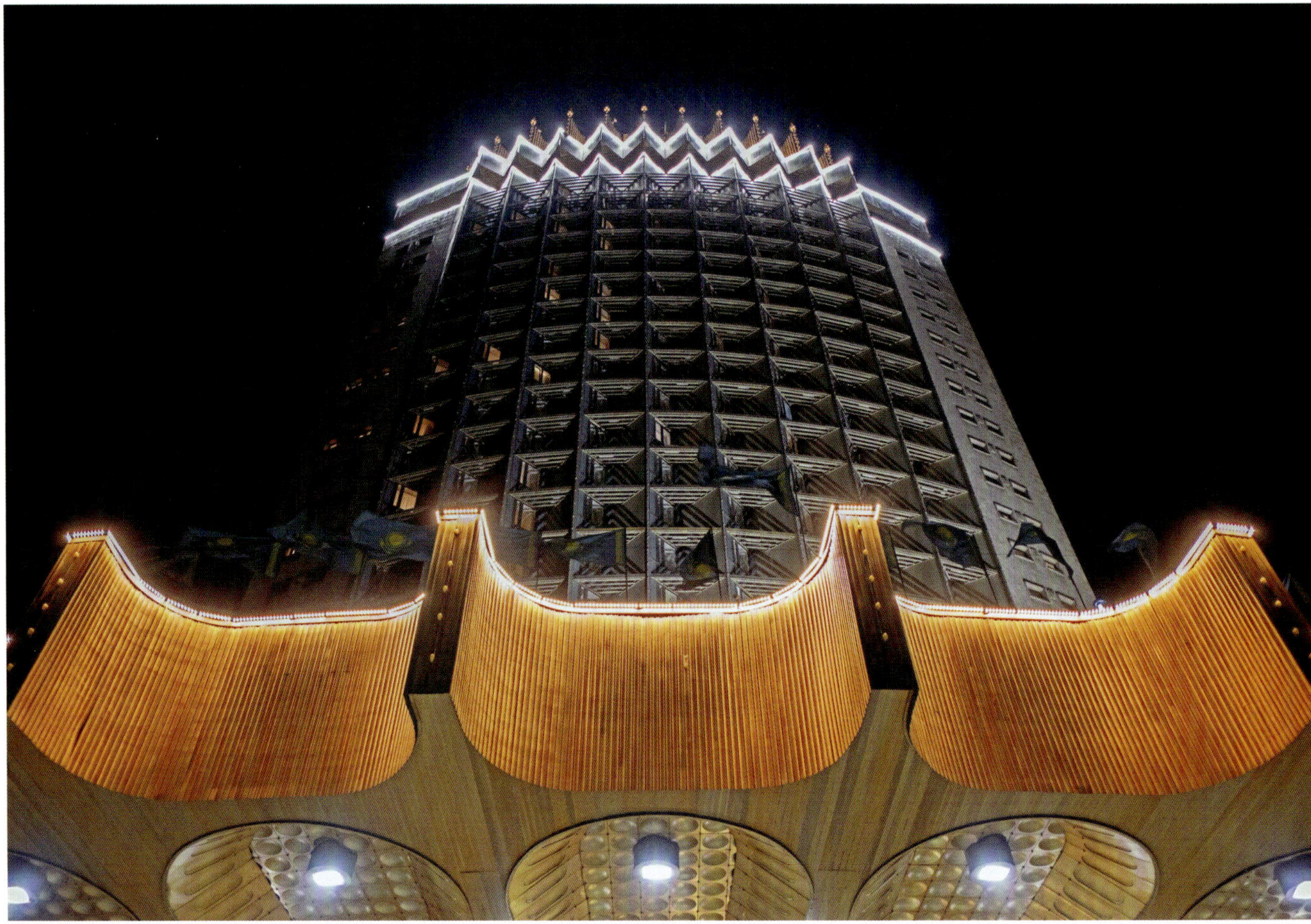

 Hotel Kazakhstan, Almaty, Kazakhstan

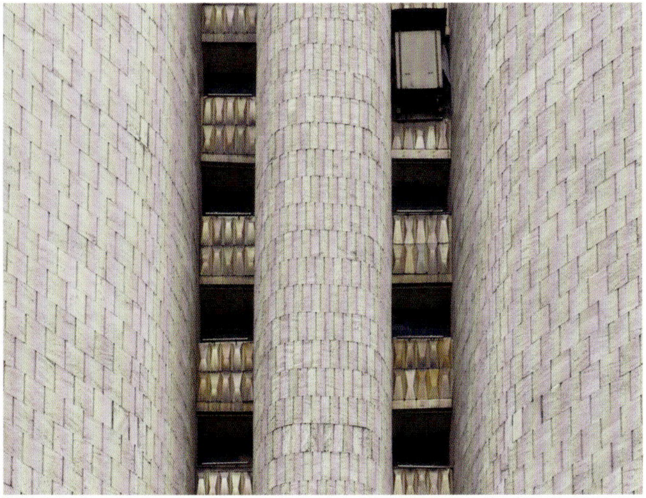

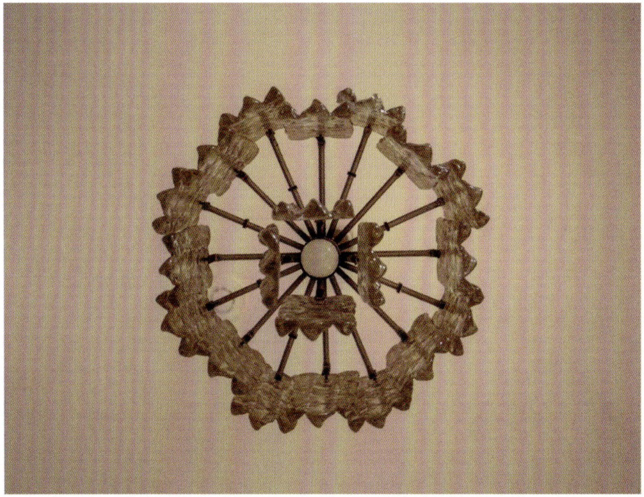

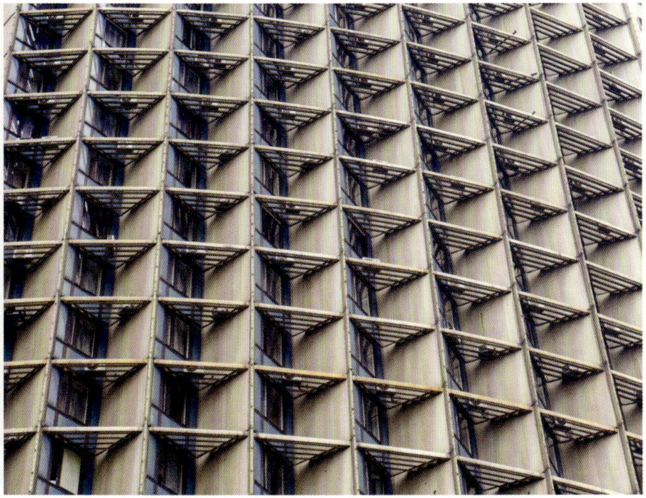

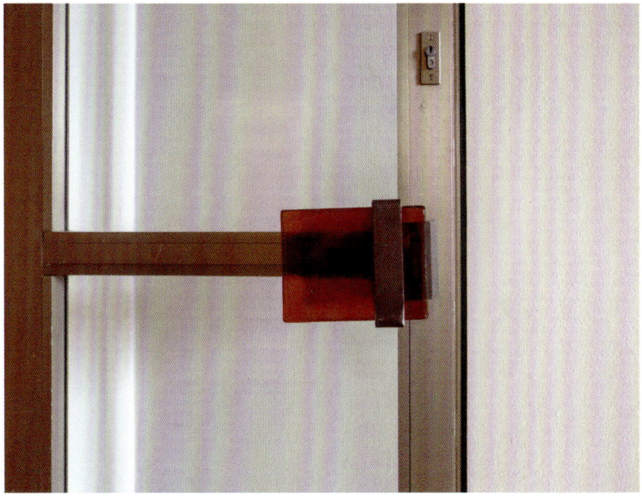

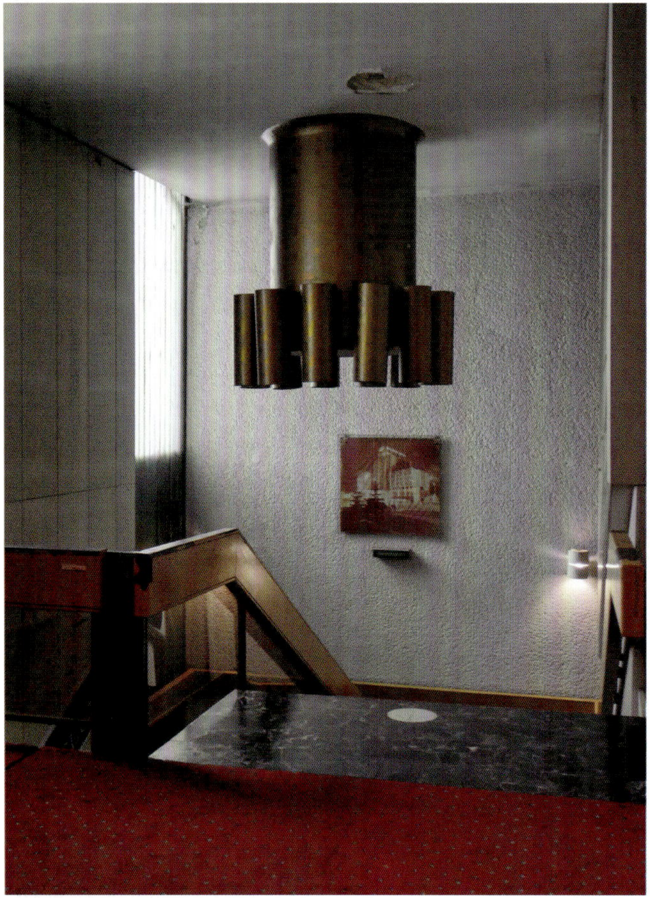

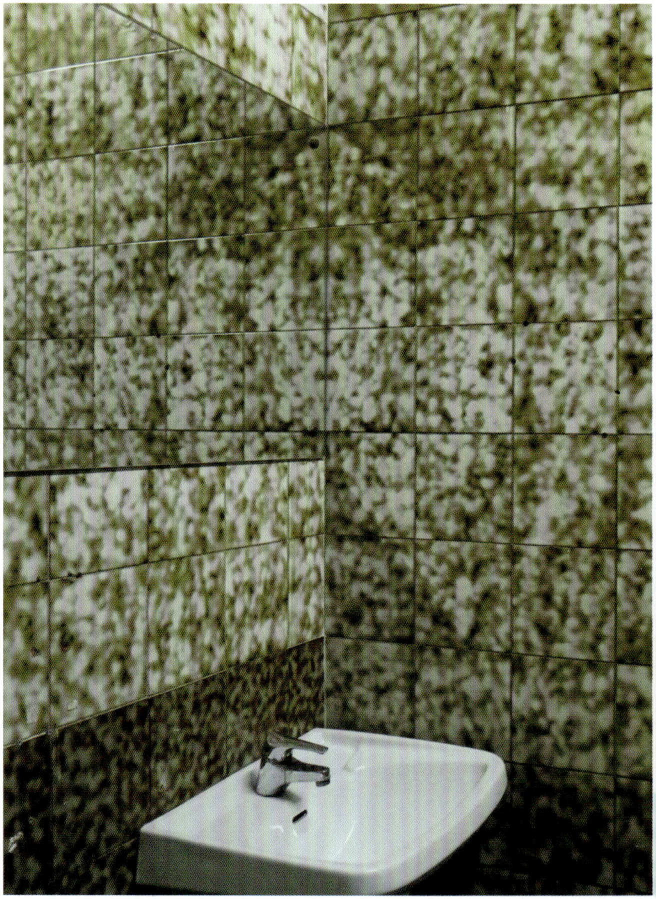

 Grand Hotel Prishtina, Prishtina, Kosovo

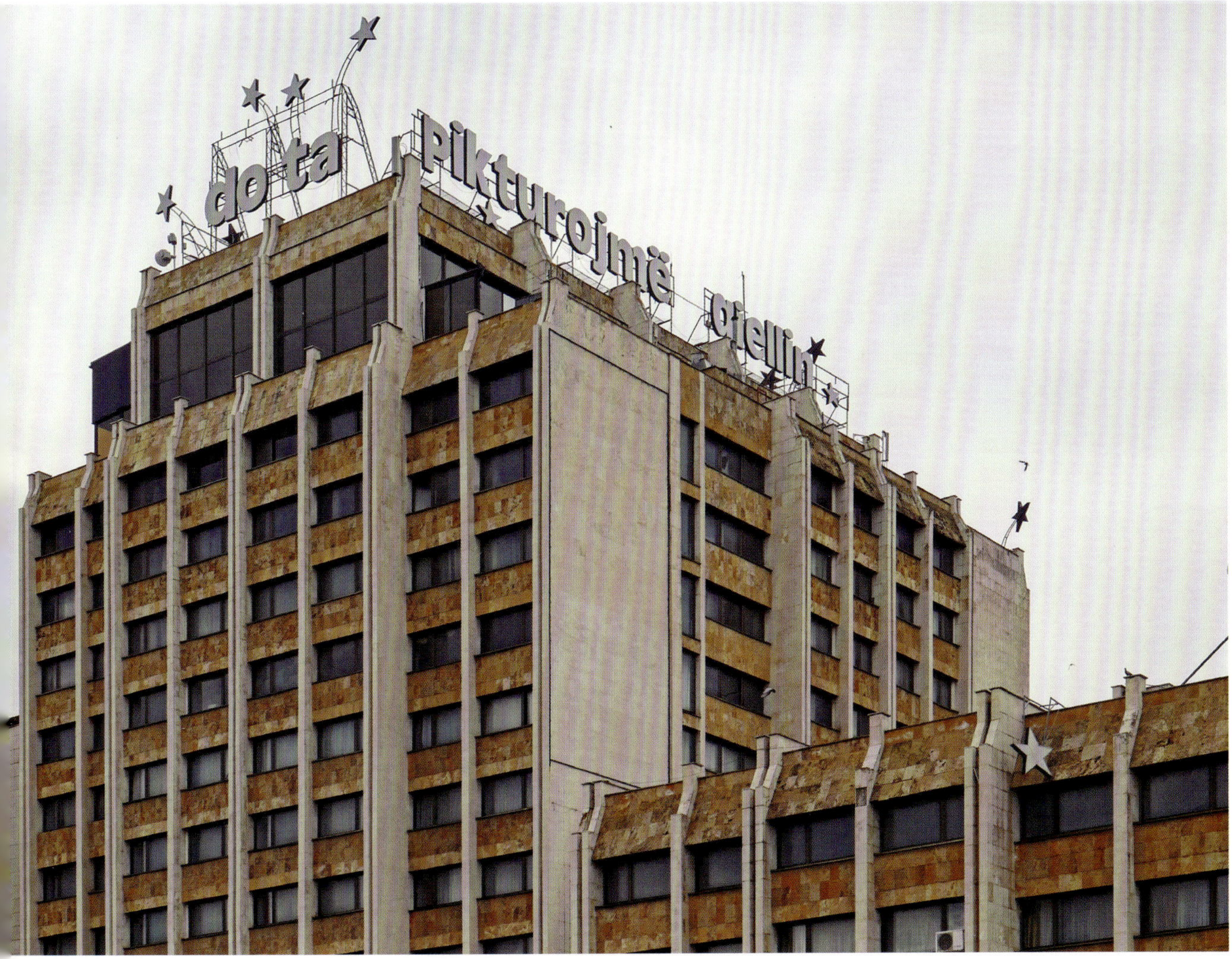
do ta
pikturojmë
qiellin

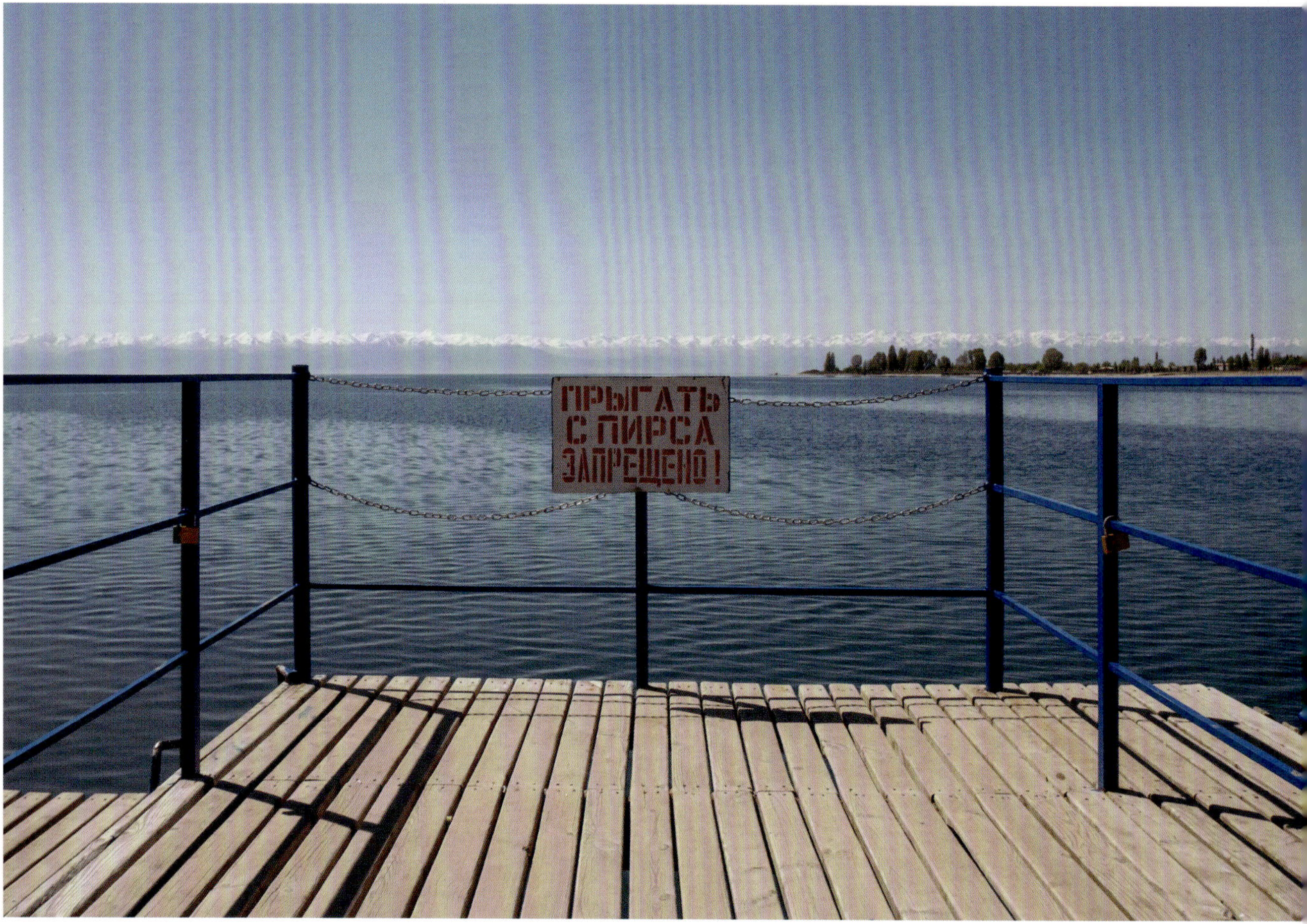

Sanatorium Goluboy Issyk-Kul, Cholpon-Ata, Kyrgyzstan

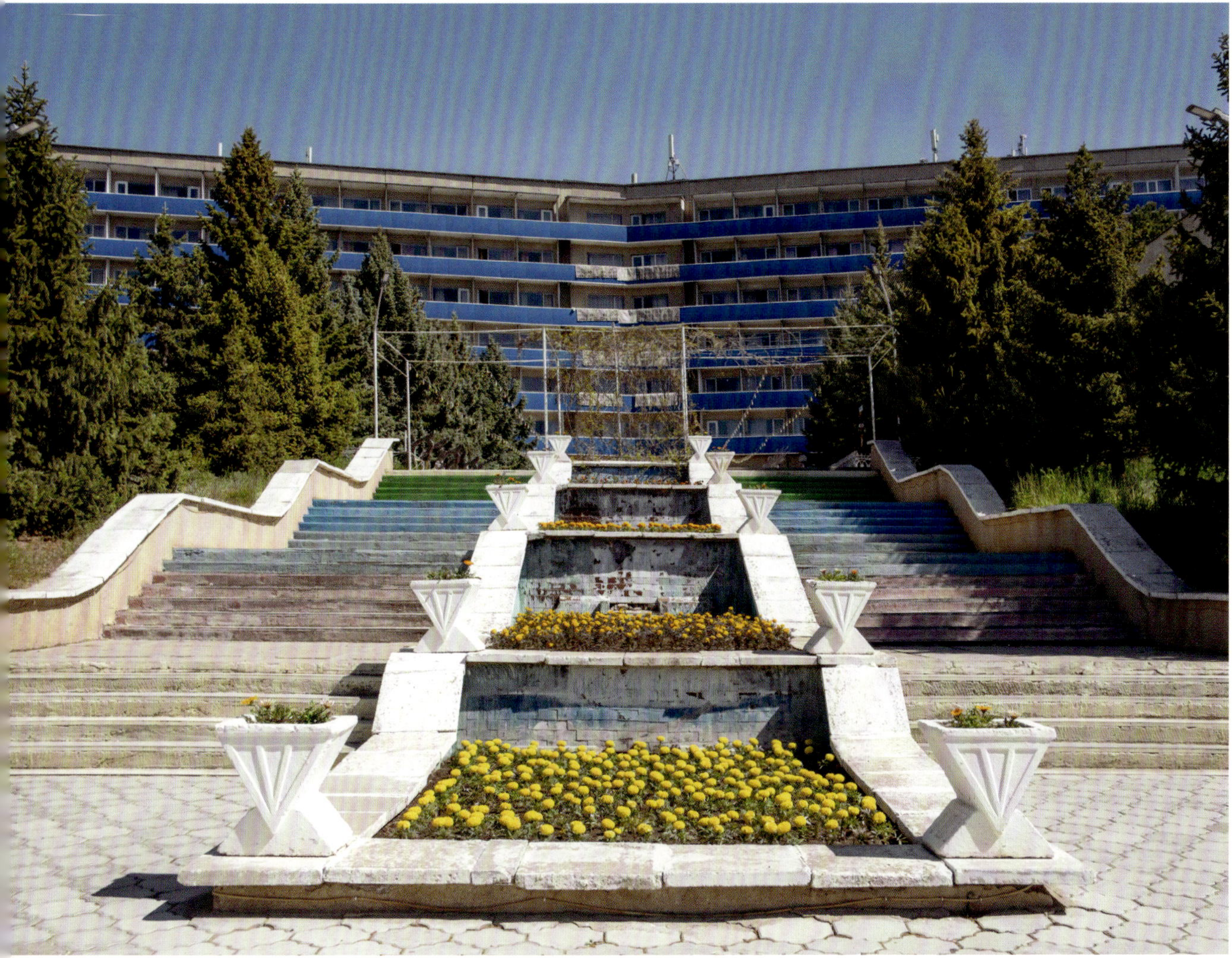

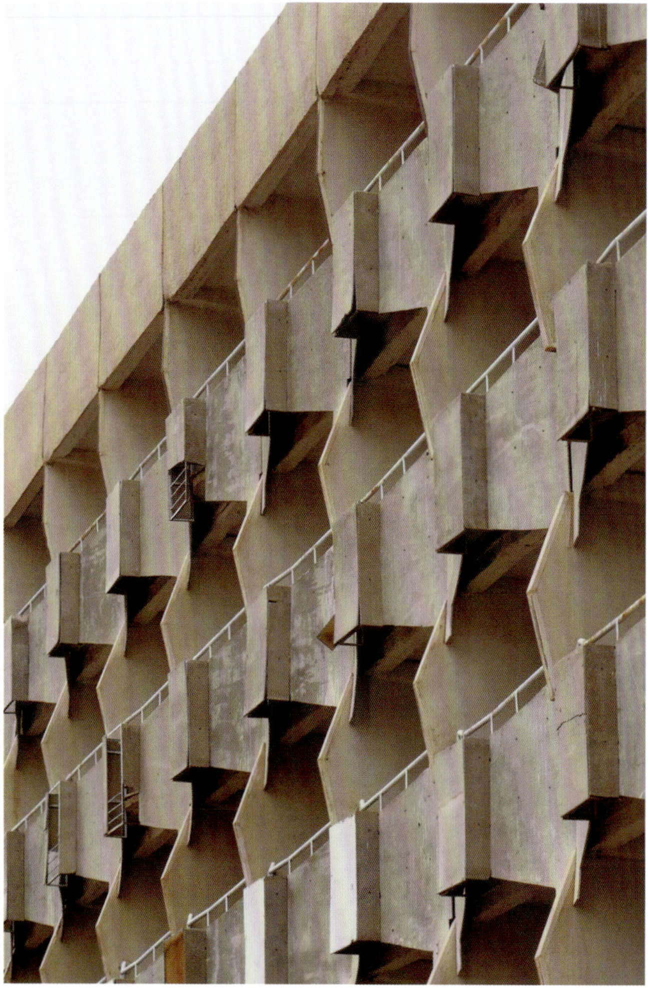

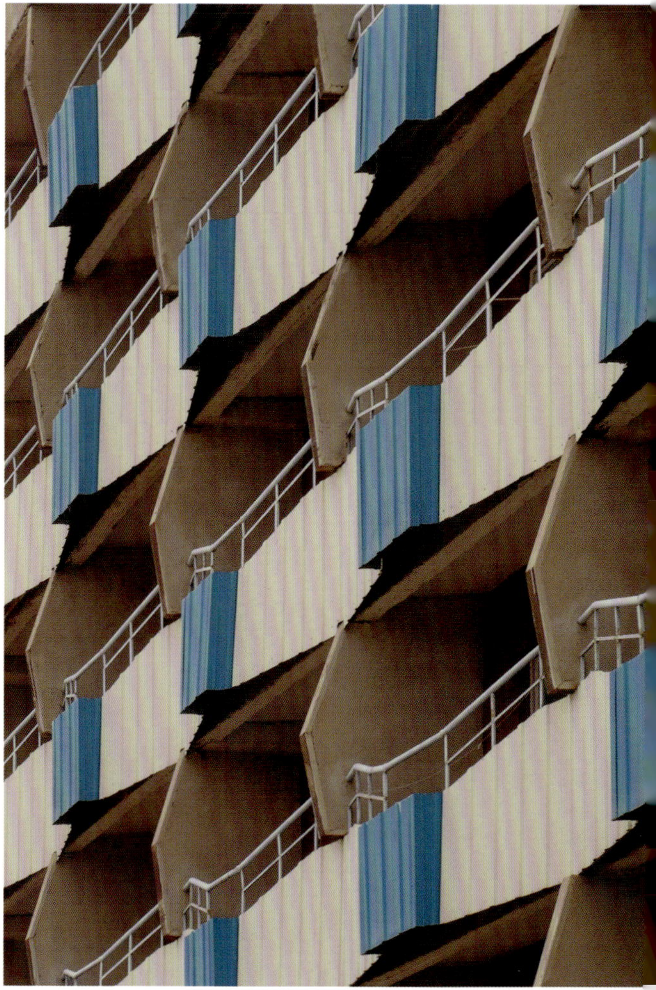

 Hotel Nur, Kaji-Say, Kyrgyzstan

right: Hotel Osh-Nuru (former Hotel Intourist), Osh, Kyrgyzsta

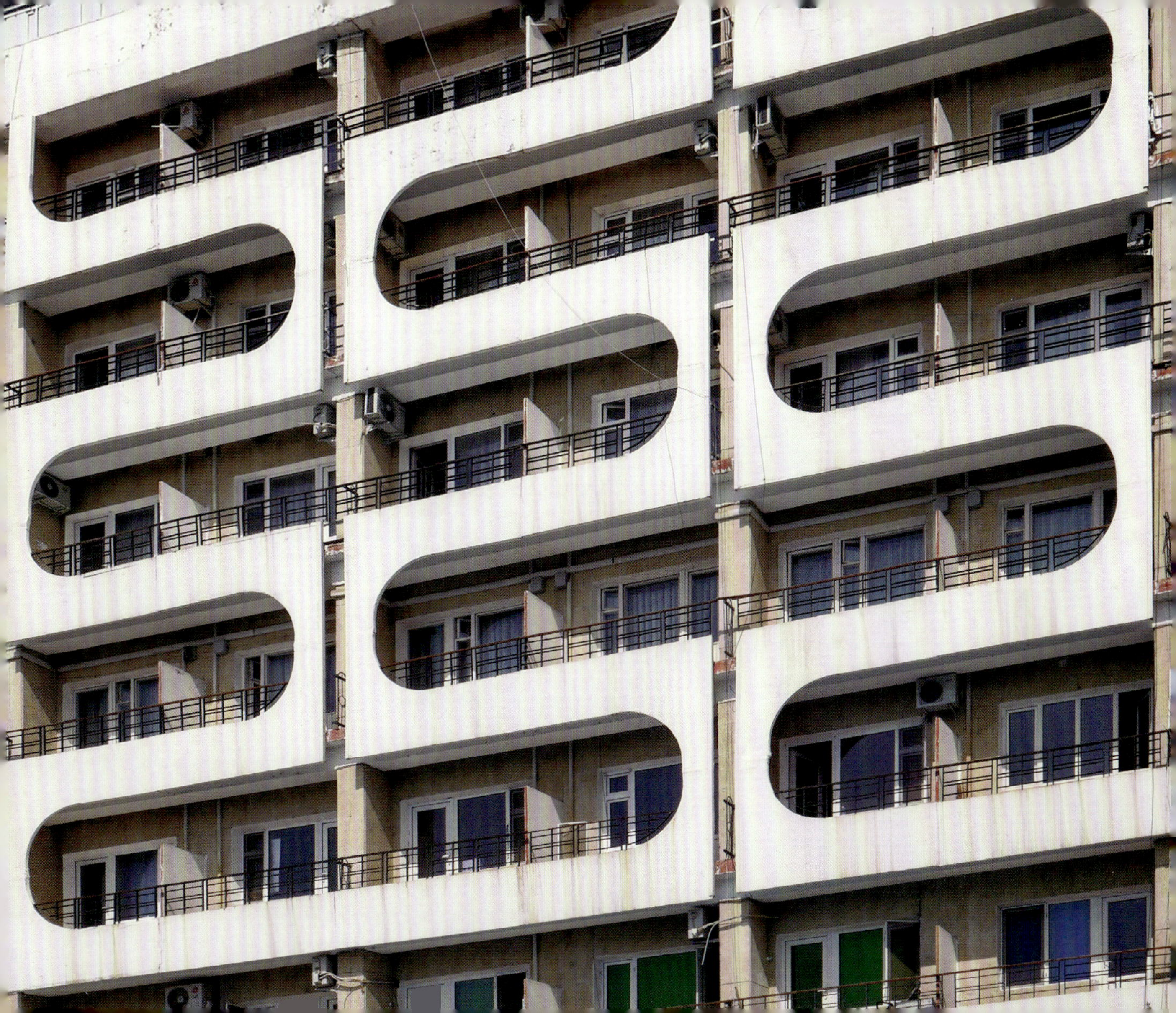

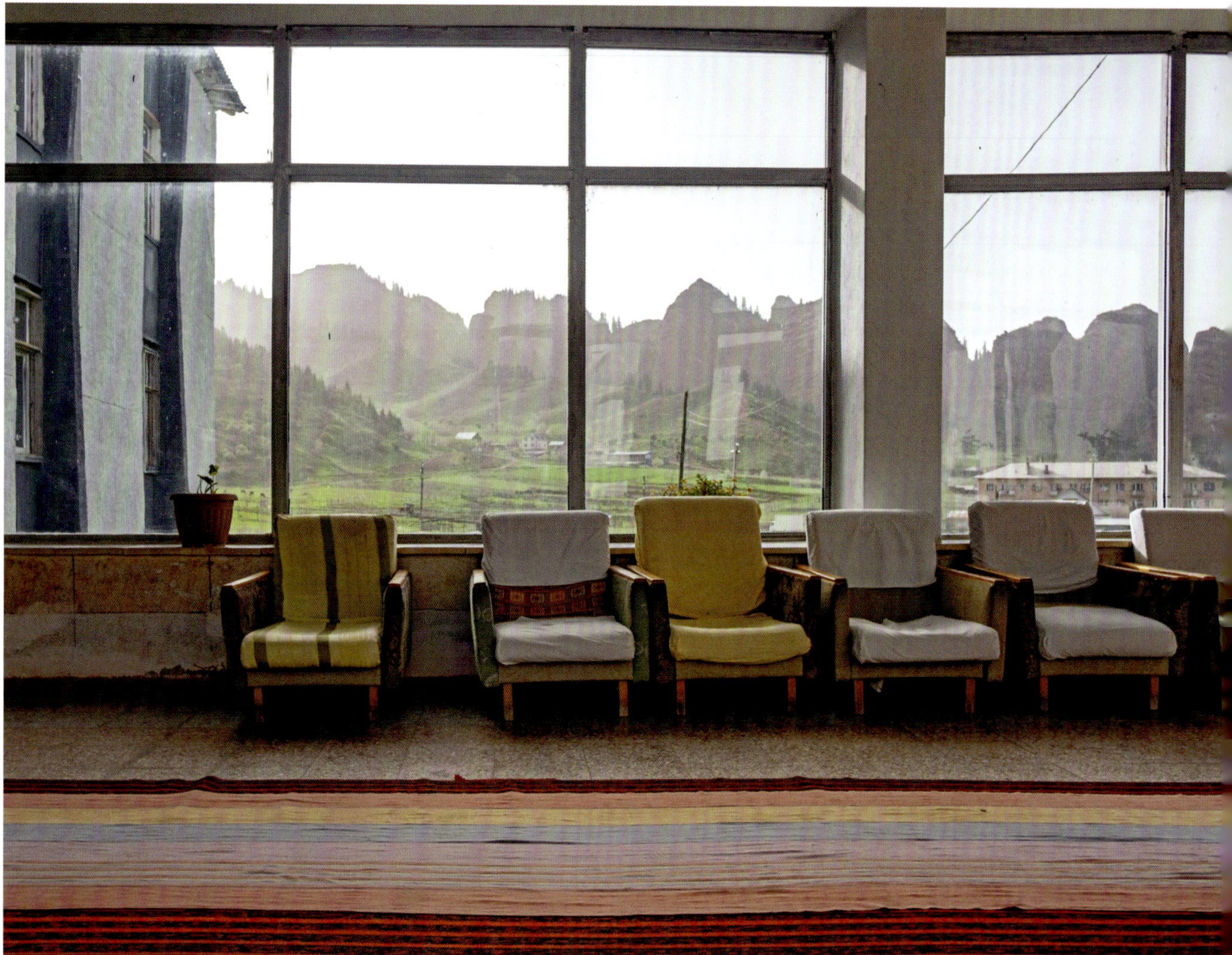

Sanatorium Zheti-Oguz, Kyrgyzstan

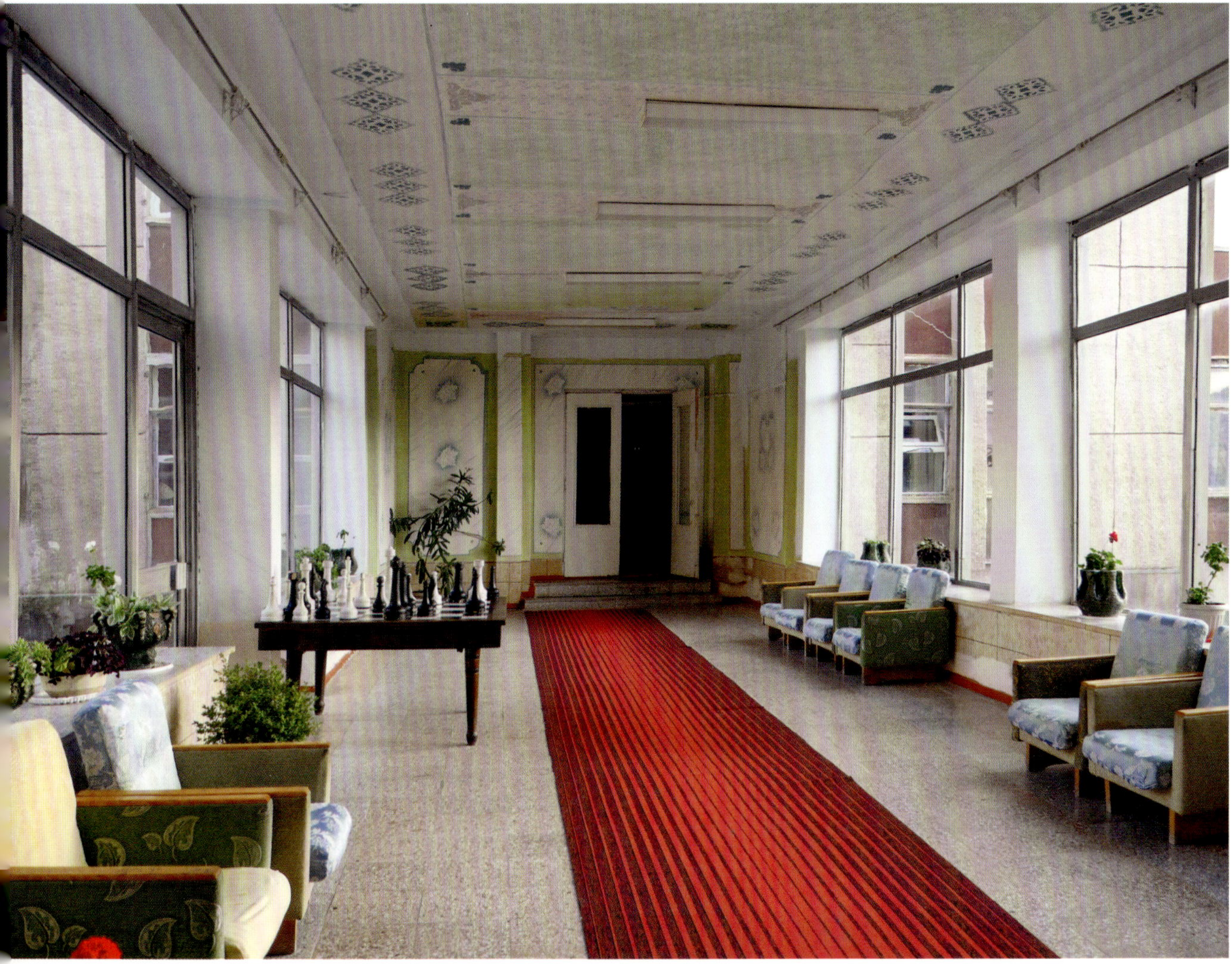

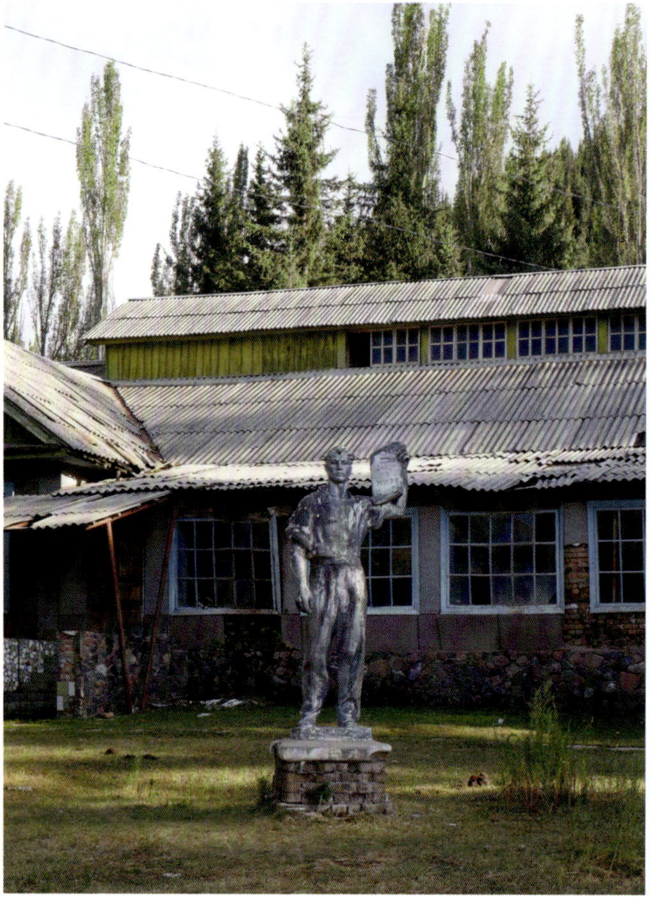

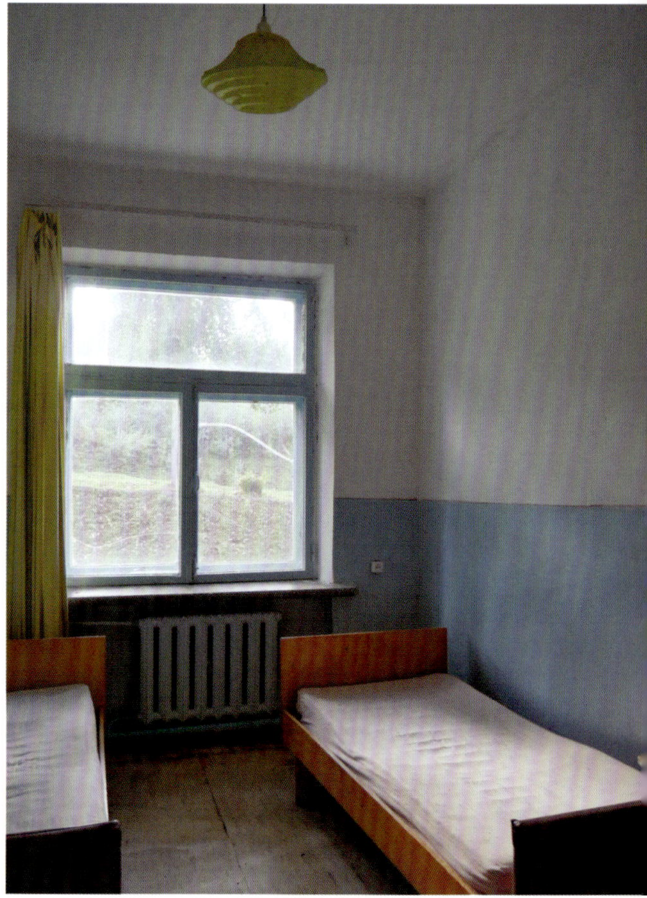

 Sanatorium Zheti-Oguz, Kyrgyzstan

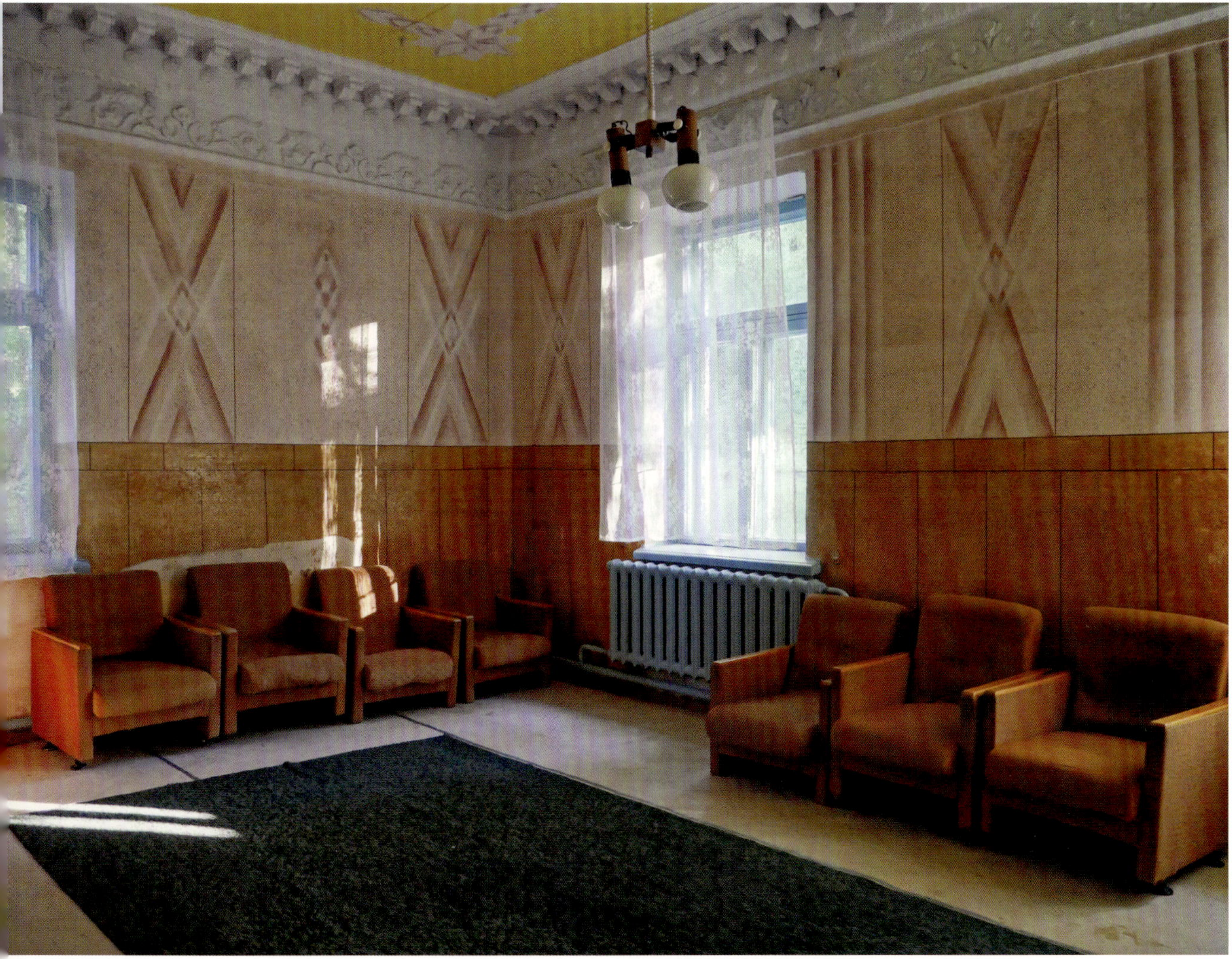

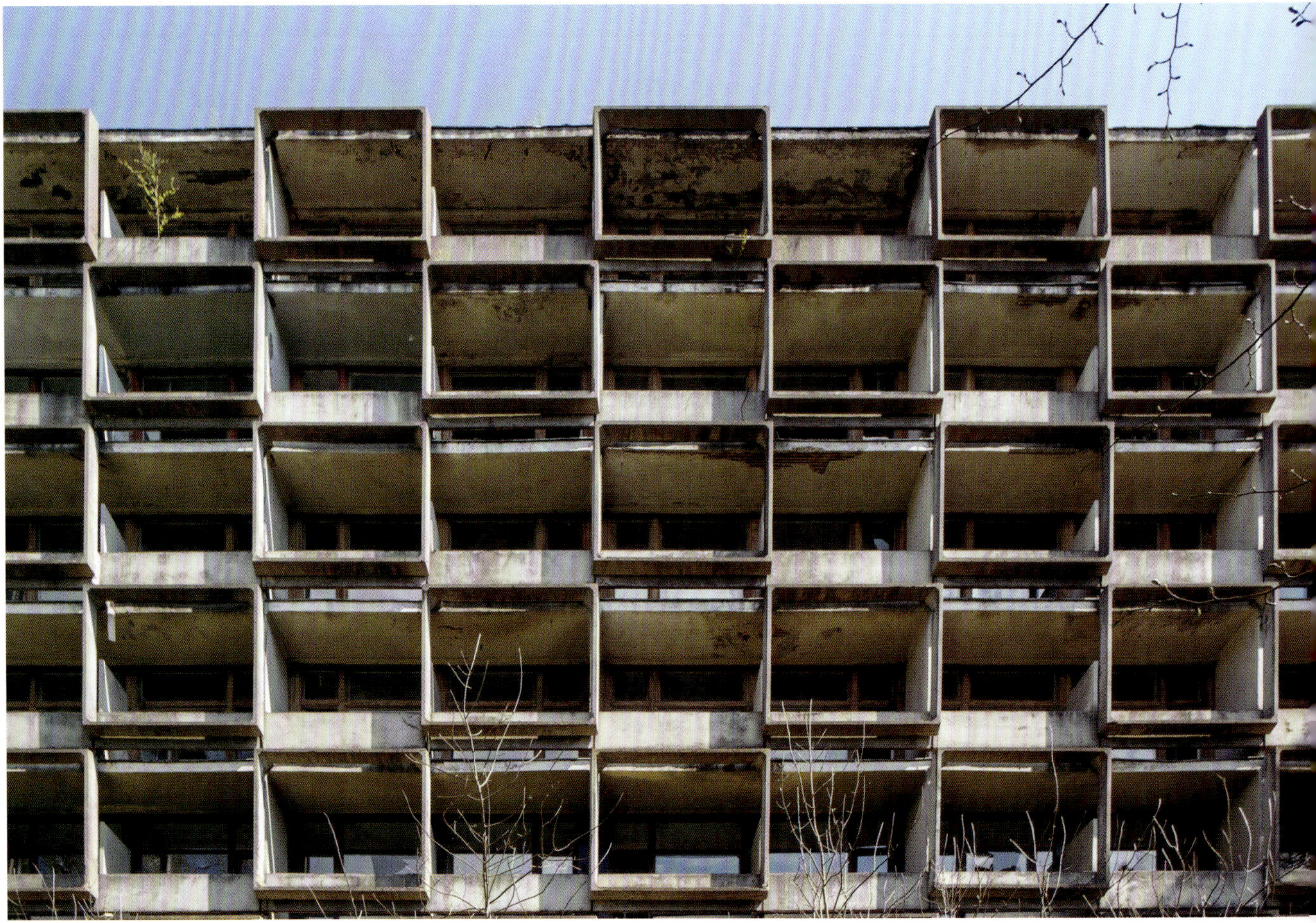

Sanatorium Baltija, Jūrmala, Latvia

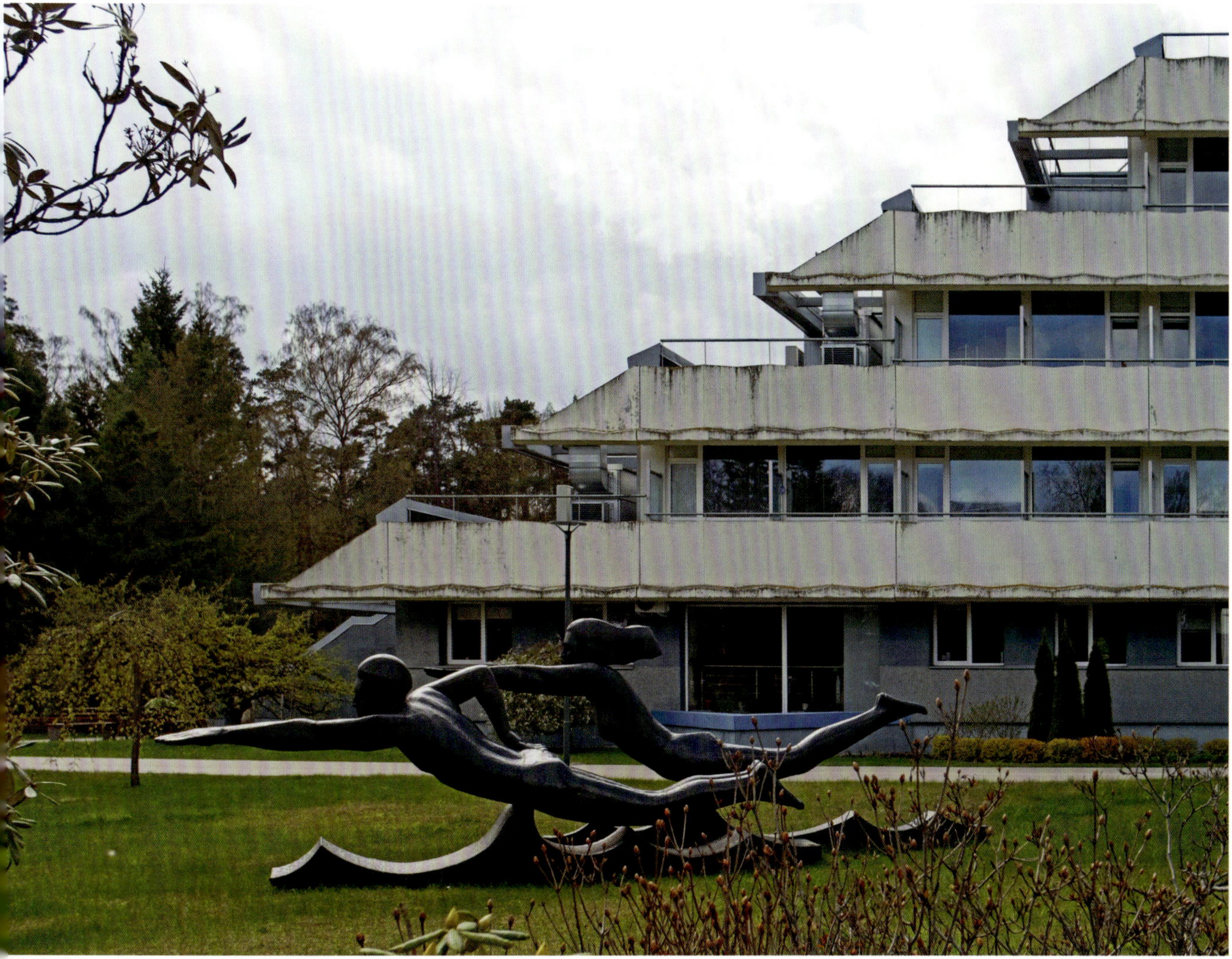

Sanatorium Vaivari (former All-Union Pansionat Start), Jūrmala, Latvia

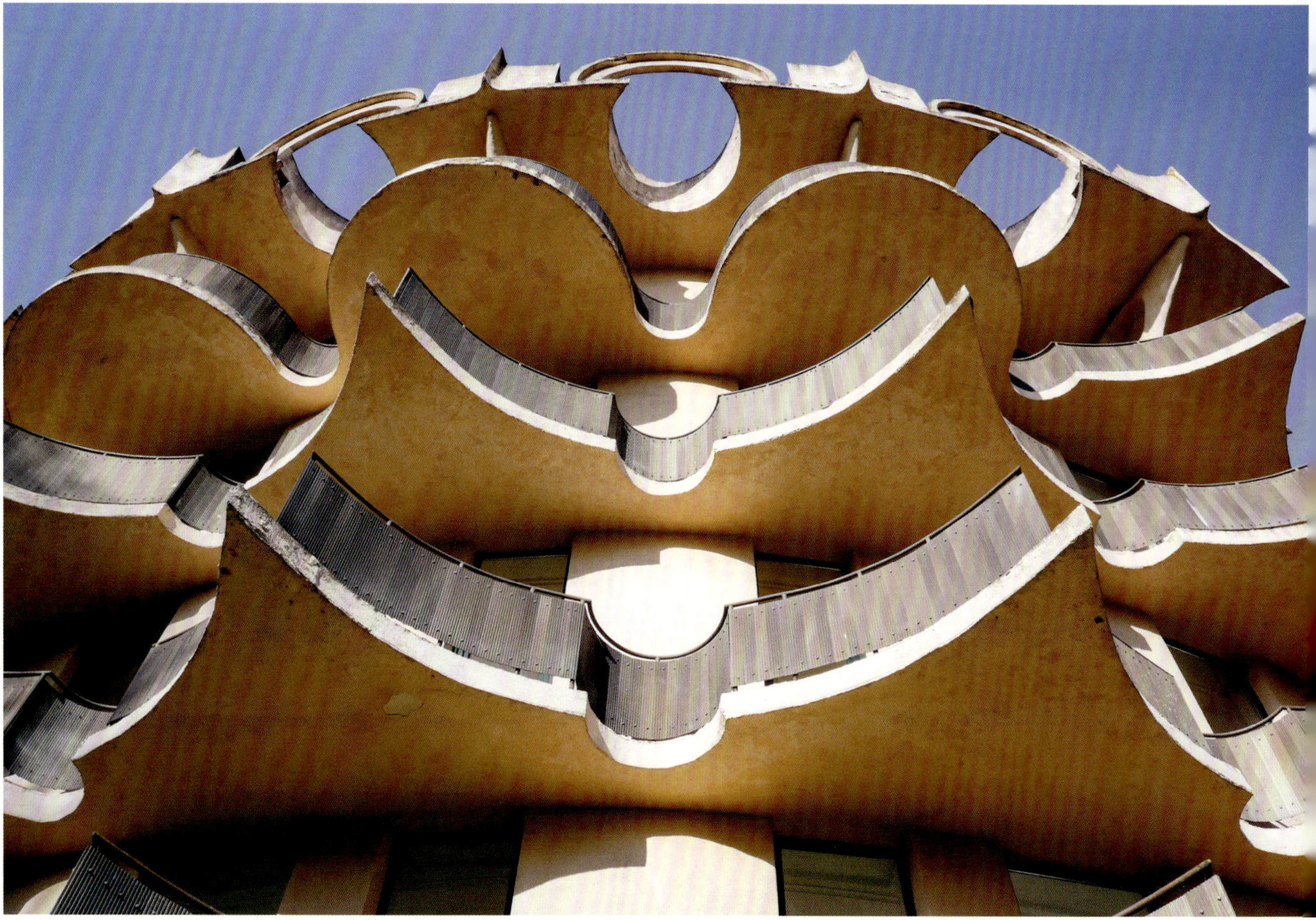

 Hotel Pusynas (former Hotel Sūrutis), Druskininkai, Lithuania

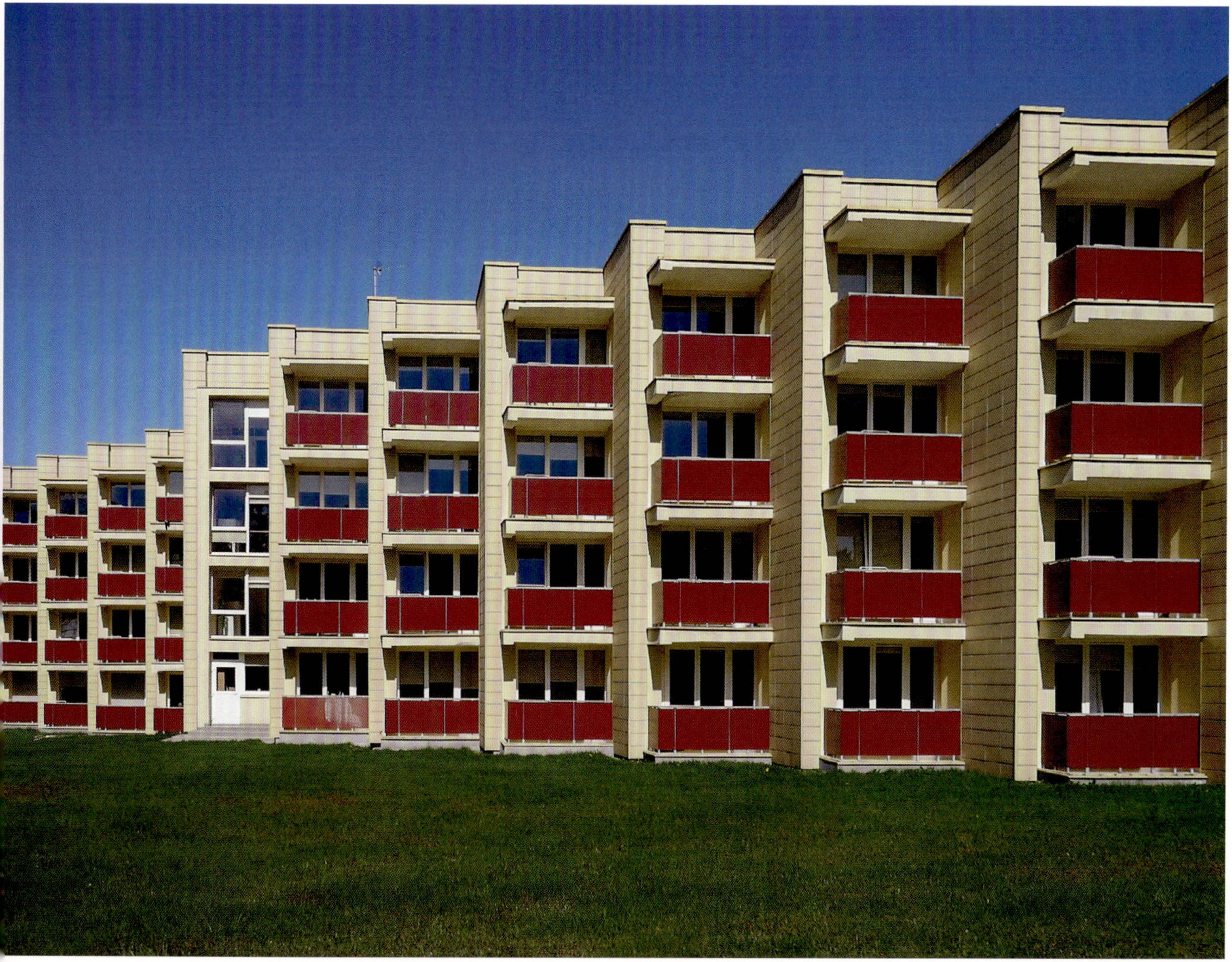

Sanatorium Palangos Gintaras (former Dom Otdykha Gintaras), Palanga, Lithuania

MACEDONIA

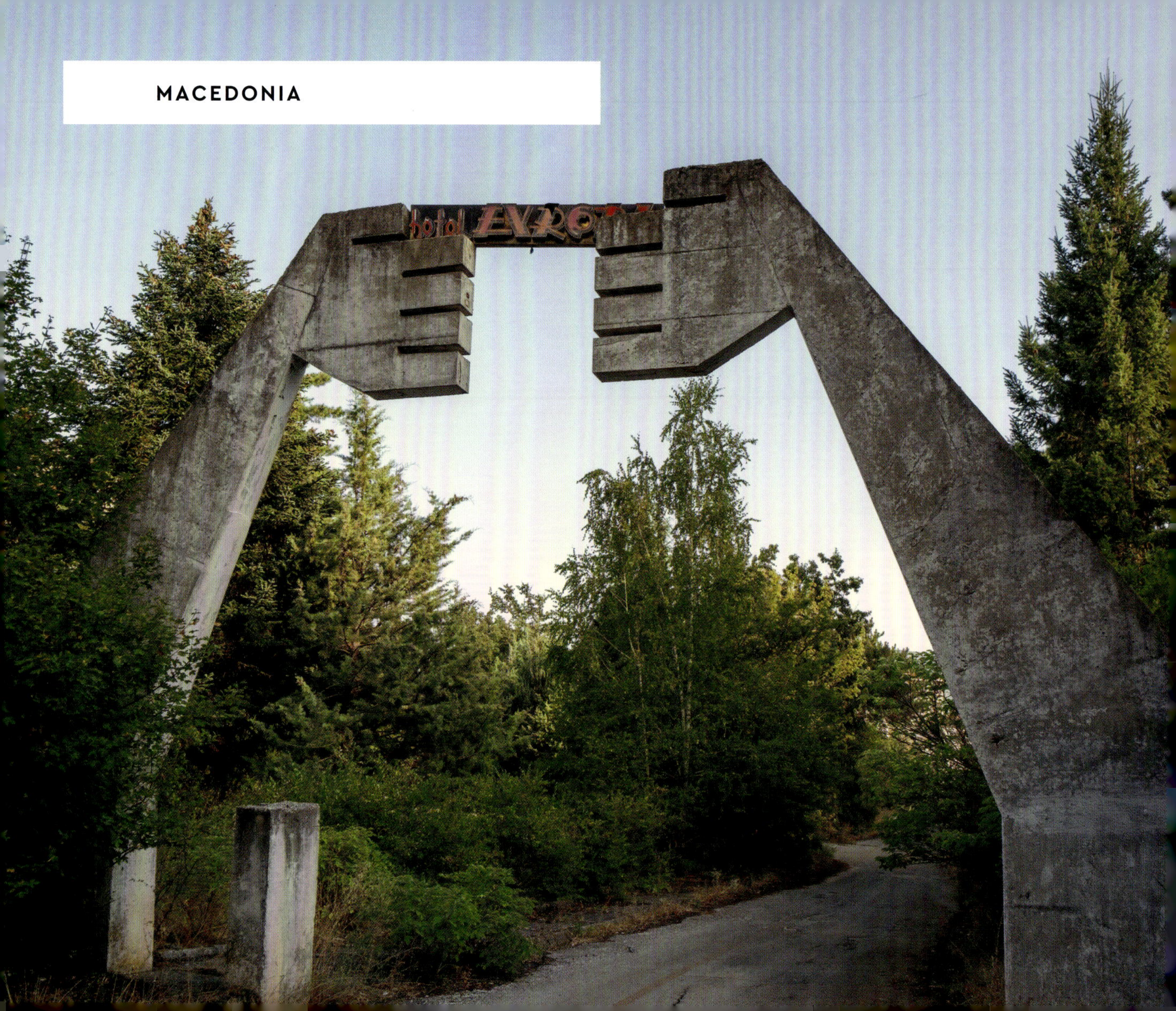

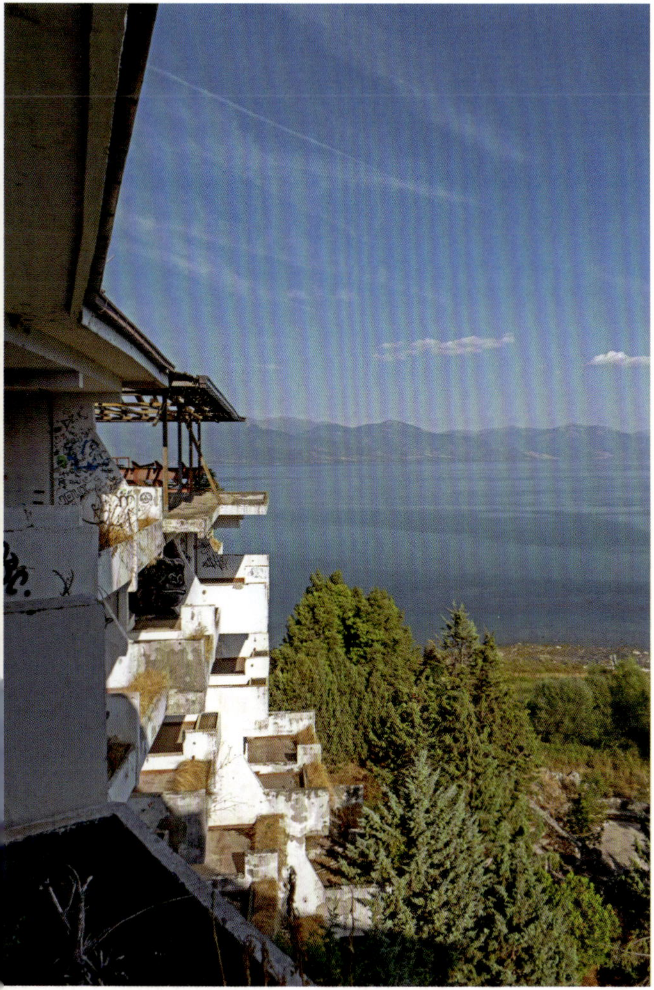

Hotel Evropa, Oteševo, Macedonia

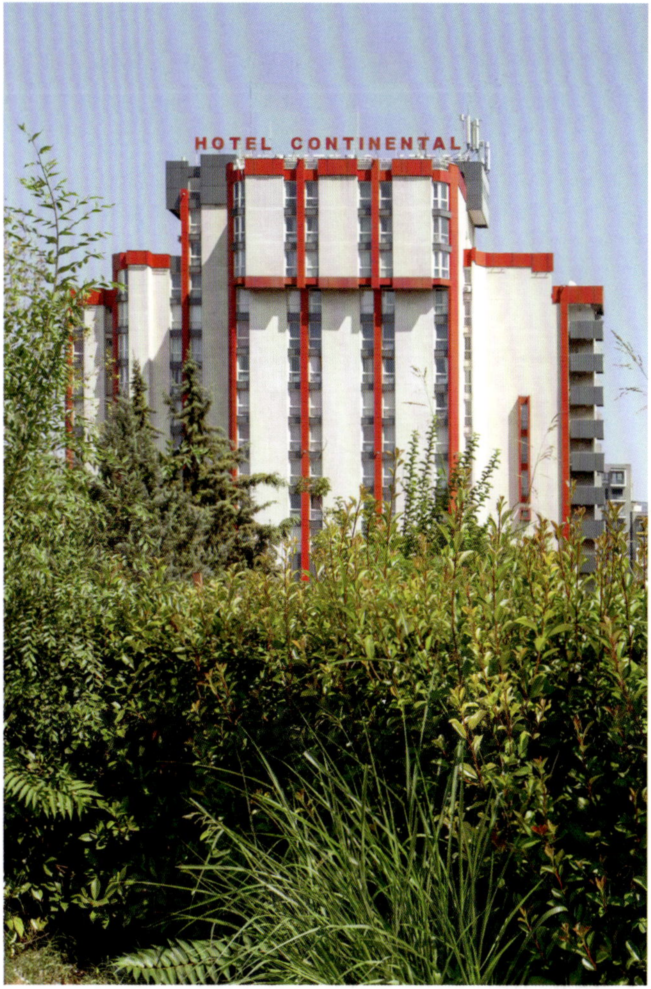

Hotel Continental, Skopje, Macedonia

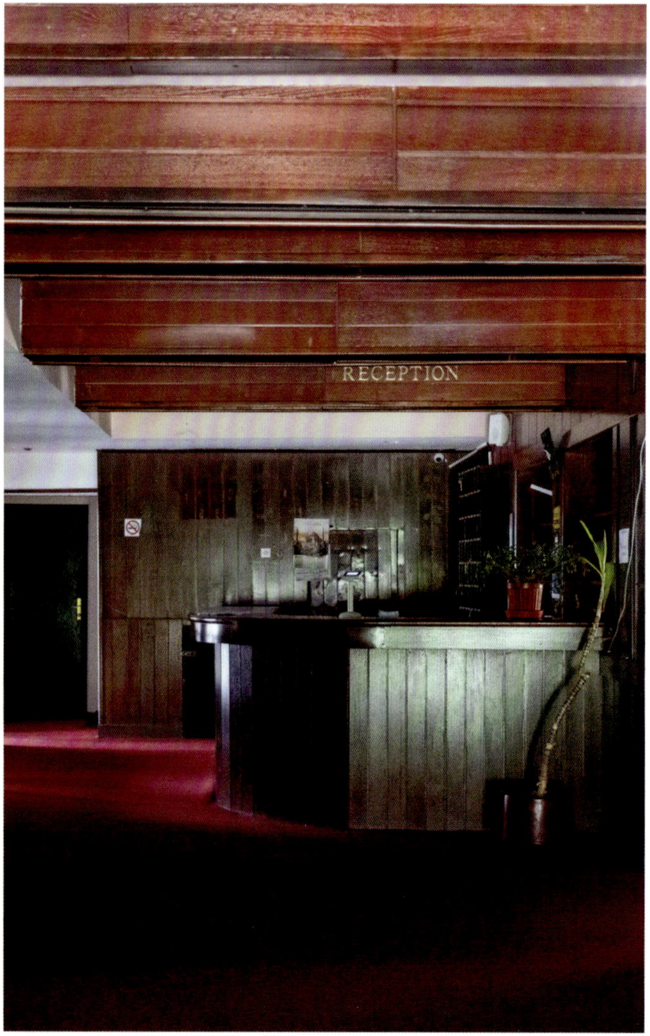

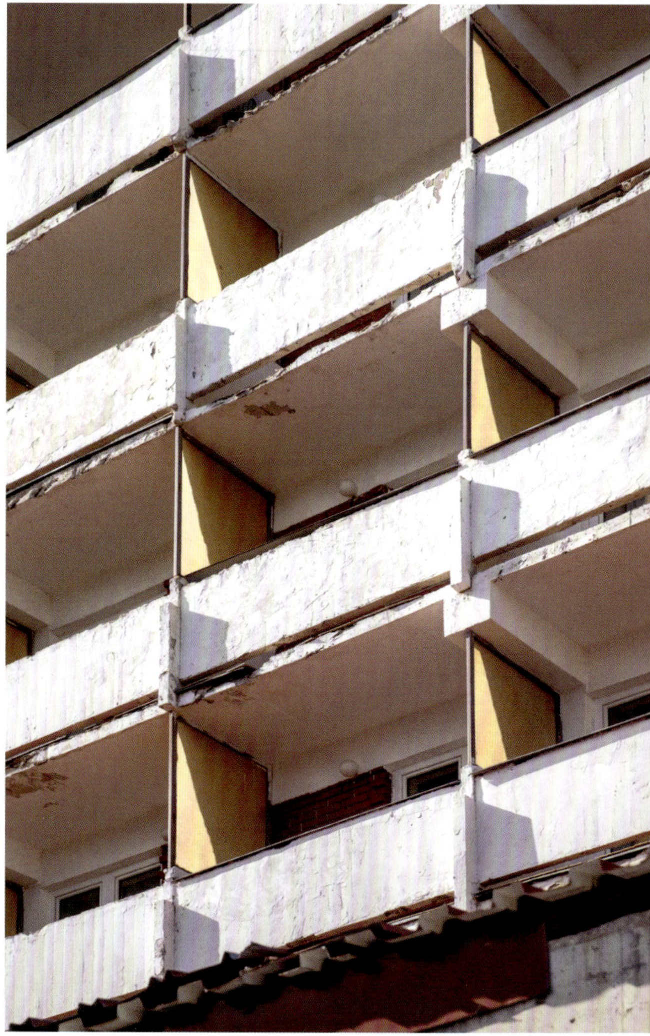

 Hotel Slavija, Popova Šapka, Macedonia

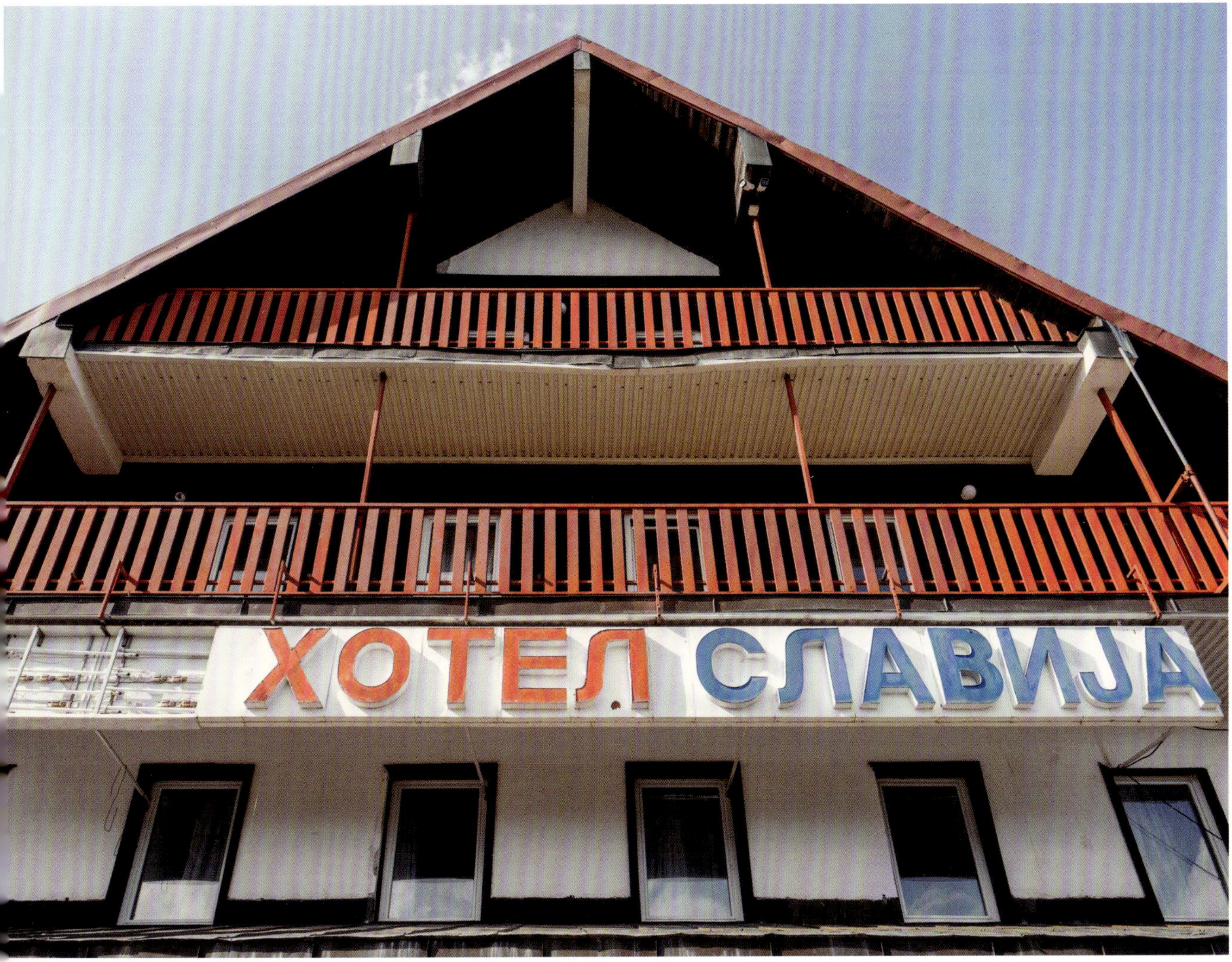
ХОТЕЛ СЛАВИЈА

MOLDOVA

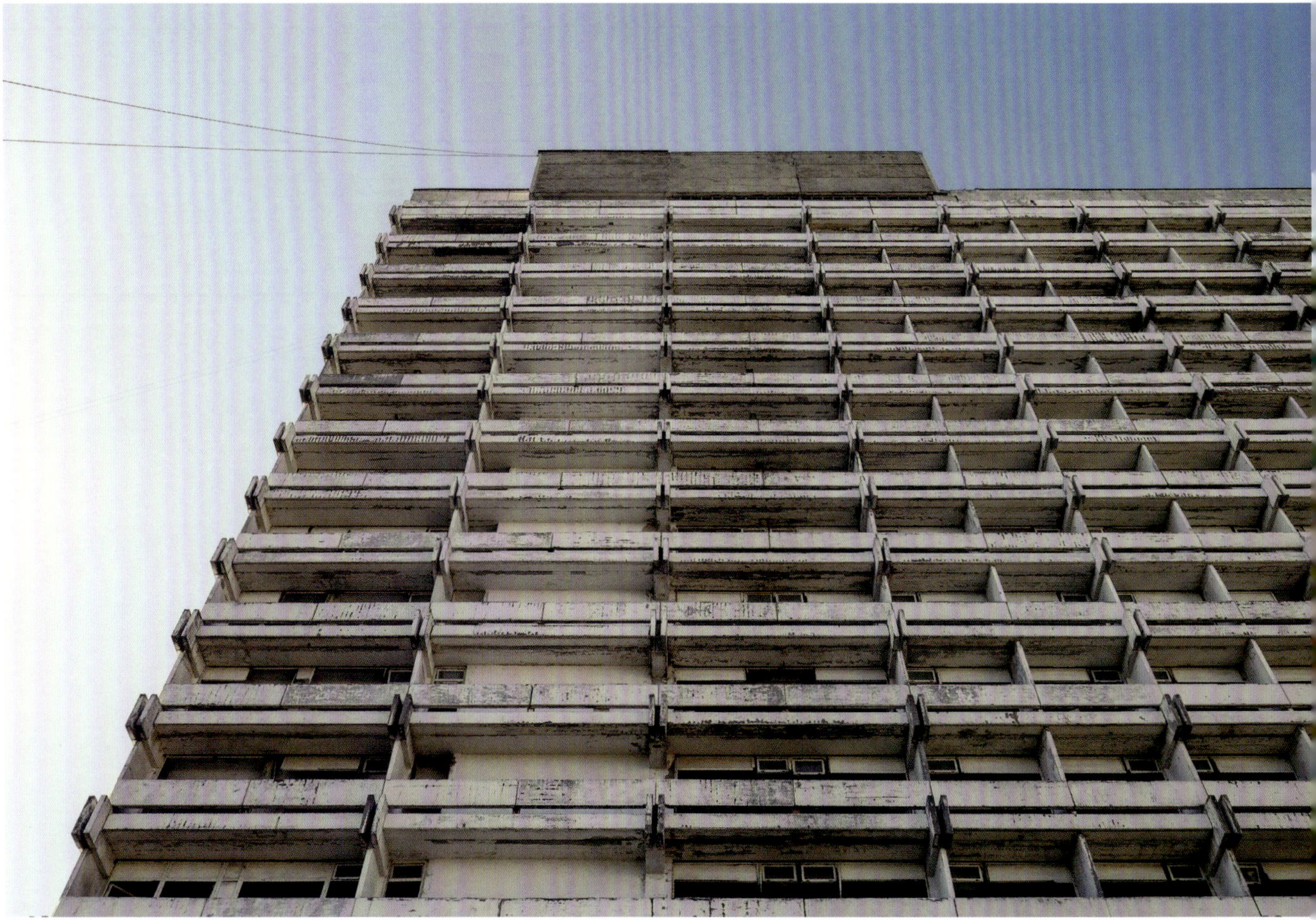

 Hotel Național (former Hotel Intourist), Chișinău, Moldova

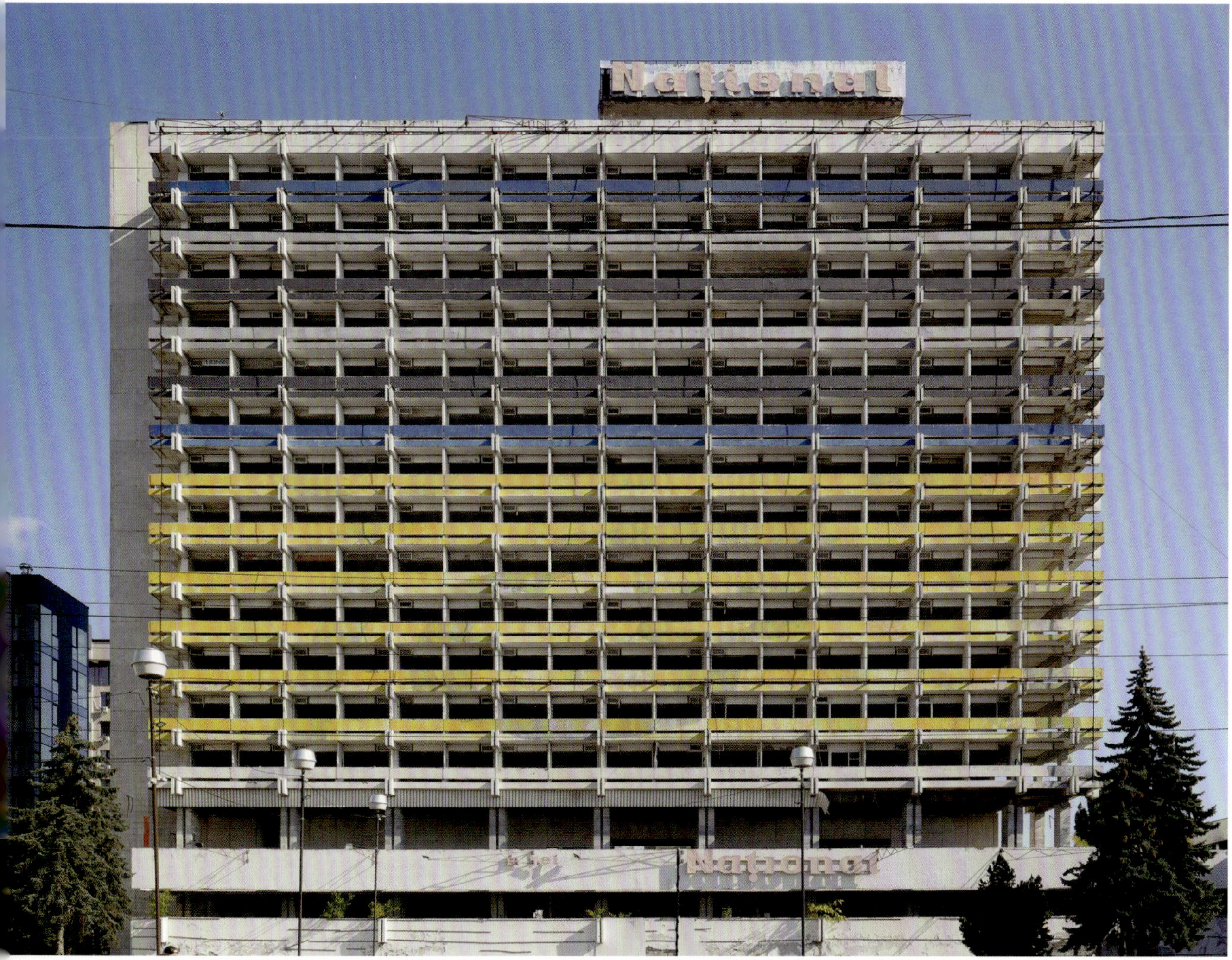
Național
Național

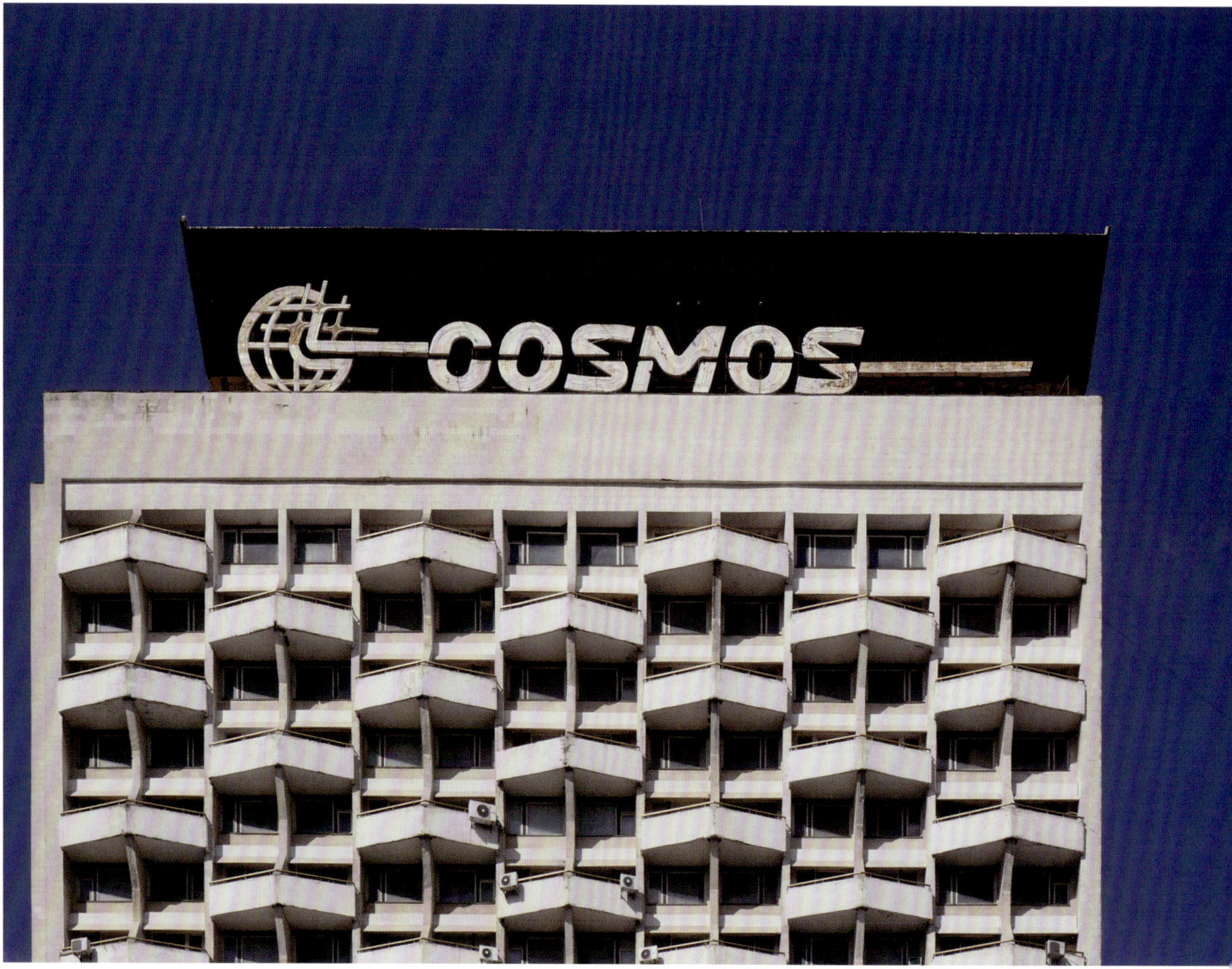

 Hotel Cosmos, Chișinău, Moldova

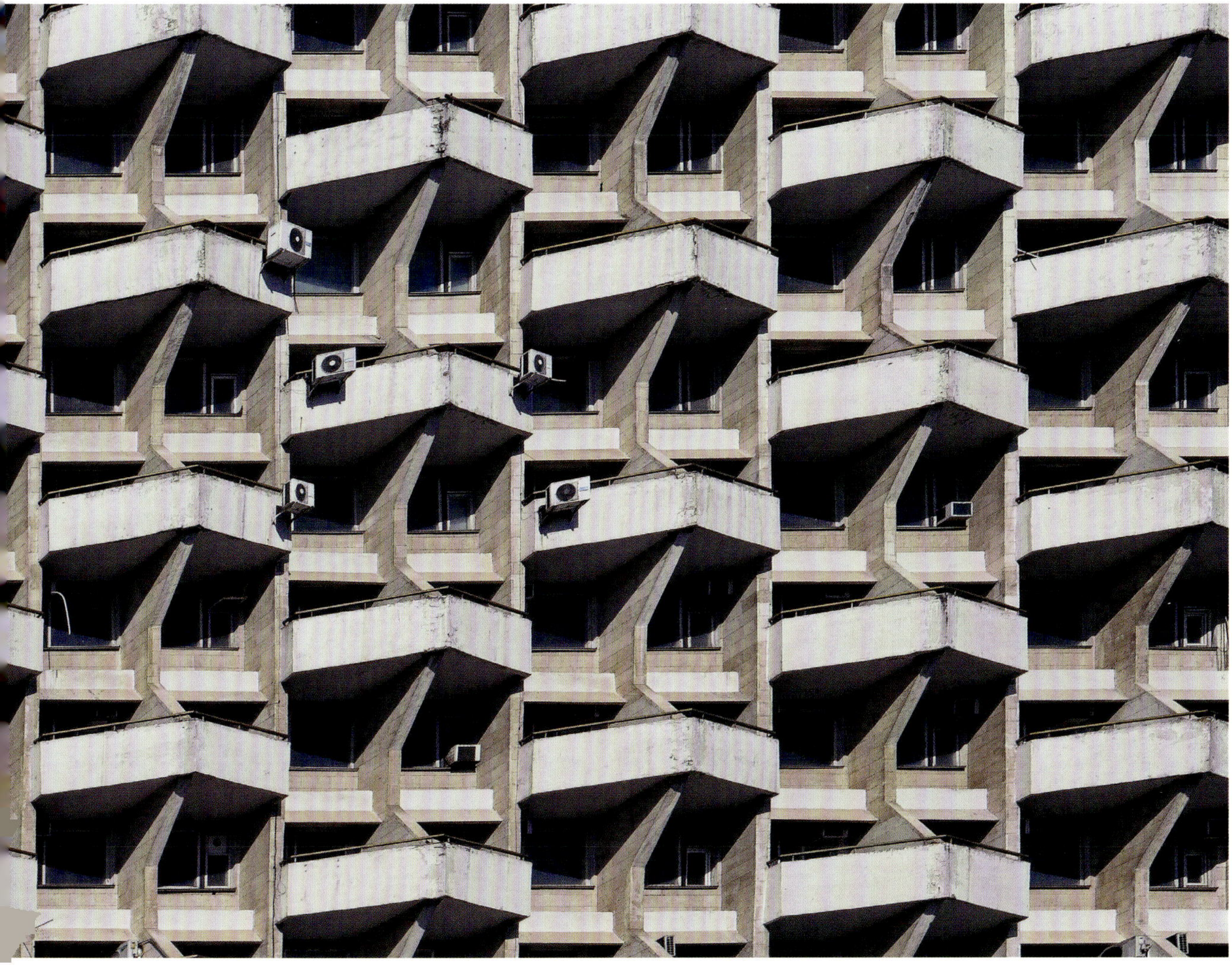

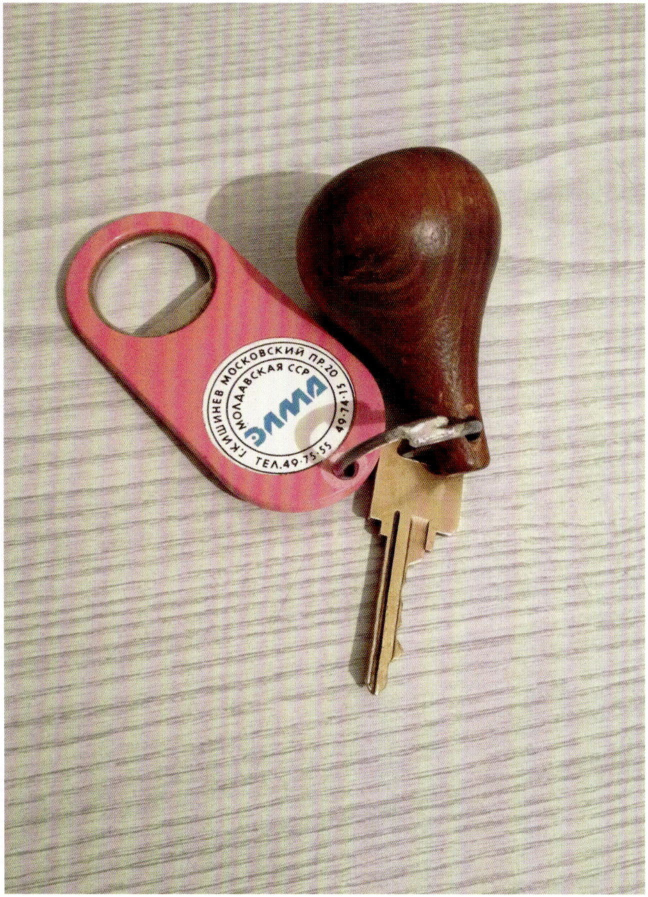

Hotel Cosmos, room key

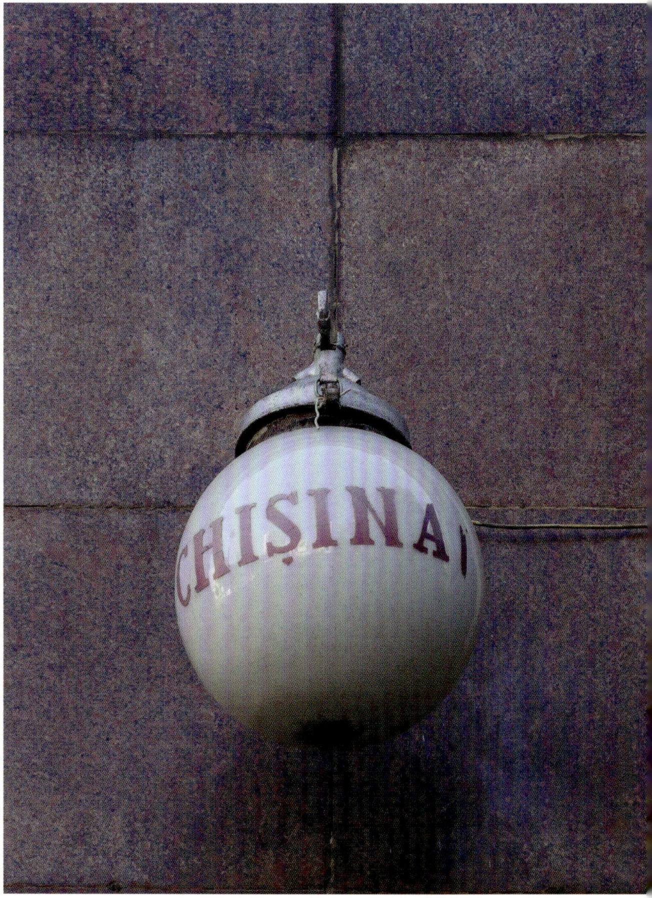

Hotel Chișinău, Chișinău, Moldova

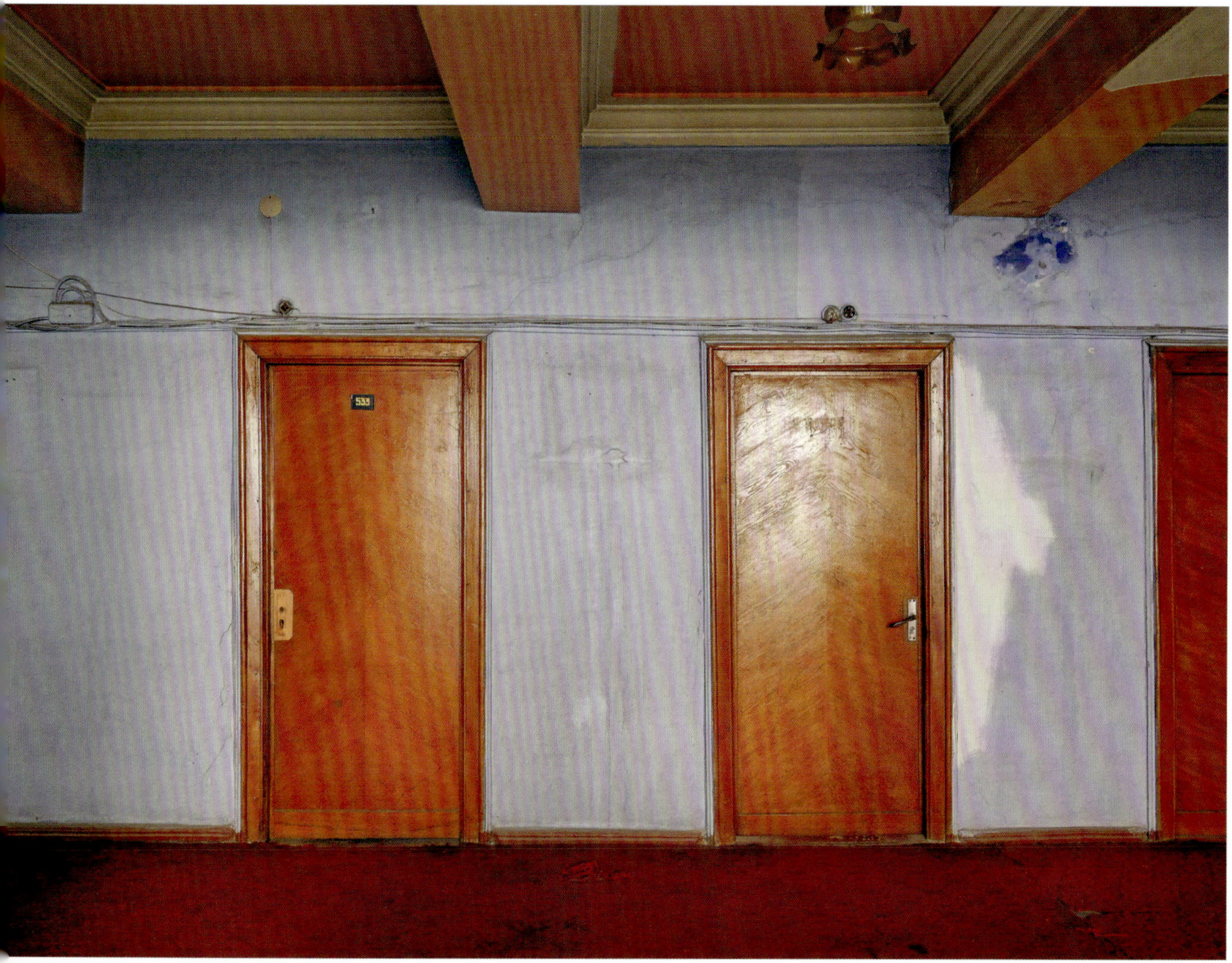
533

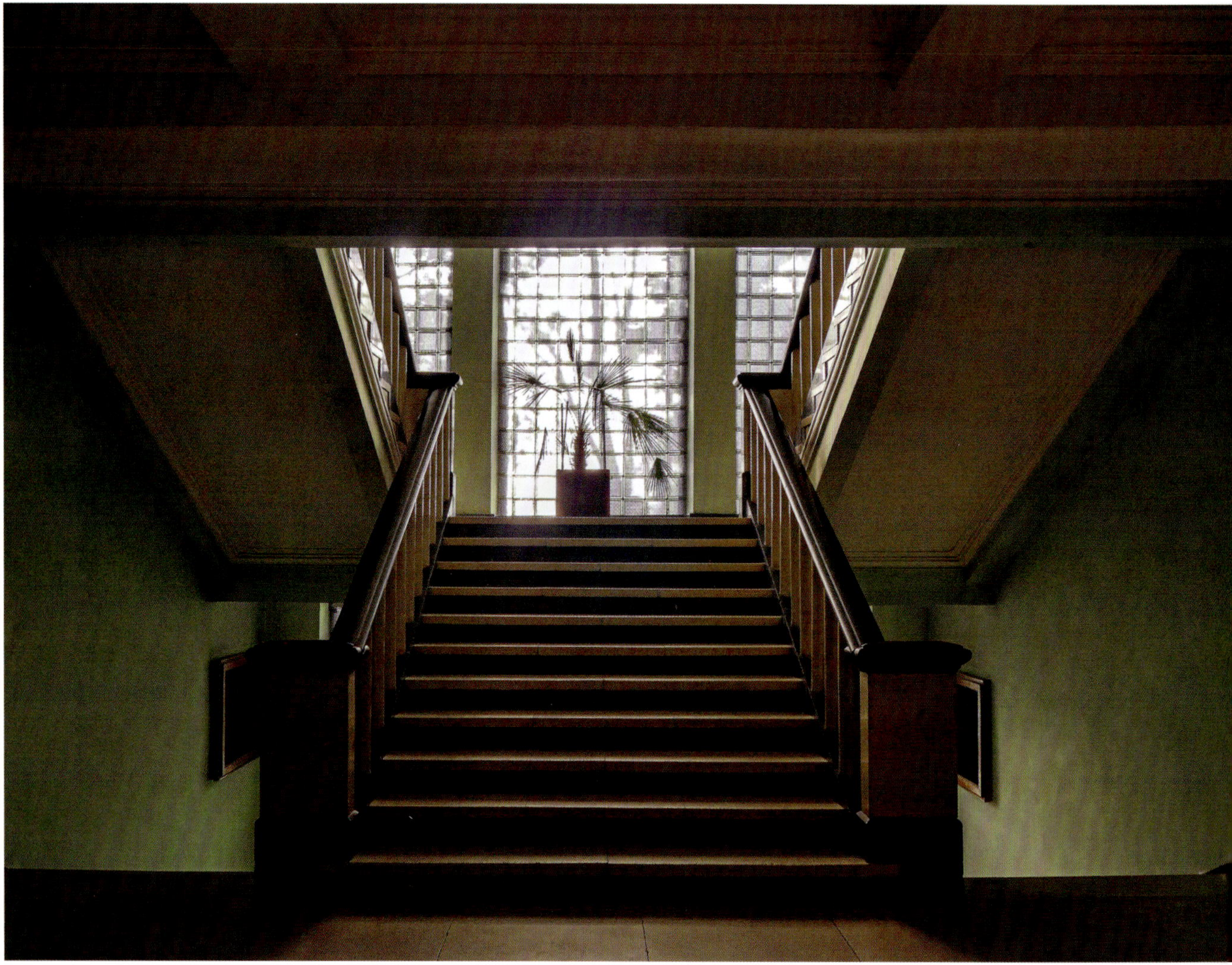

 Hotel Chișinău, Chișinău, Moldova

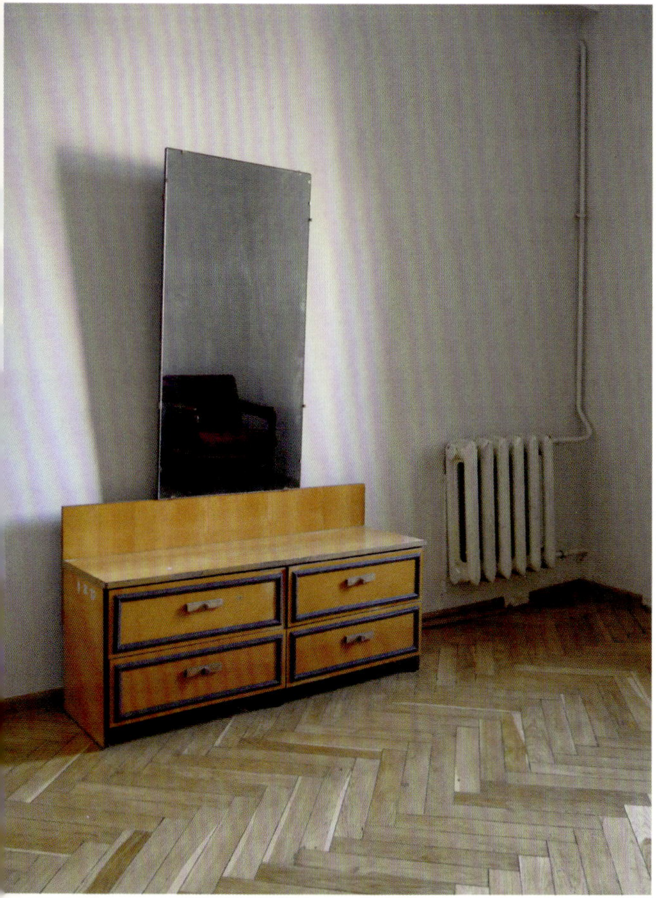

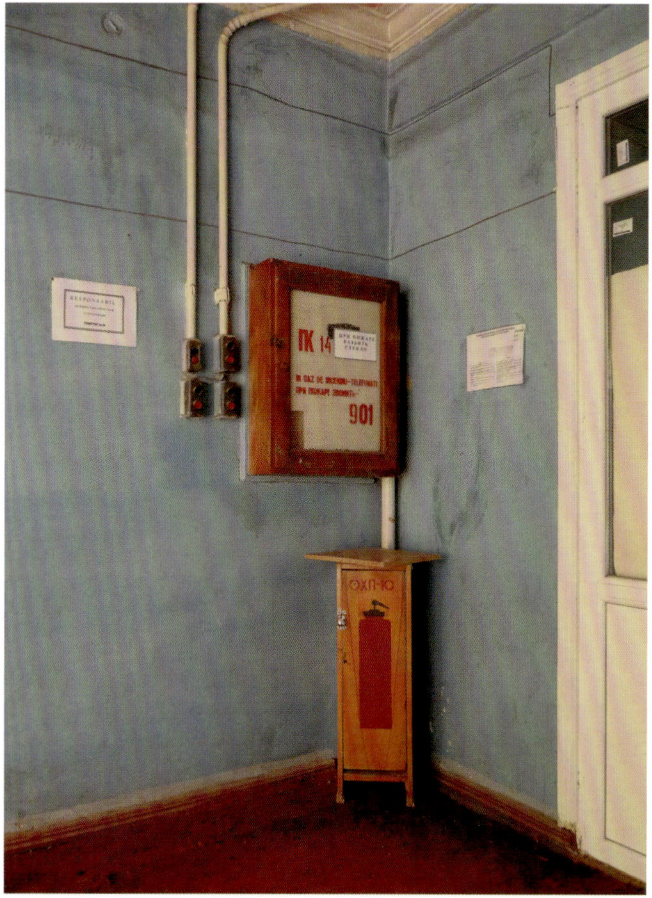
ПК 14
901

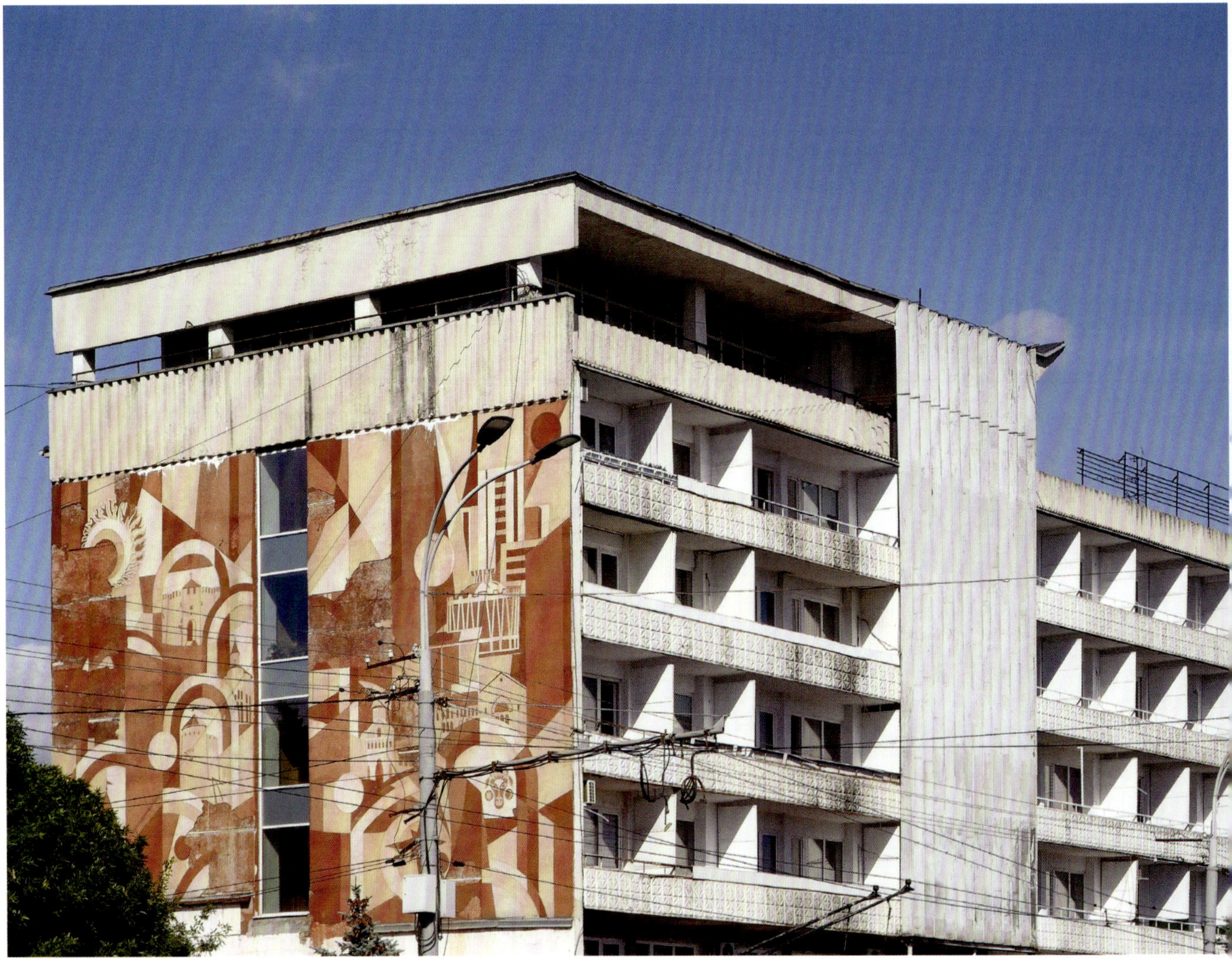

 Hotel Turist, Chișinău, Moldova

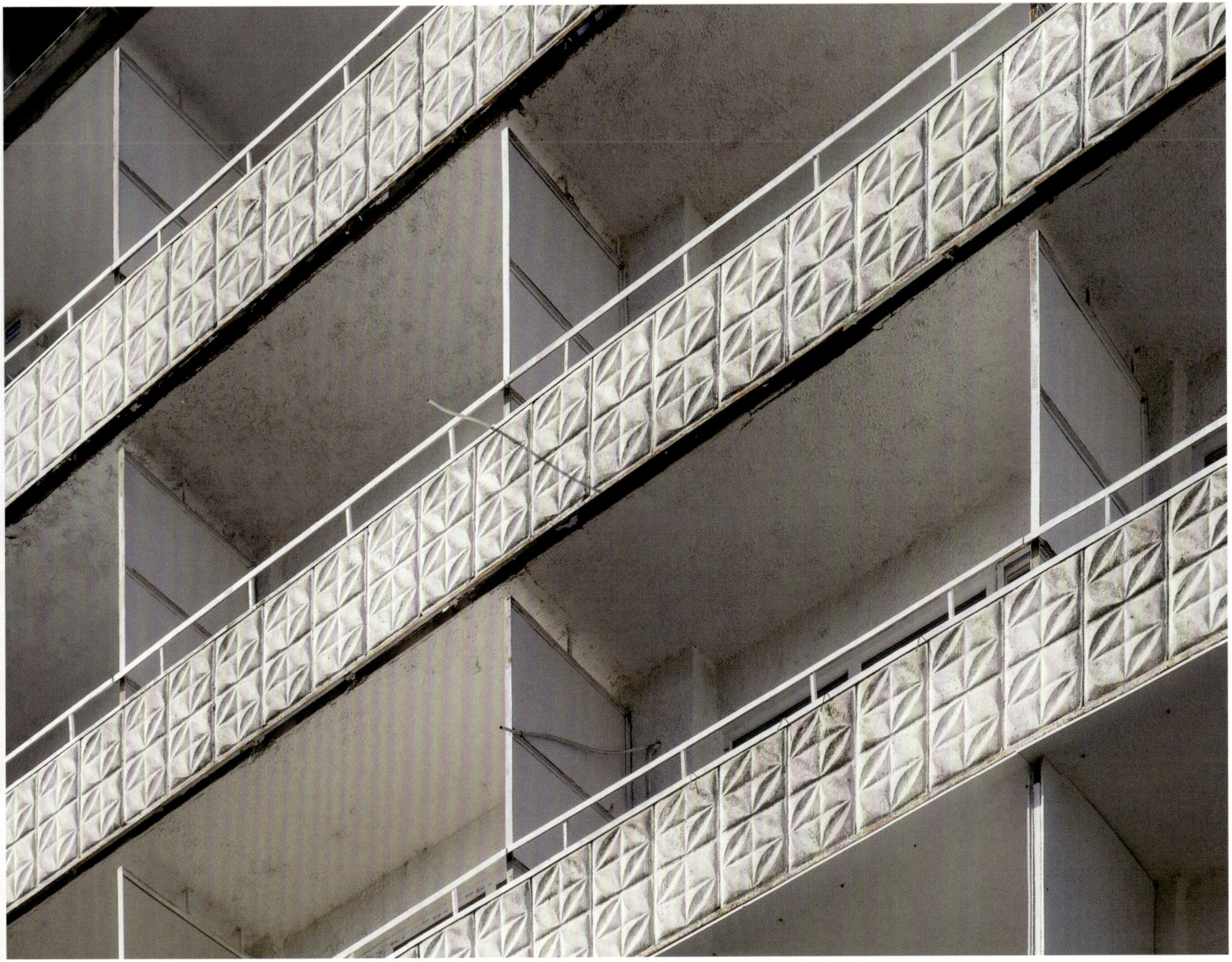

MONTENEGRO

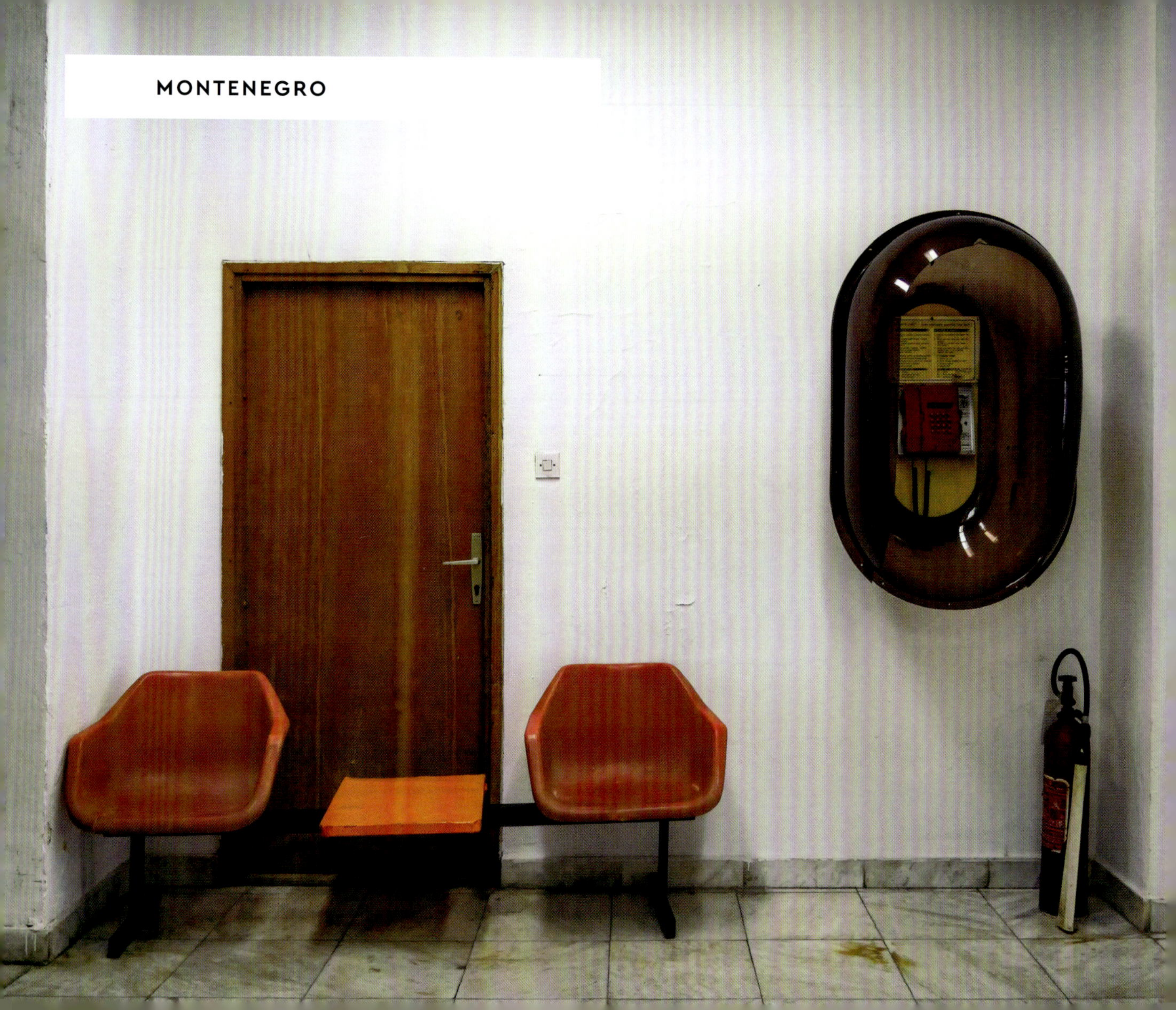

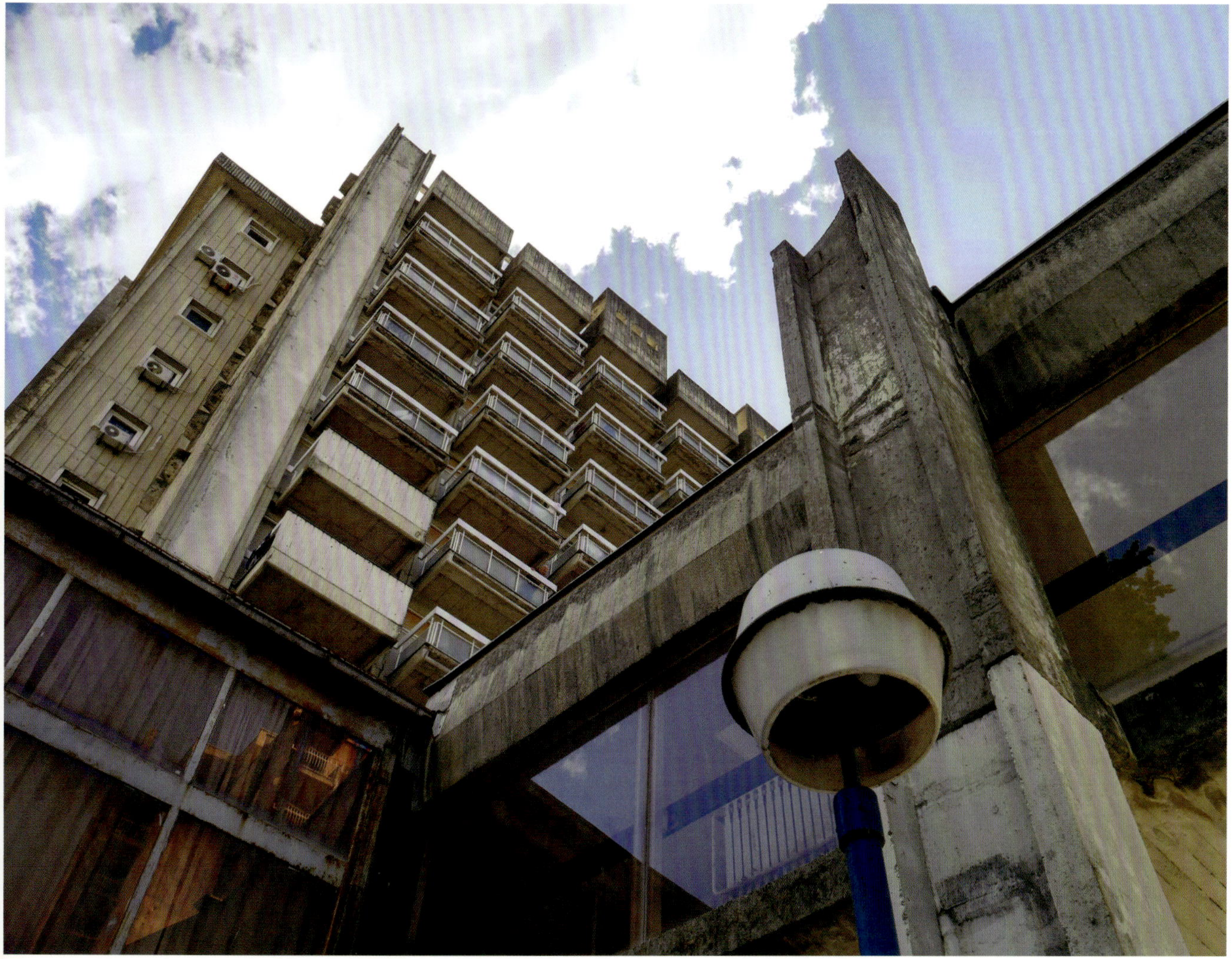

Hotel Igalo SPA, Igalo, Montenegro

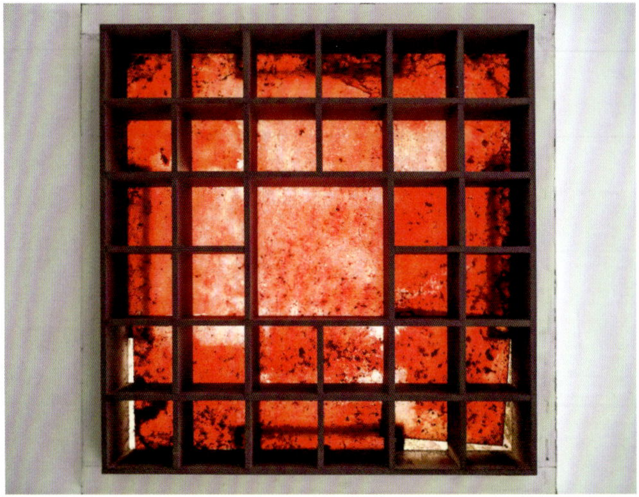

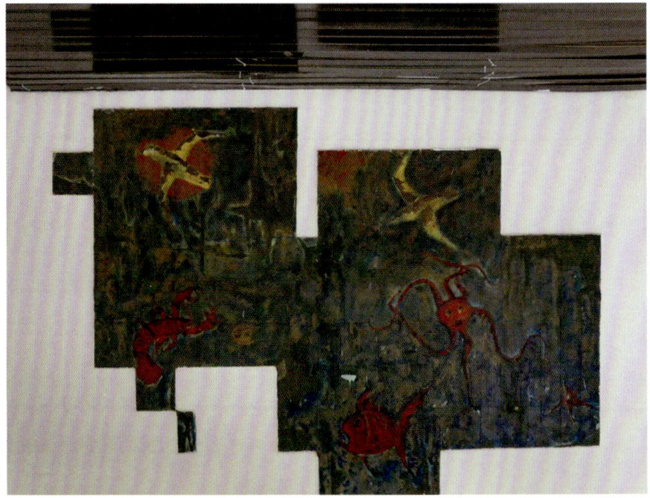

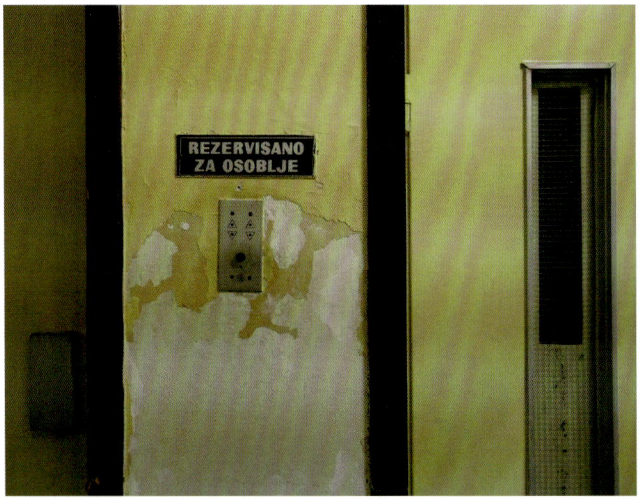
REZERVISANO
ZA OSOBLJE

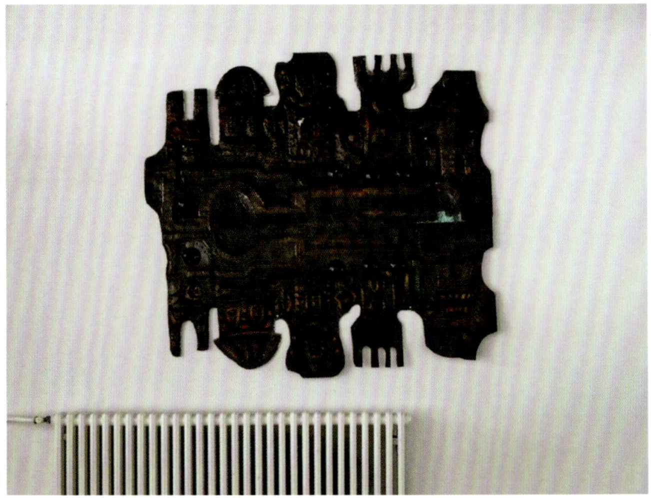

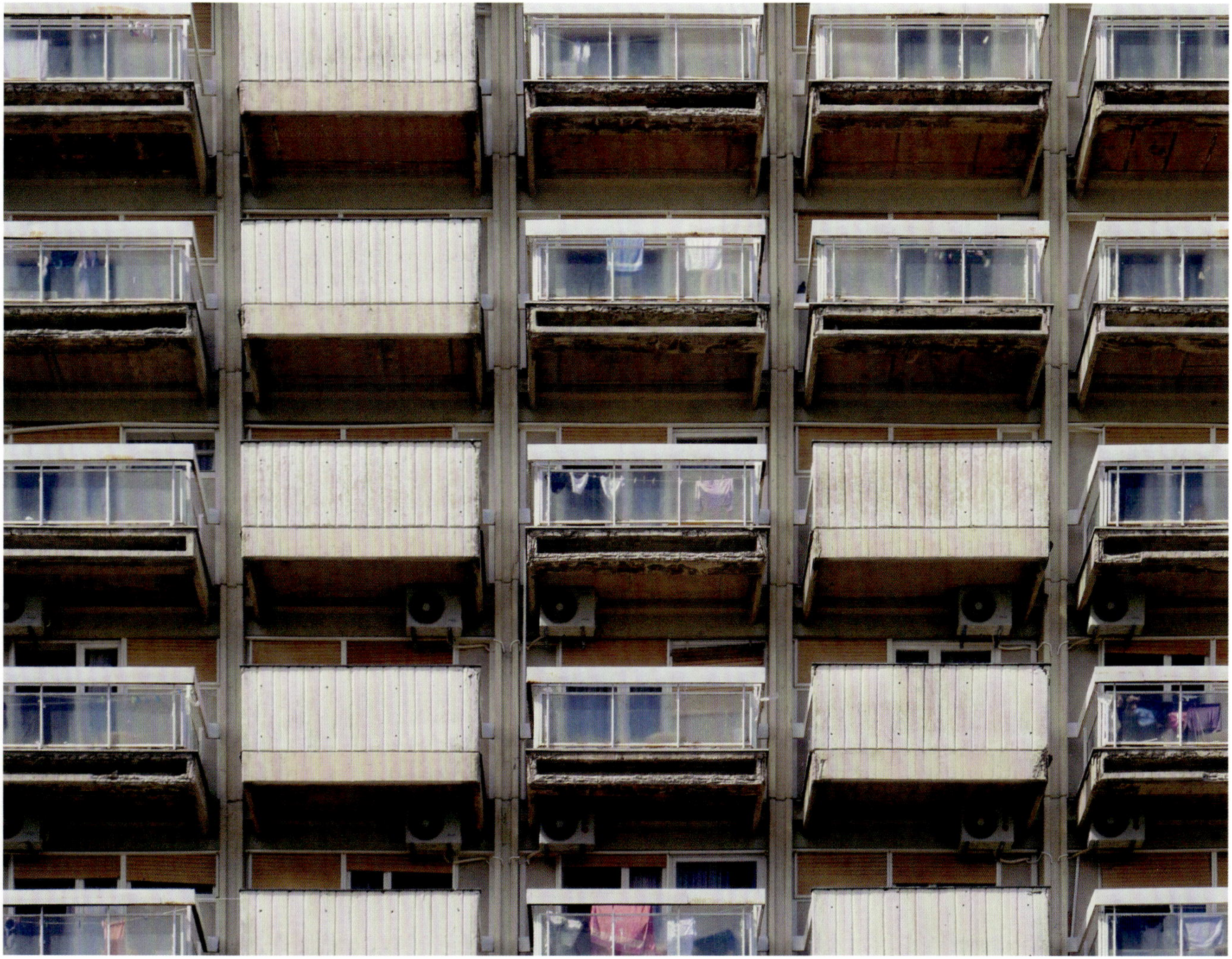

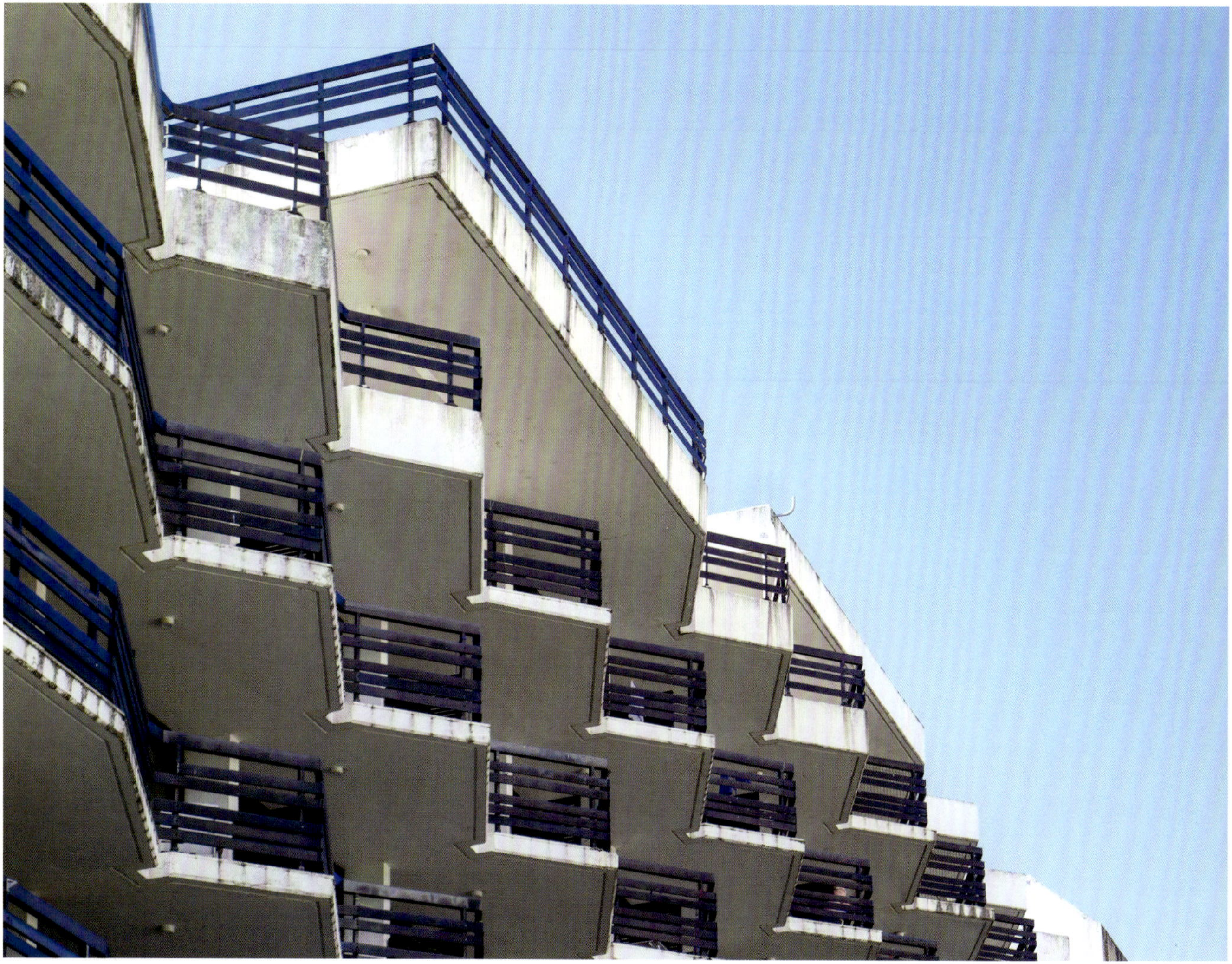

 Hotel Igalo SPA 2, Herceg Novi, Montenegro

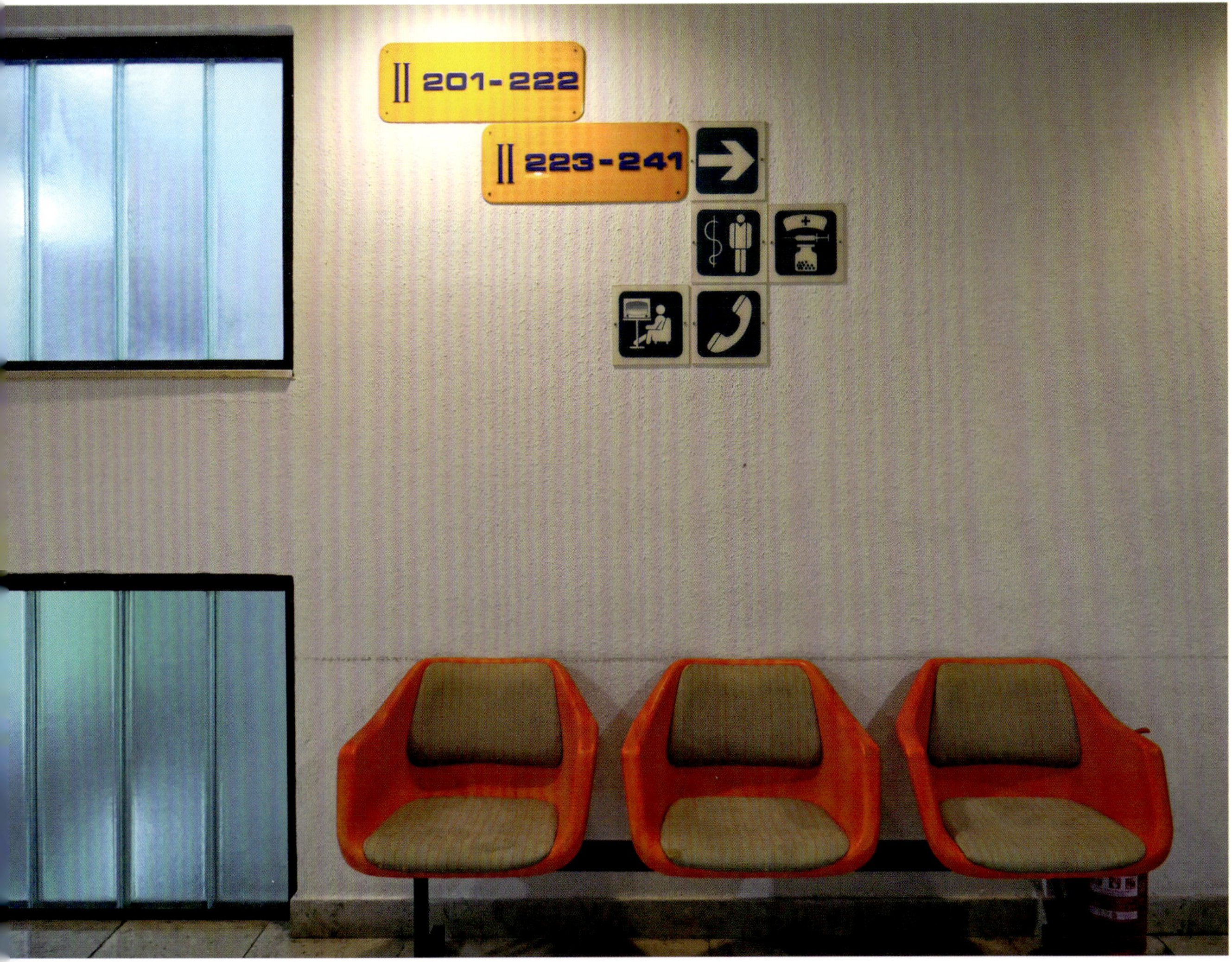
201-222
223-241

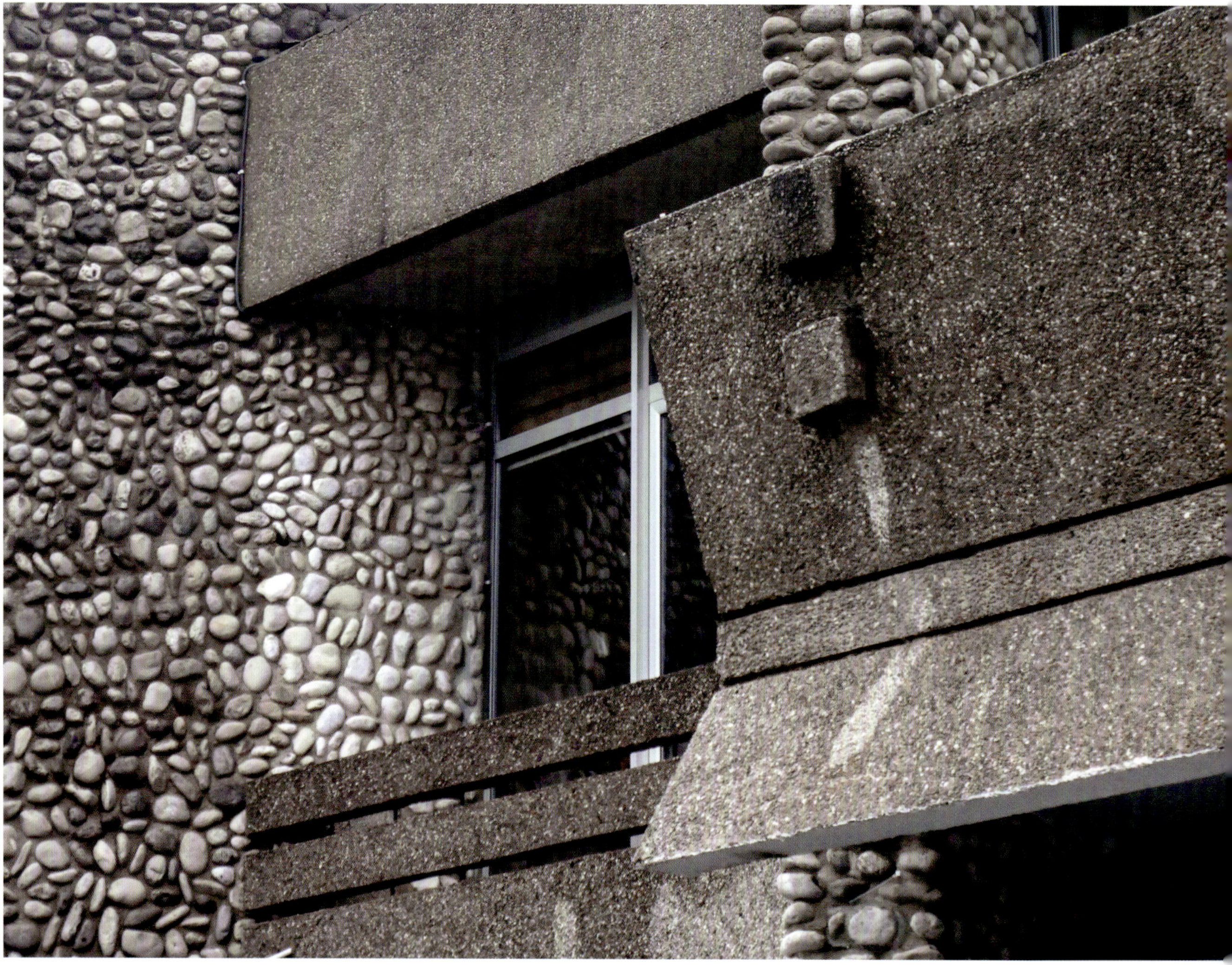

 Hotel Podgorica, Podgorica, Montenegro

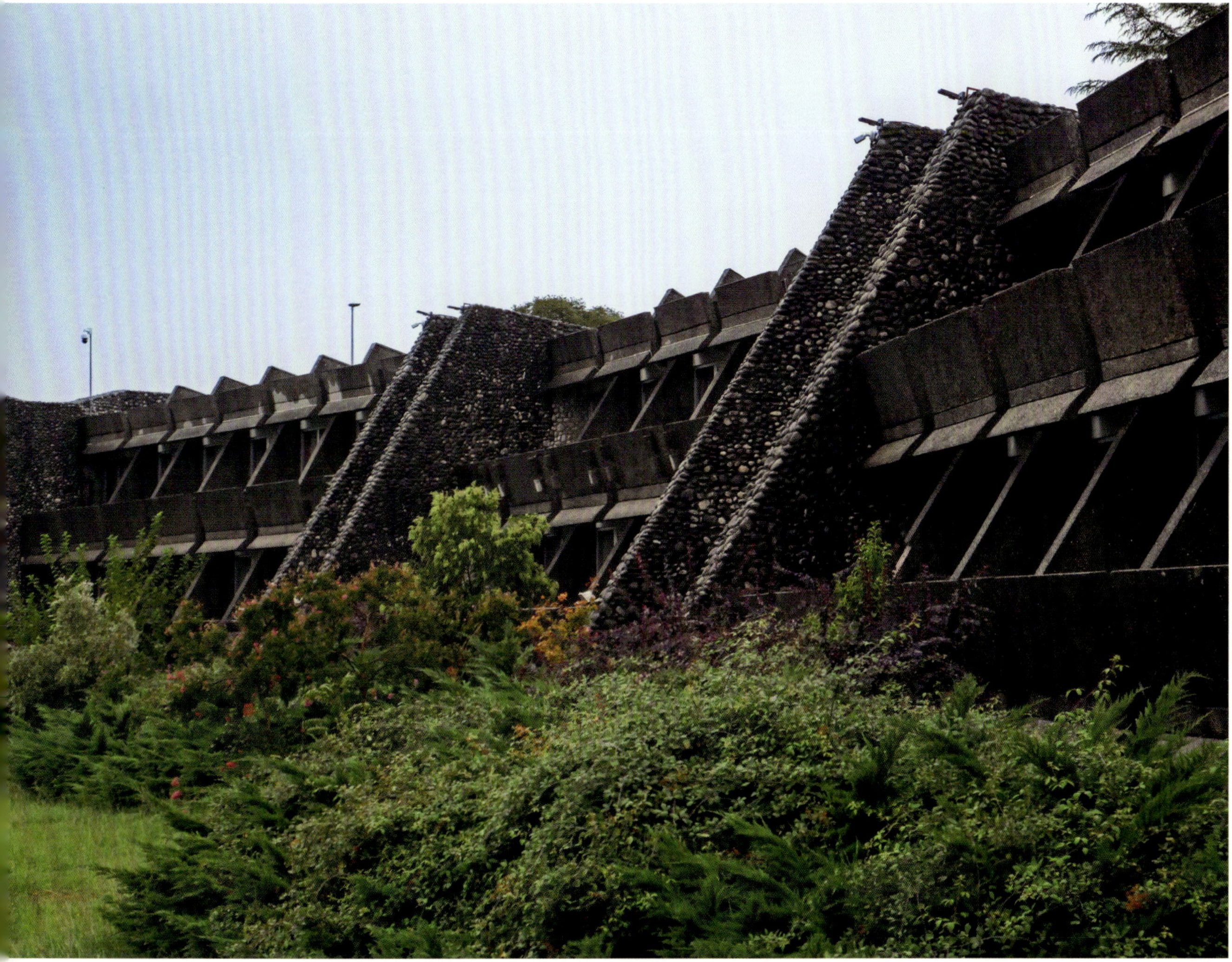

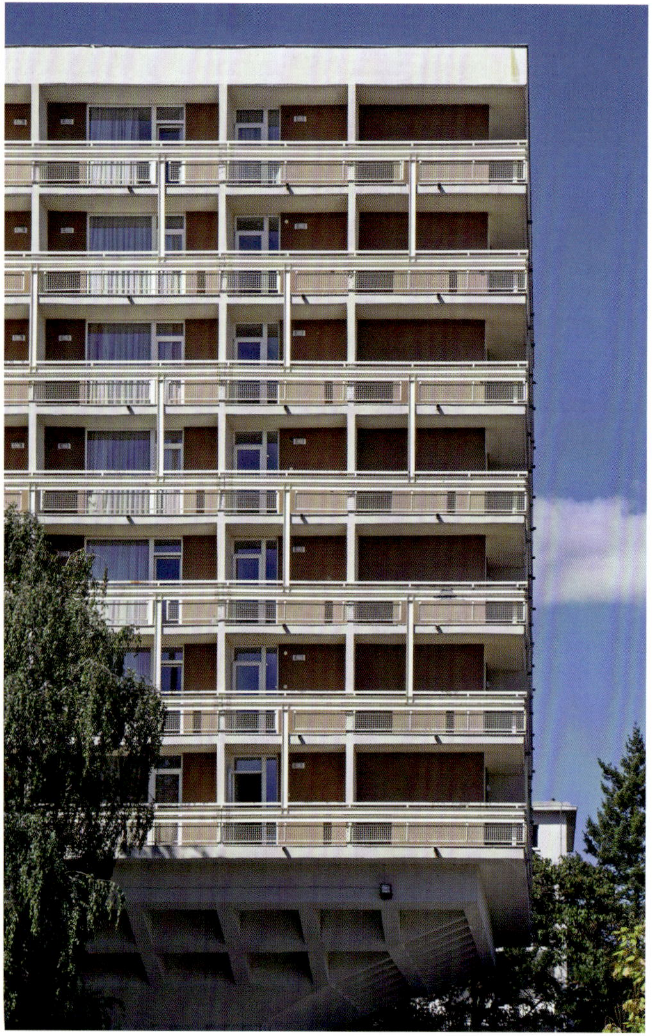

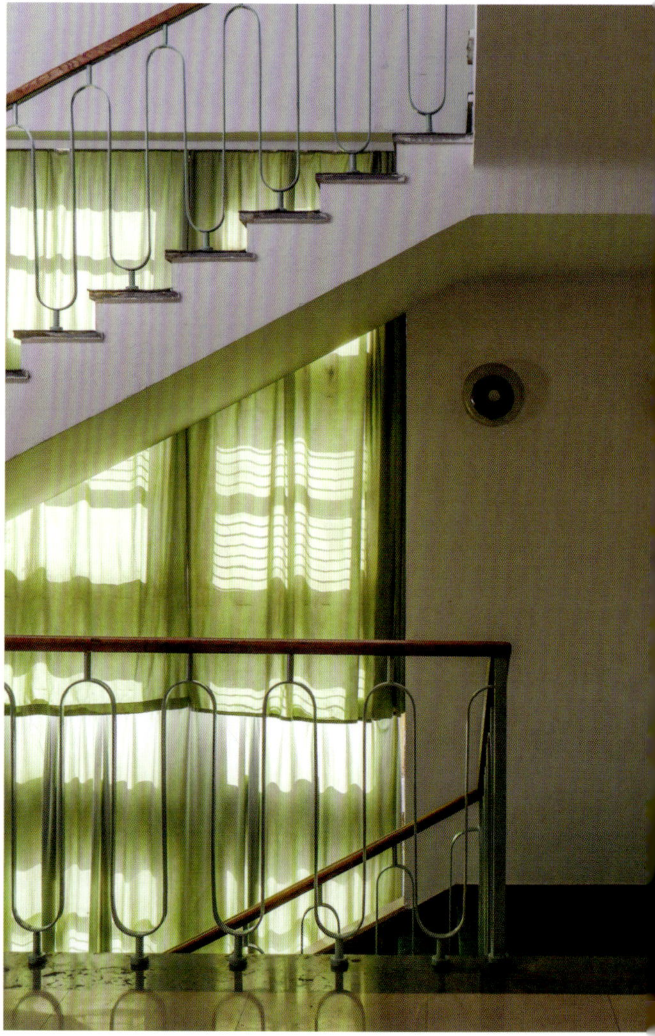

 Hotel Onogošt, Nikšić, Montenegro

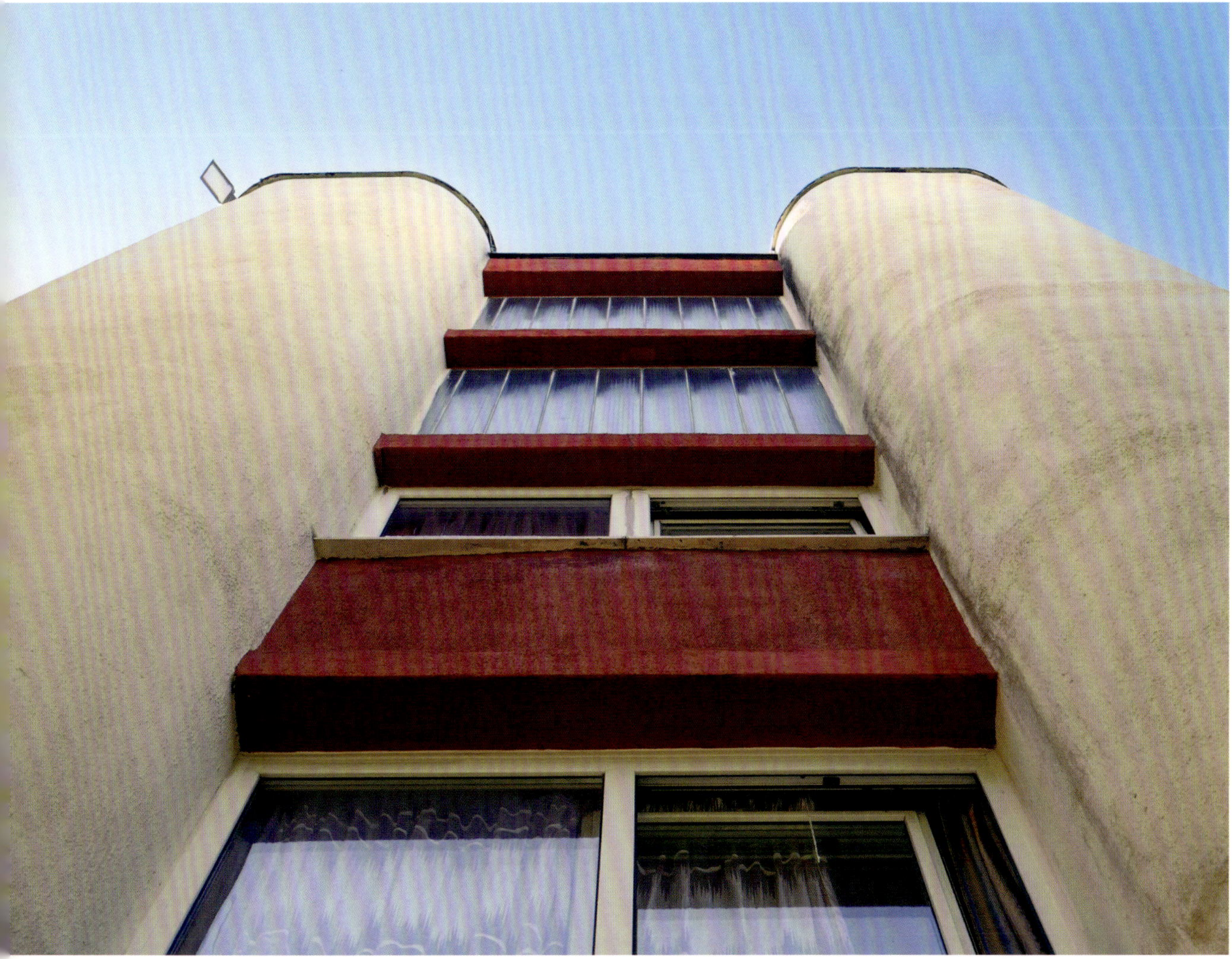

Hotel Sidro, Bar, Montenegro

POLAND

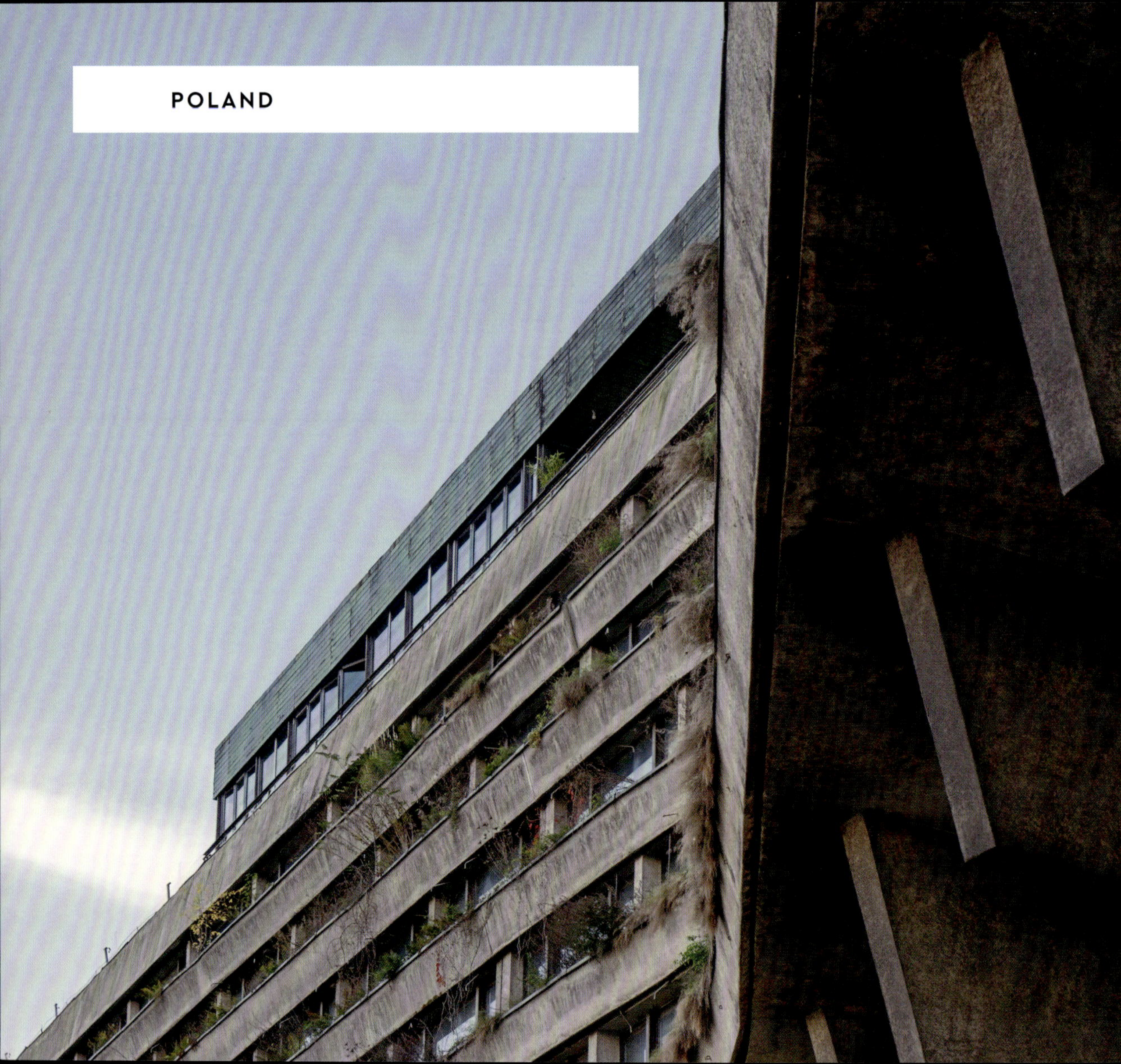

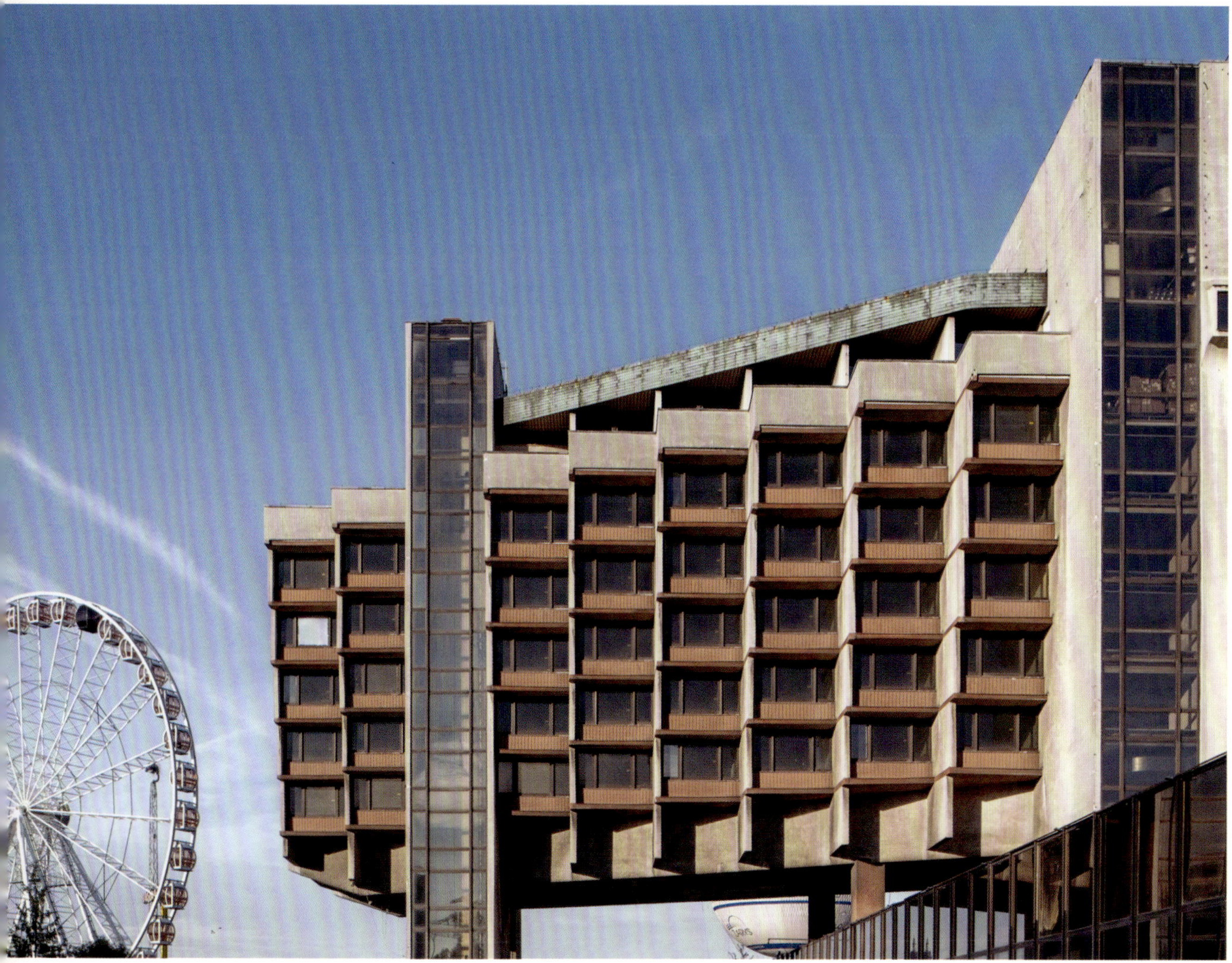

Hotel Forum, Krakow, Poland

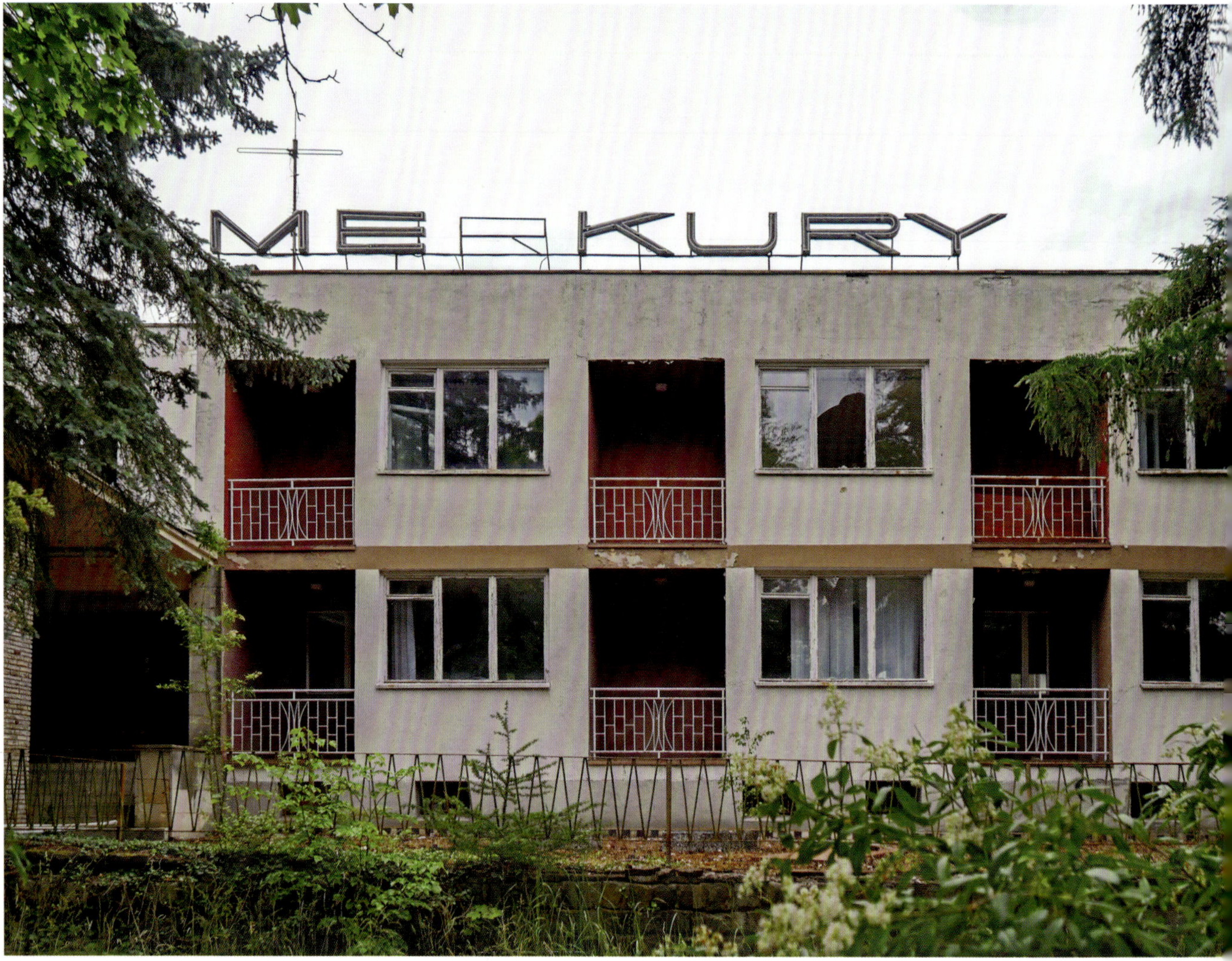

 Hotel Merkury, Kiekrz, Poland

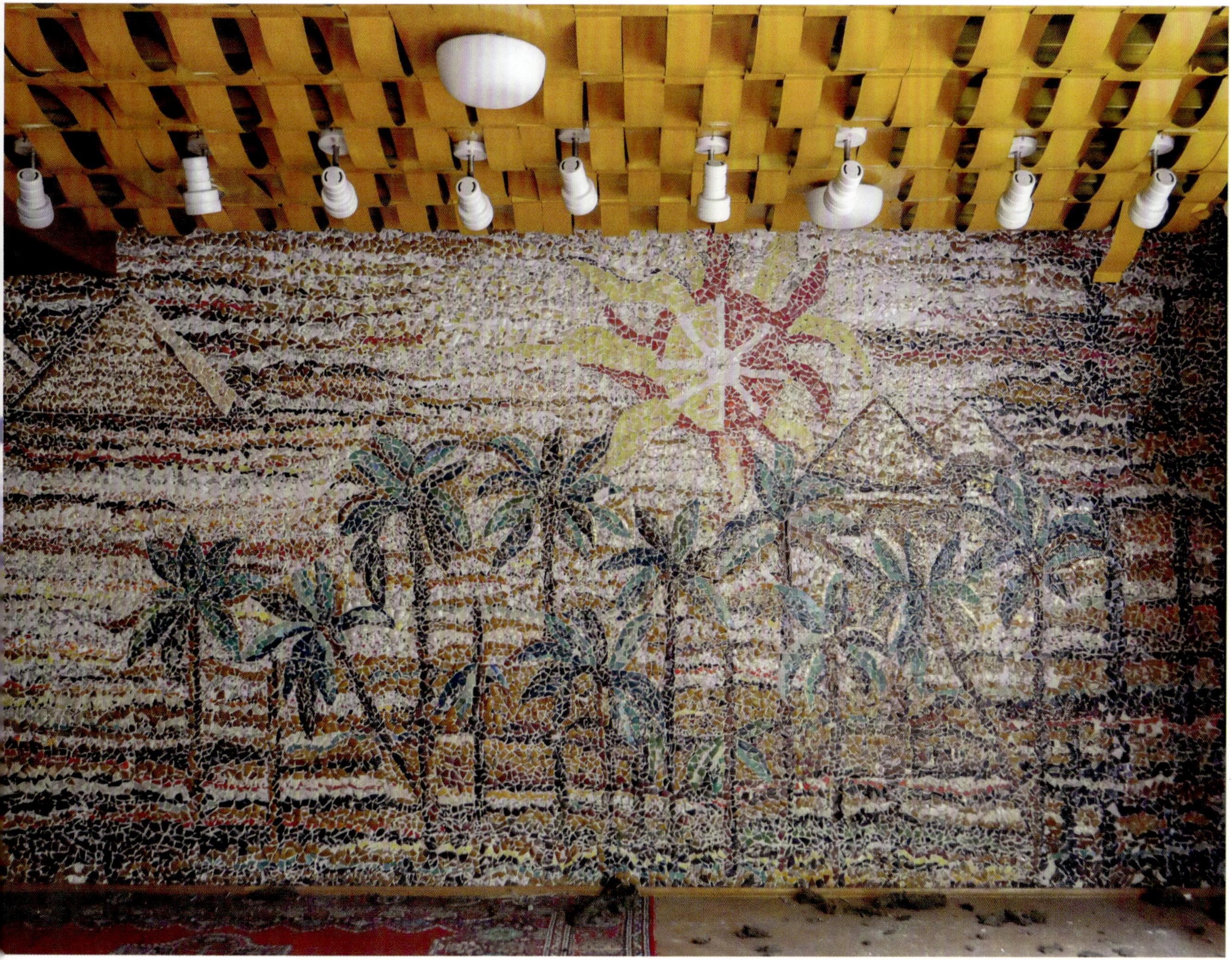

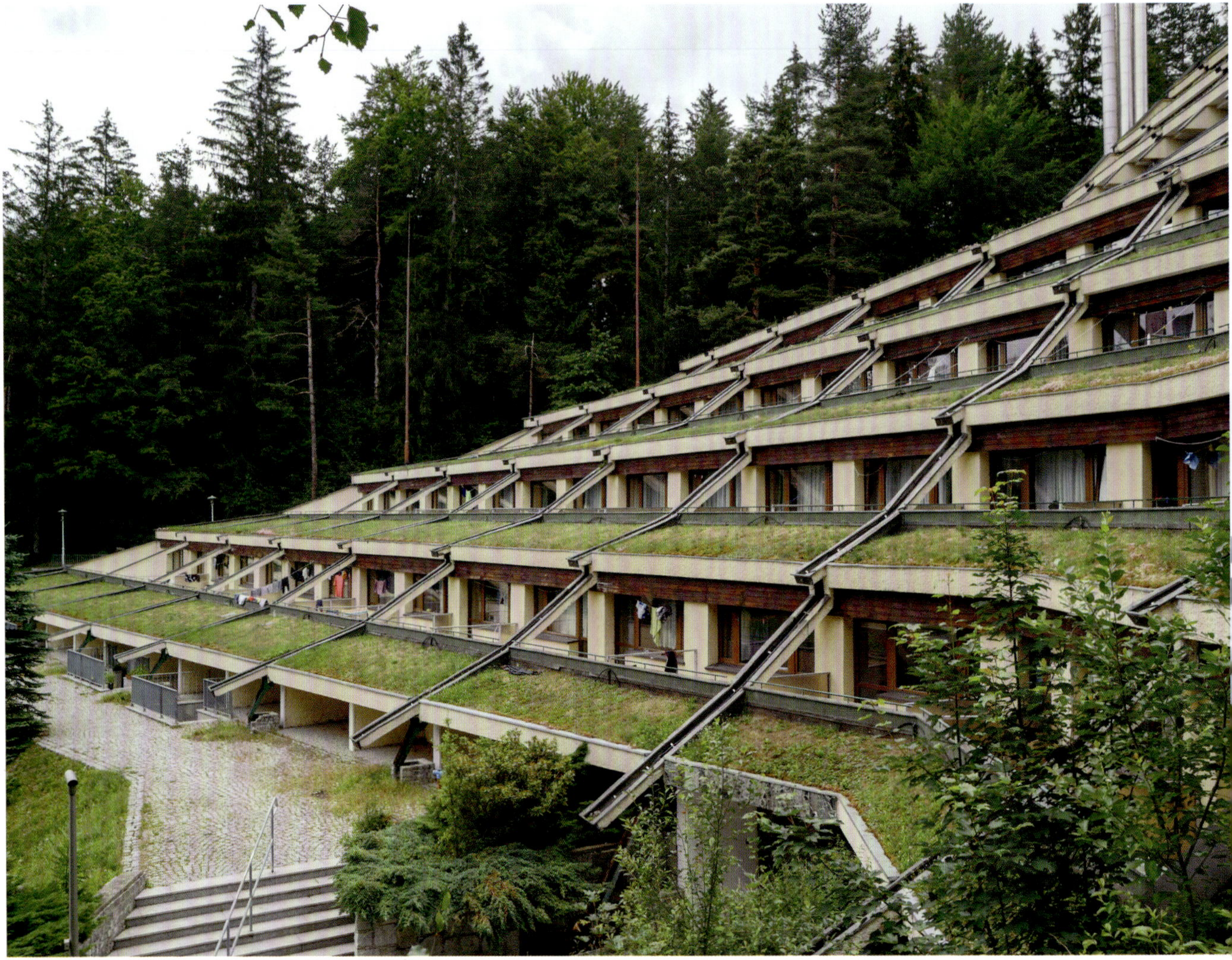

 Hotel Granit (former Granit Holiday Centre), Szklarska Poręba, Poland

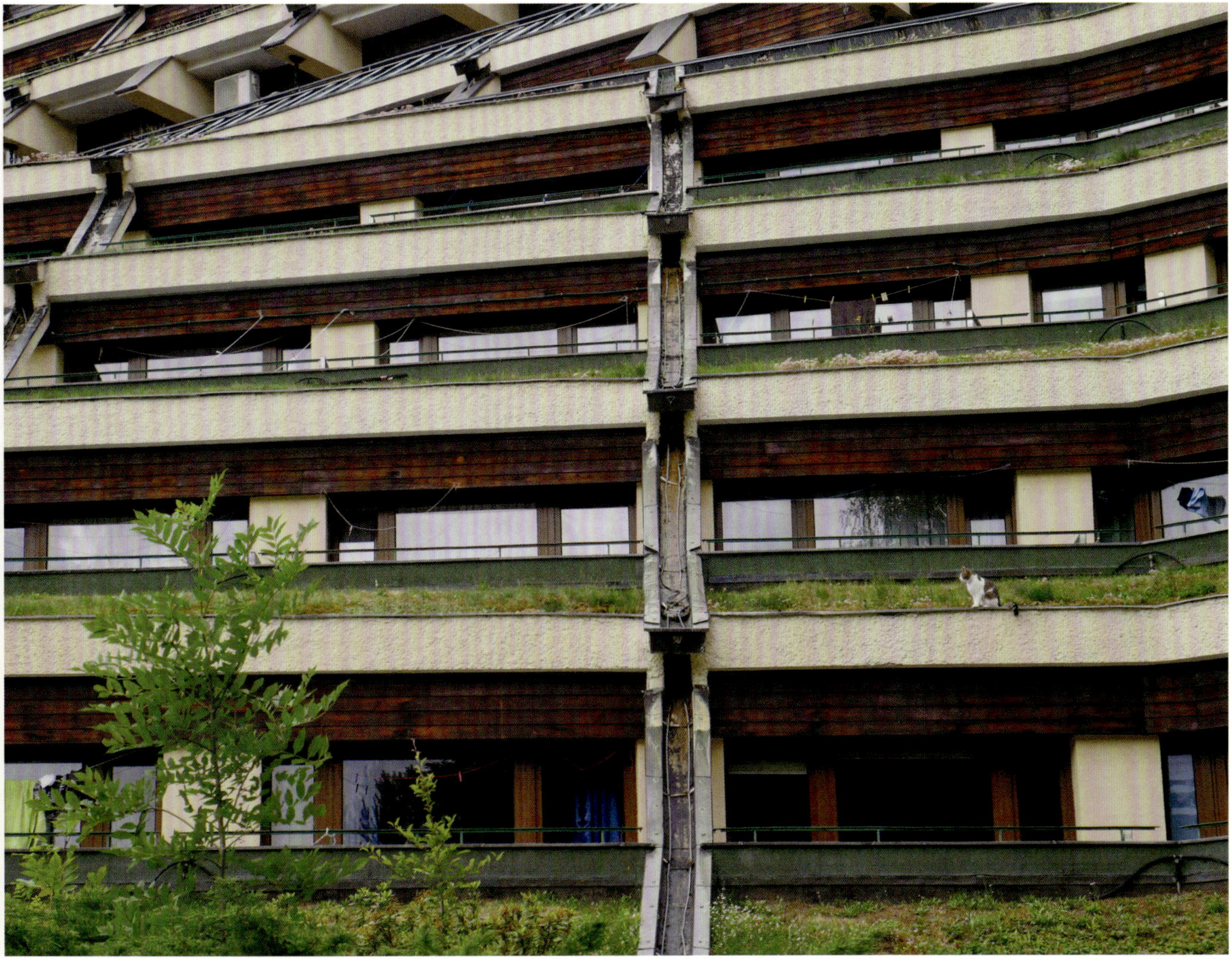

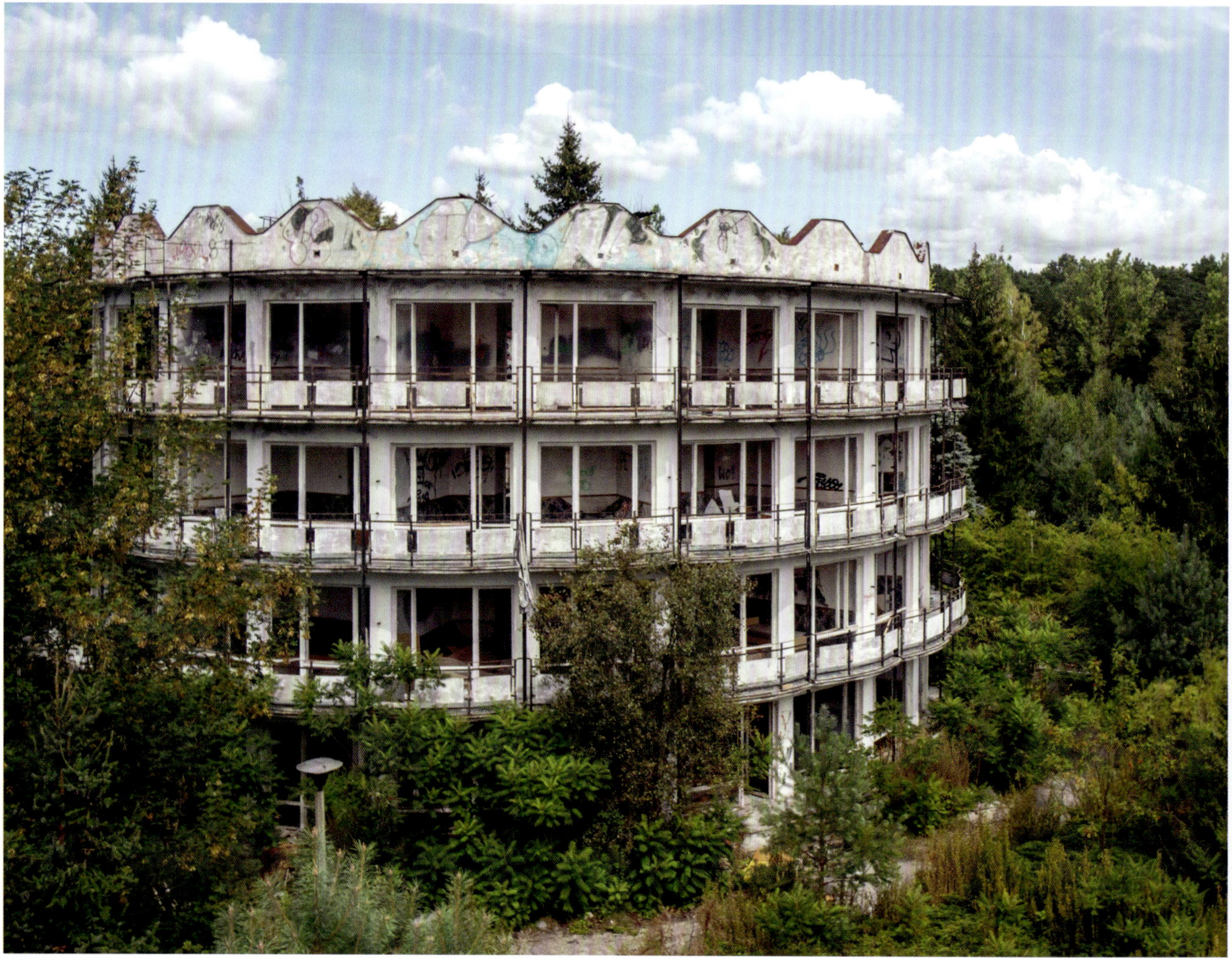

 Hotel Lucień, Miałkówek, Poland

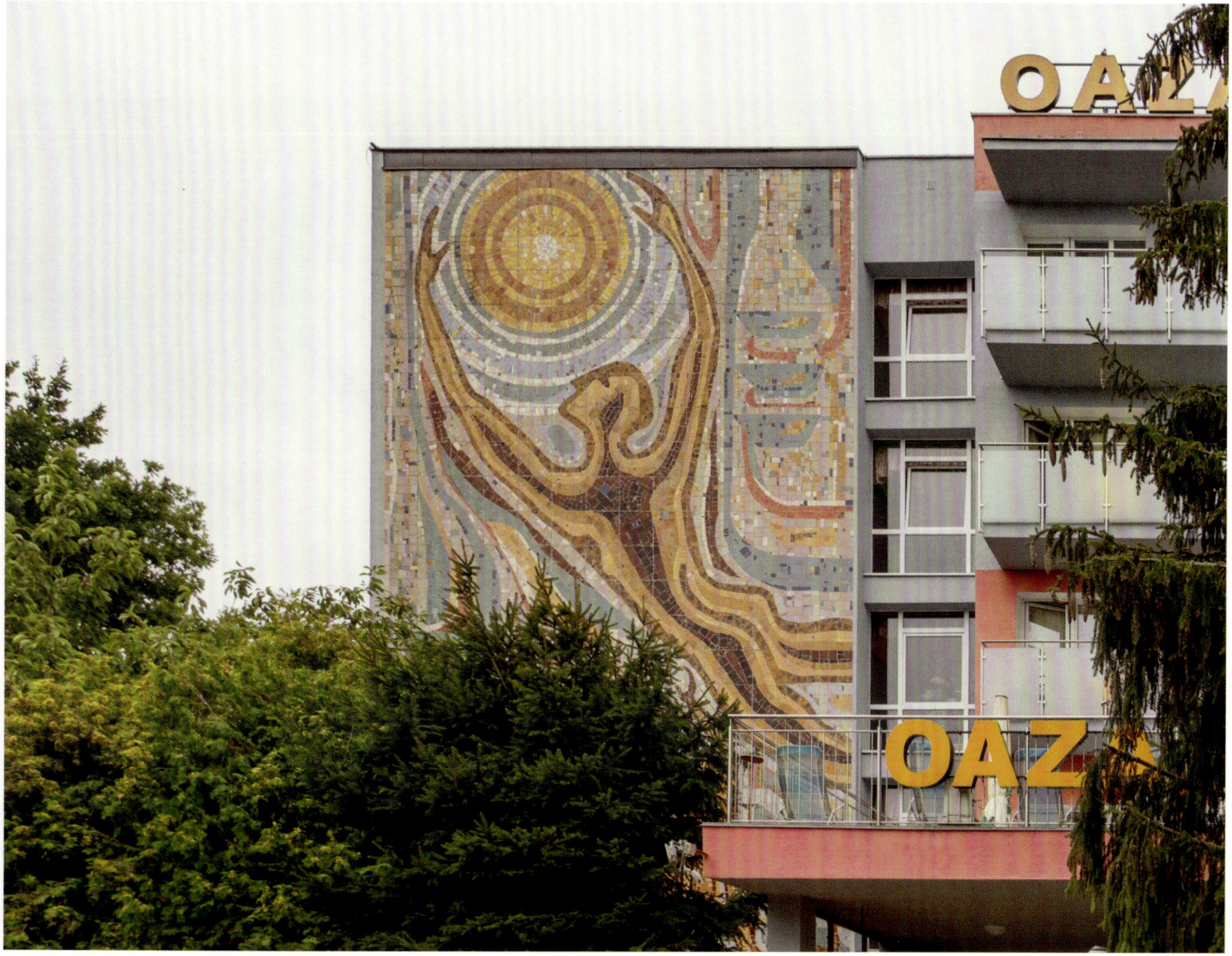

Sanatorium Oaza (former Sanatorium Metalowiec 70), Inowrocław, Poland

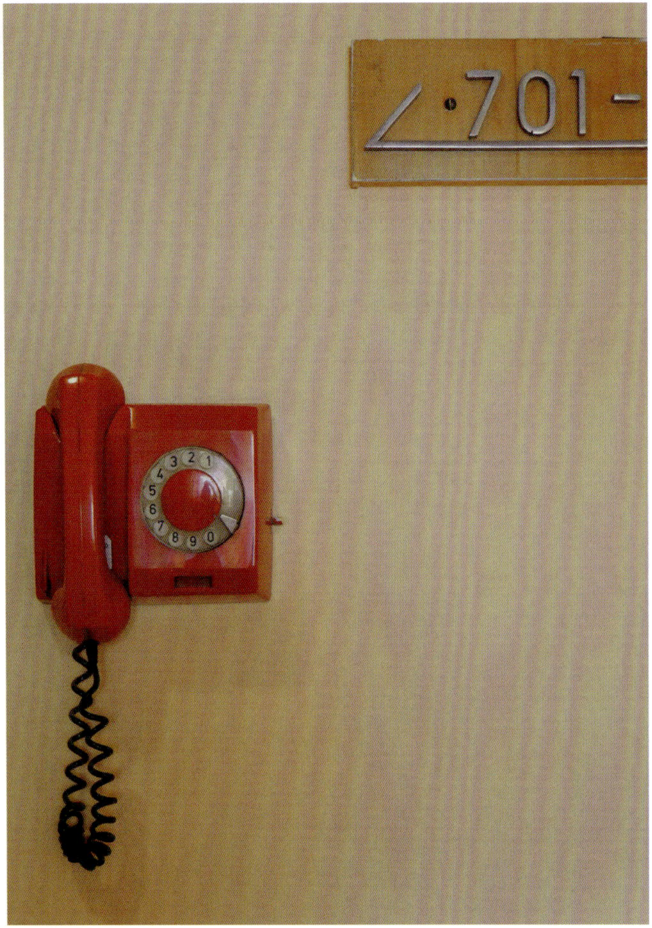

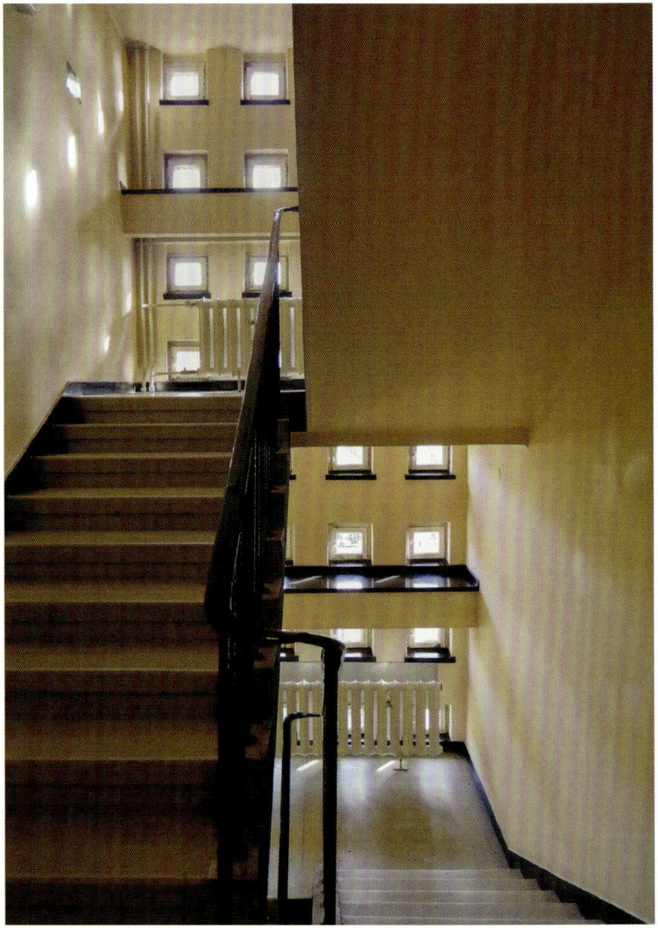

 Hotel Katowice, Katowice, Poland

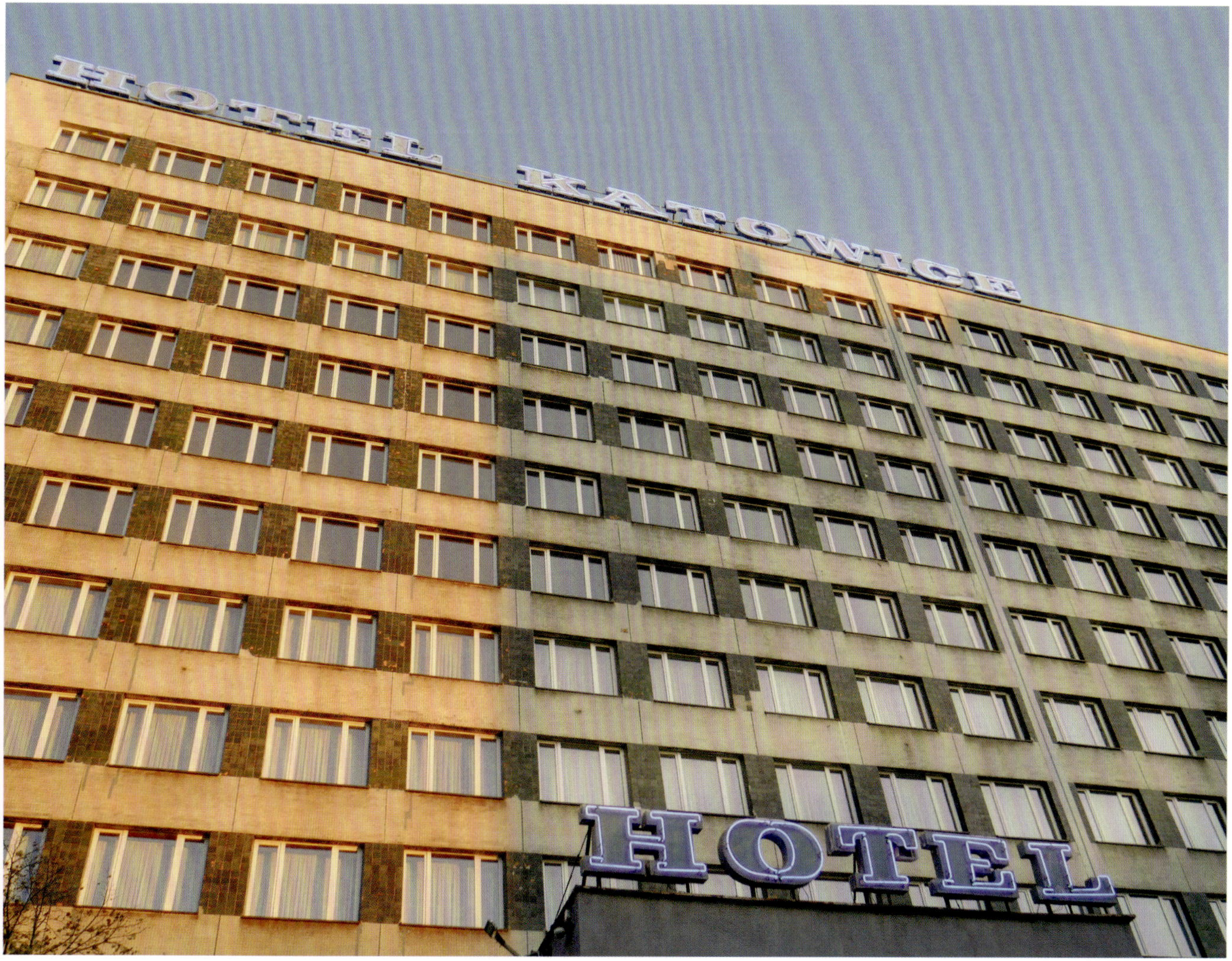
HOTEL KATOWICE
HOTEL

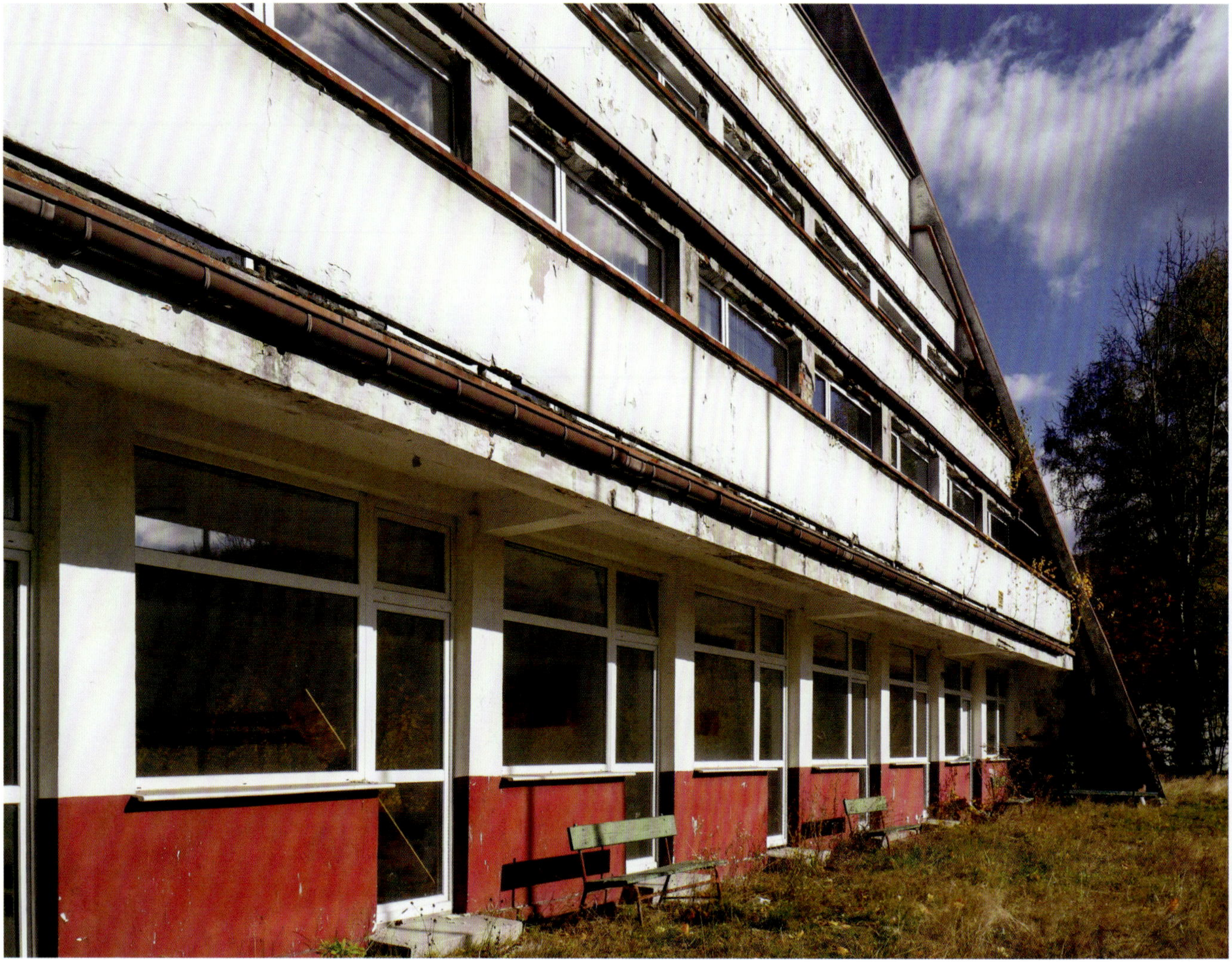

 Hostel Wiecha (former Holiday Home Wiecha), Ustroń, Poland

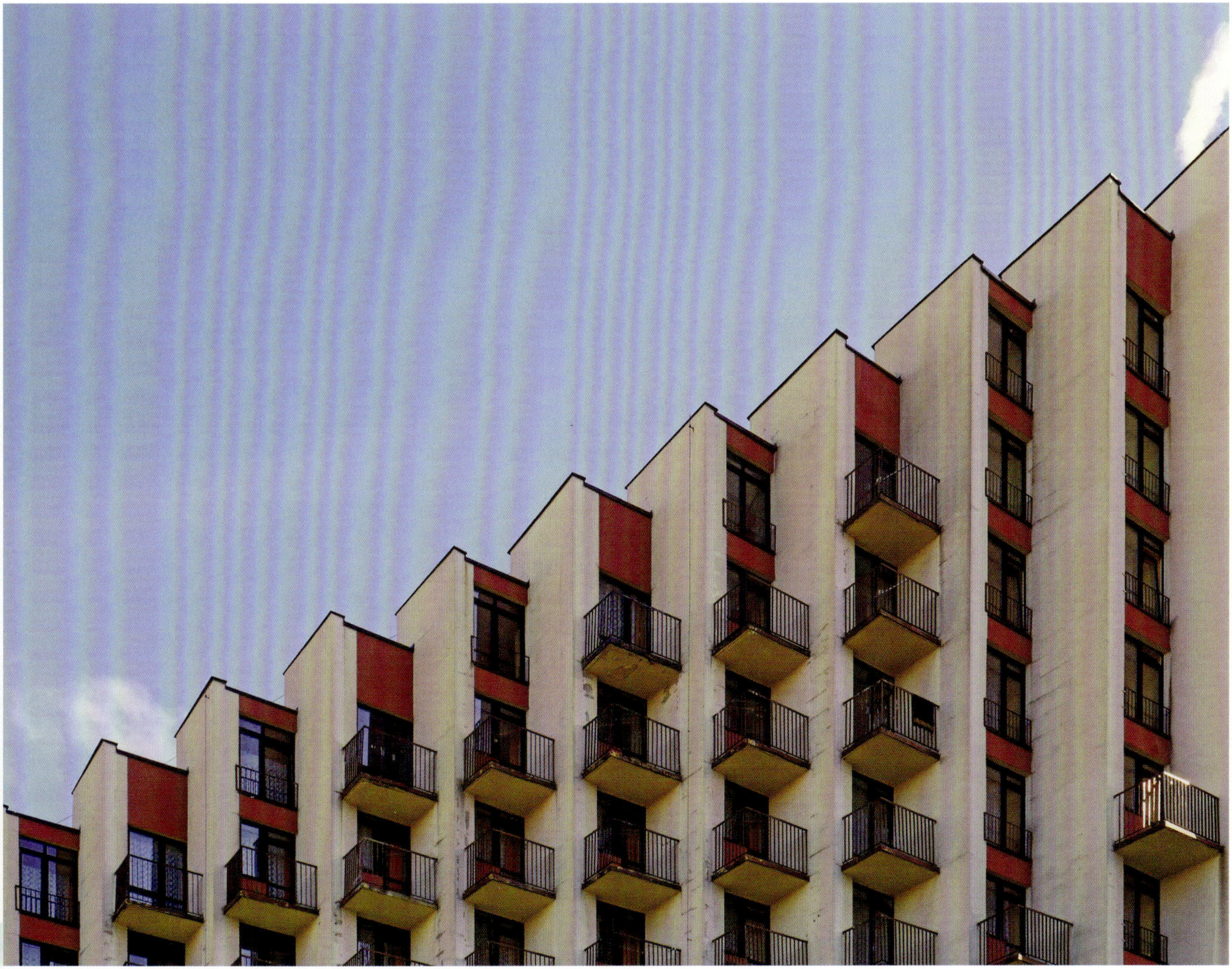

Hotel Kos (former Sanatorium Kos), Ustroń, Poland

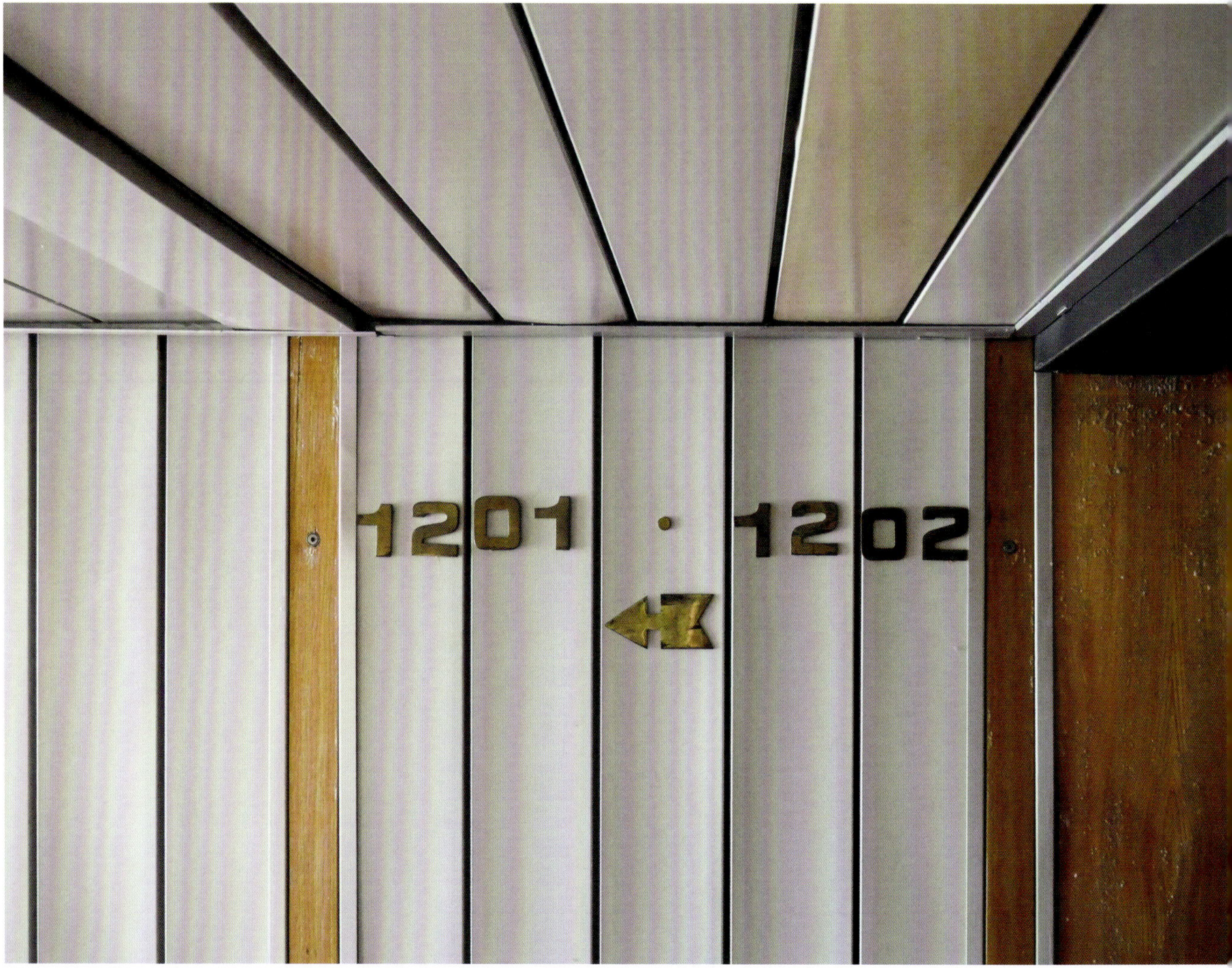

 Hotel Gromada (former Hotel Rodło), Piła, Poland

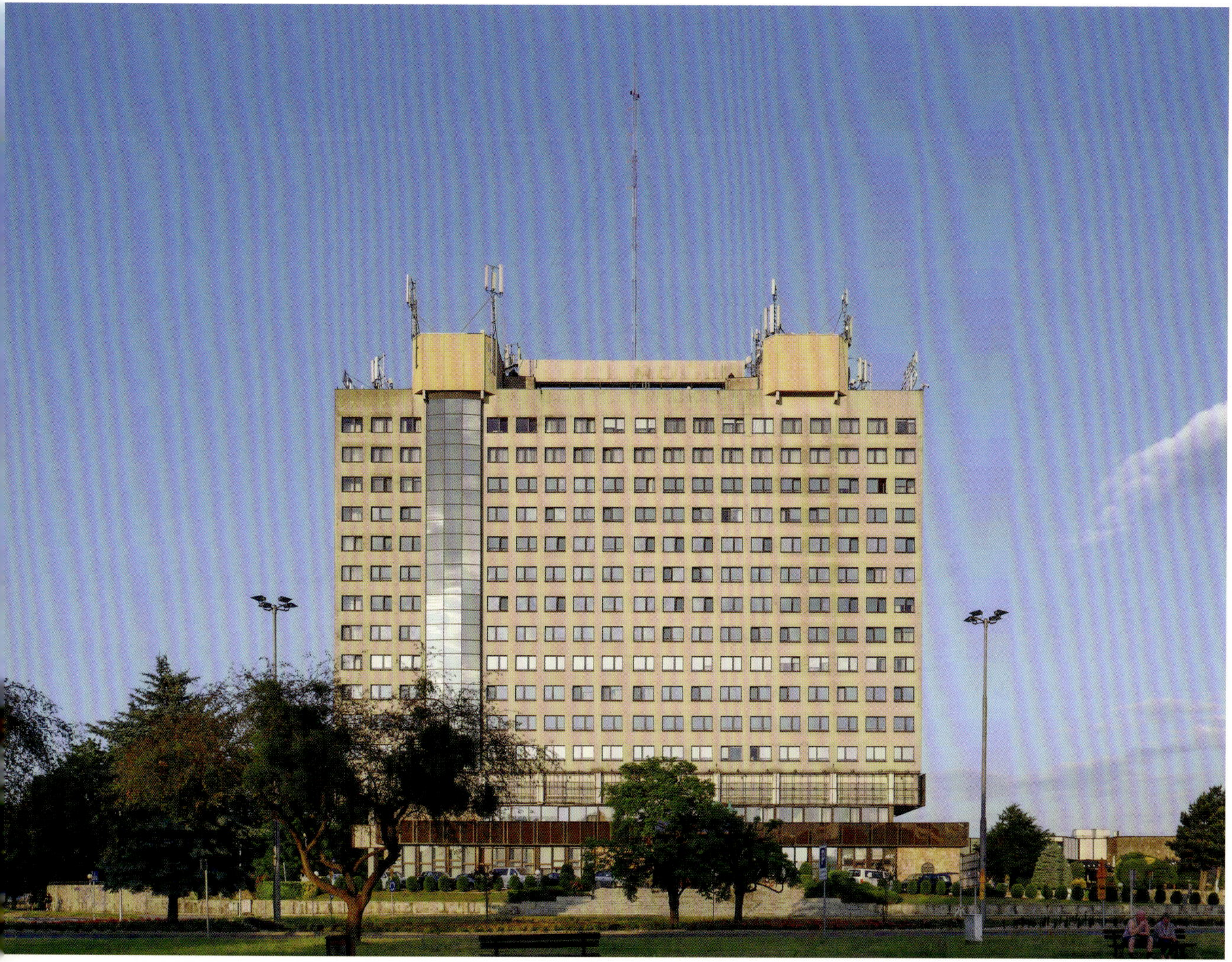

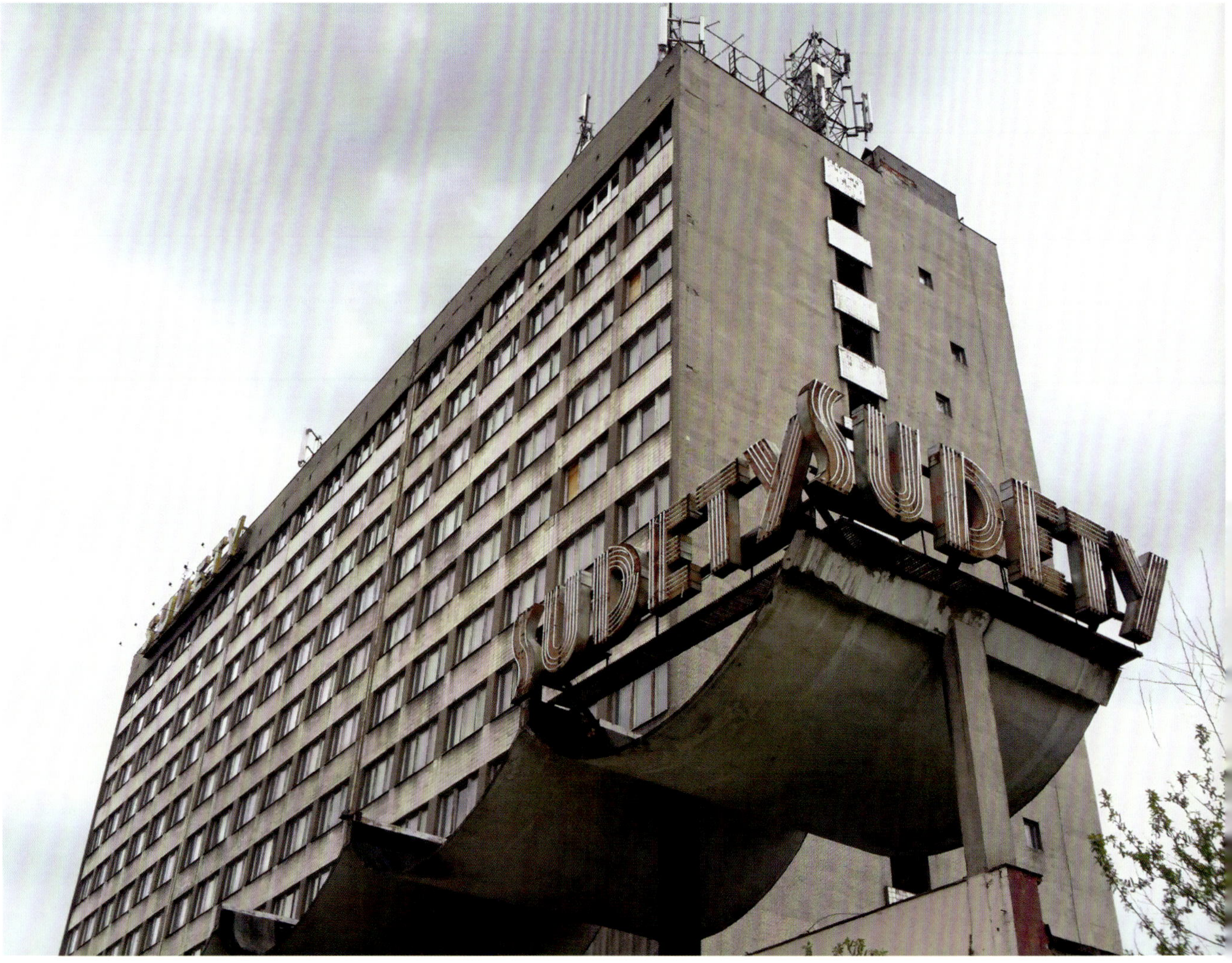

 Hotel Sudety, Wałbrzych, Poland

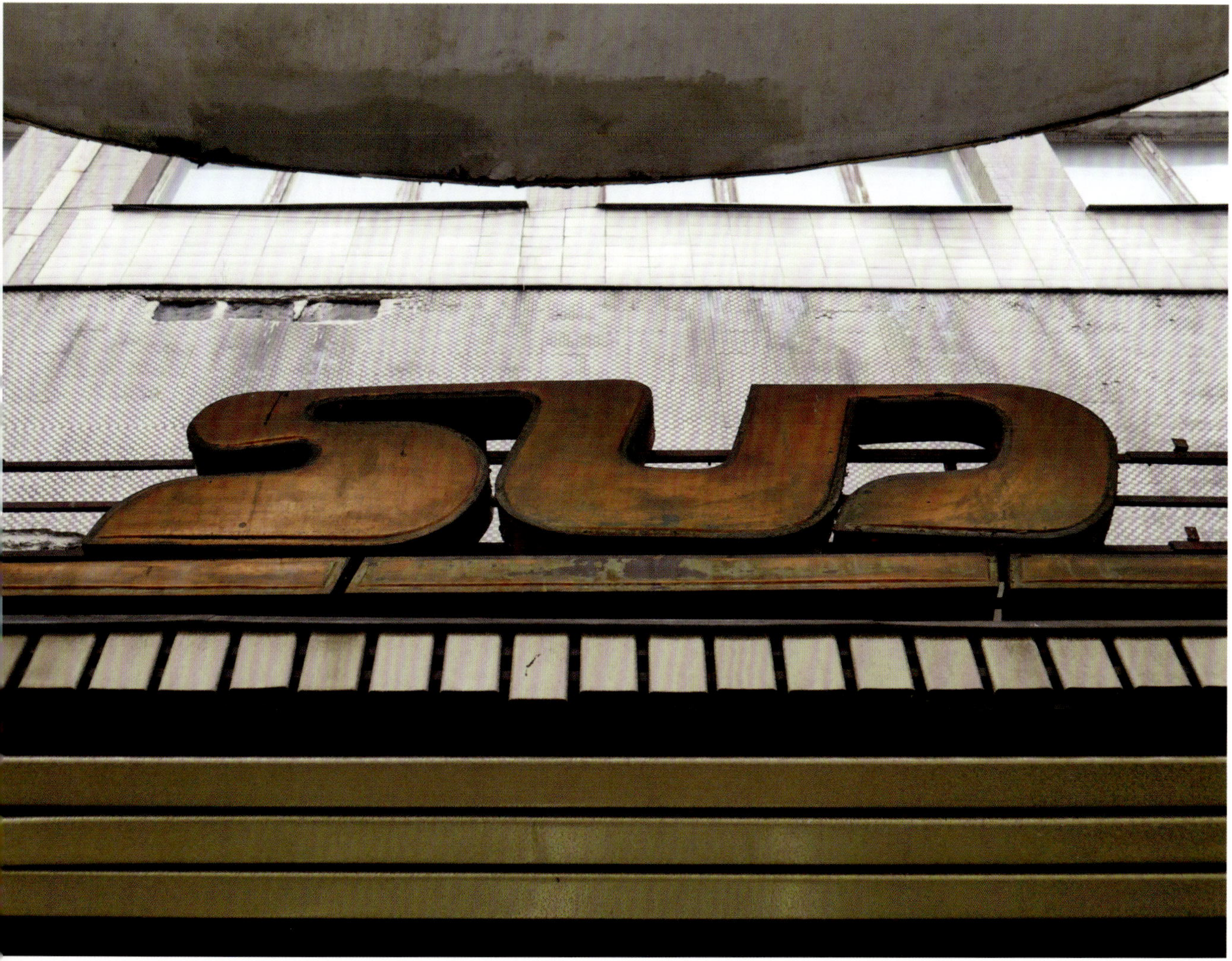

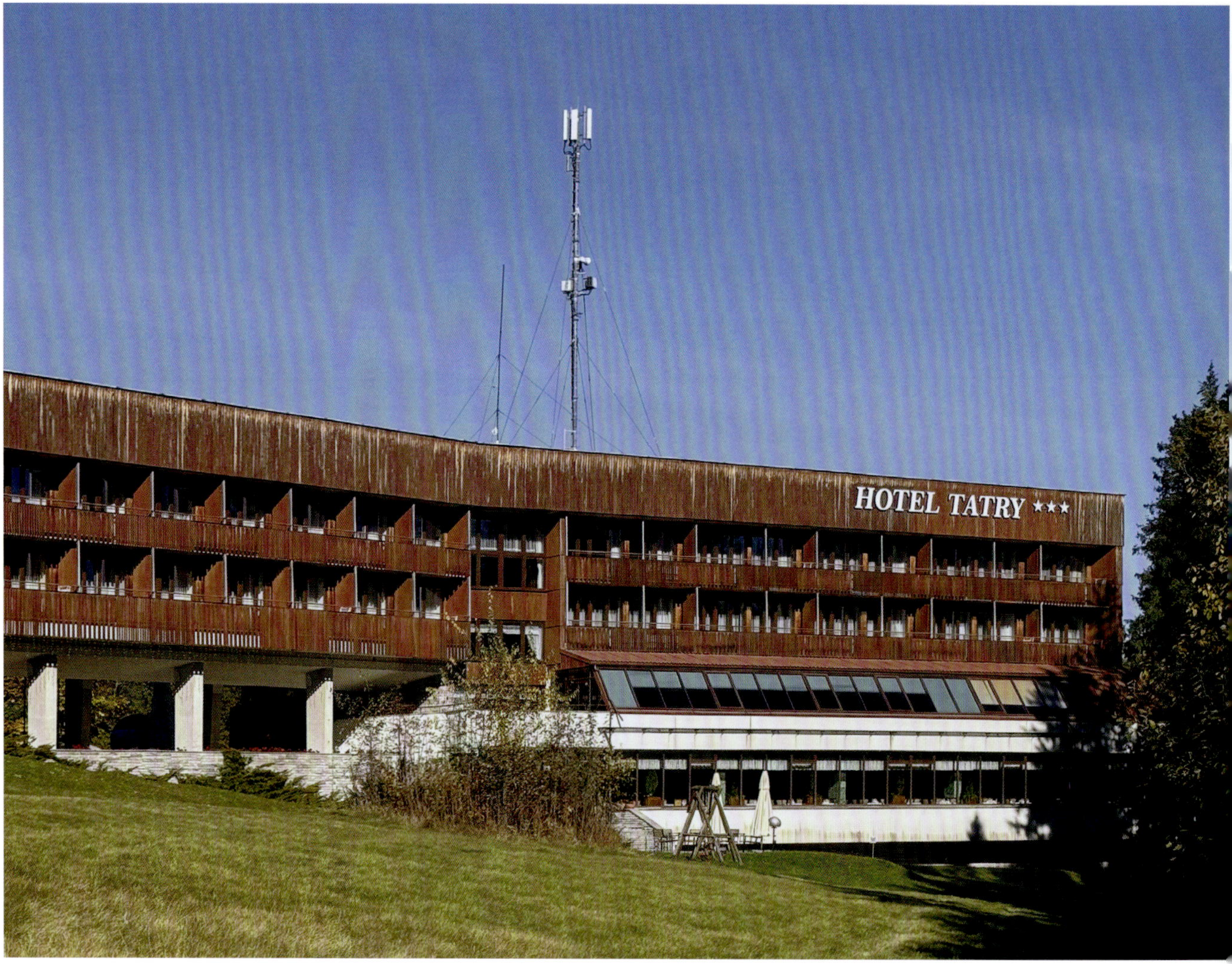

174 Hotel Tatry (former Holiday House of the Council of Ministers), Murzasichle, Poland

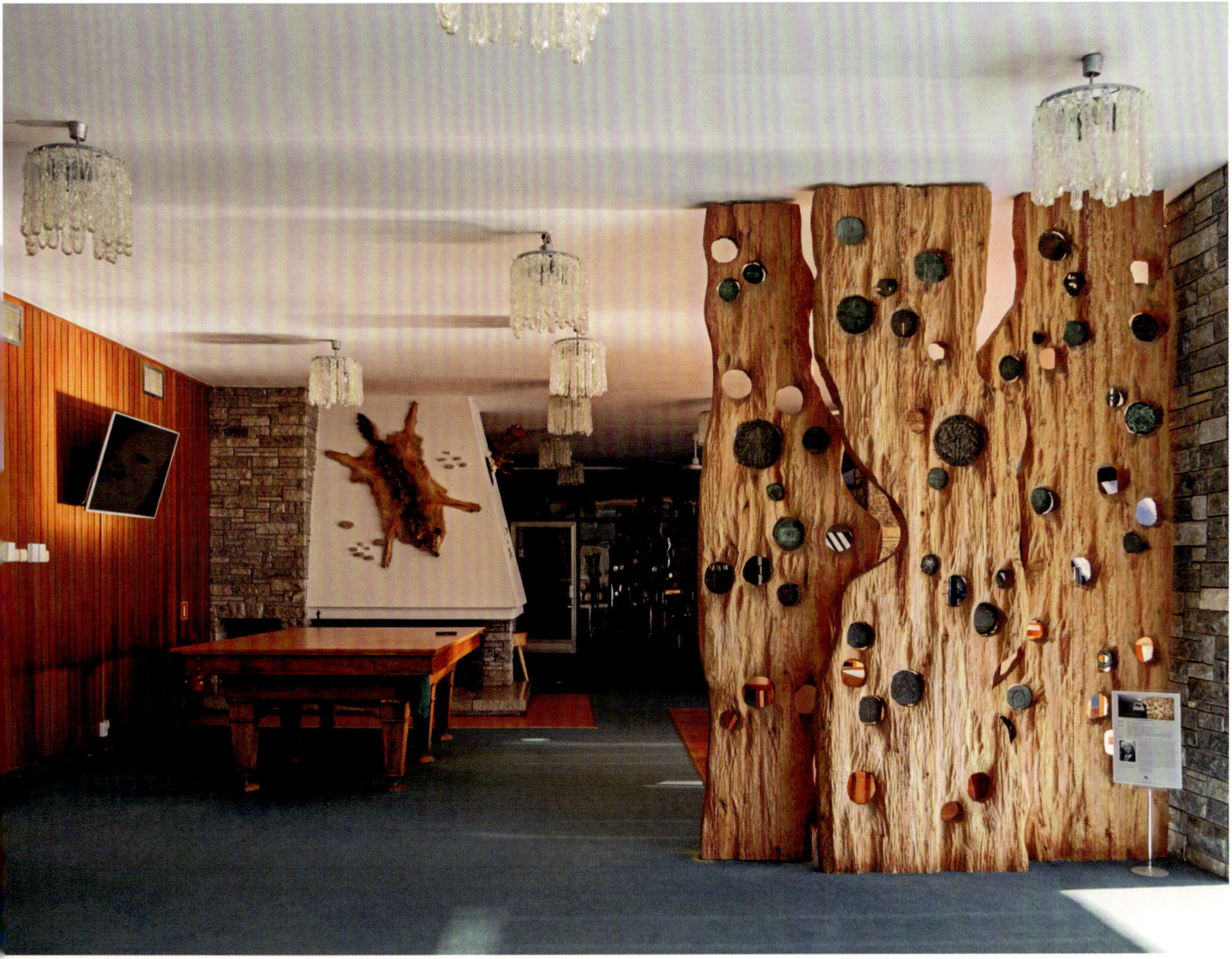

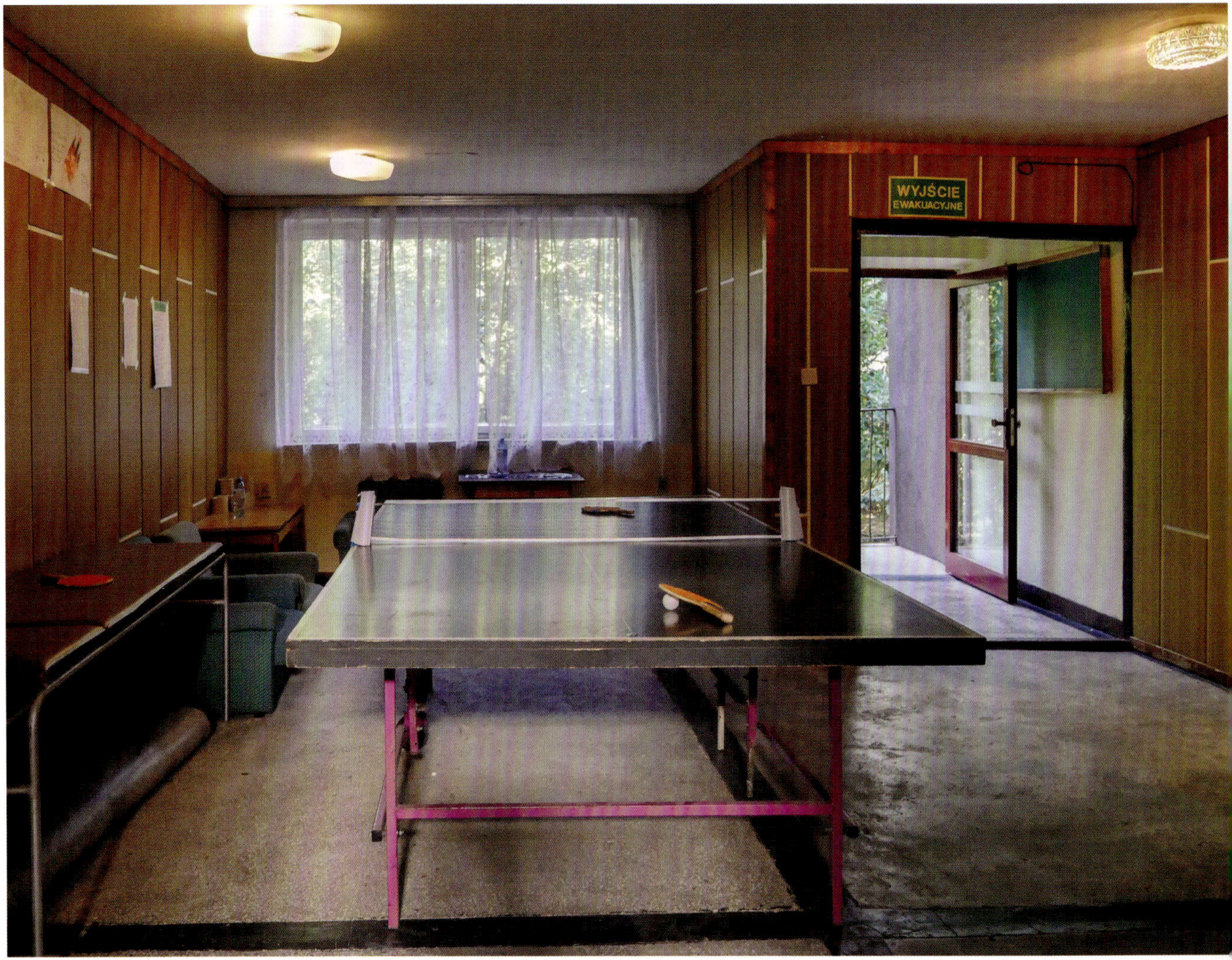

 Hotel Trojak, Rowy, Poland

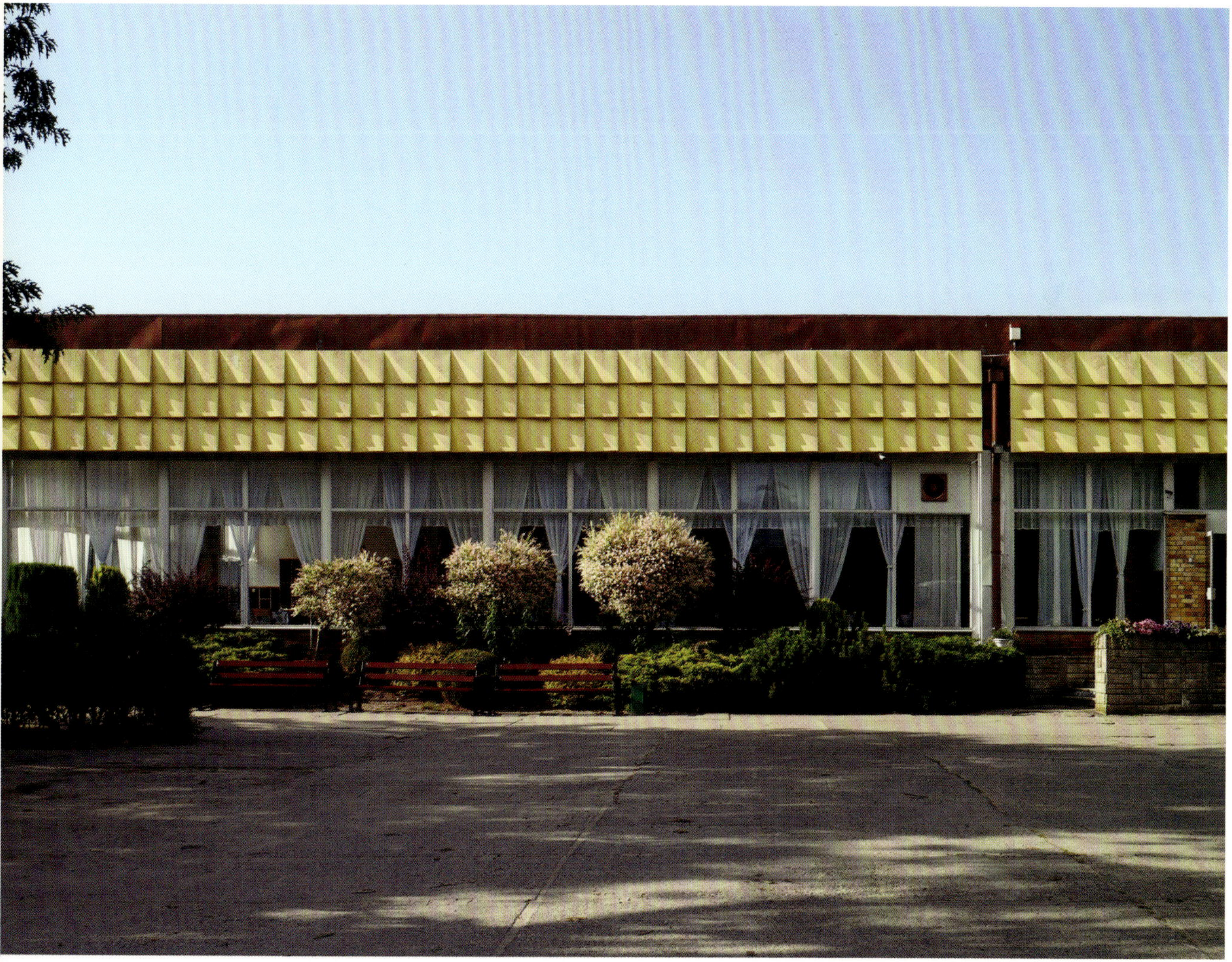

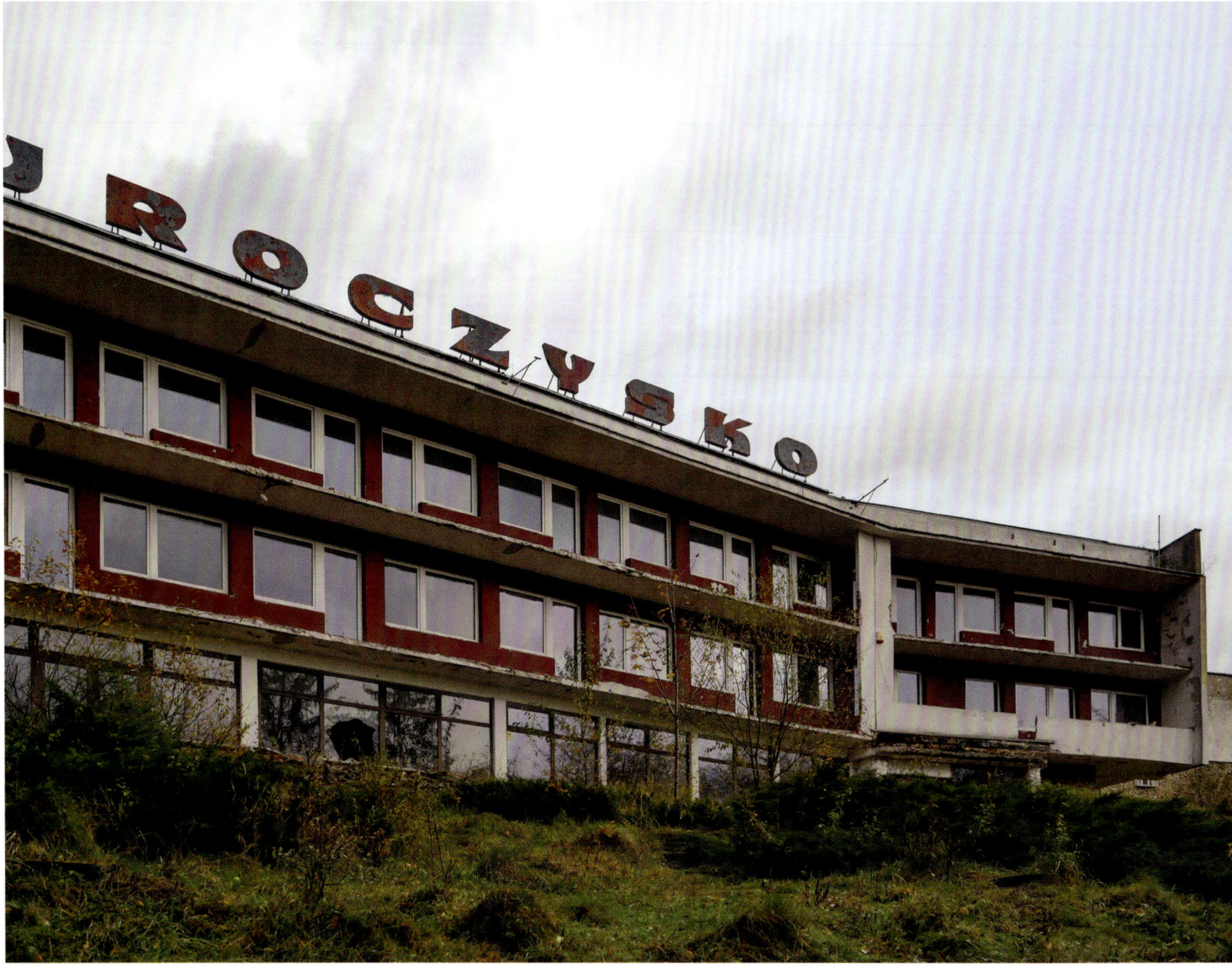

 Hotel Uroczysko, Cedzyna, Poland

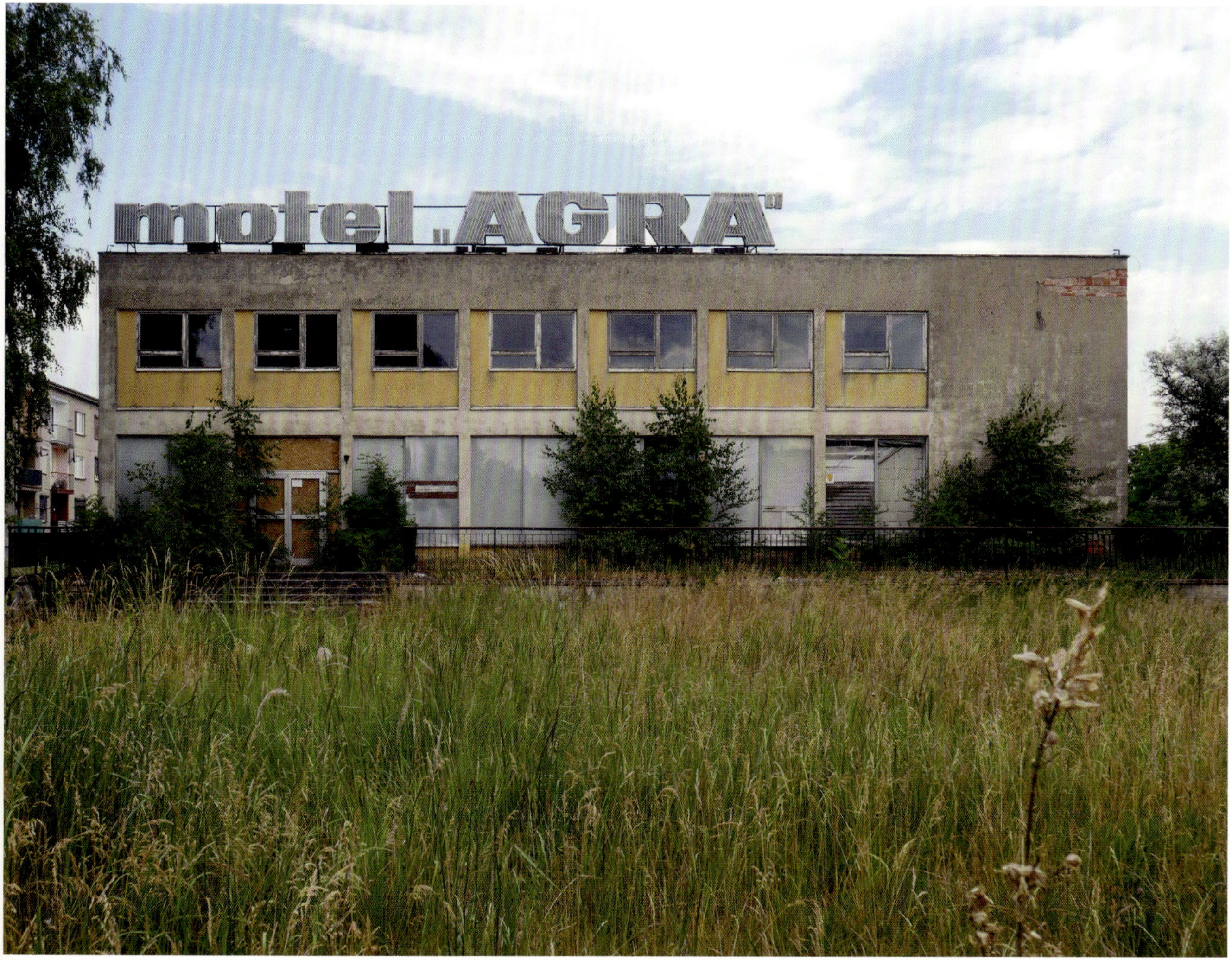

Motel Agra, Raszewy, Poland

ROMANIA

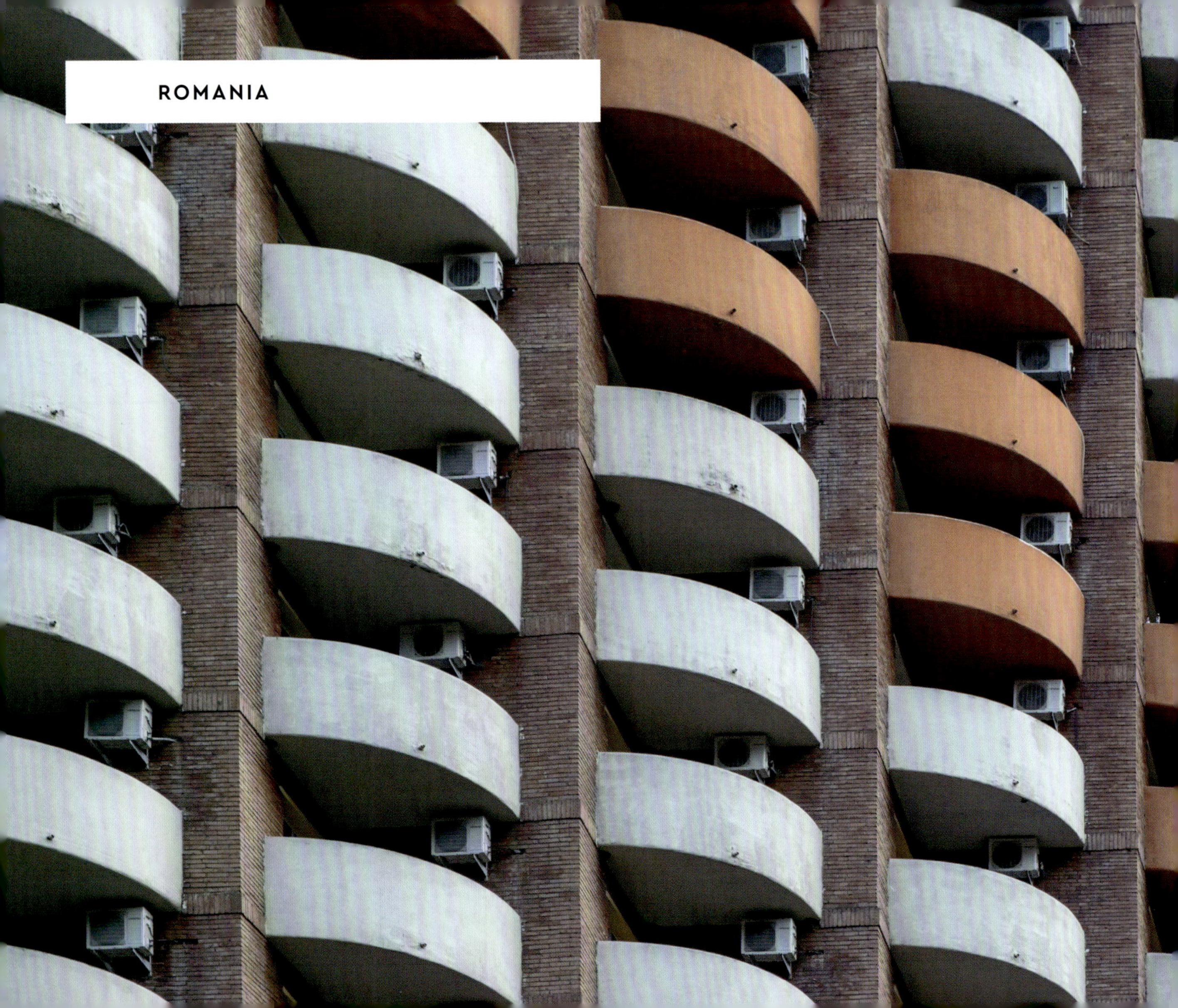

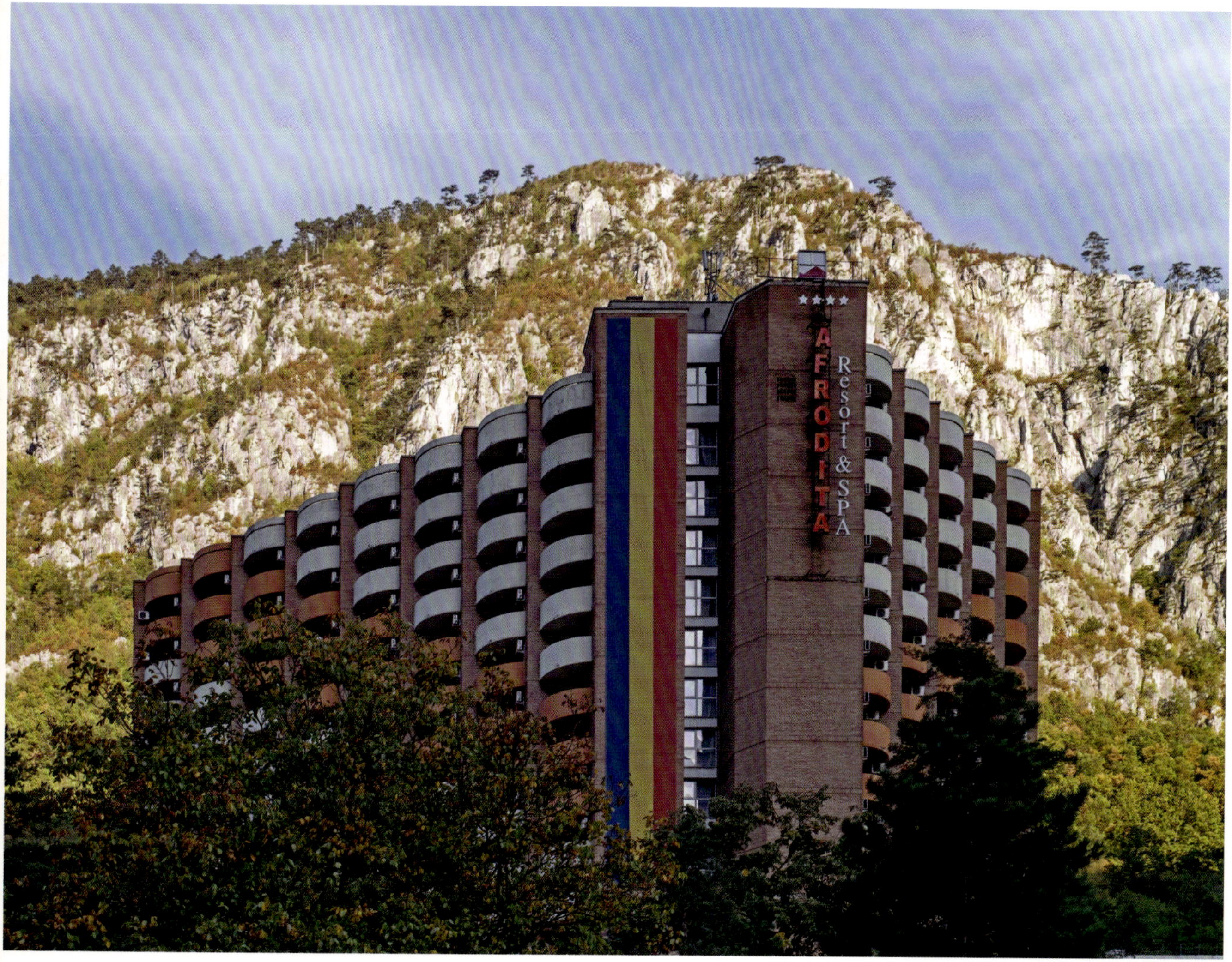

Hotel Afrodita, Băile Herculane, Romania

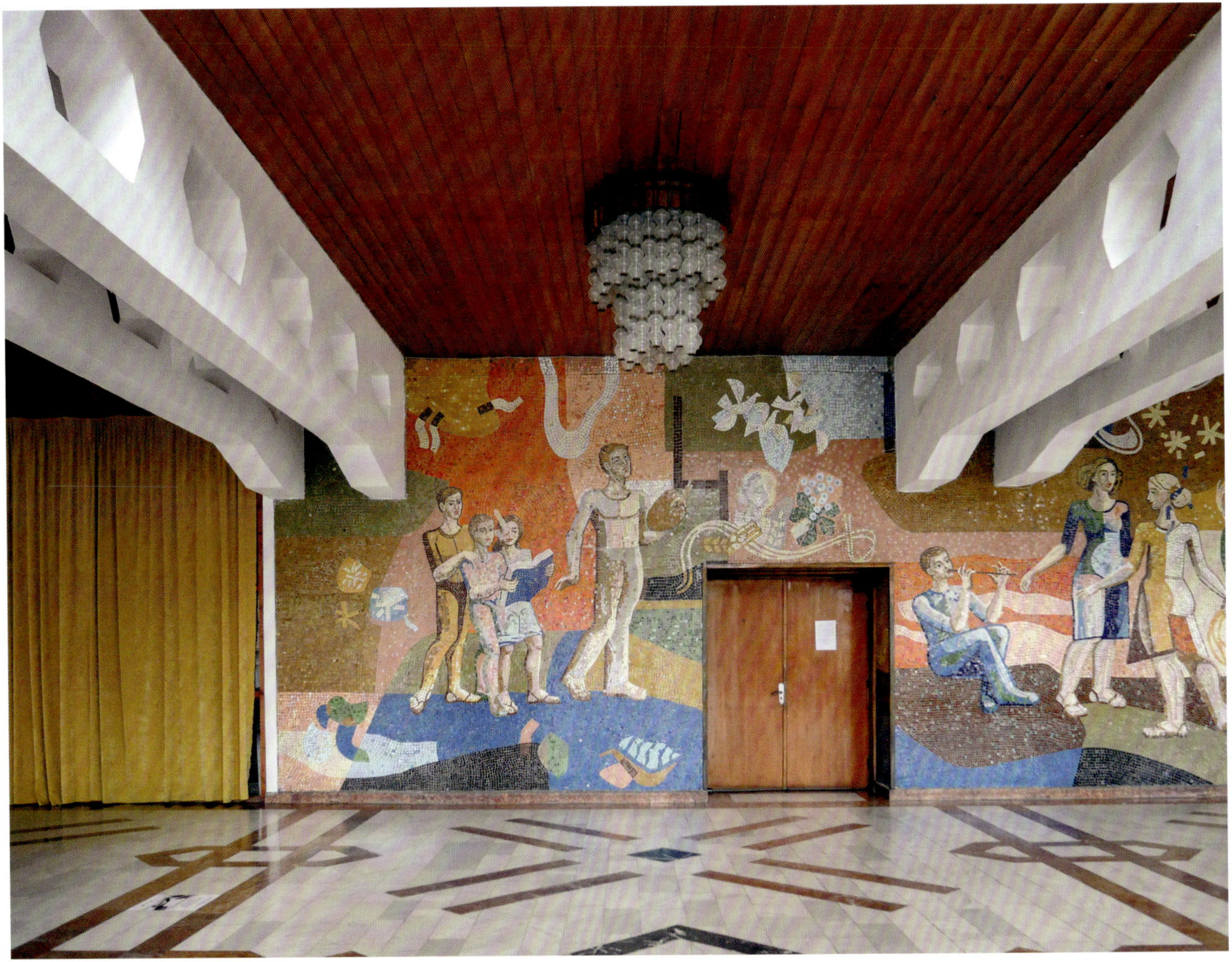

 Hotel Casa Tineretului, Câmpina, Romania

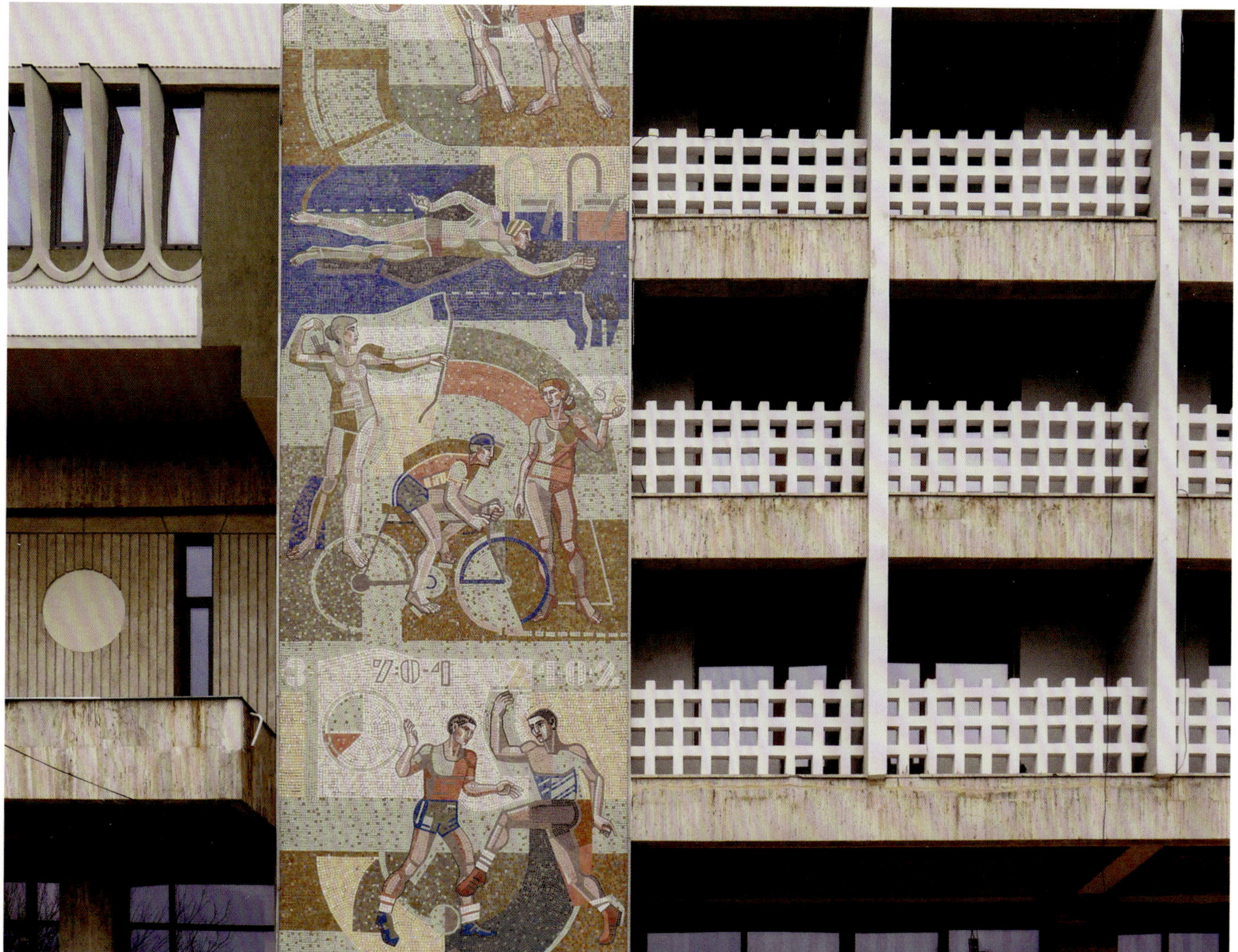

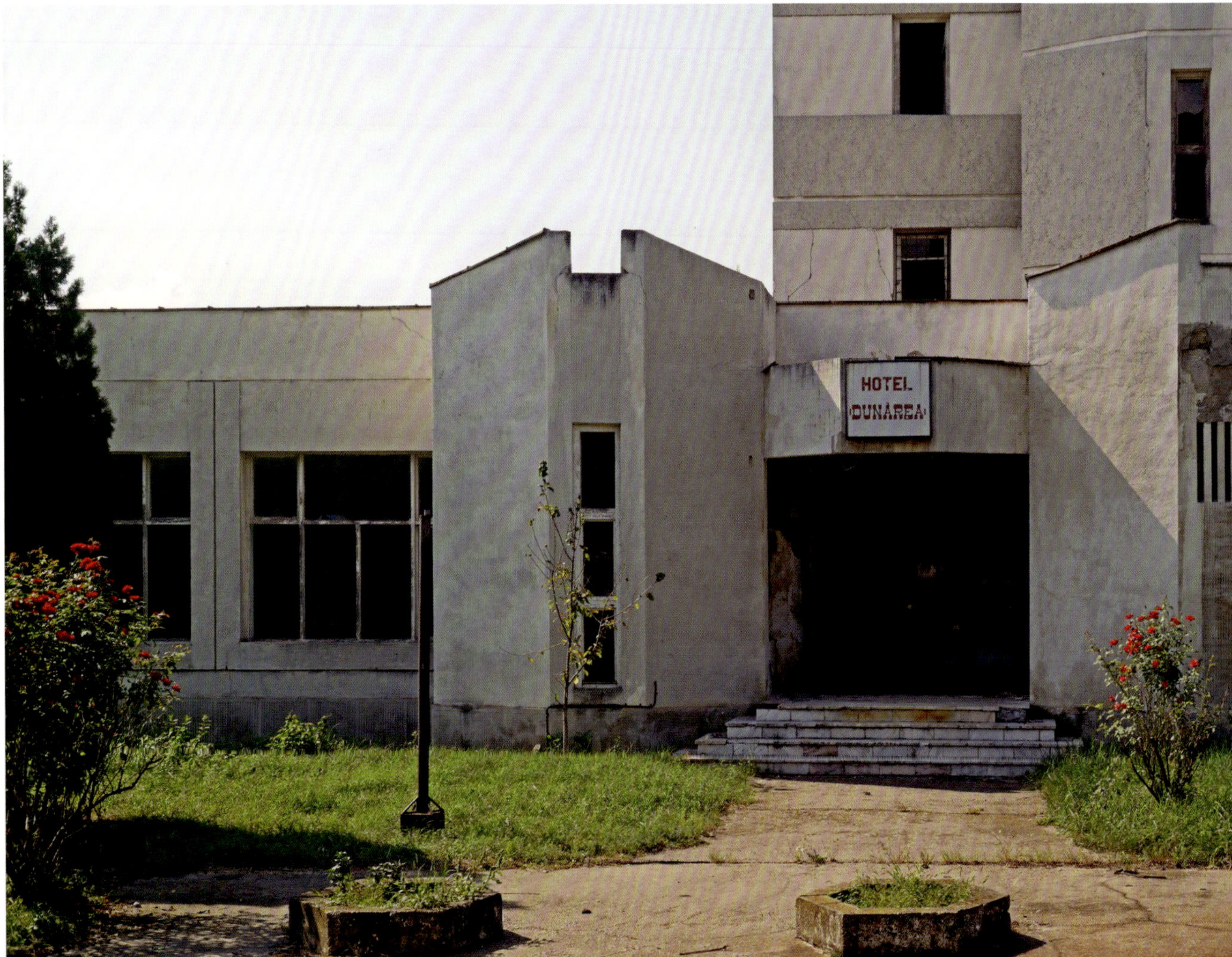

 Hotel Dunărea, Moldova Nouă, Romania

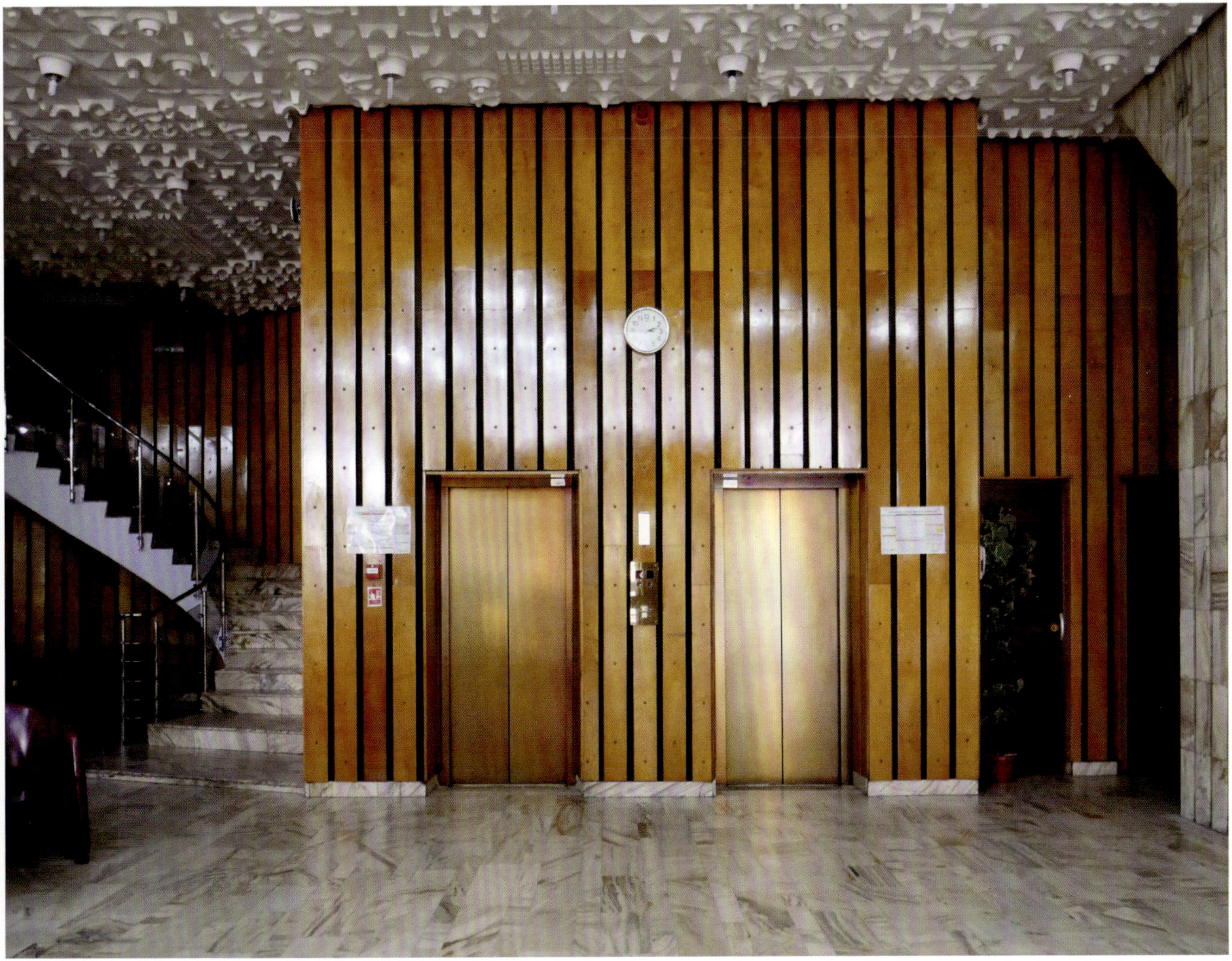

Hotel Decebal, Bacău, Romania

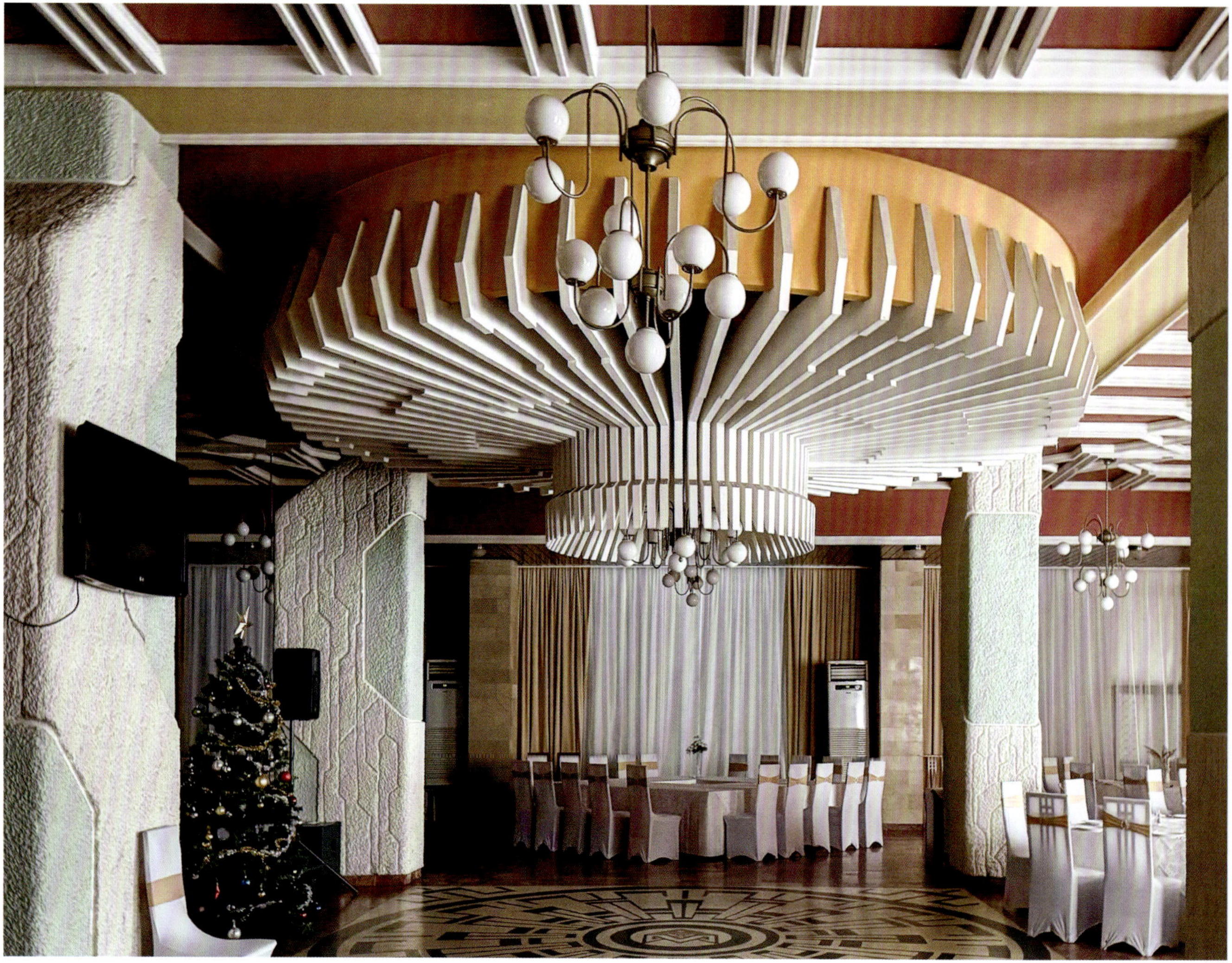

 Hotel Moldova, Iași, Romania

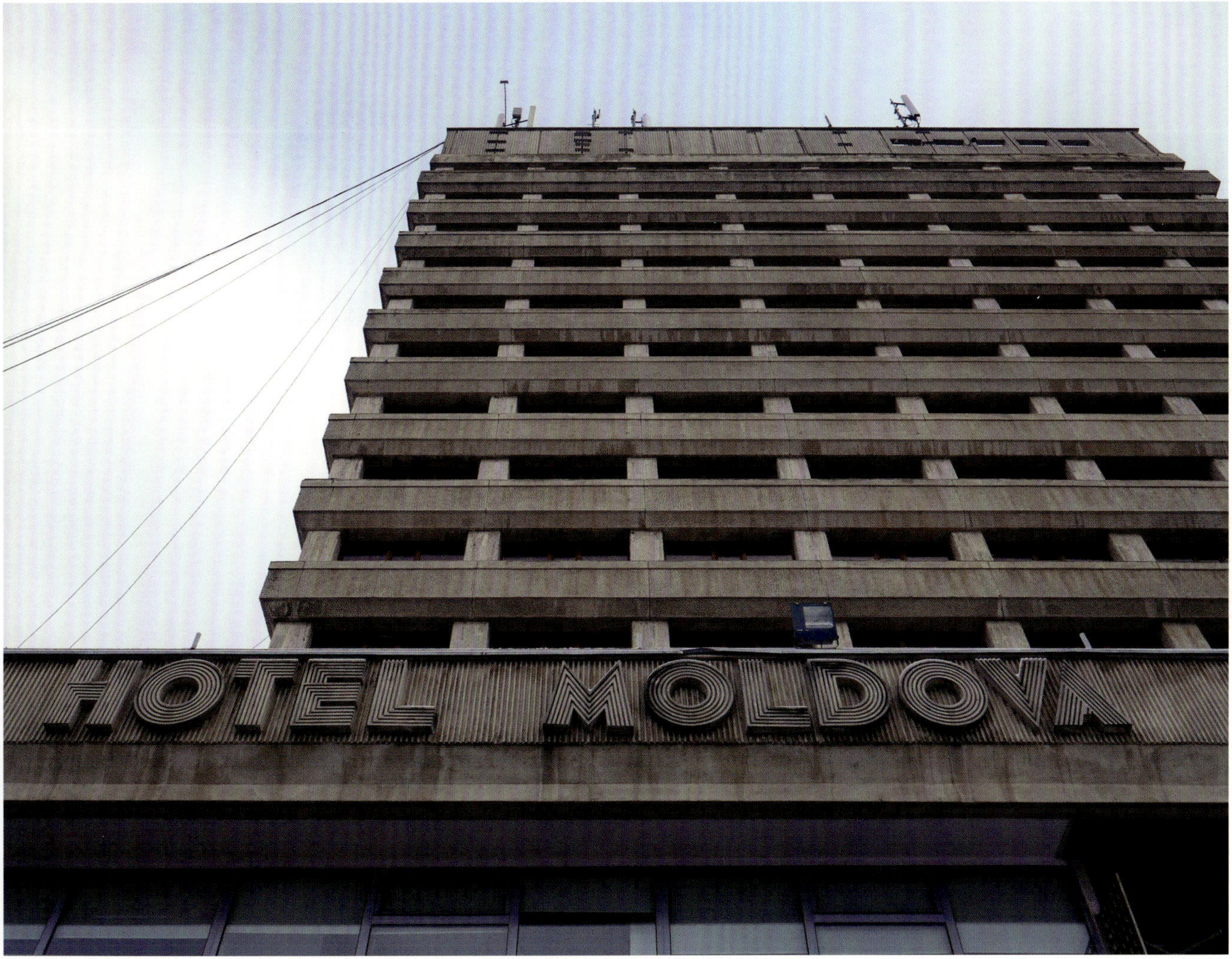
HOTEL MOLDOVA

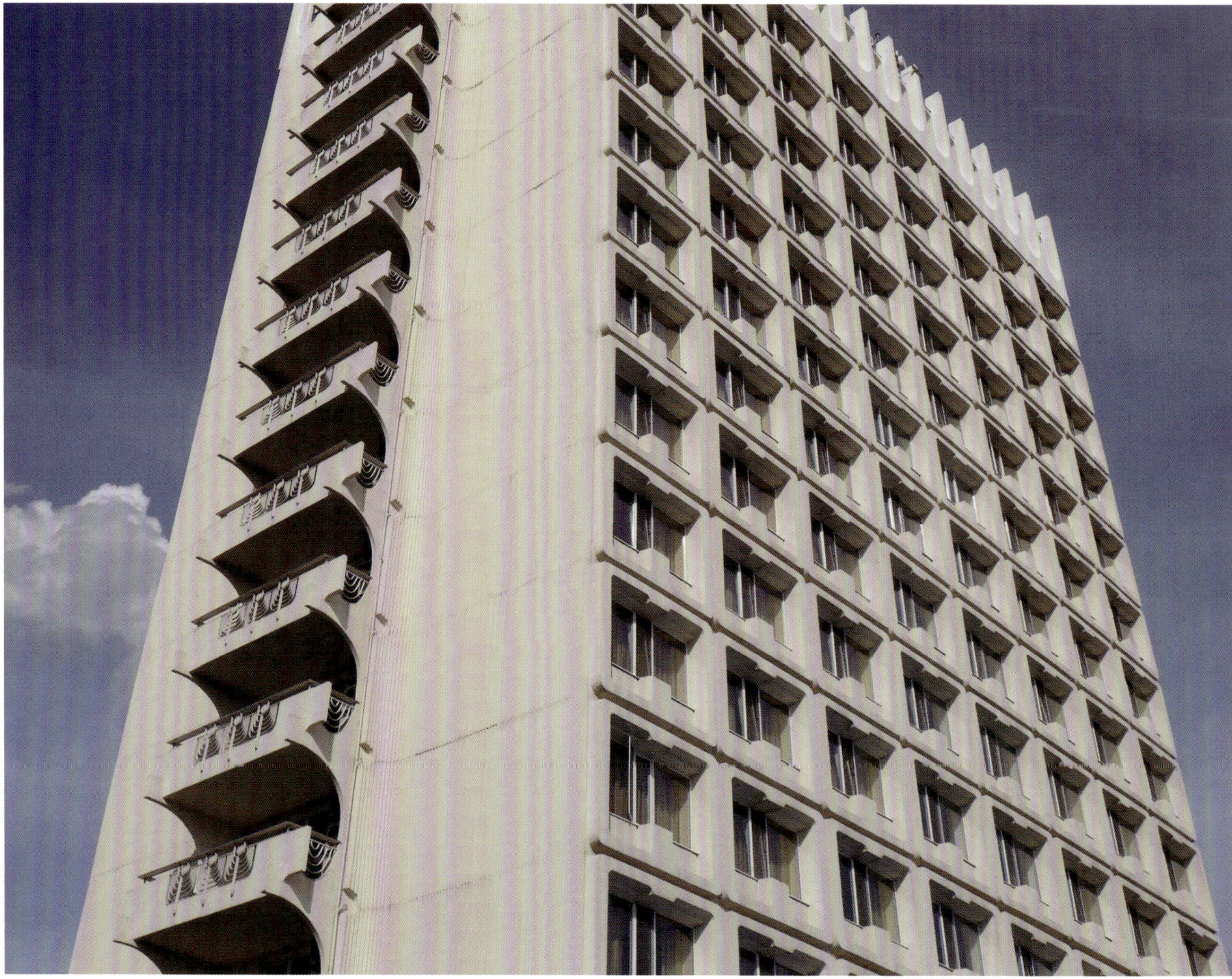

Hotel Continental, Timișoara, Romania

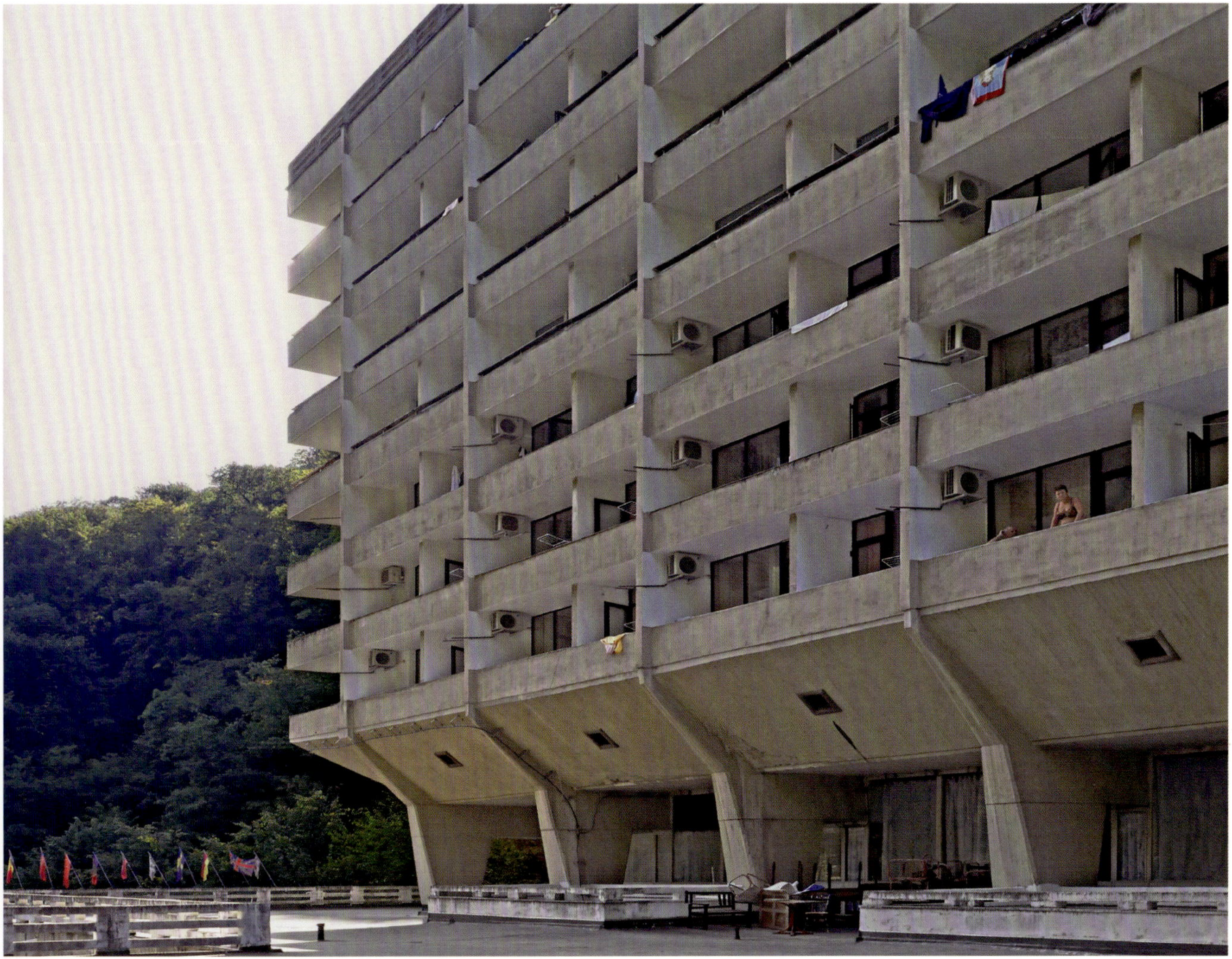

Hotel Roman (former Hotel Trajan), Băile Herculane, Romania

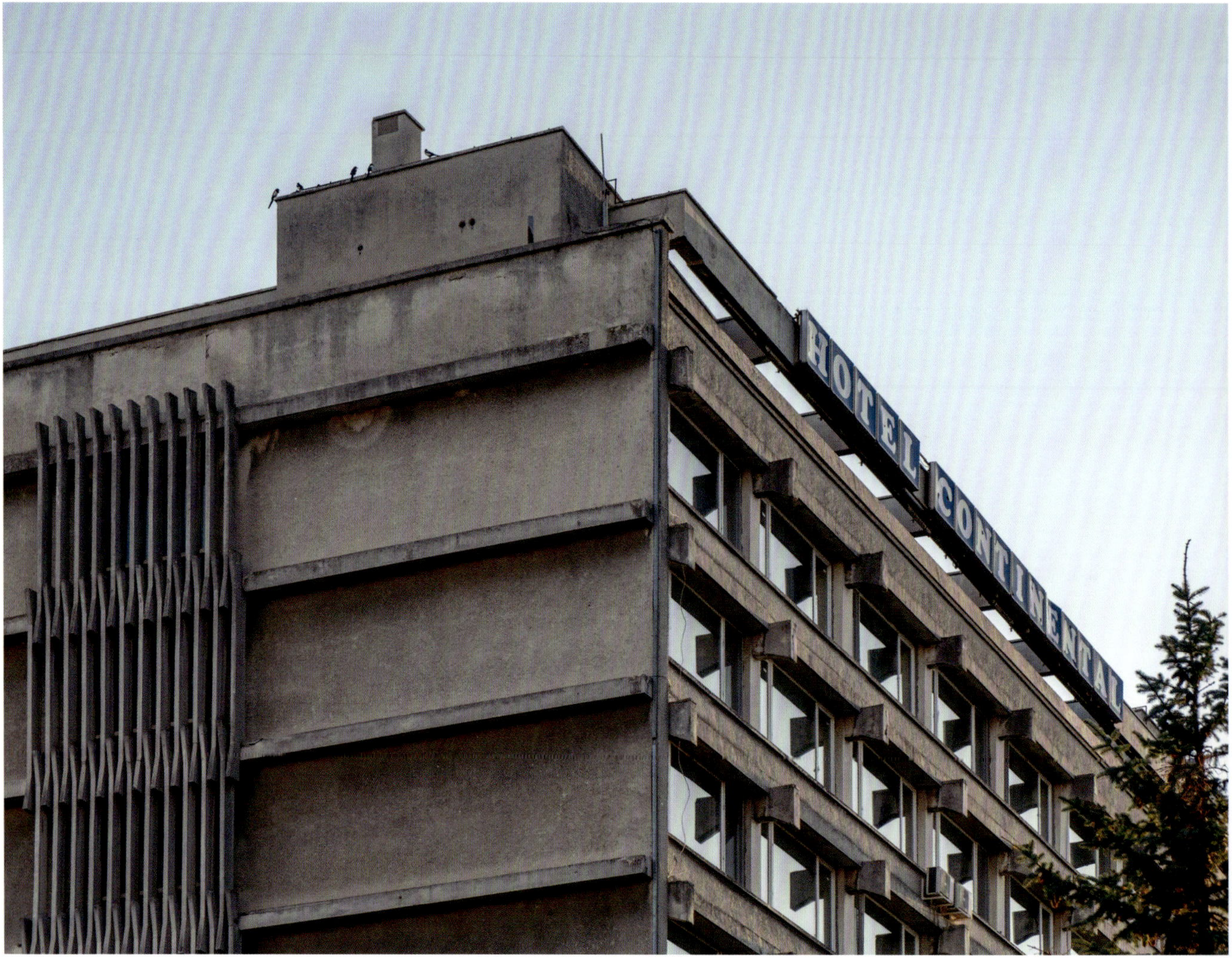

 Hotel Continental (former Hotel Parc), Drobeta-Turnu Severin, Romania

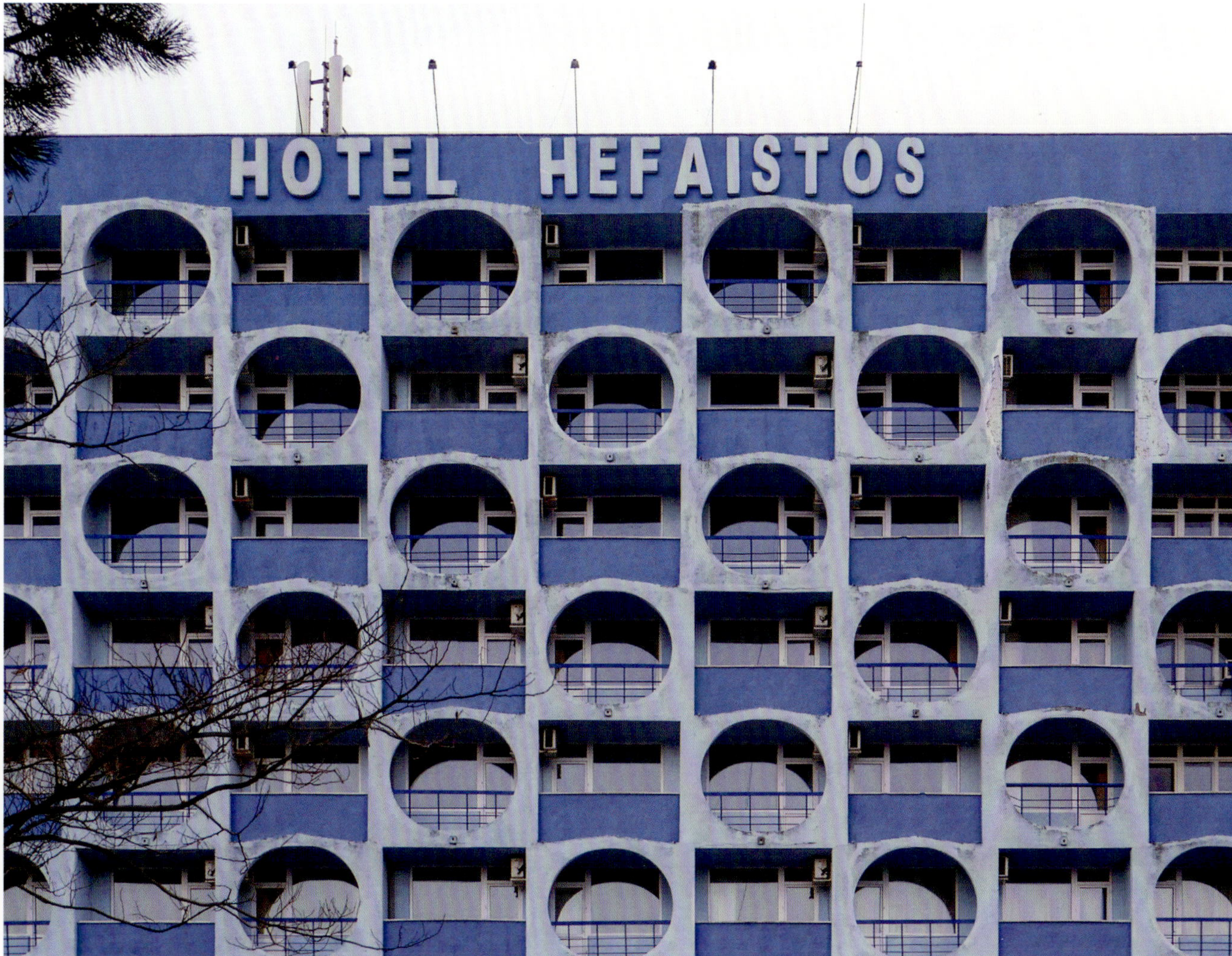

Hotel Hefaistos (former Hotel Cascom), Eforie Nord, Romania

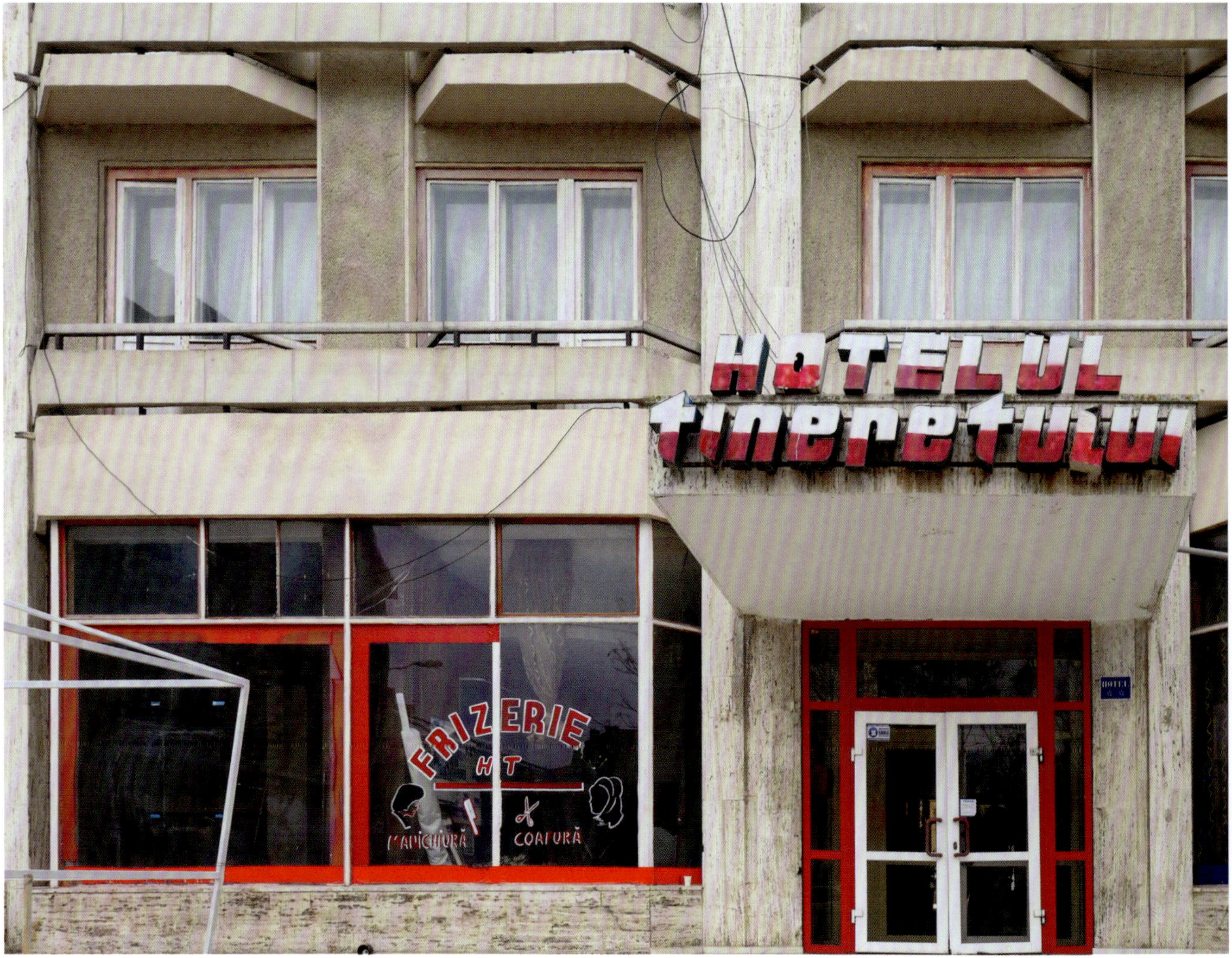

 Hotel Tineretului, Constanța, Romania

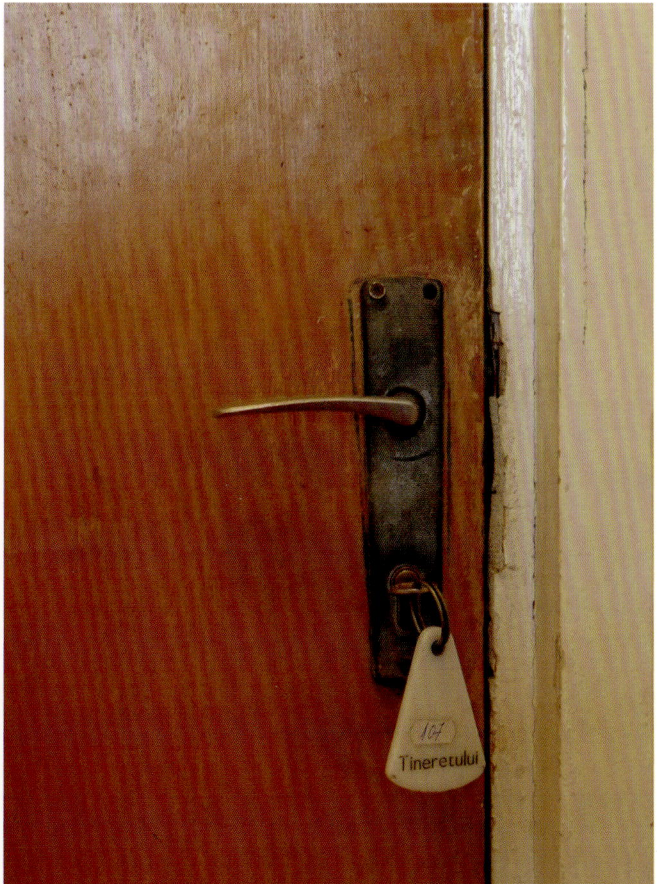
107
Tineretului

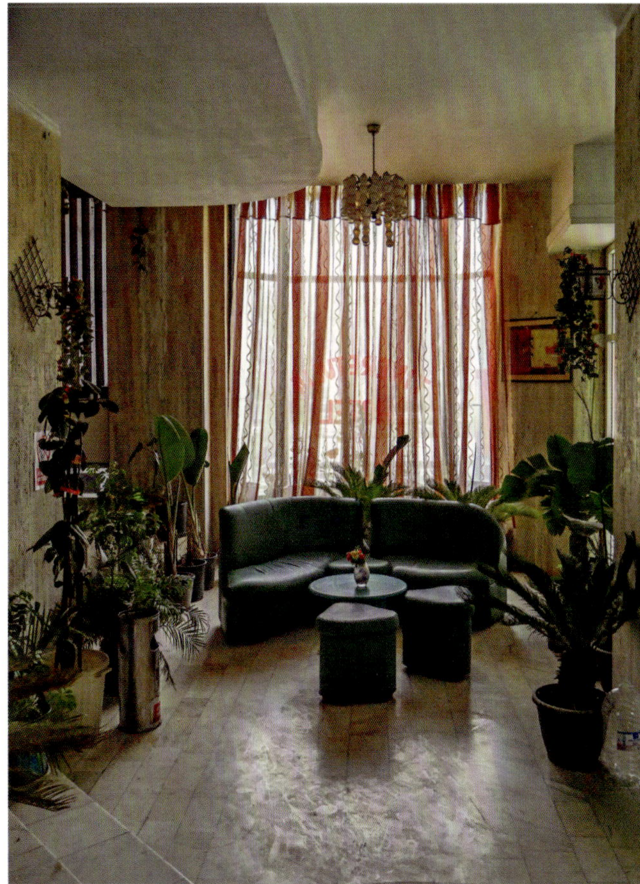

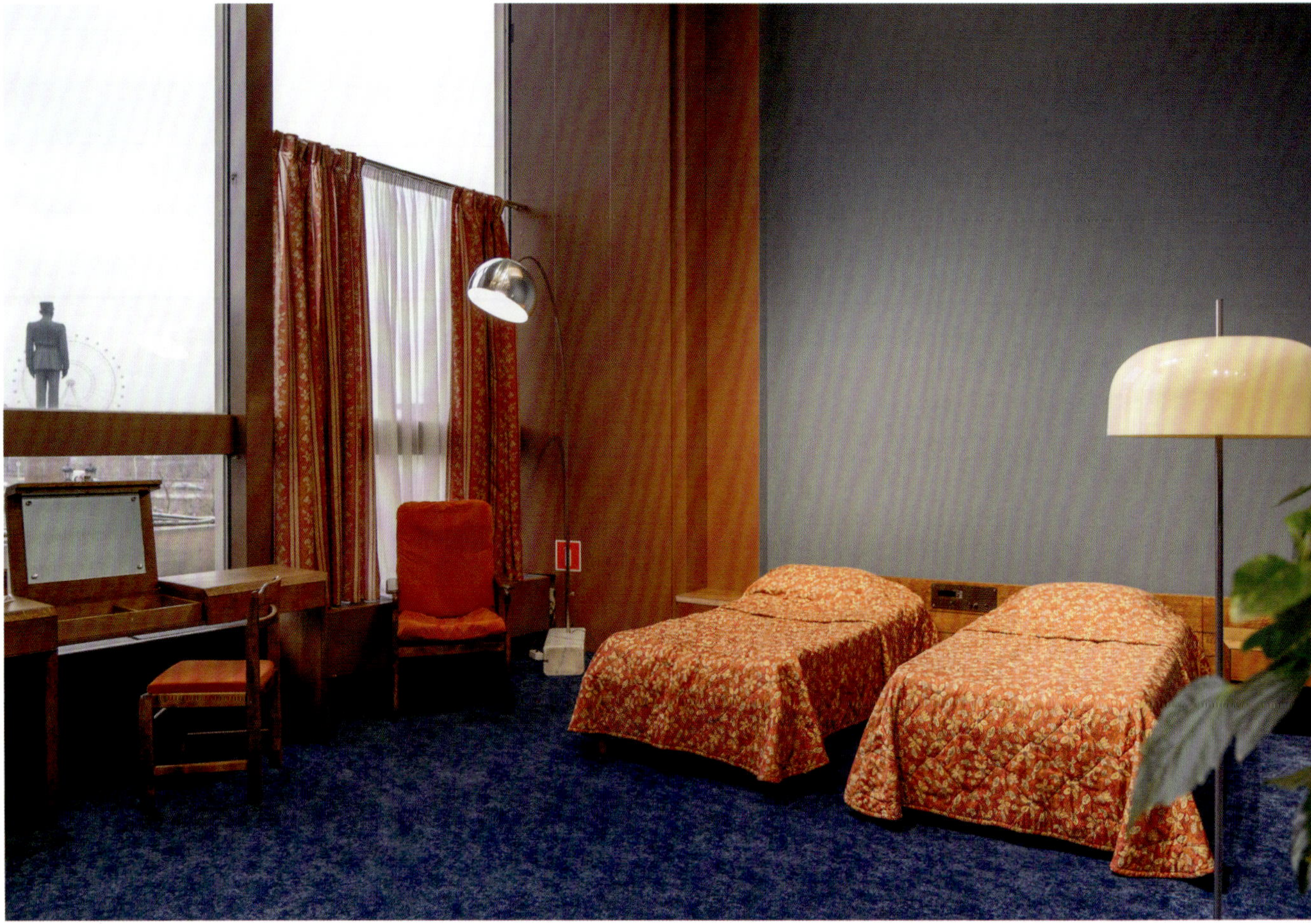

 Hotel Cosmos, Moscow, Russia

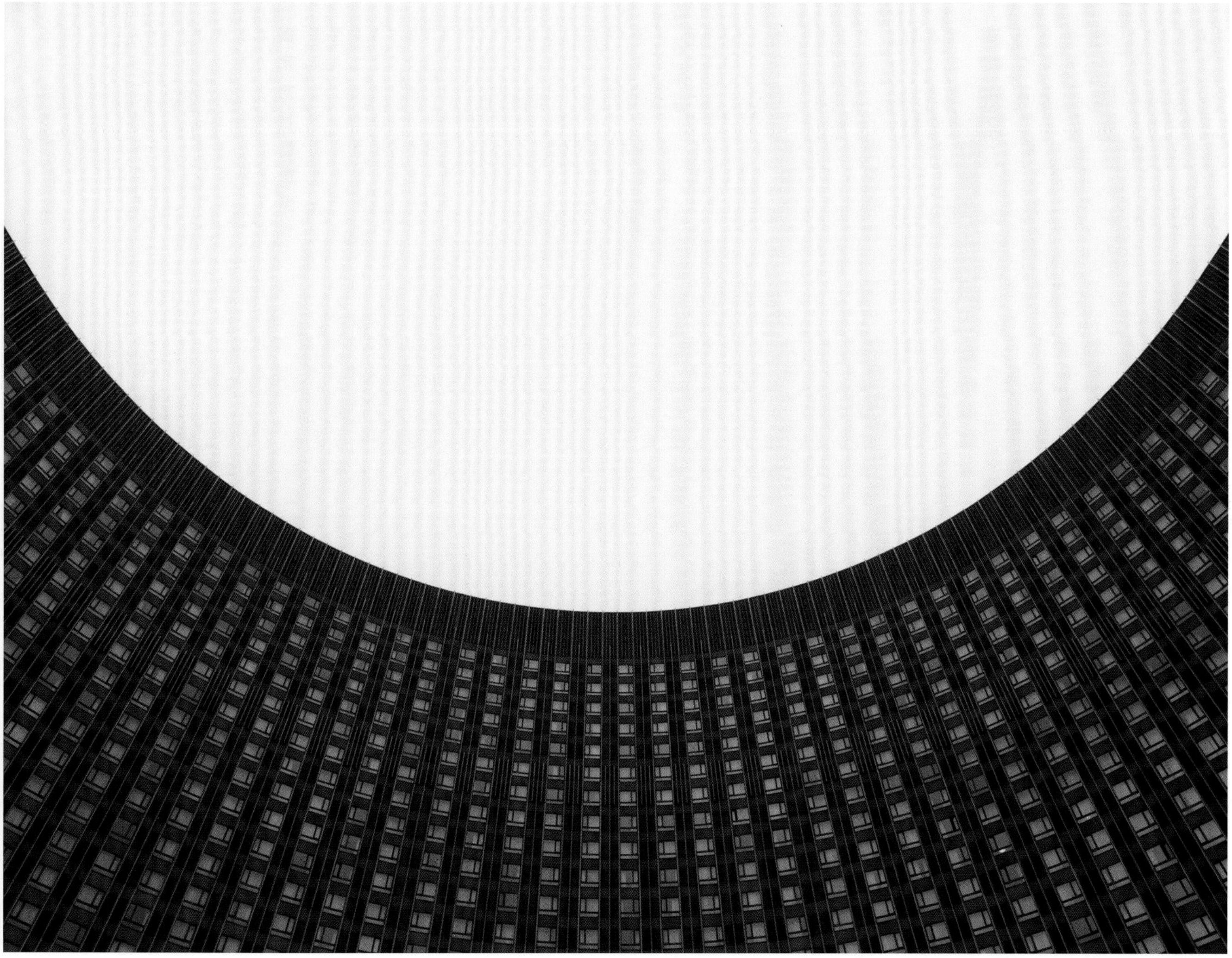

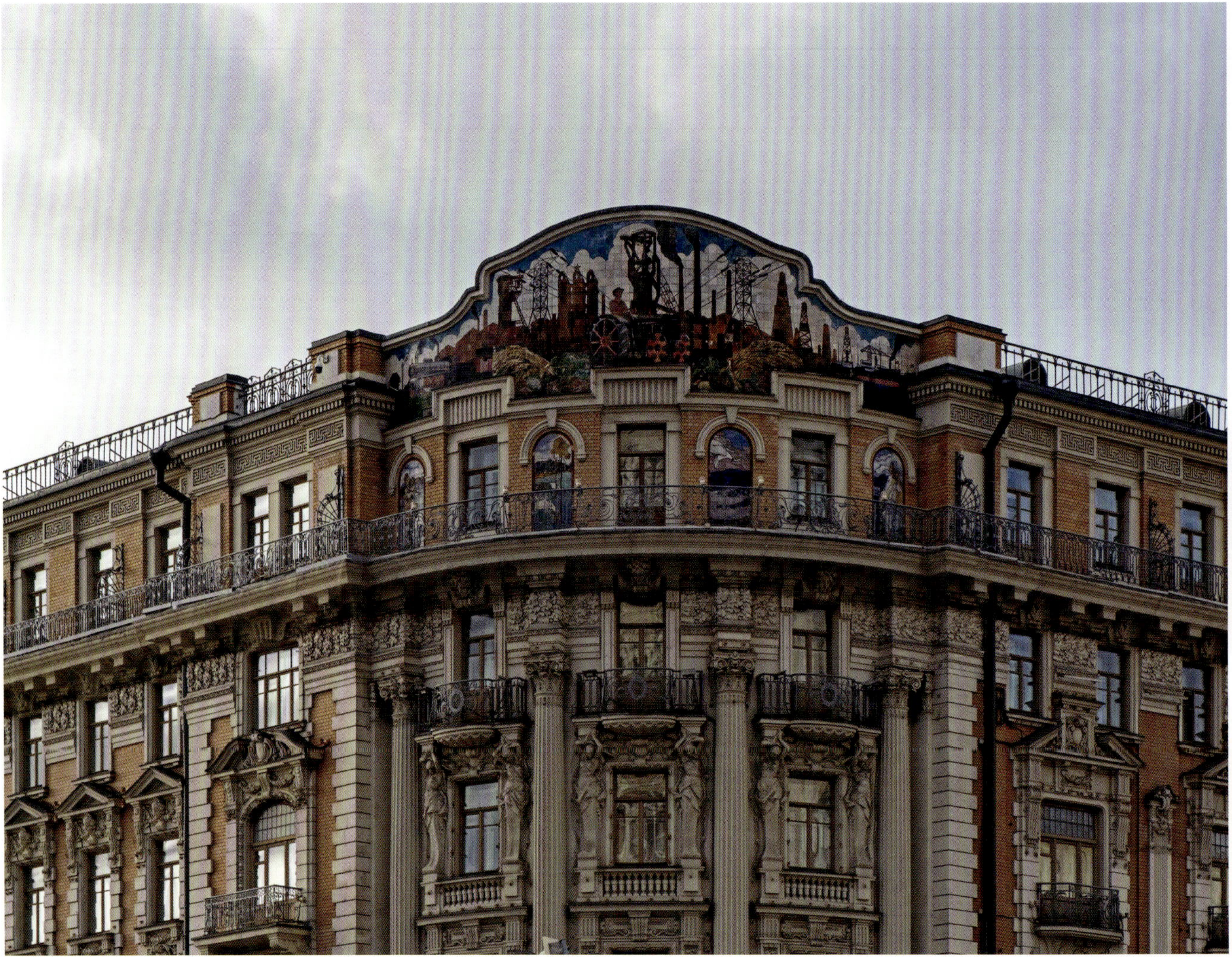

Hotel National, Moscow, Russia

right: Hotel Ukraina, Moscow, Russia

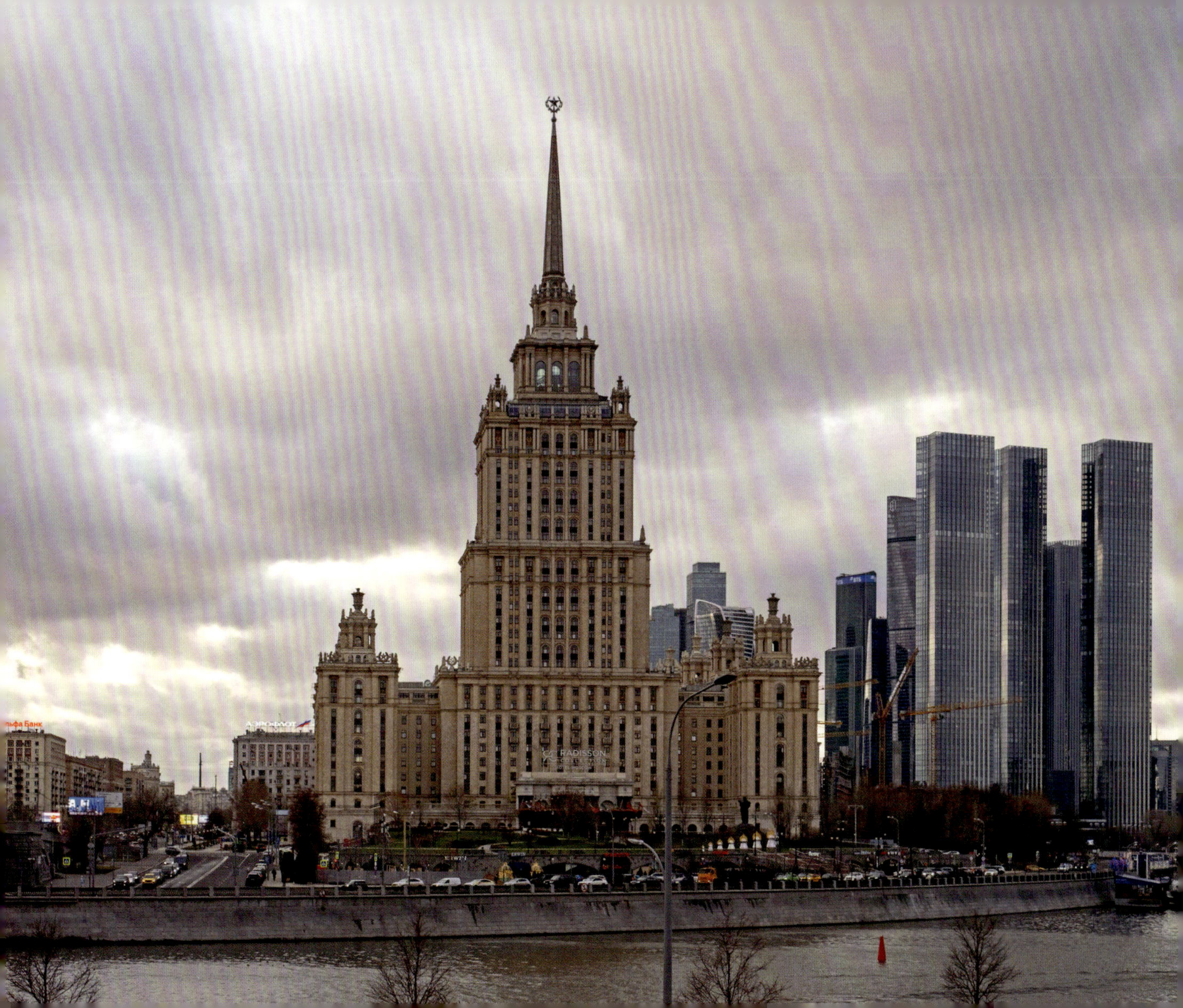
RADISSON

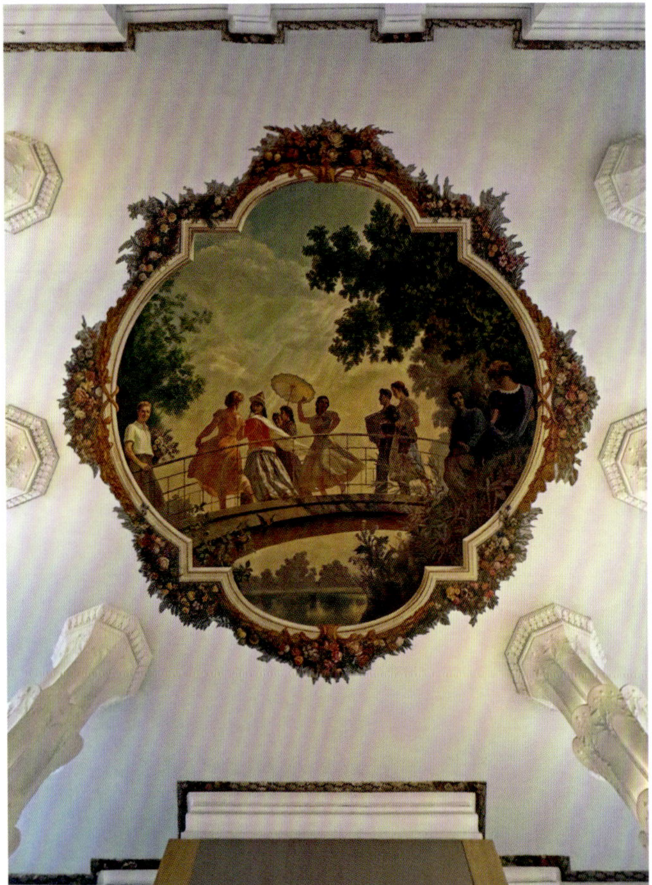

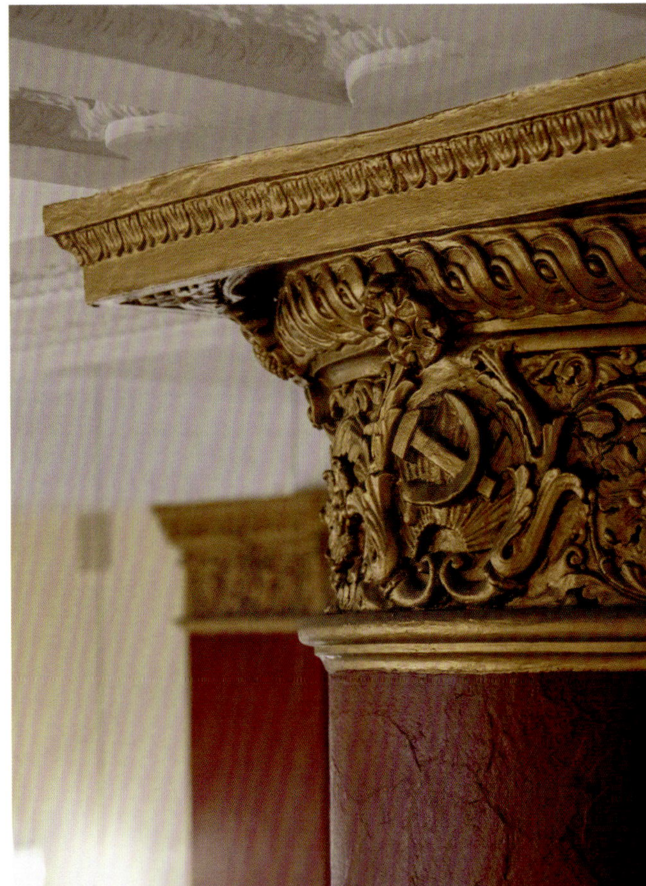

 Hotel Peking, Moscow, Russia

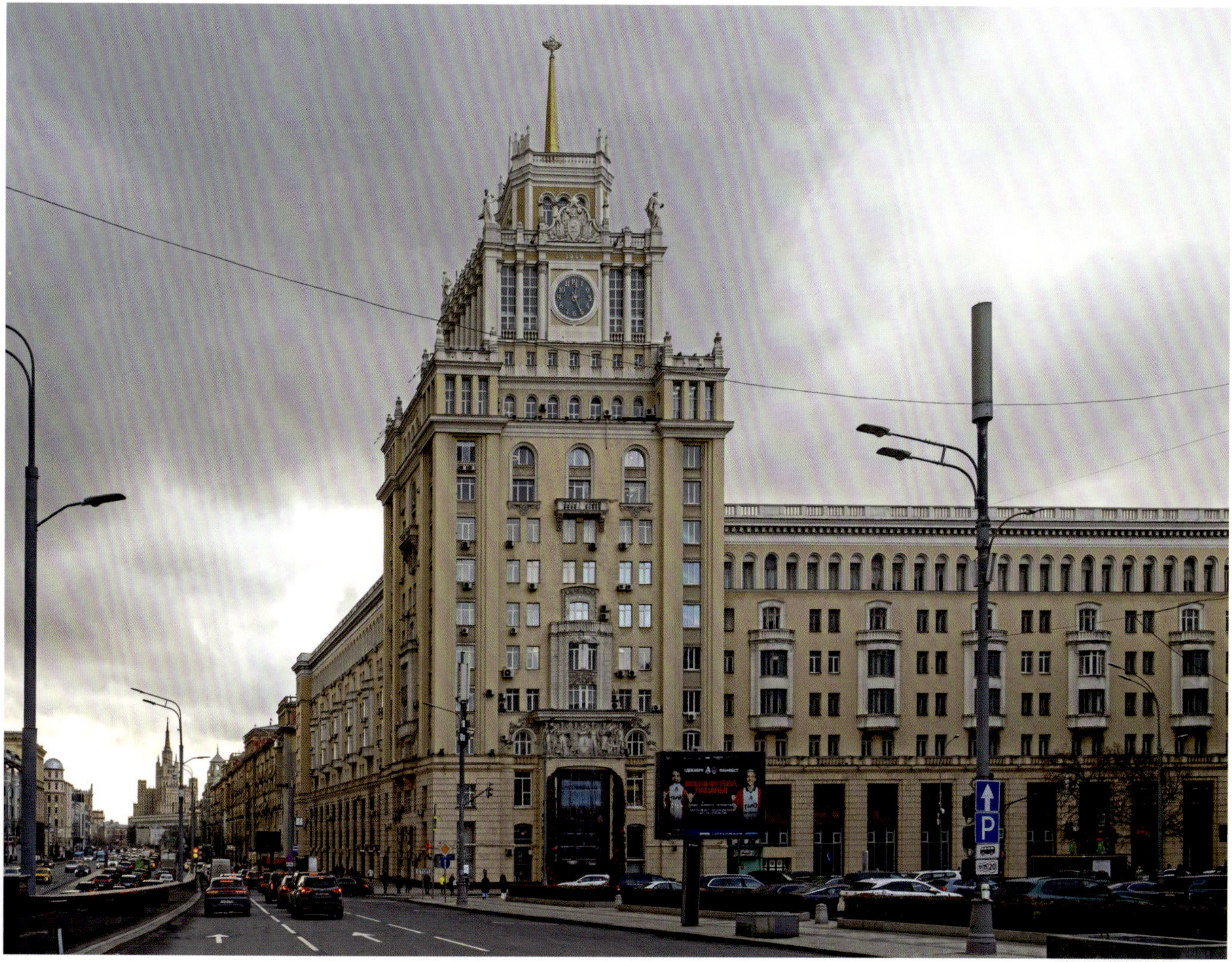

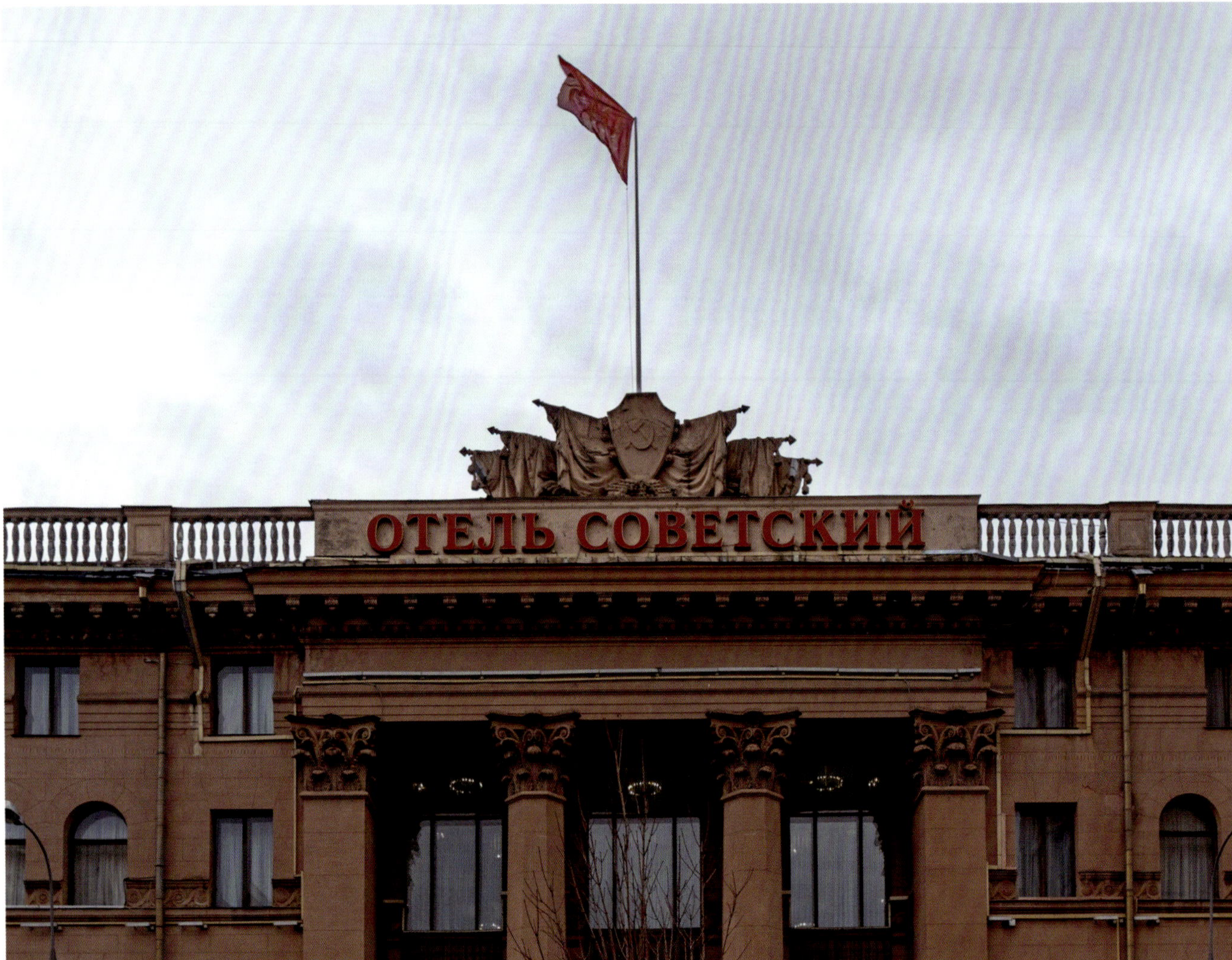

 Hotel Sovietsky, Moscow, Russia

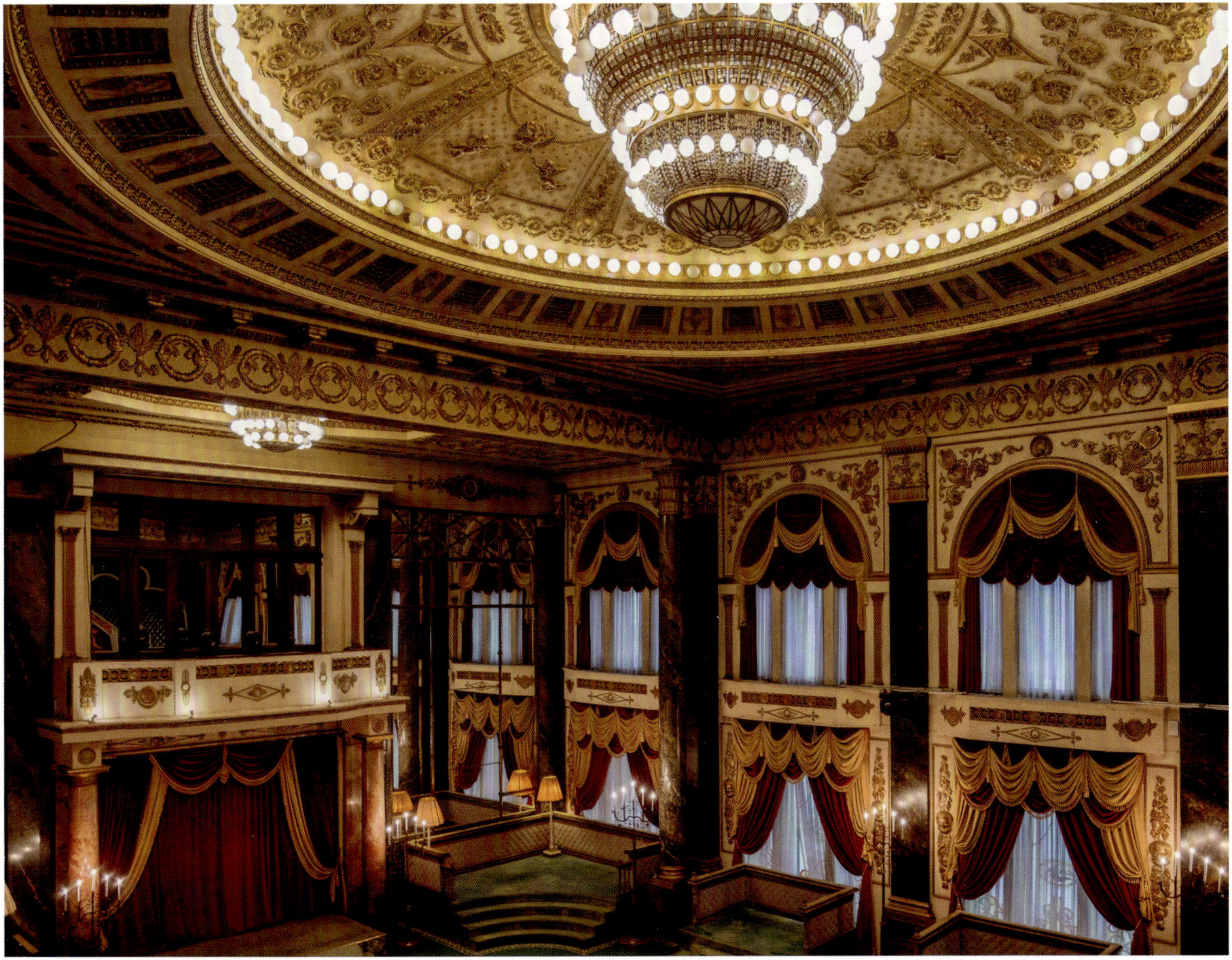

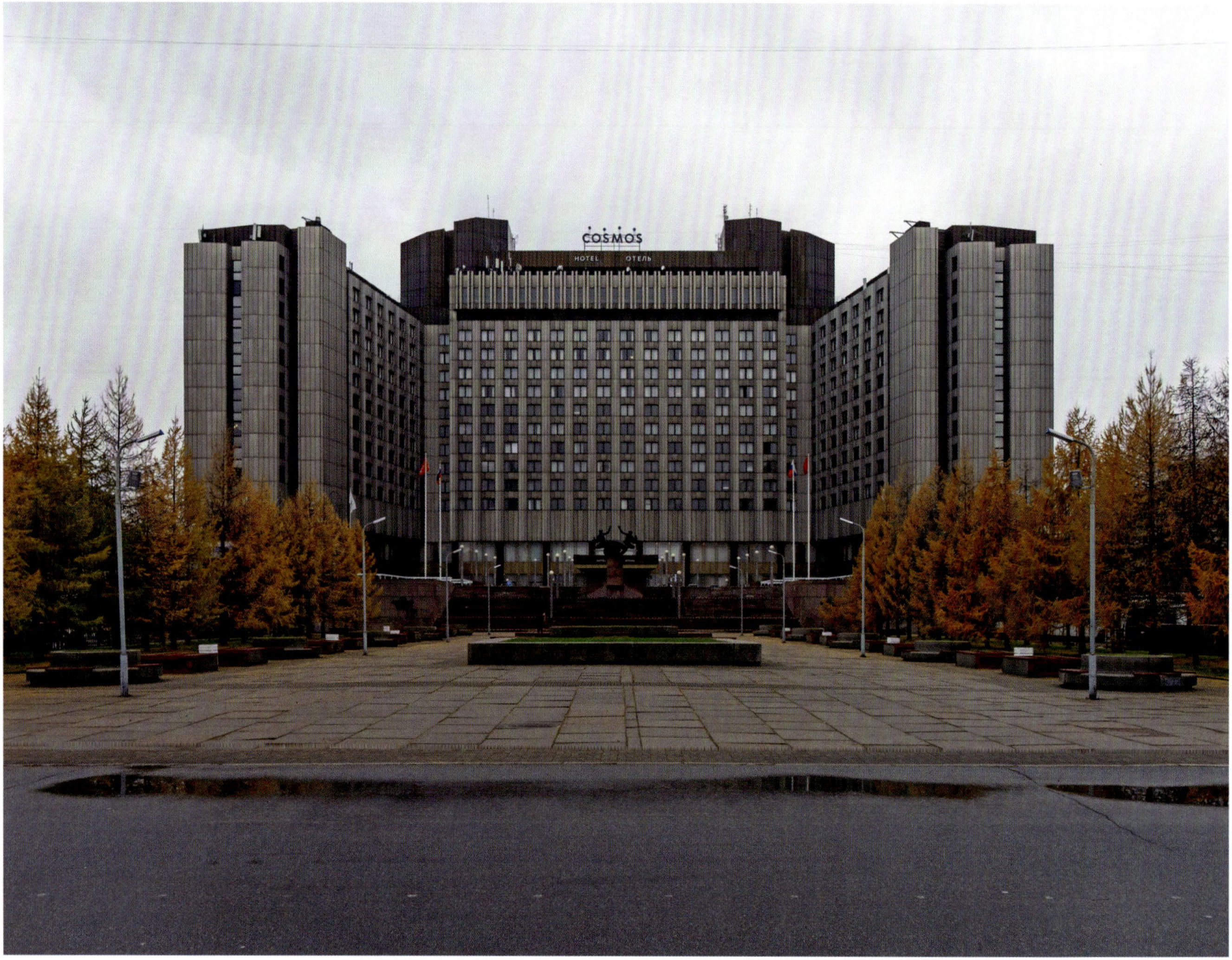

 Hotel Pribaltiyskaya, Saint Petersburg, Russia

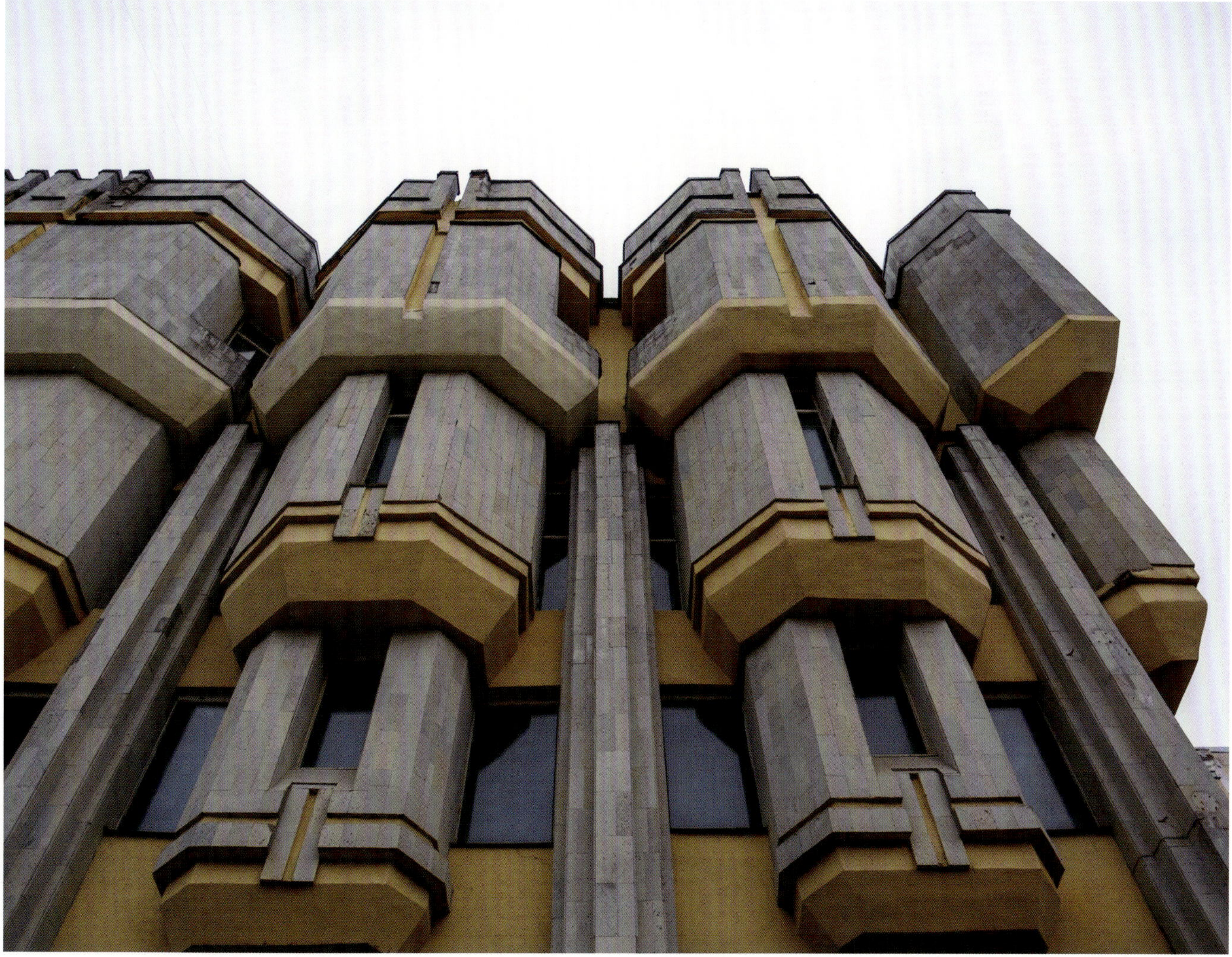

Hotel Russ, Saint Petersburg, Russia

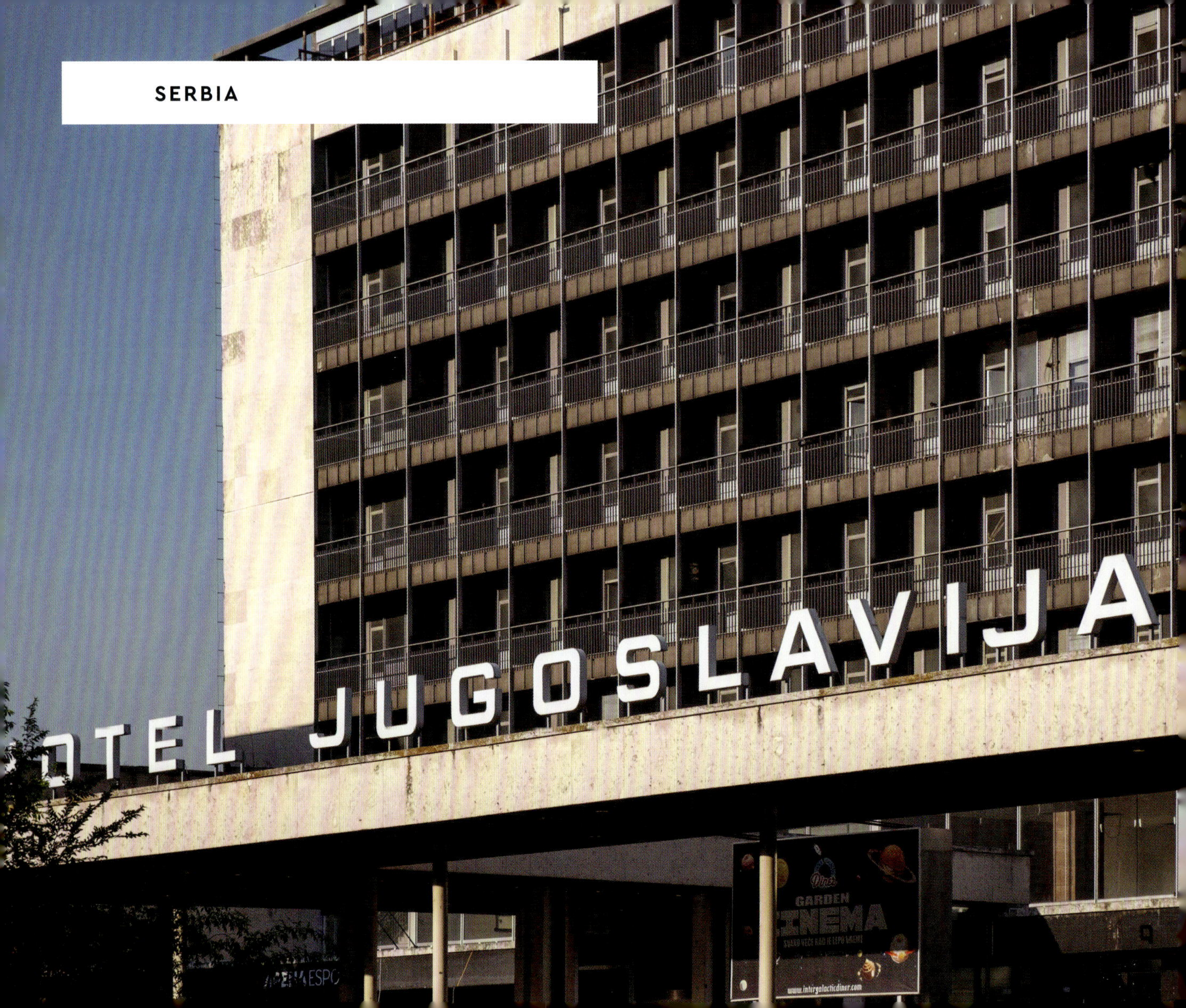
OTEL JUGOSLAVIJA
GARDEN
INEMA

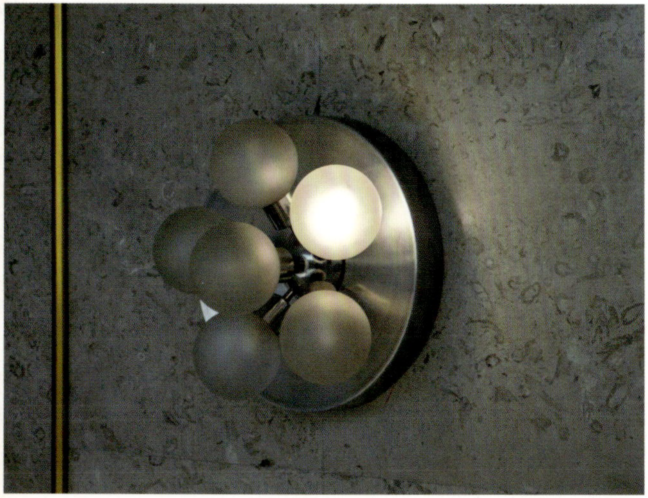
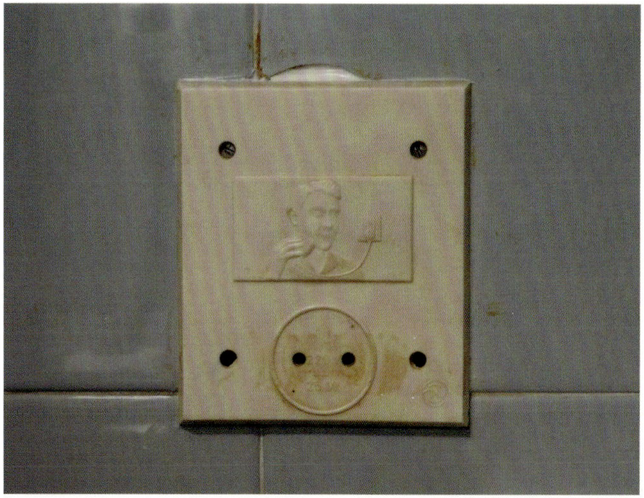
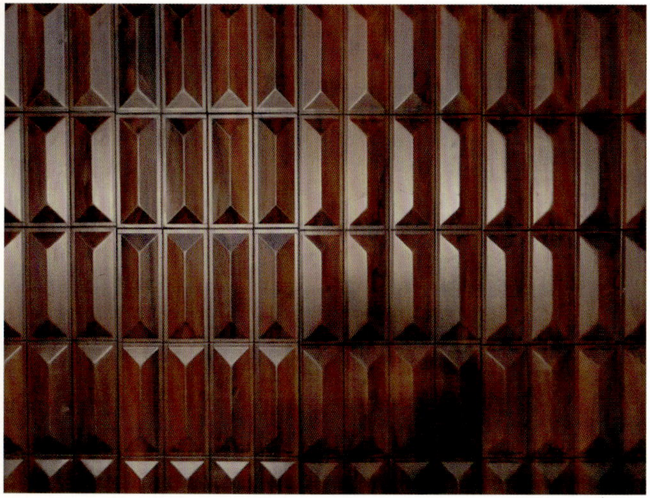
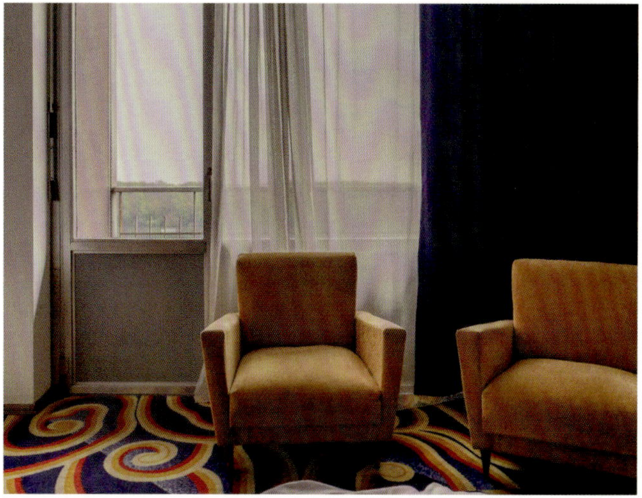

Hotel Jugoslavija, Belgrade, Serbia

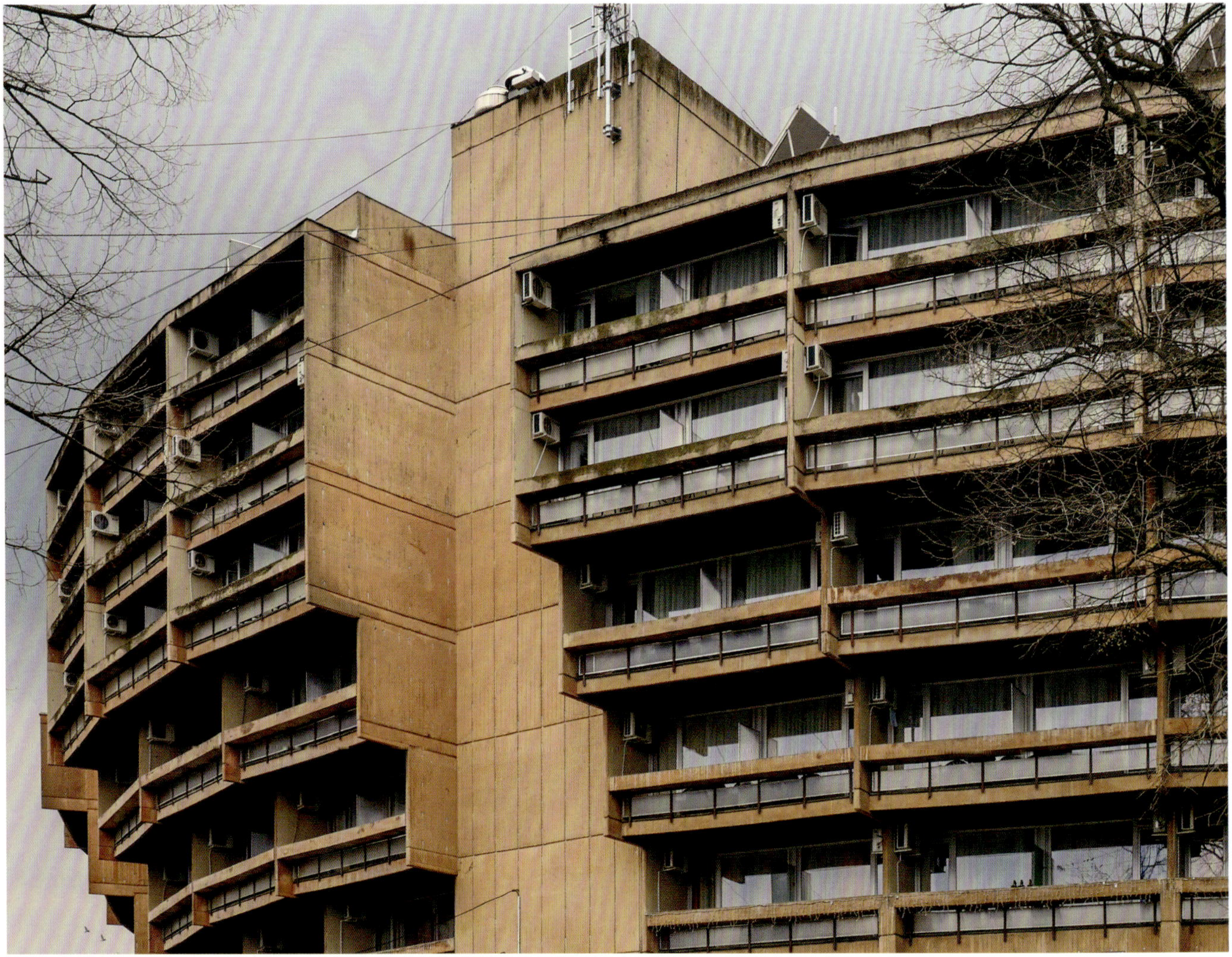

Hotel Merkur, Vrnjačka Banja, Serbia

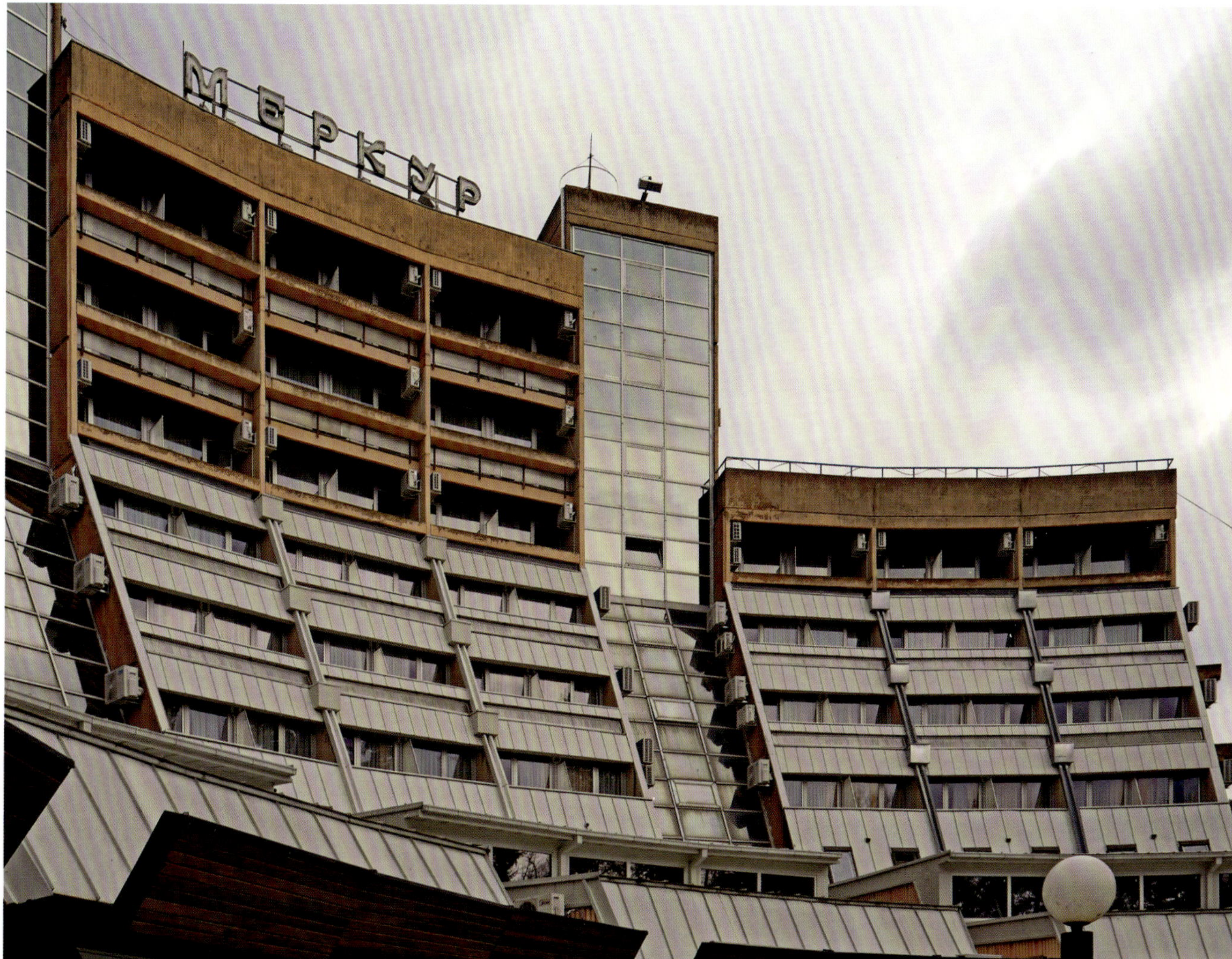
МЕРКУР

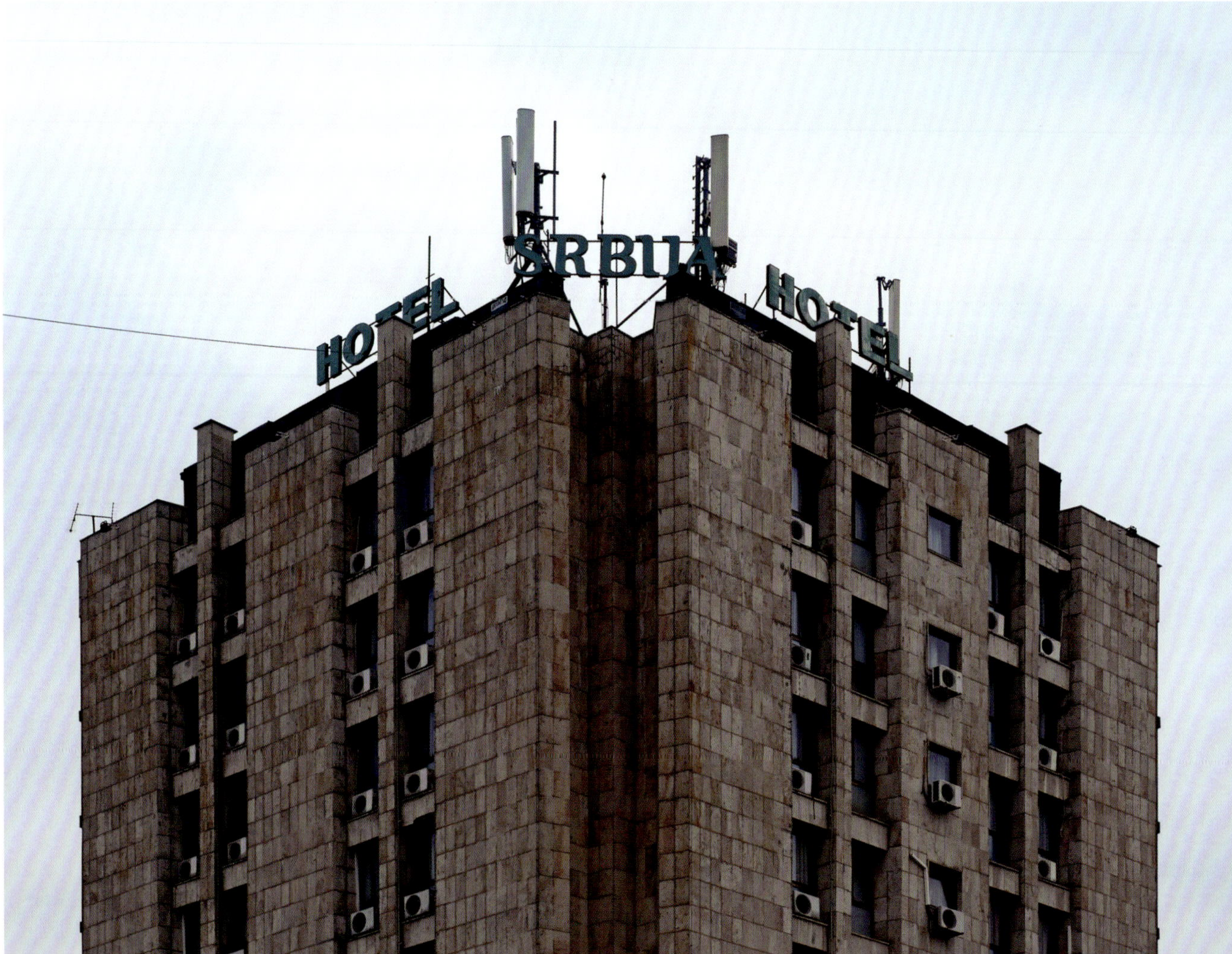

 Hotel Srbija, Vršac, Serbia

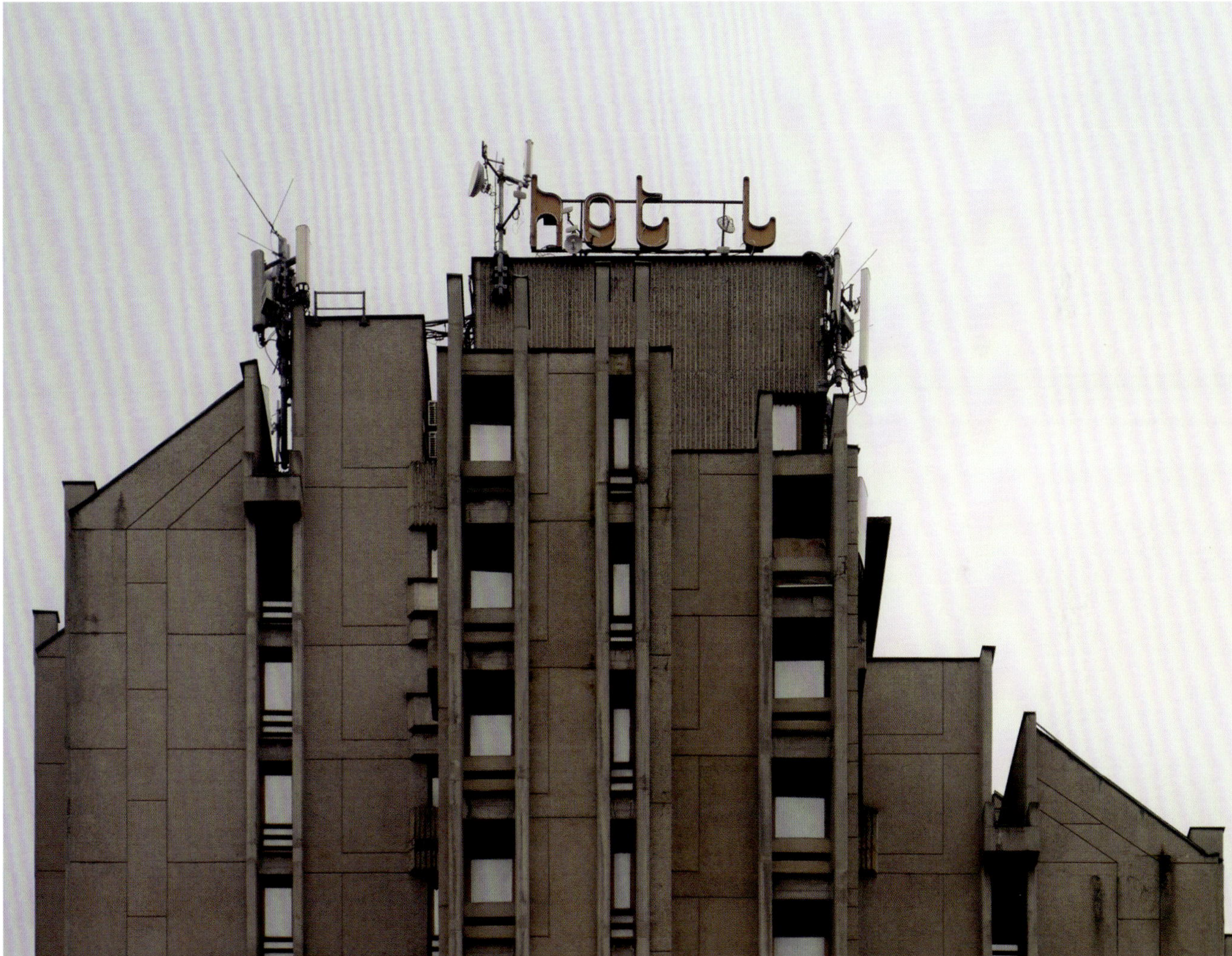

Hotel Zlatibor, Užice, Serbia

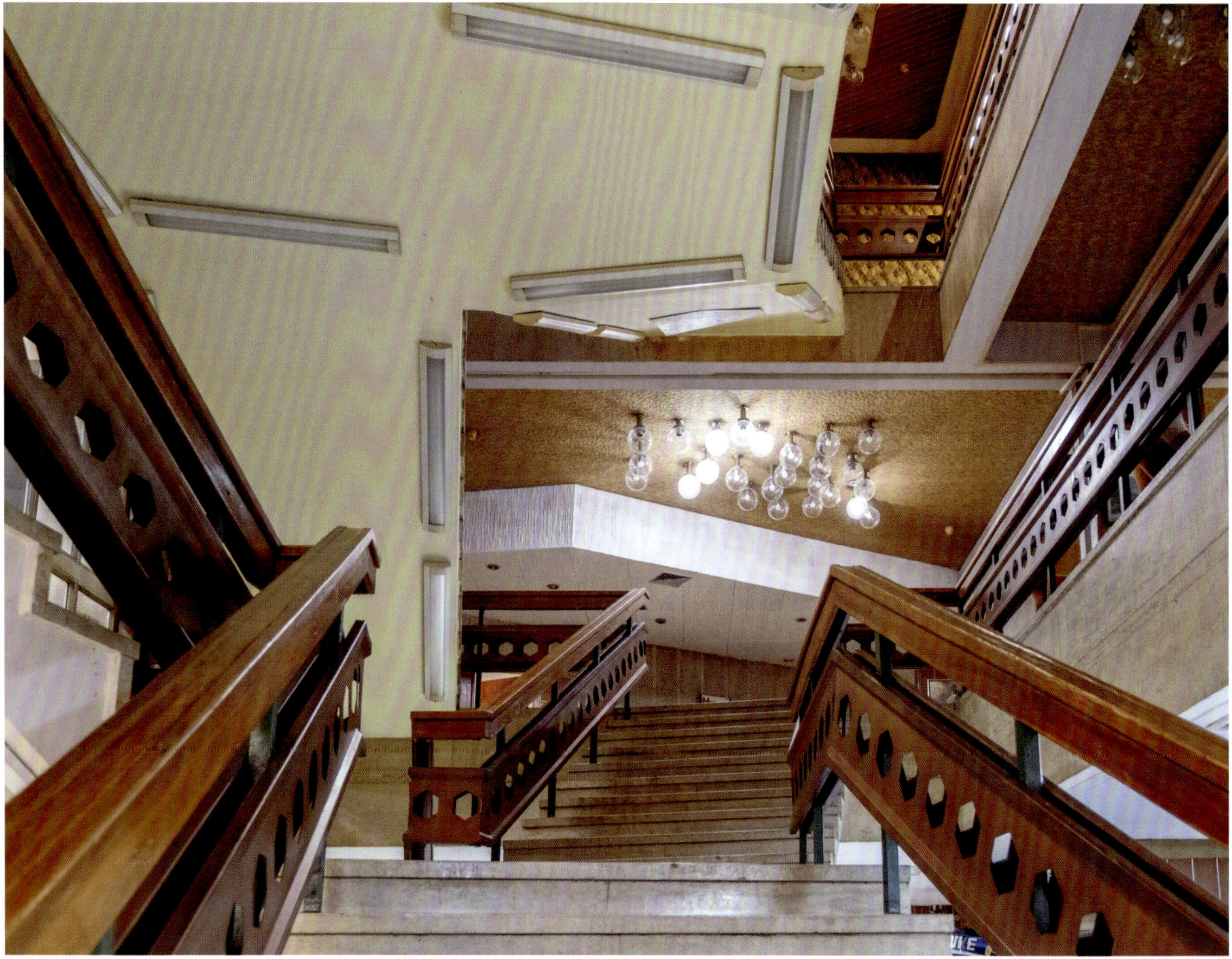

 Hotel Omorika, Tara National Park, Serbia

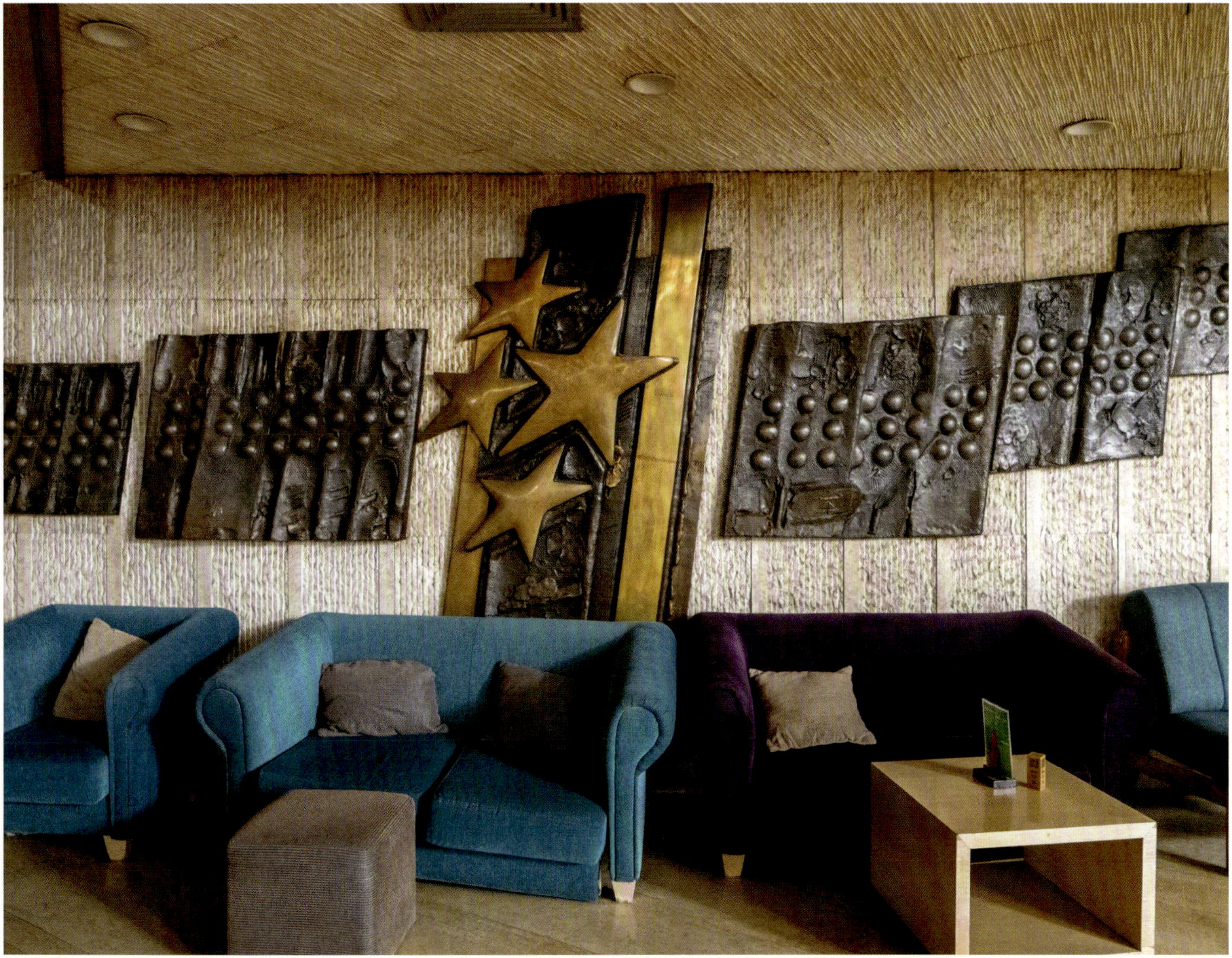

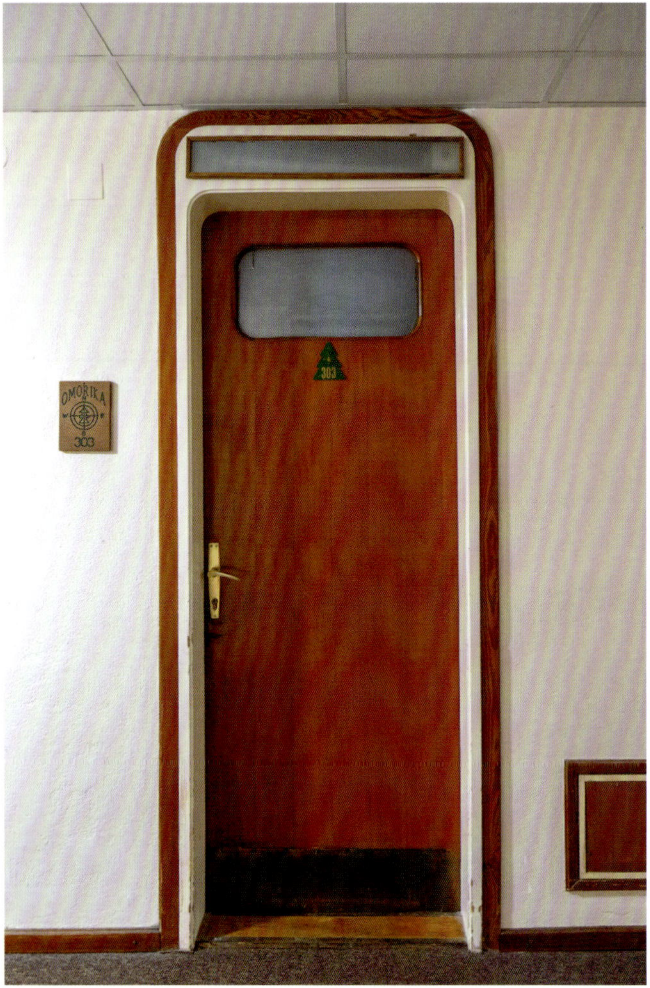

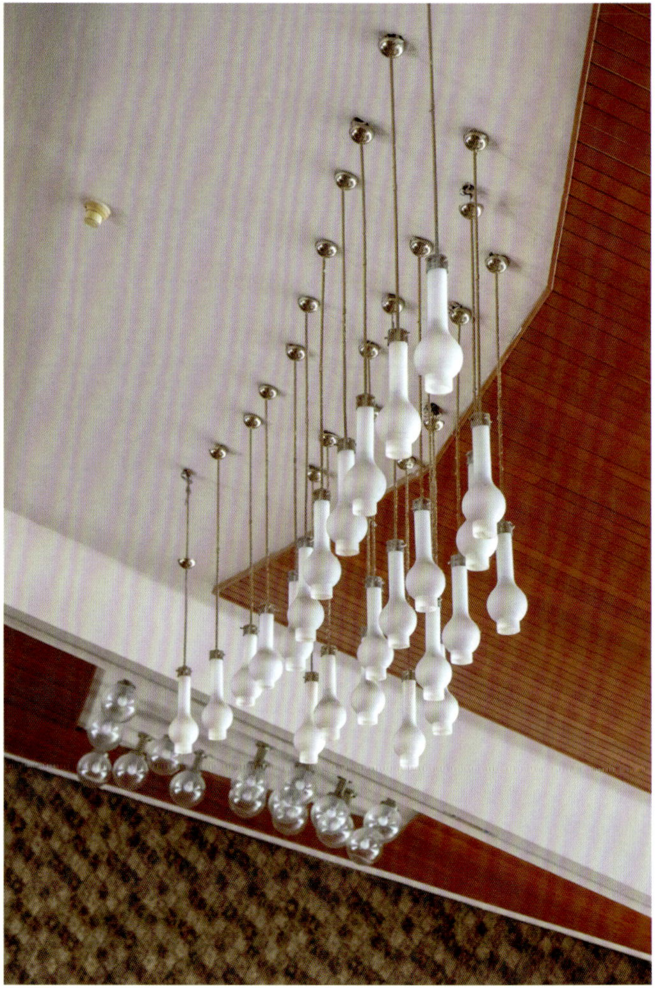

 Hotel Omorika, Tara National Park, Serbia

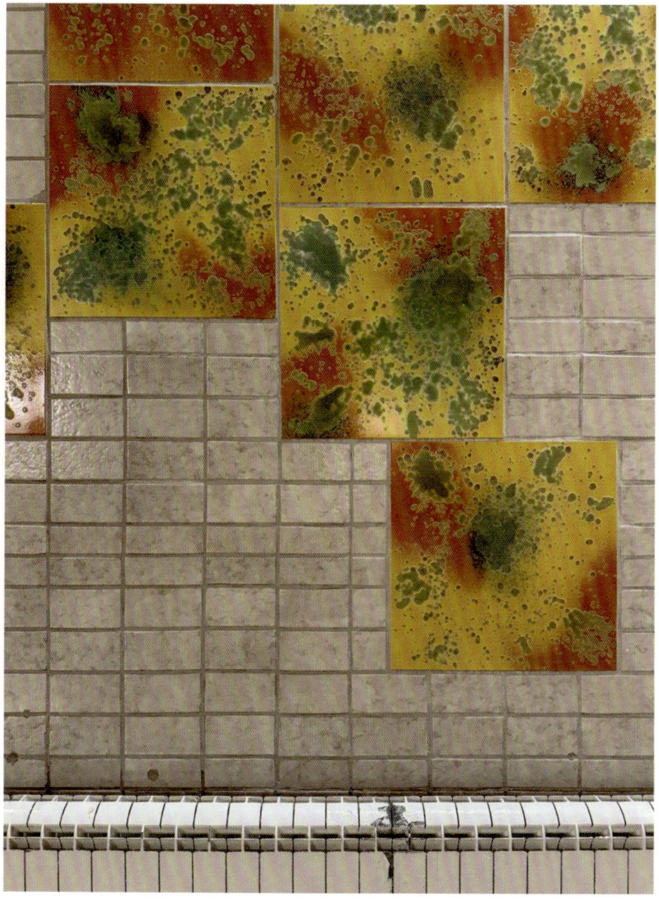
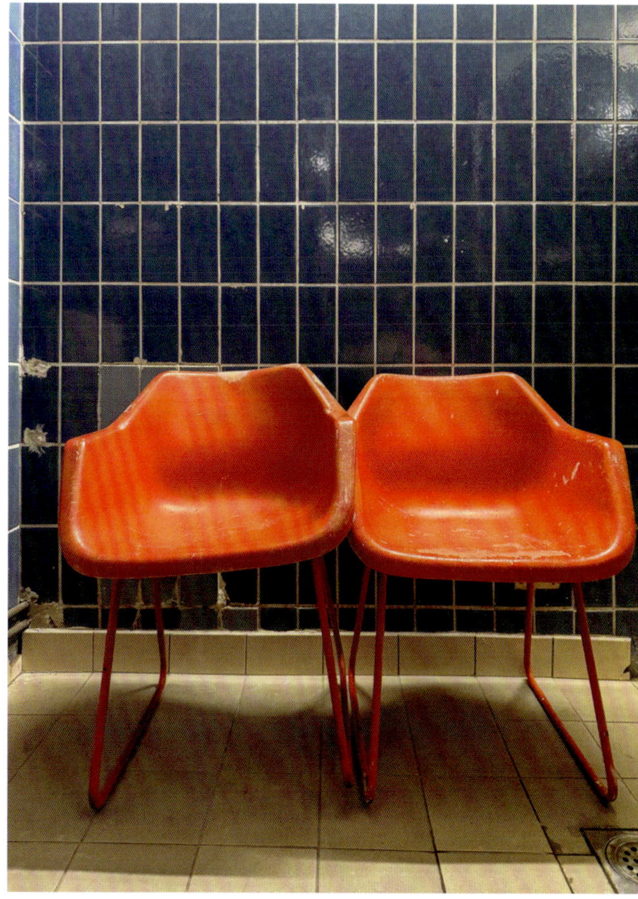

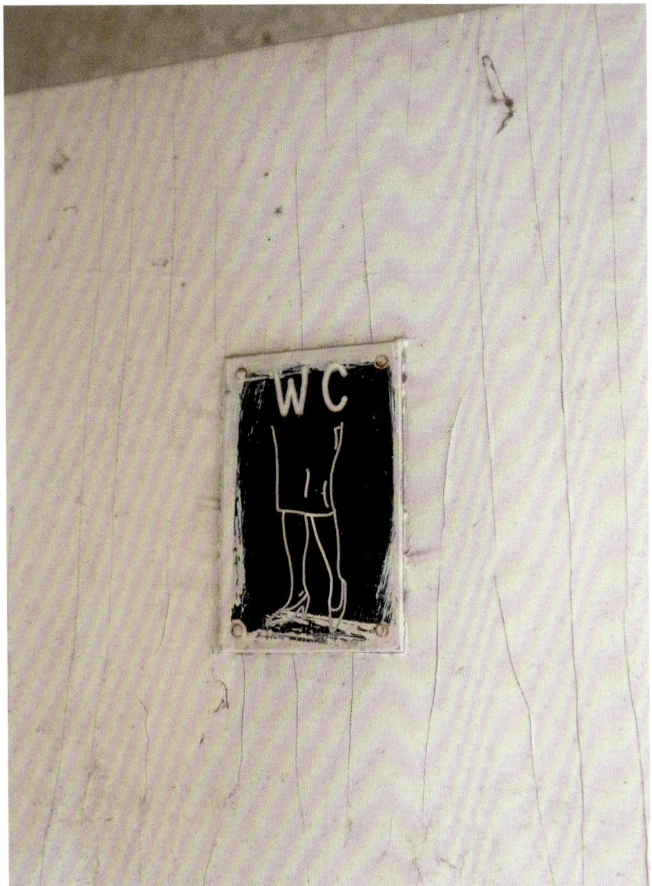

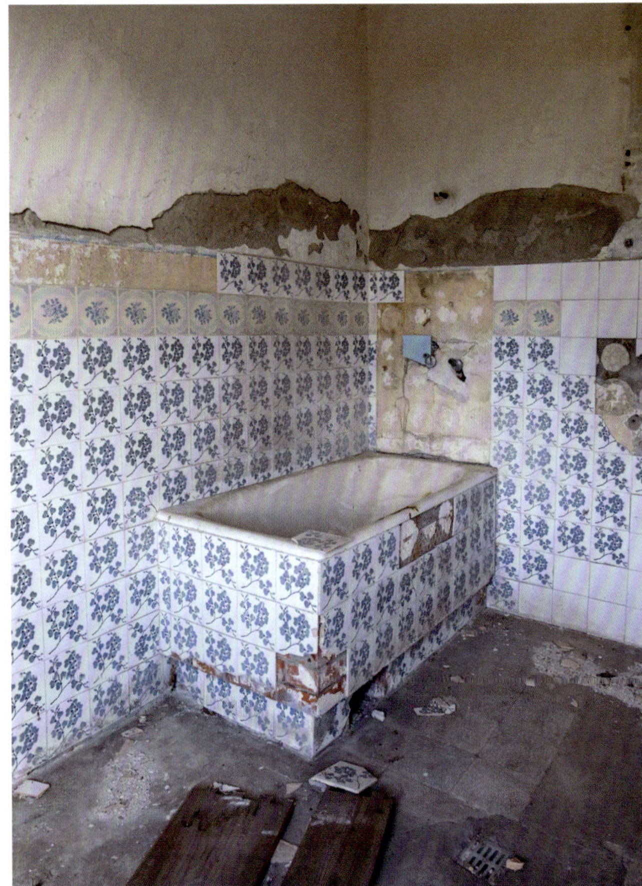

Hotel Venac (former Hotel Prvi Maj), Iriški Venac, Serbia

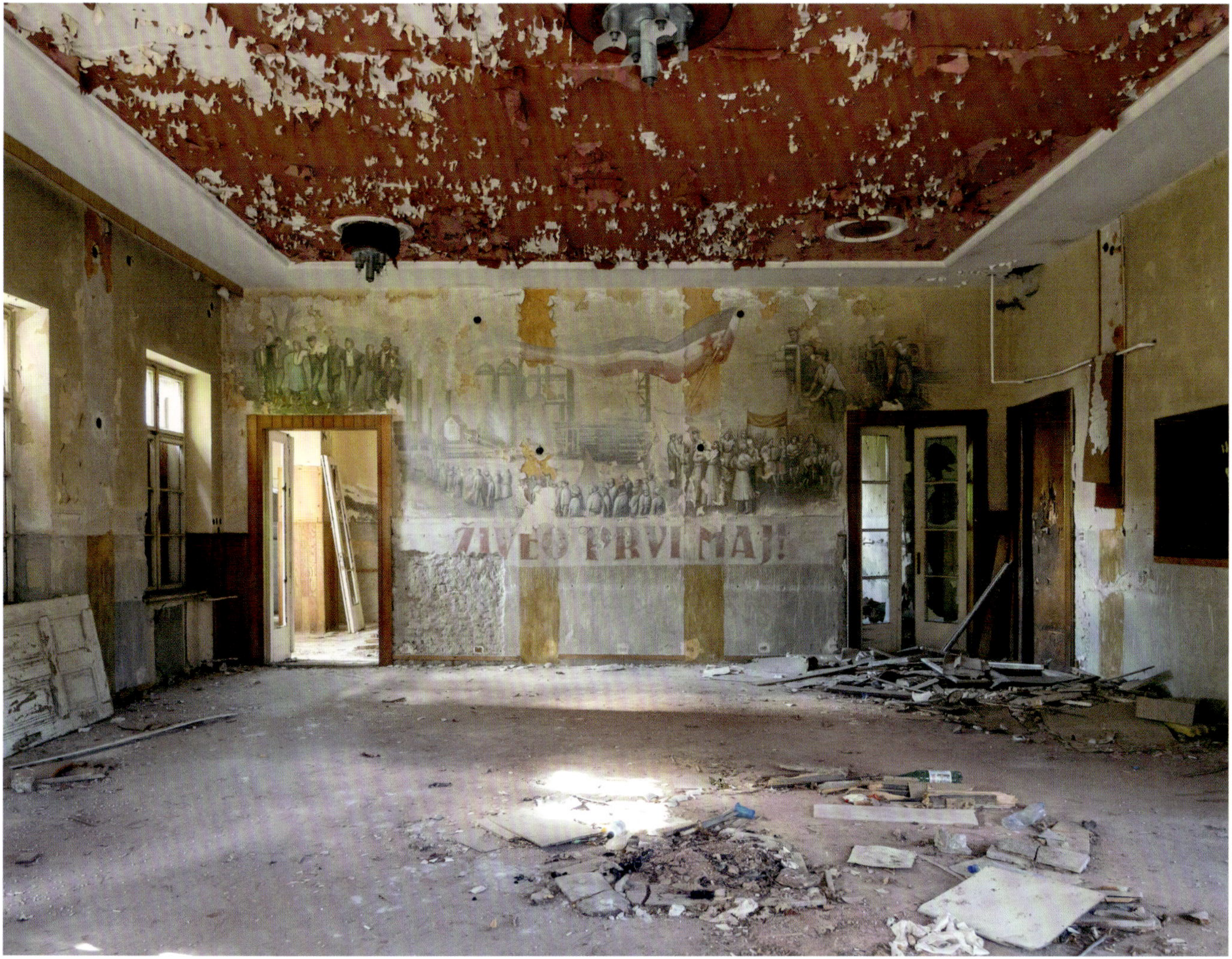
ŽIVEO PRVI MAJ!

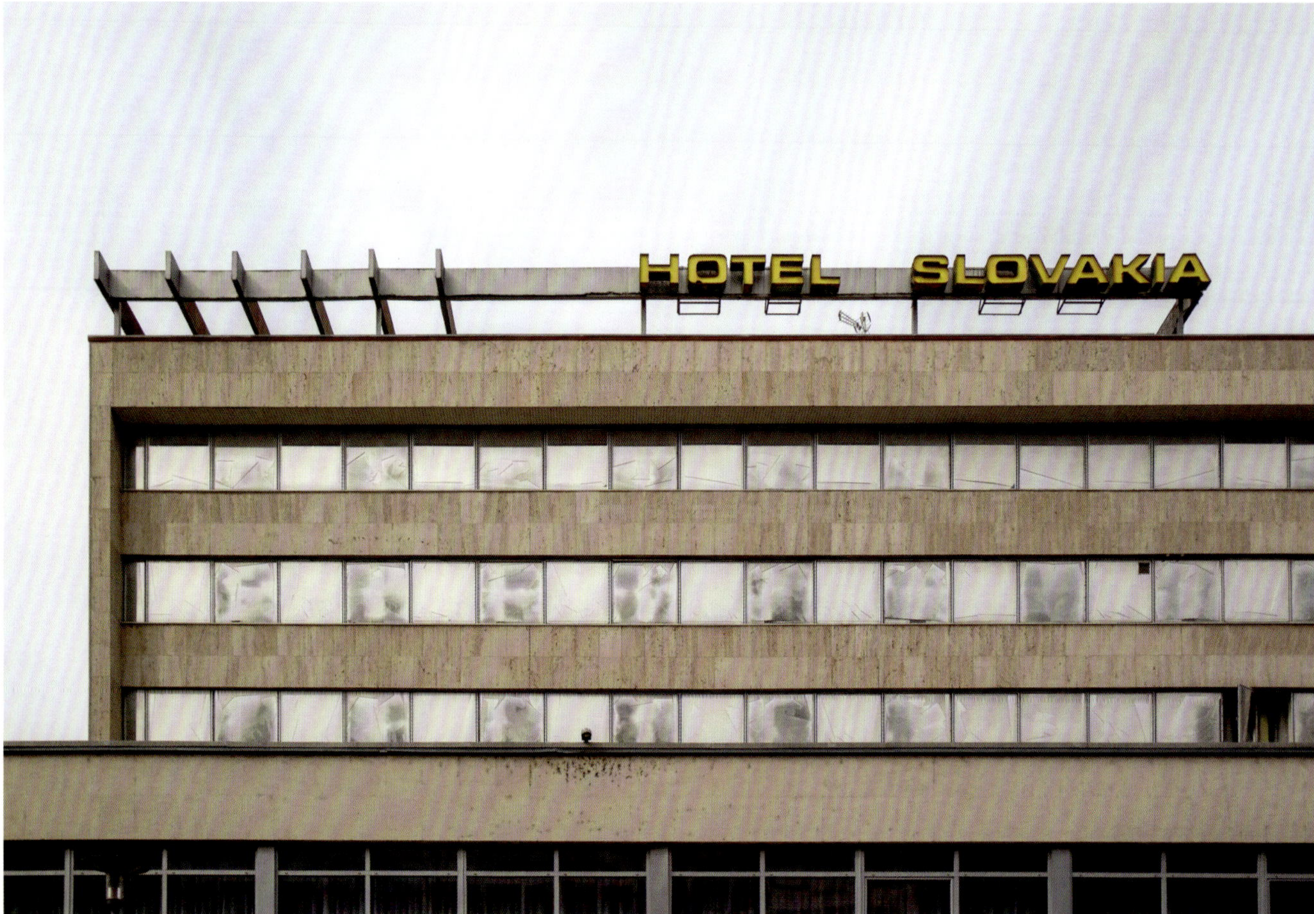

Hotel Slovakia, Žilina, Slovakia

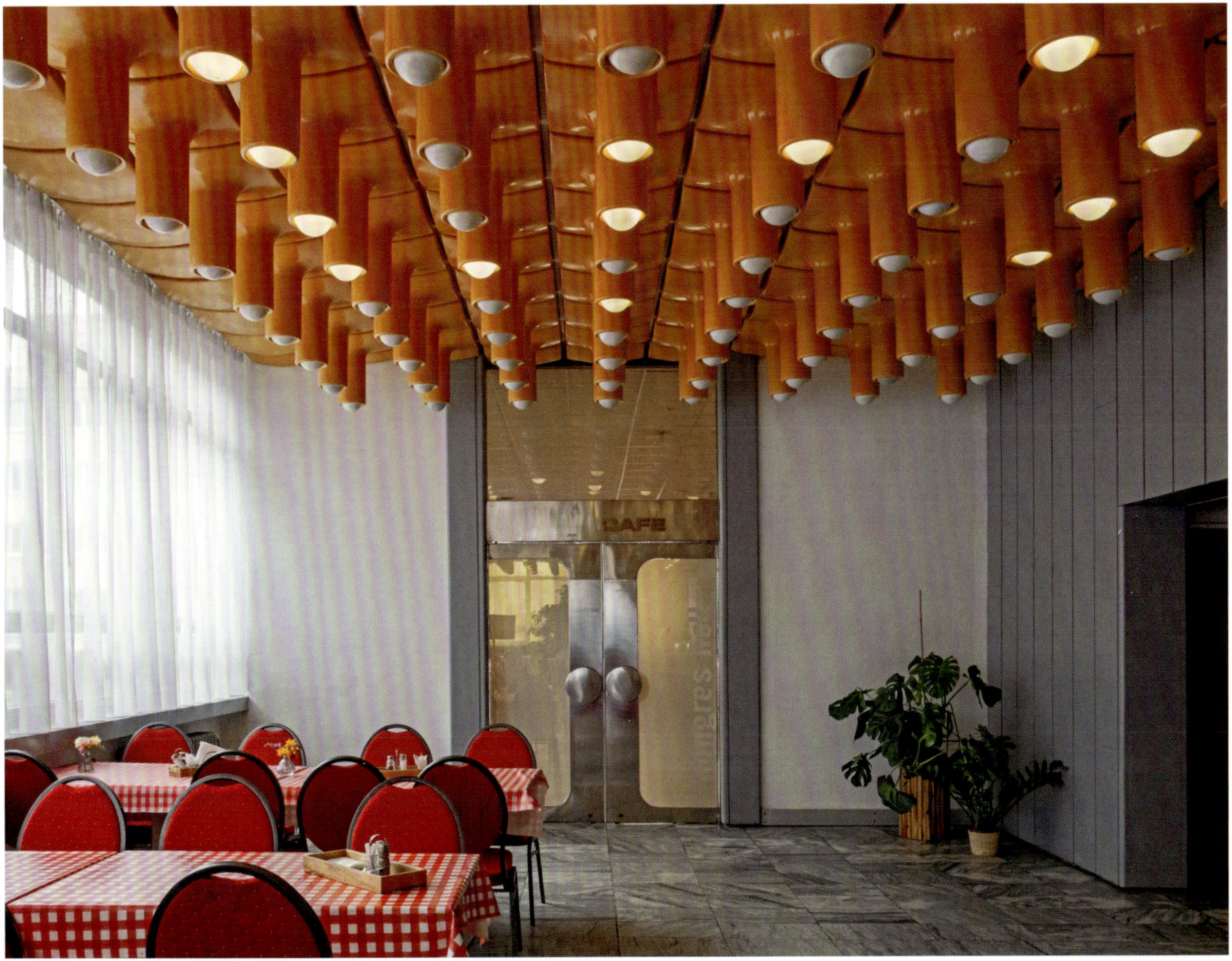
CAFE

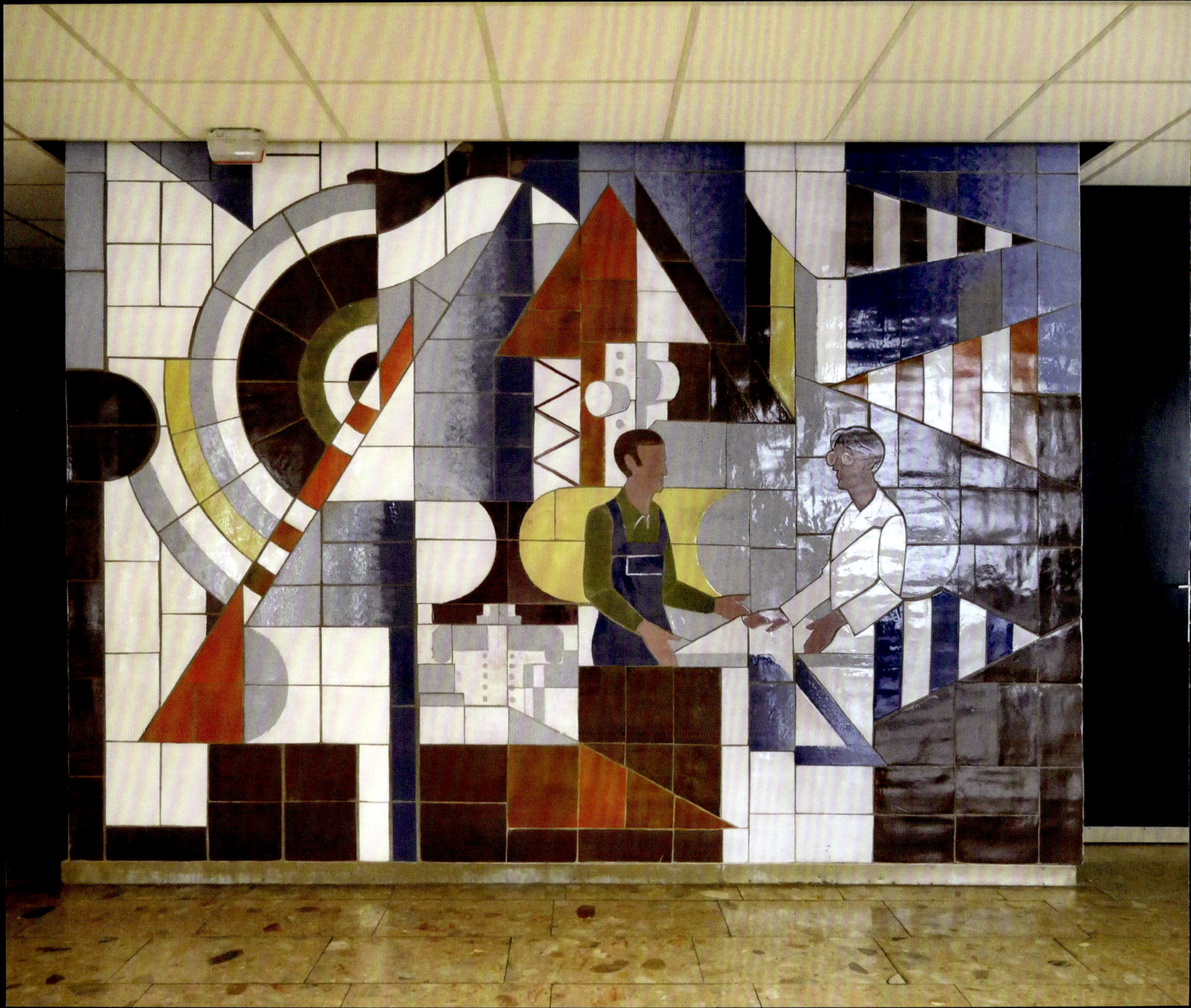

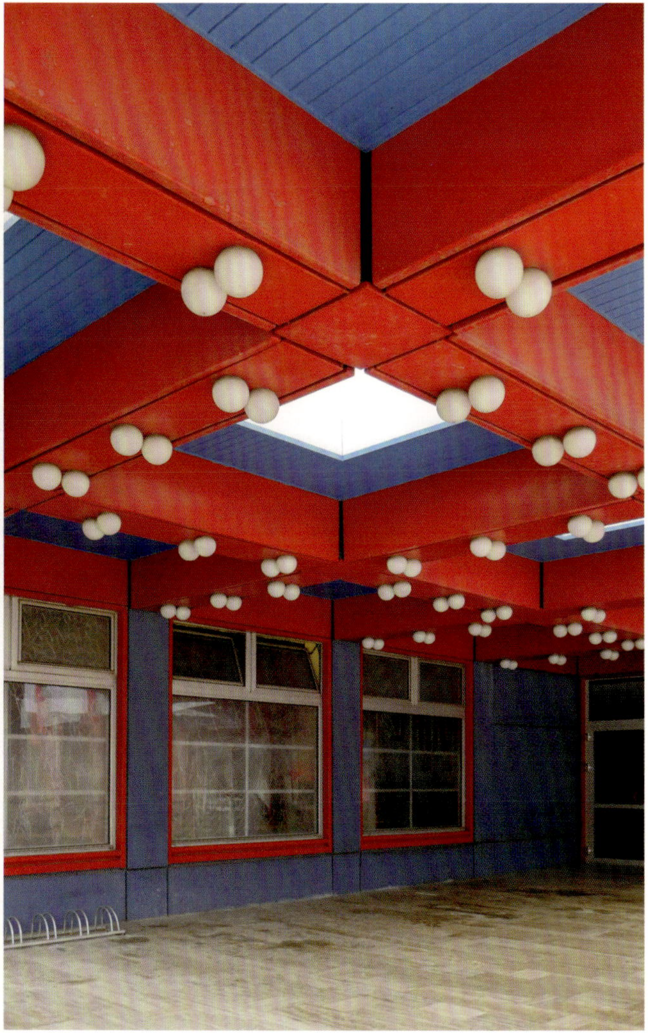

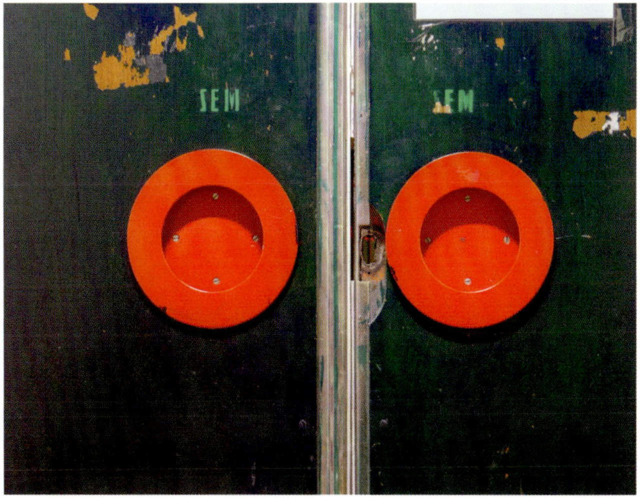

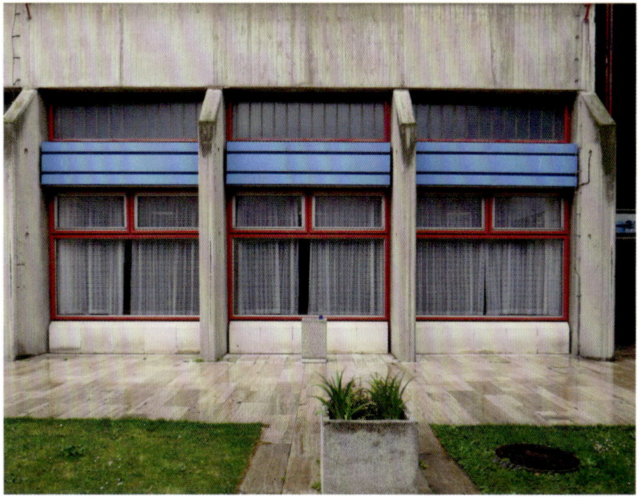

Hotel Družba, Bratislava, Slovakia

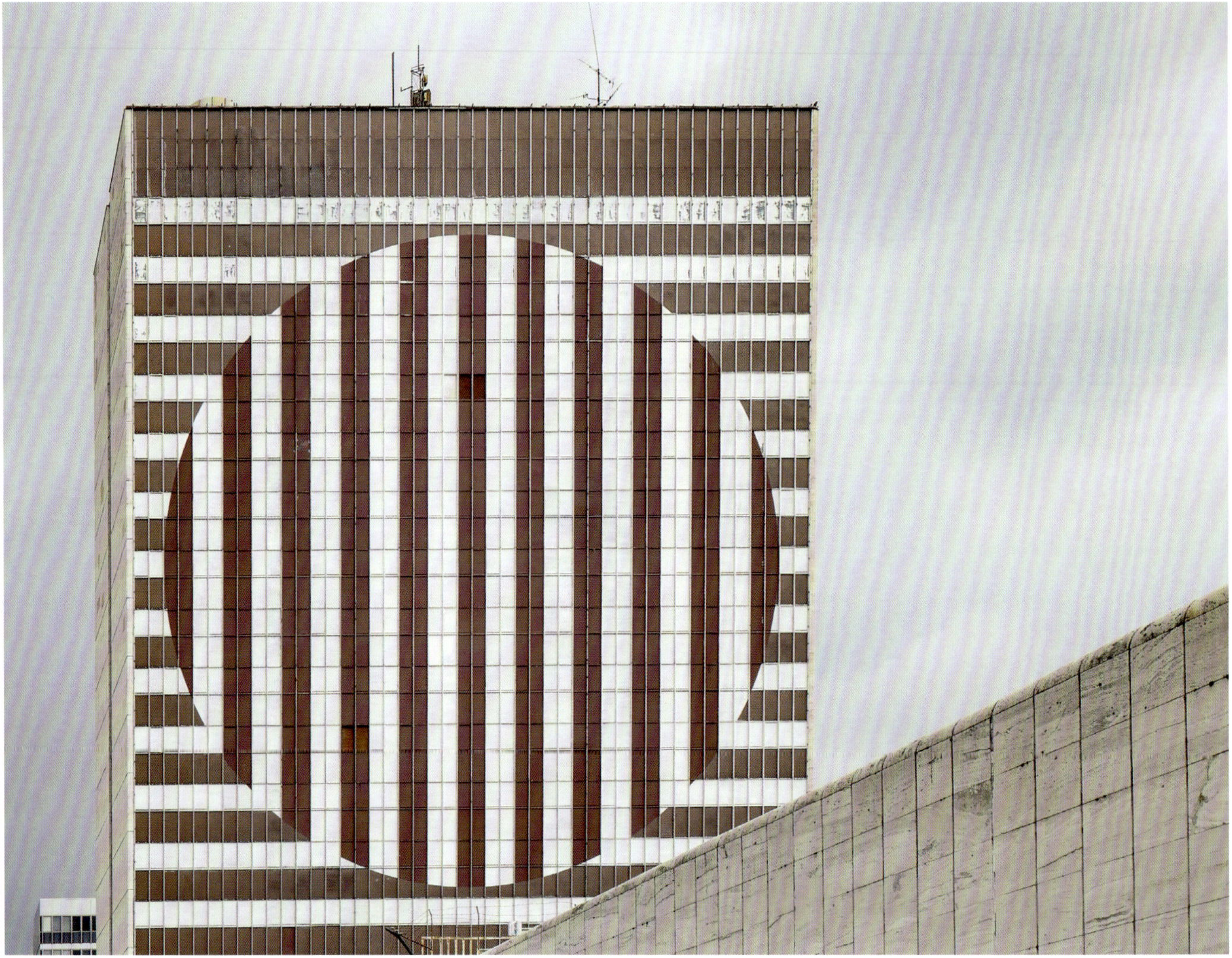

 Hotel Kyjev, Bratislava, Slovakia

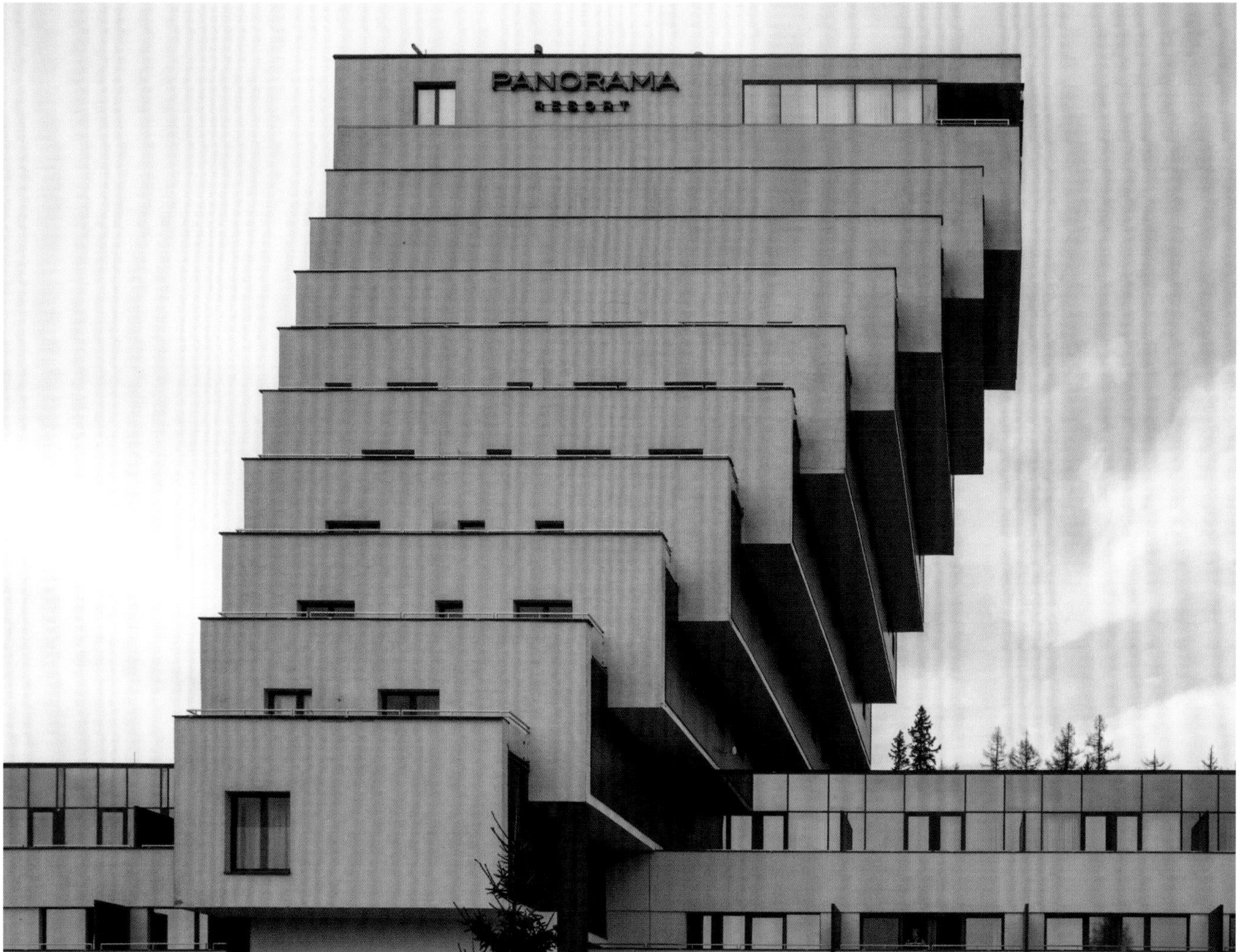

Hotel Panorama, Štrbské Pleso, Slovakia

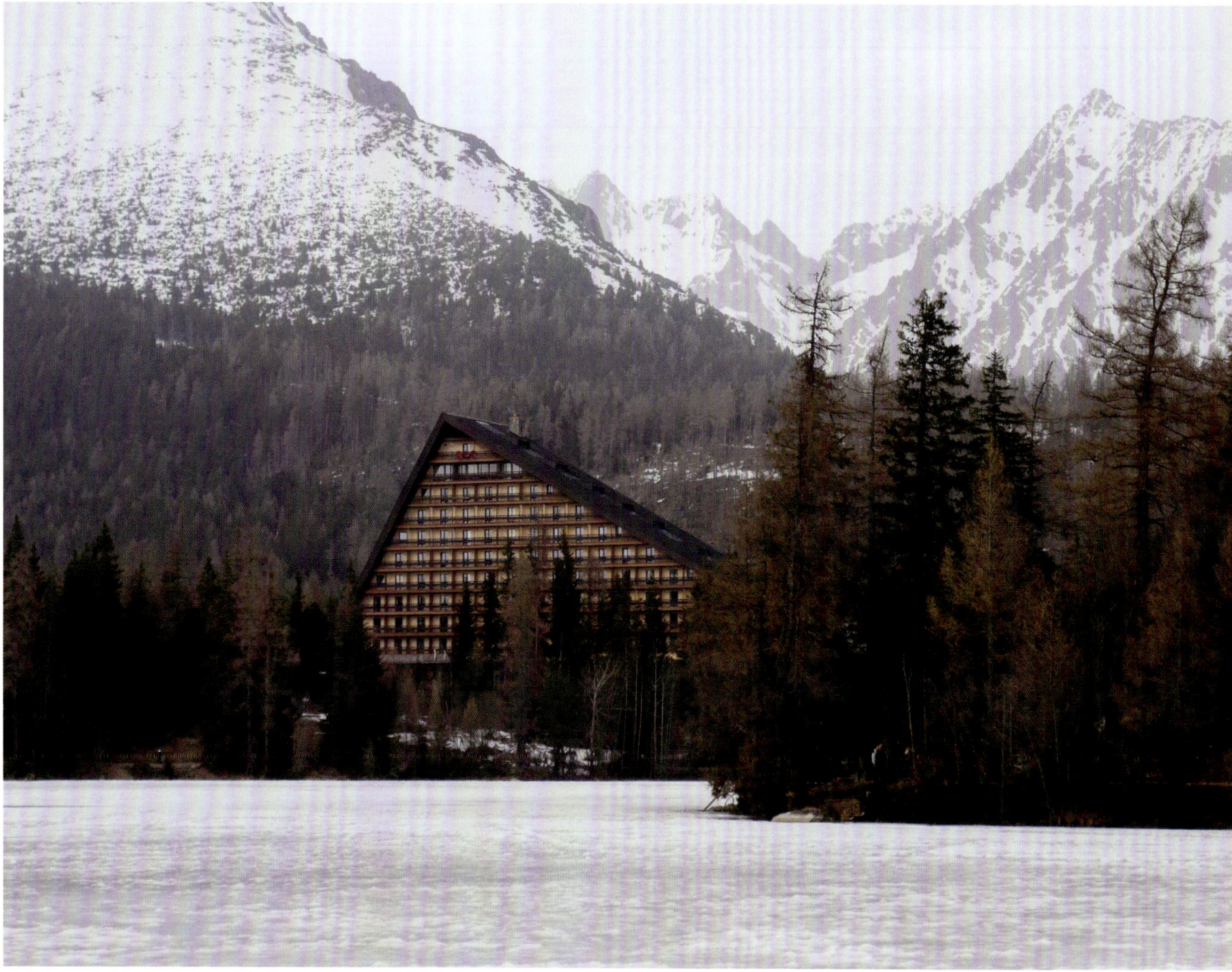

 Interhotel Patria, Štrbské Pleso, Slovakia

right: Hotel Montfort (former Hotel Poľana), Tatranská Javorina, Slovakia

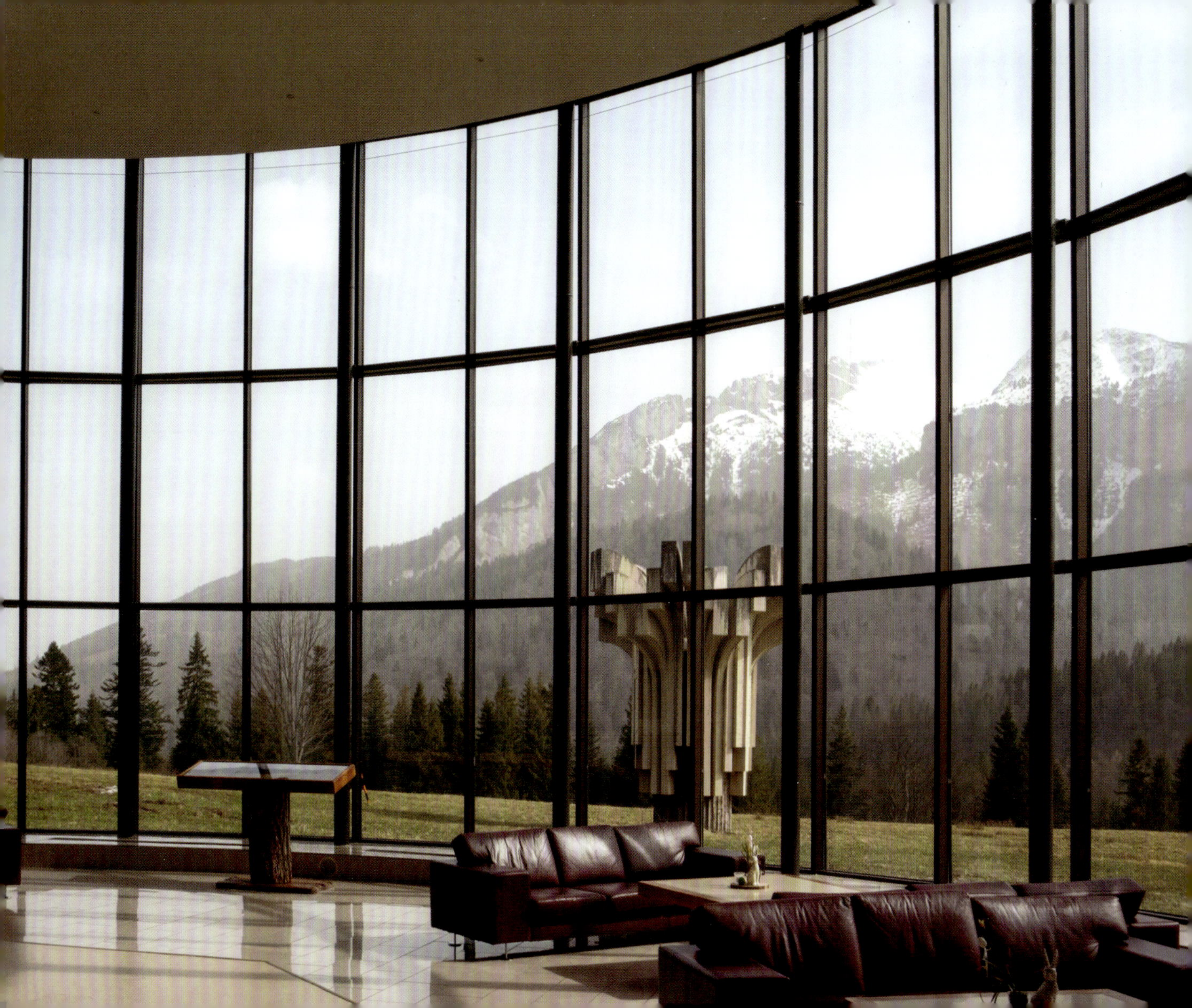

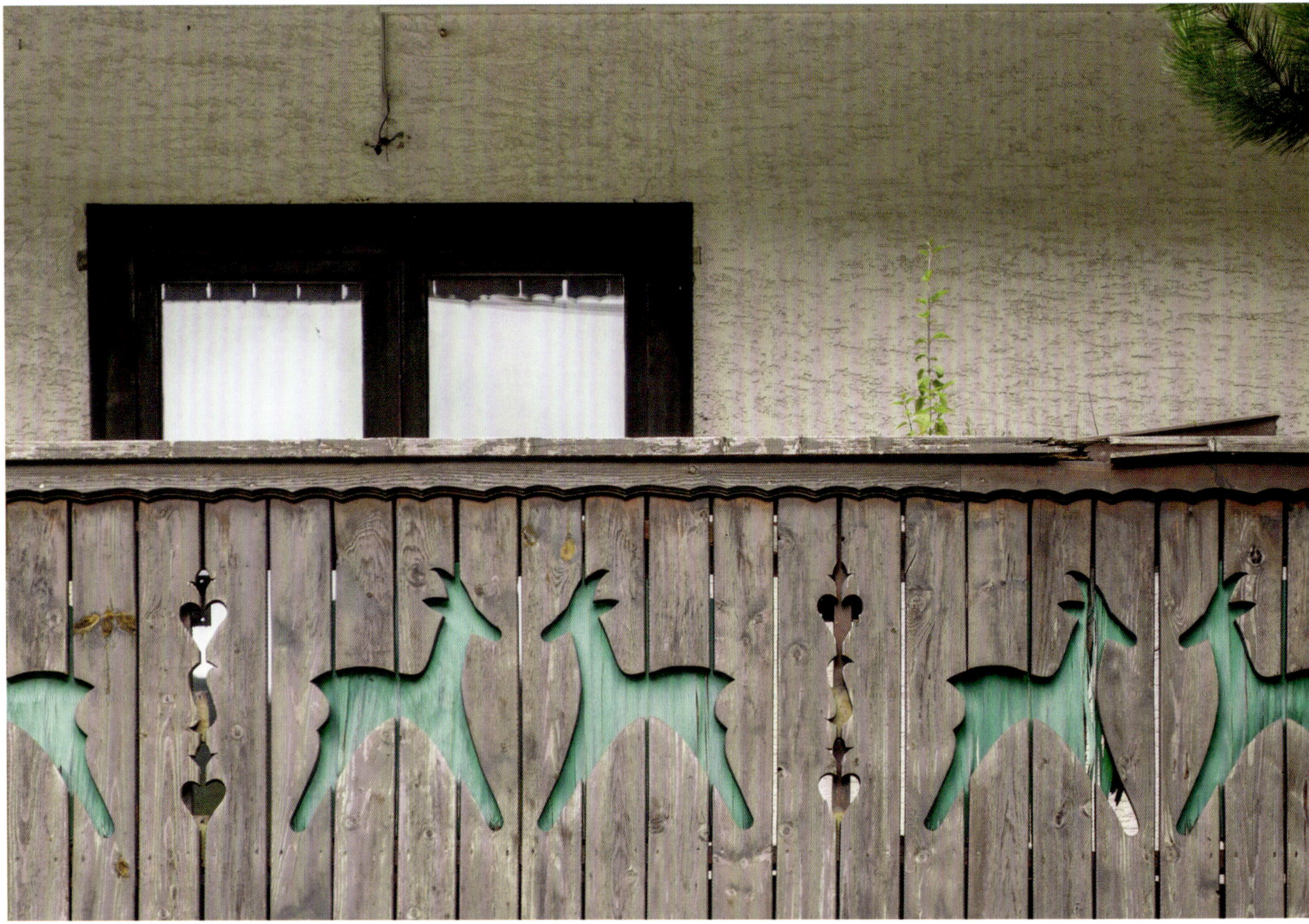

 Hotel Zlatorog, Ukanc, Slovenia

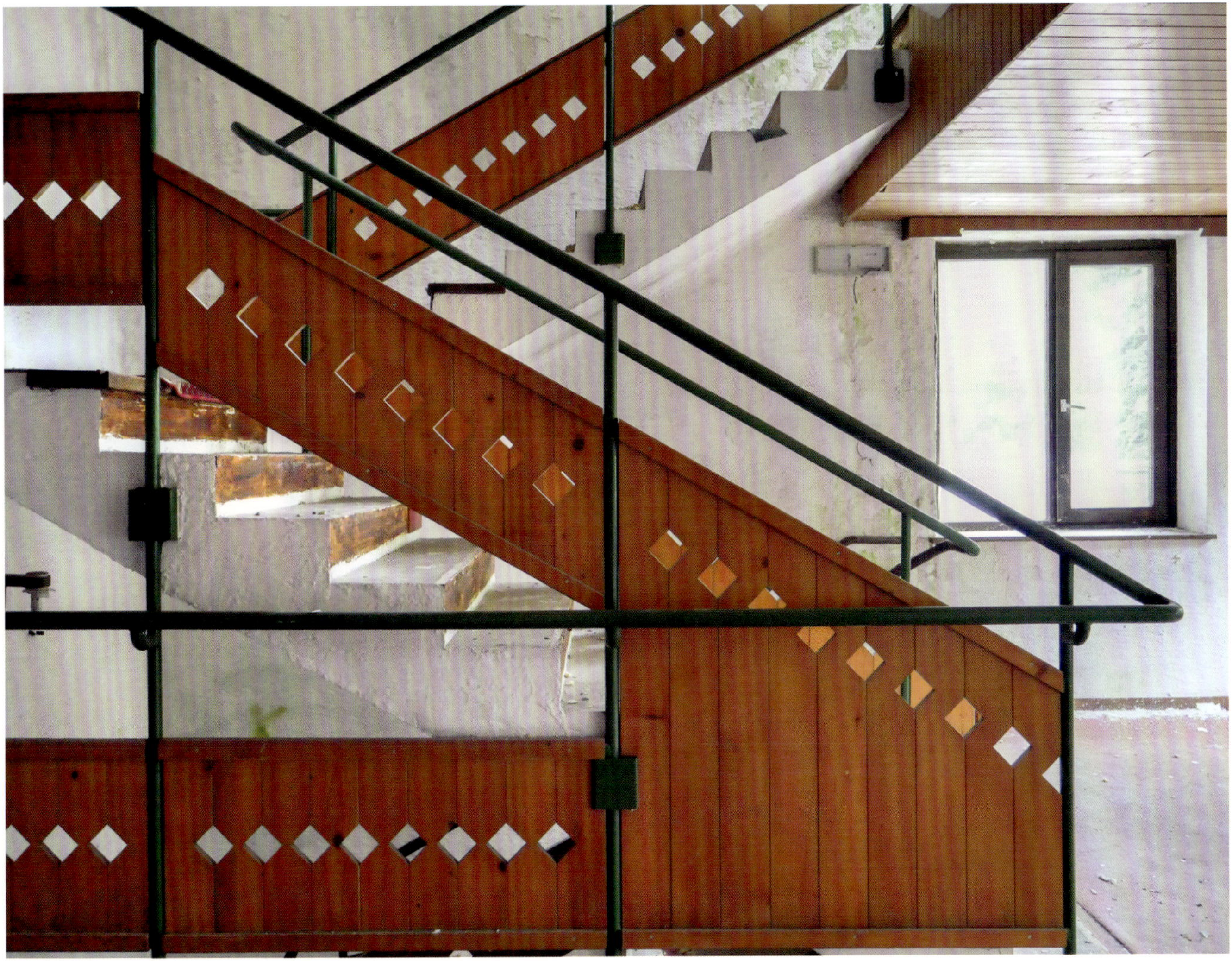

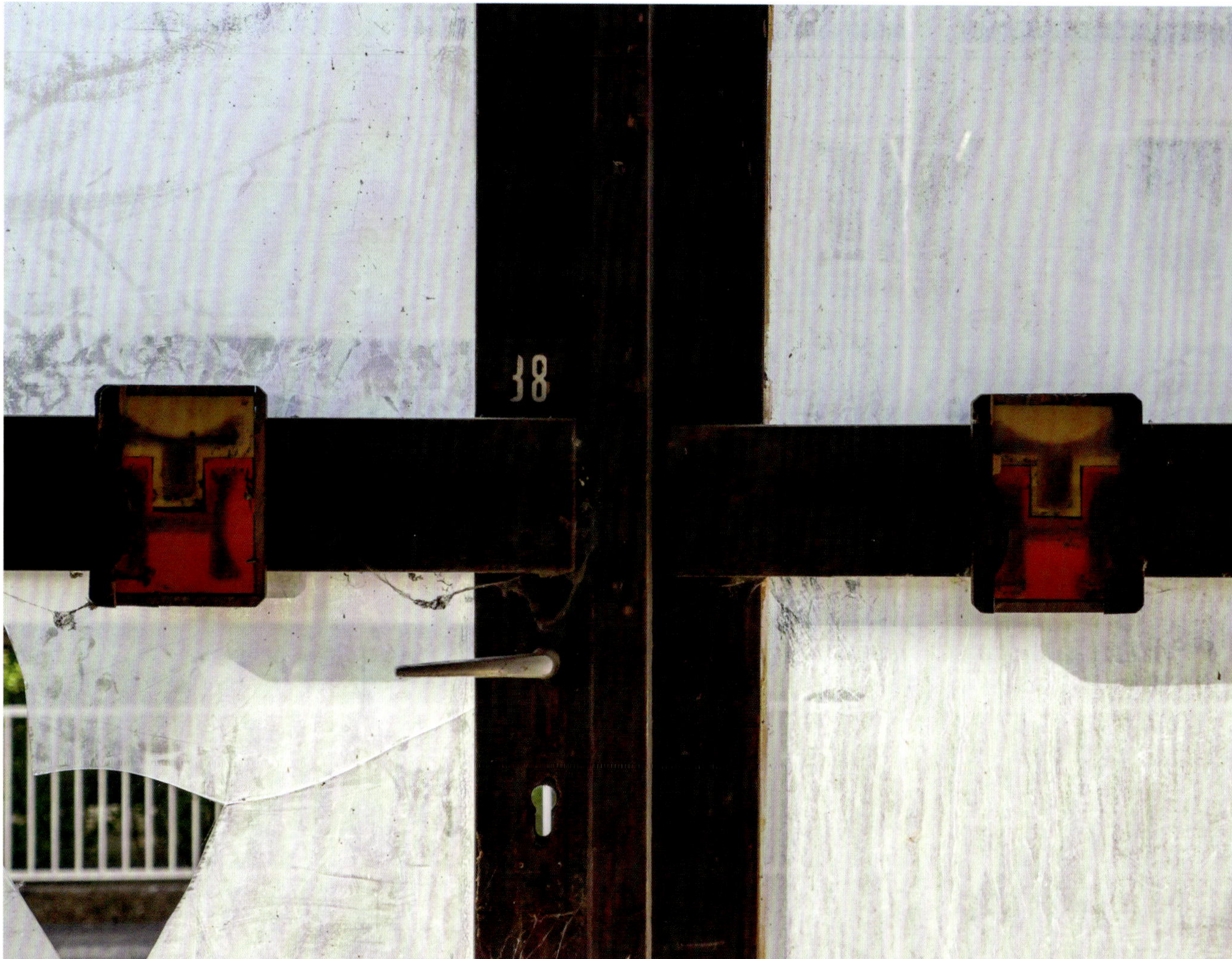

 Hotel Turist, Ilirska Bistrica, Slovenia

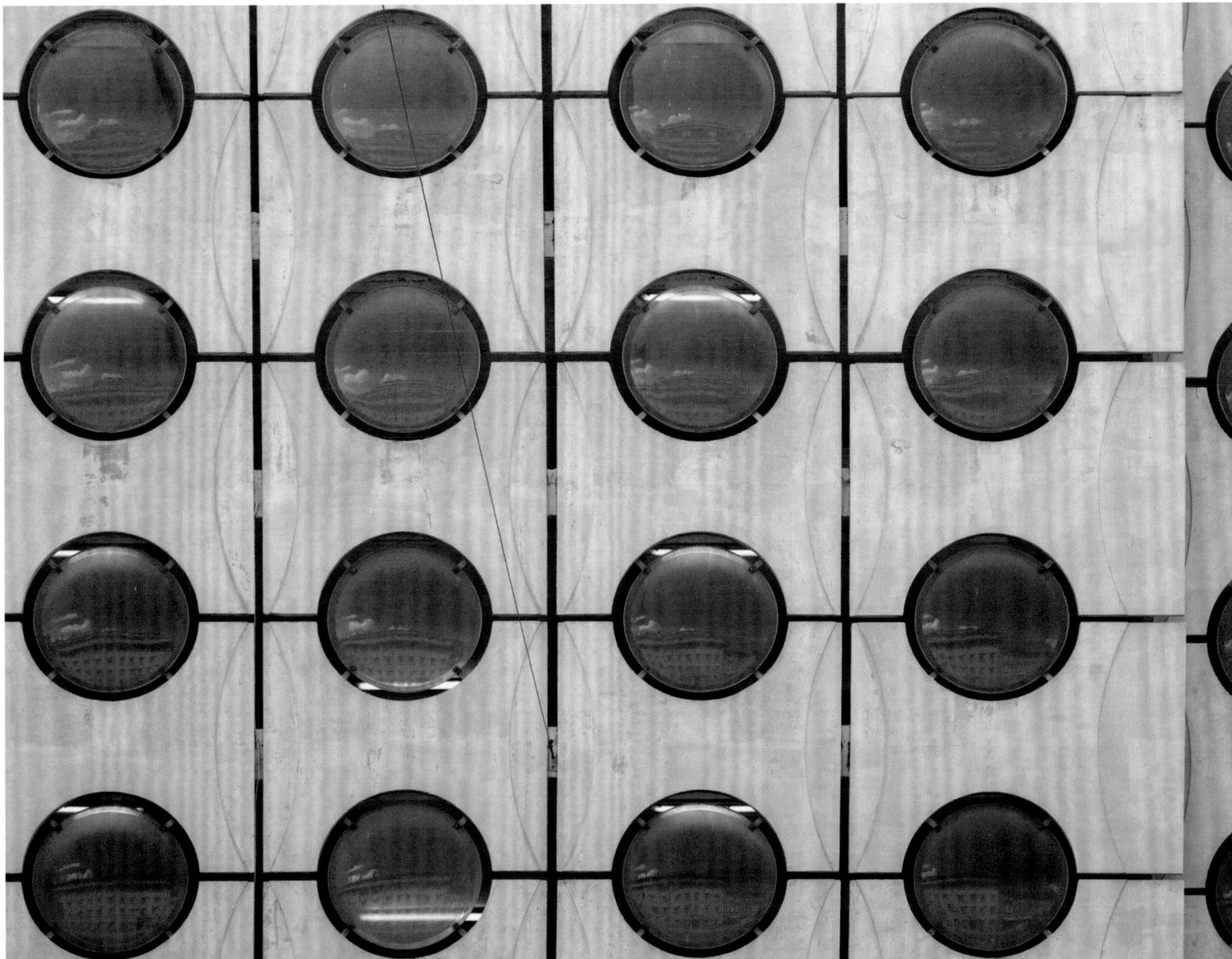

Hotel Central, Ljubljana, Slovenia

TAJIKISTAN

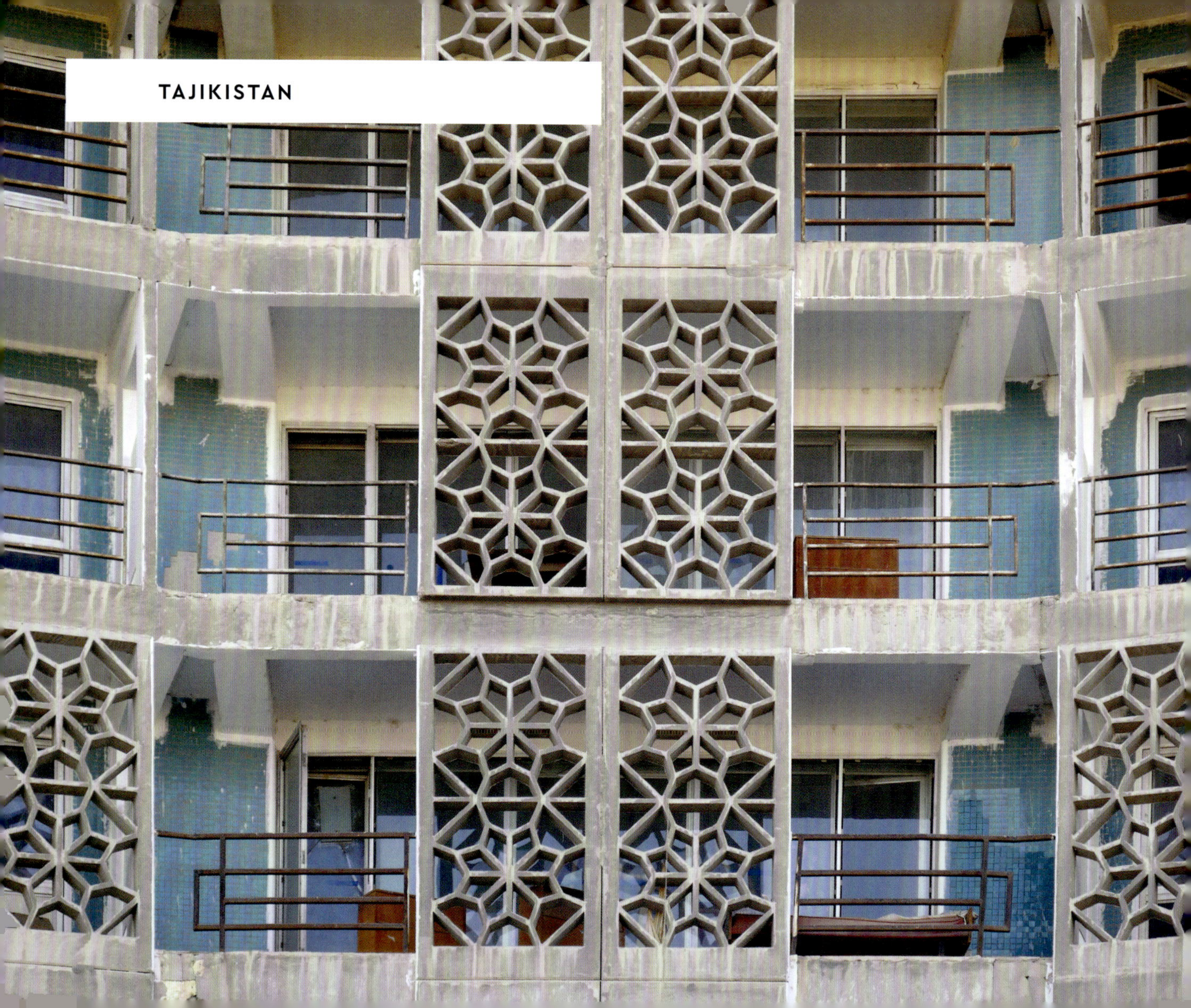

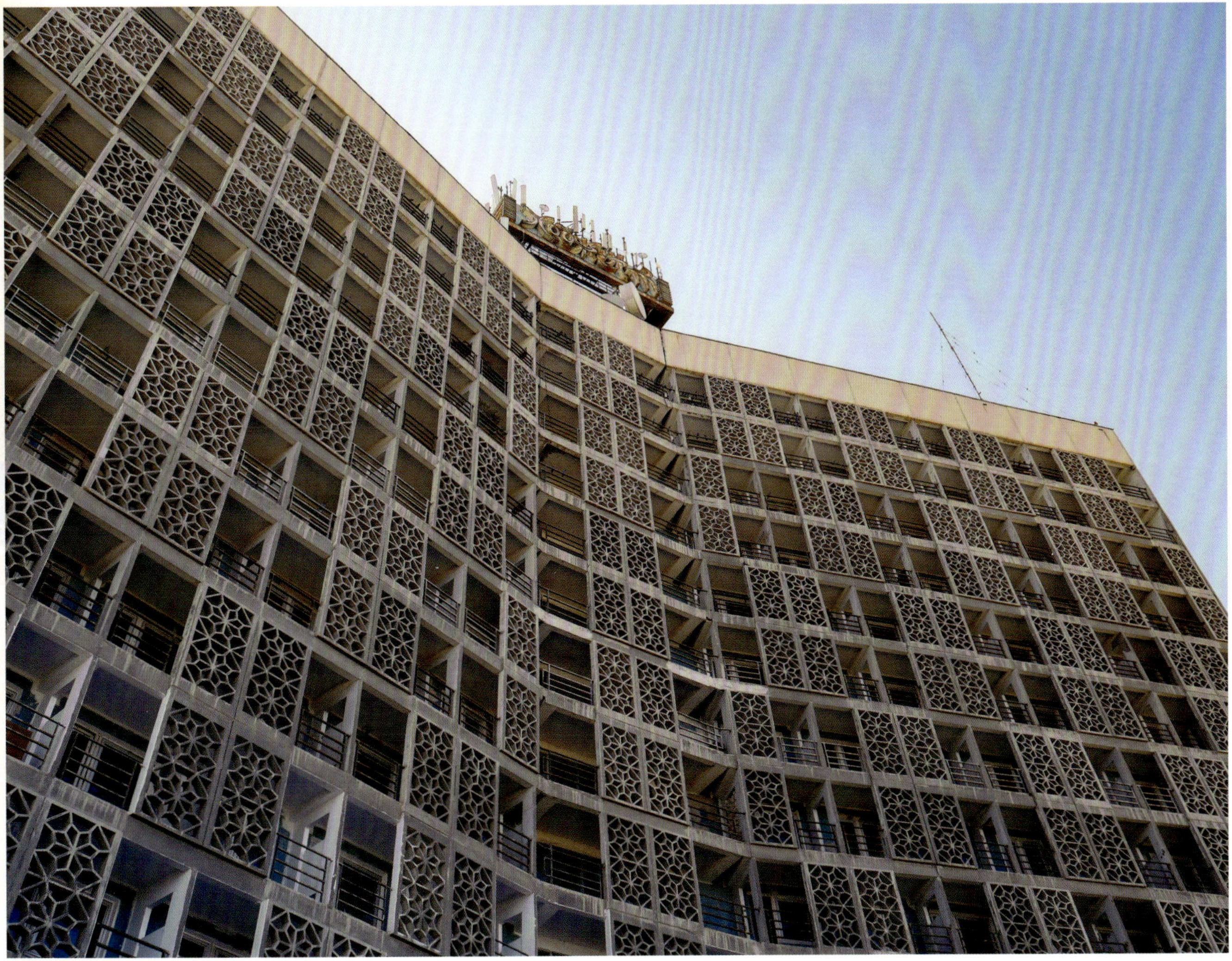

Hotel Khuzhand, Buston, Tajikistan

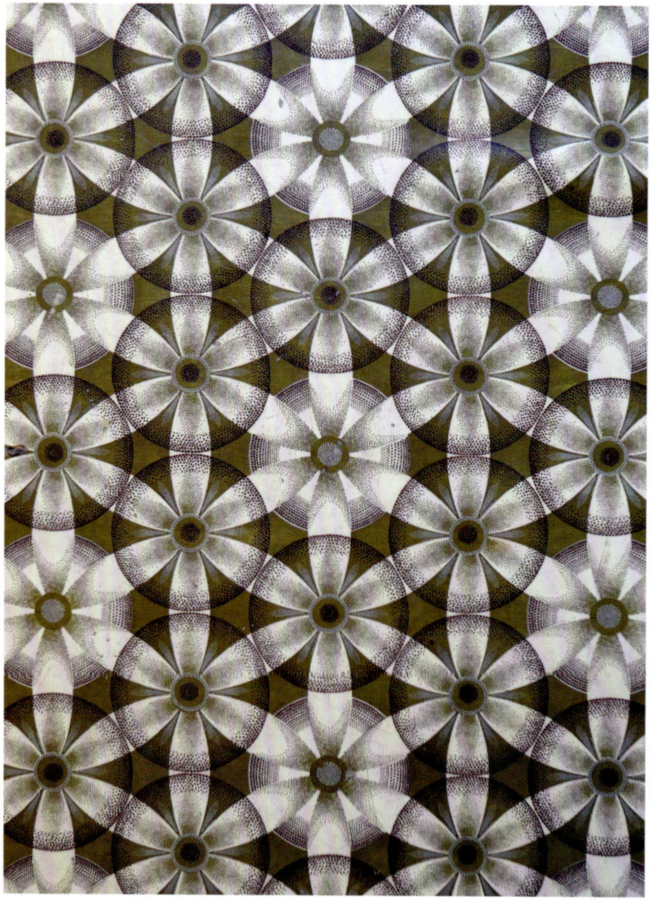

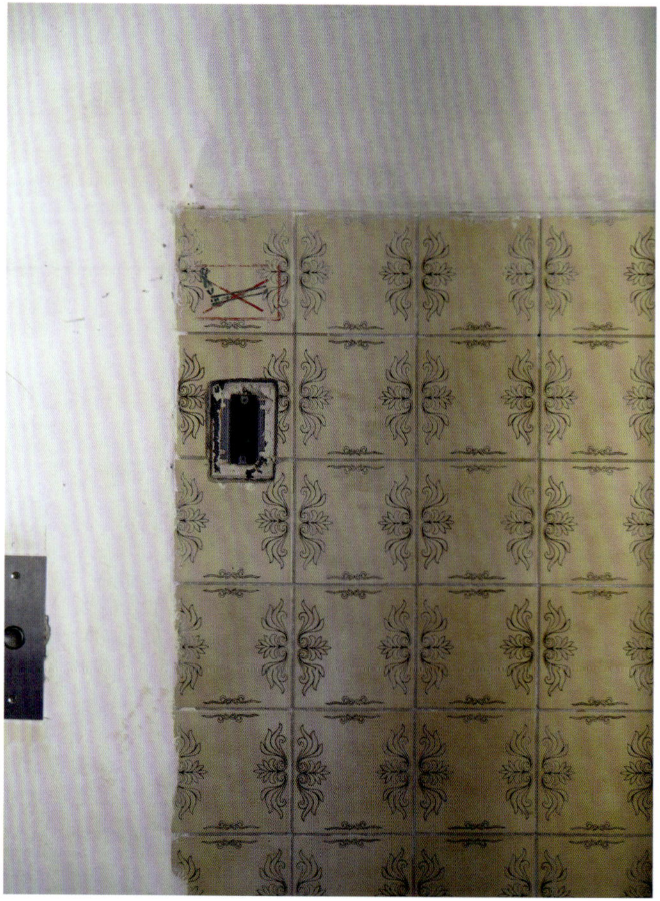

 Hotel Avesto (former Hotel Oktyabrskaya), Dushanbe, Tajikistan

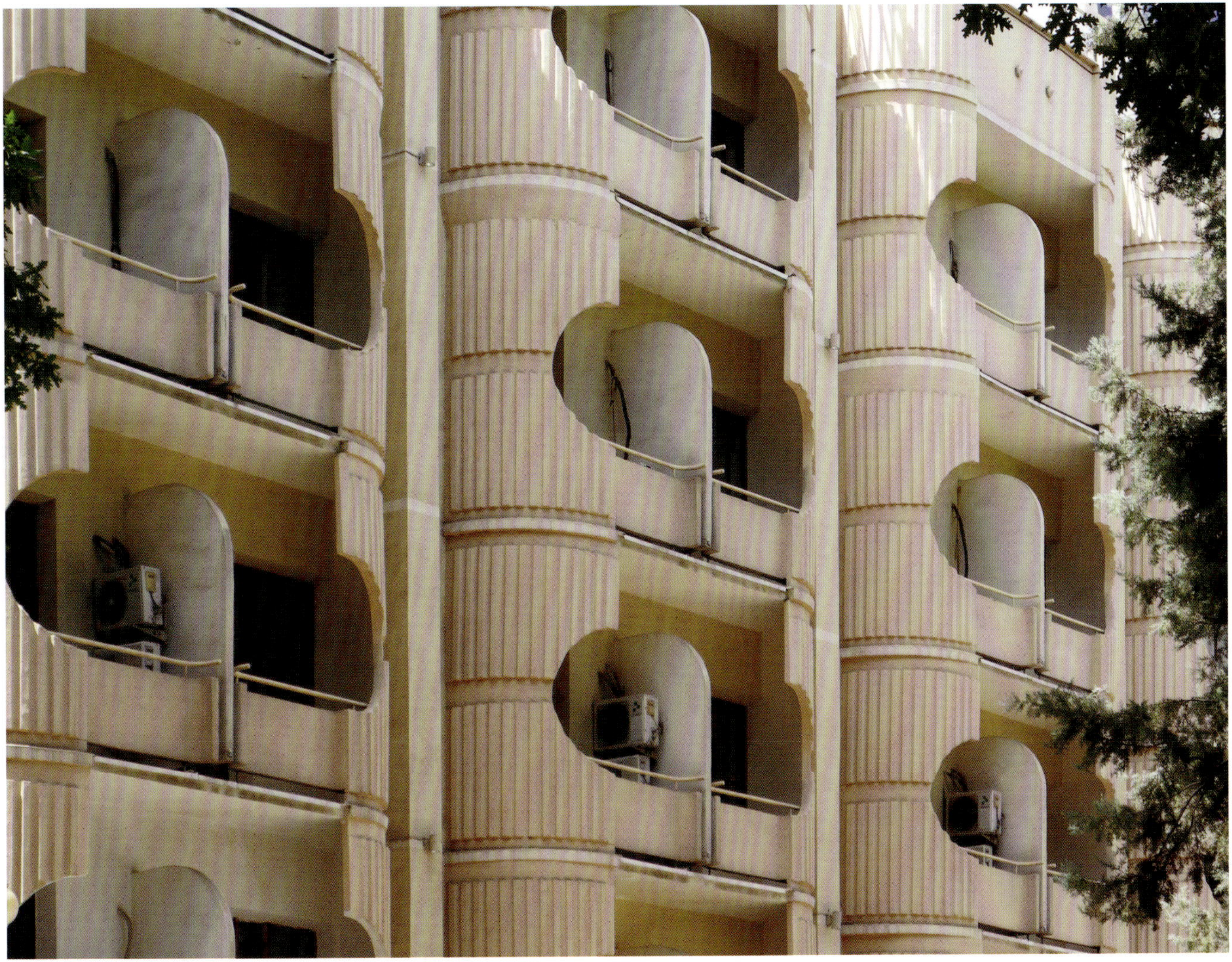

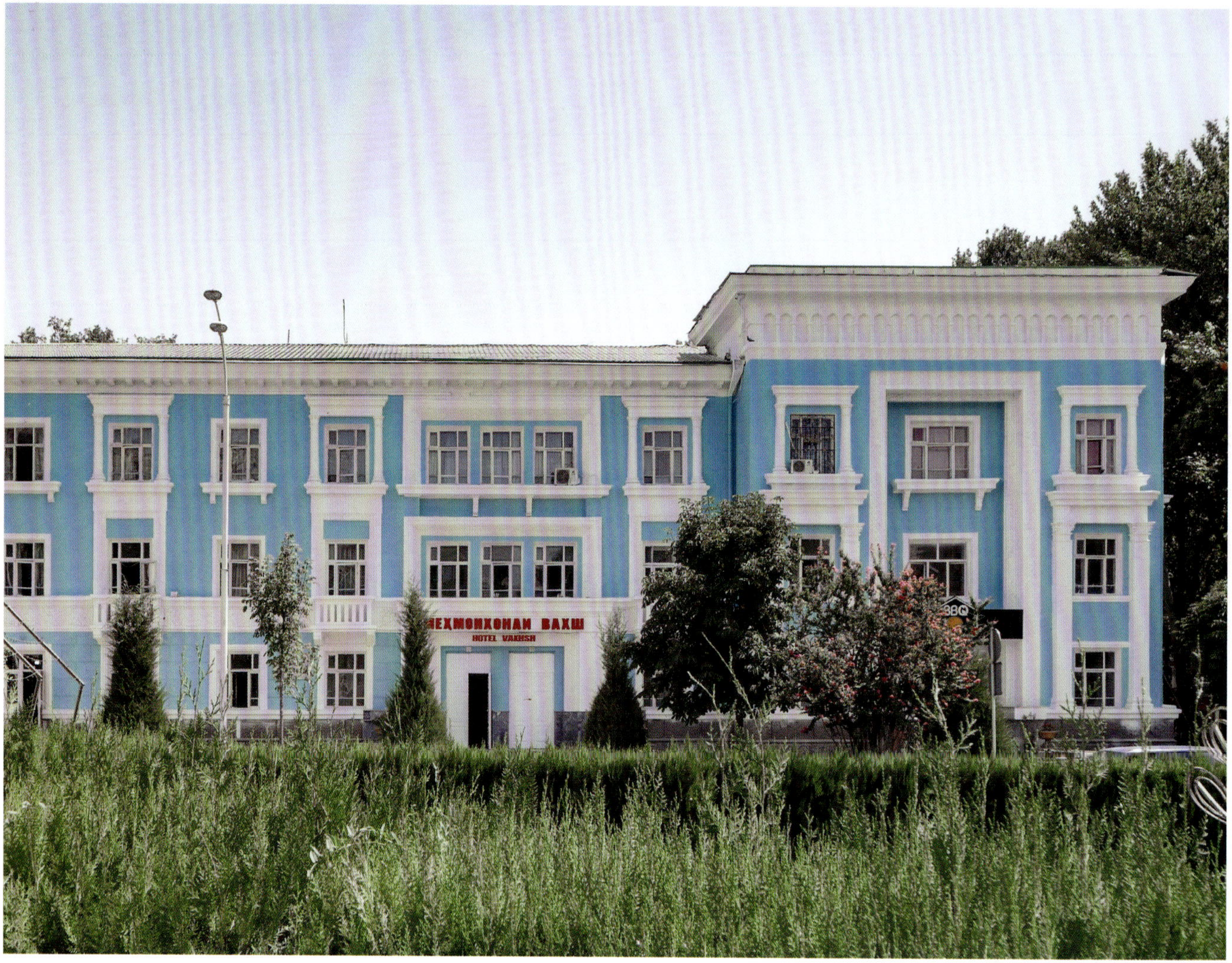

Hotel Vakhsh (former Hotel Stalinabad), Dushanbe, Tajikistan

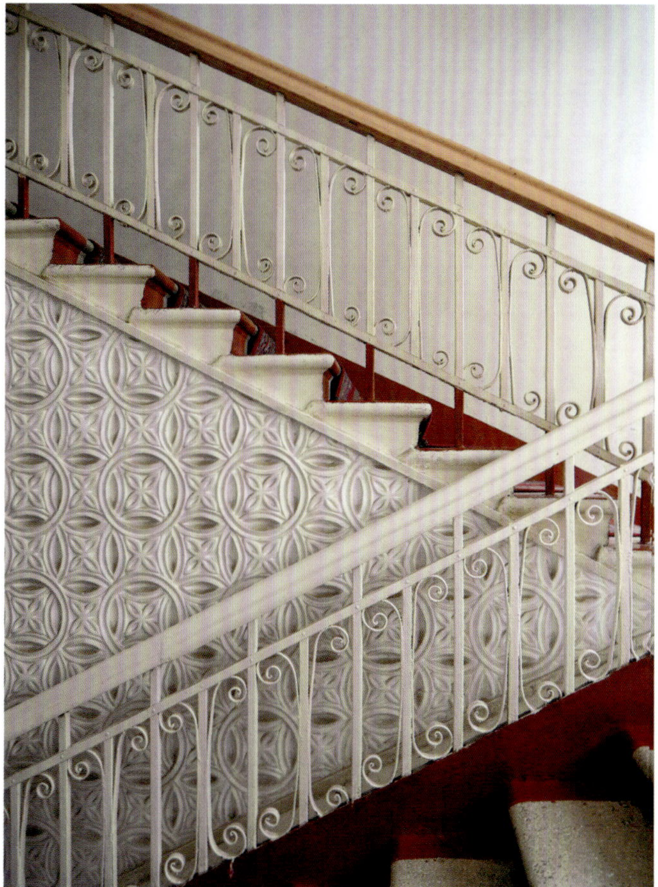

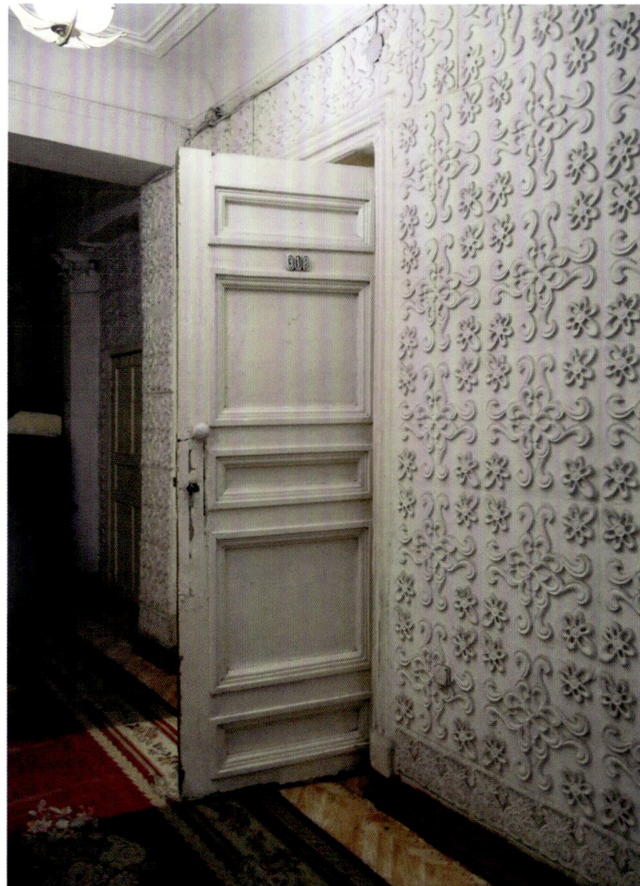
308

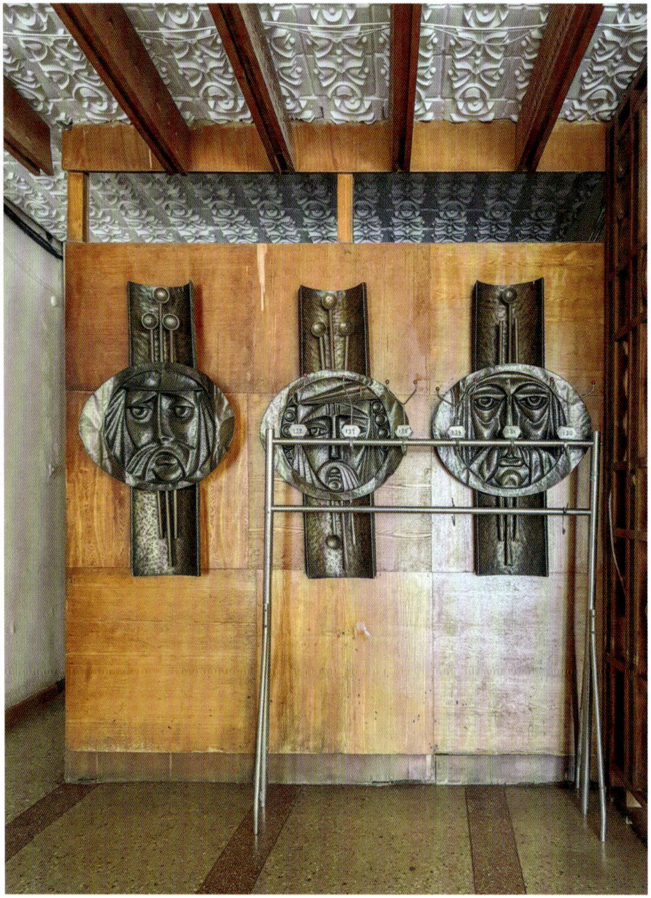

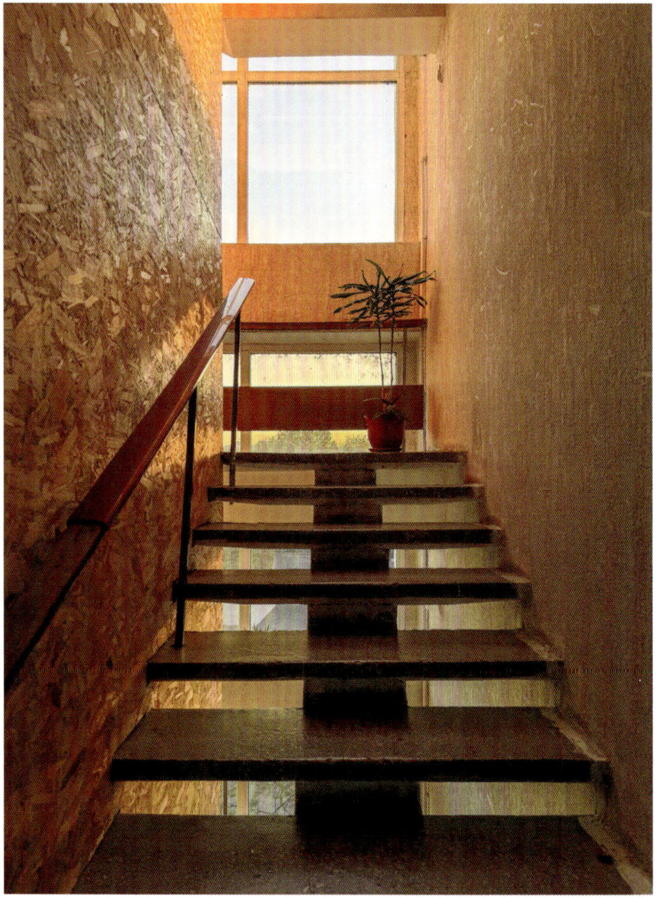

 Hotel Prietenia, Bender, Transnistria

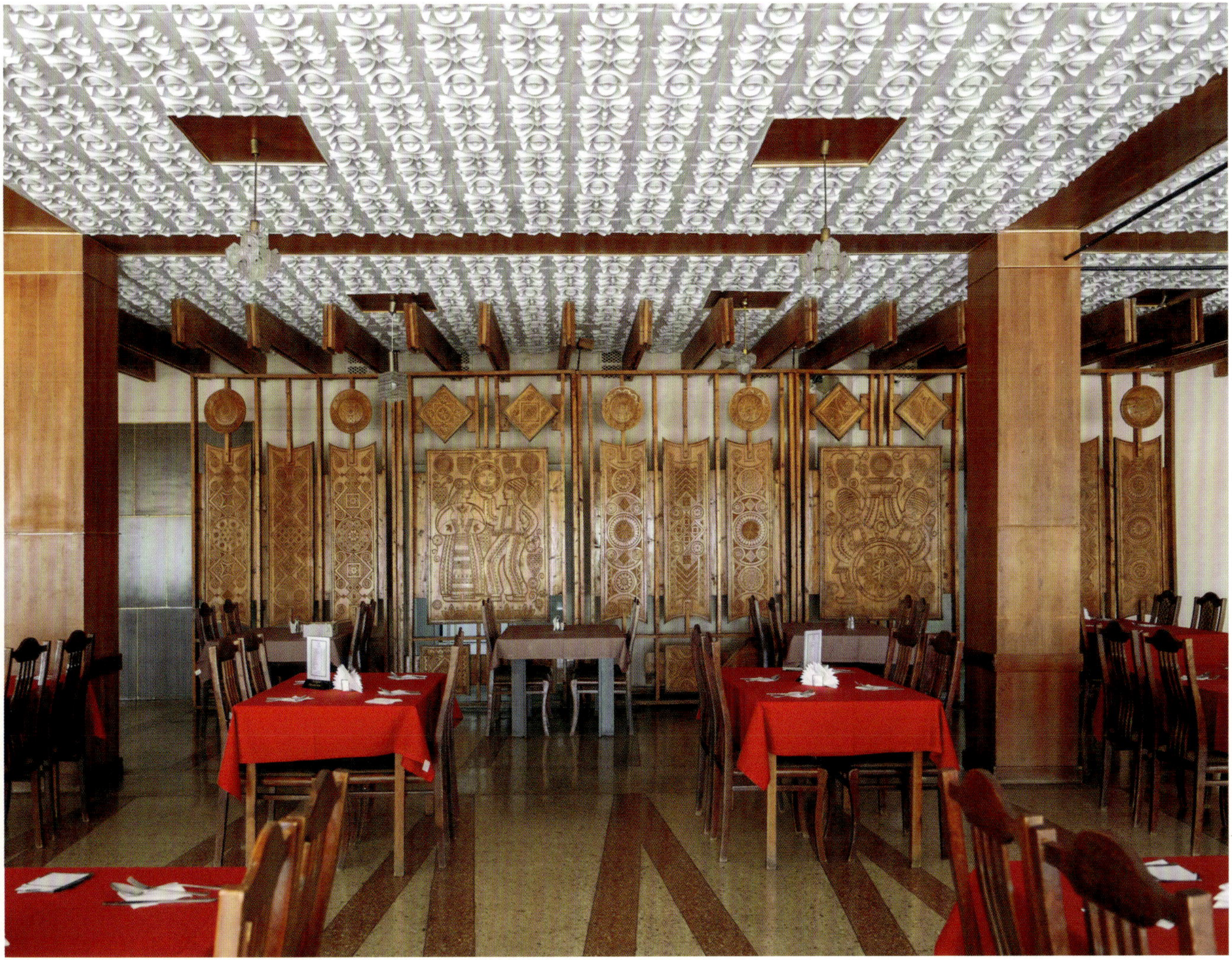

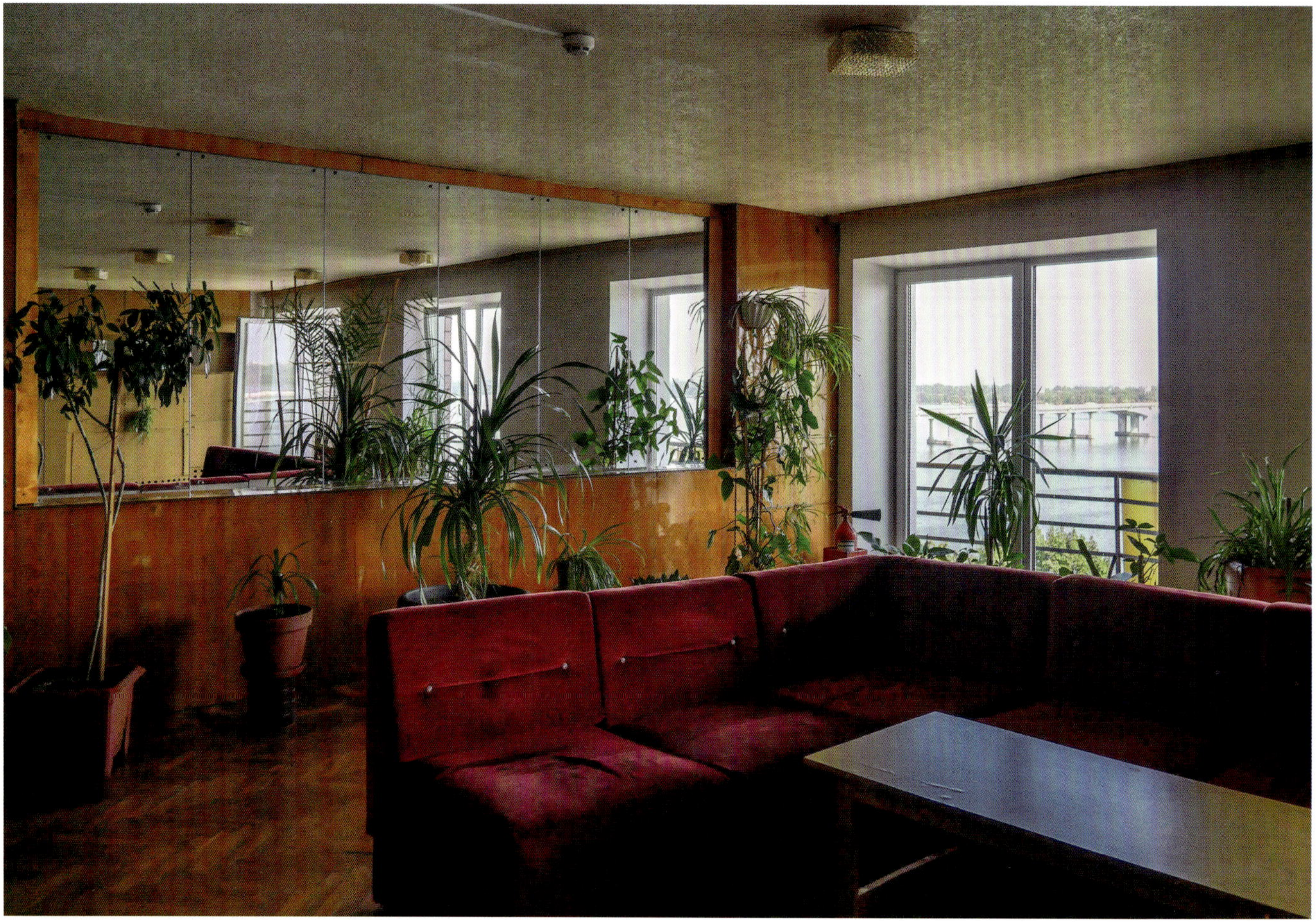

 Hotel Dnepropetrovsk, Dnipro, Ukraine

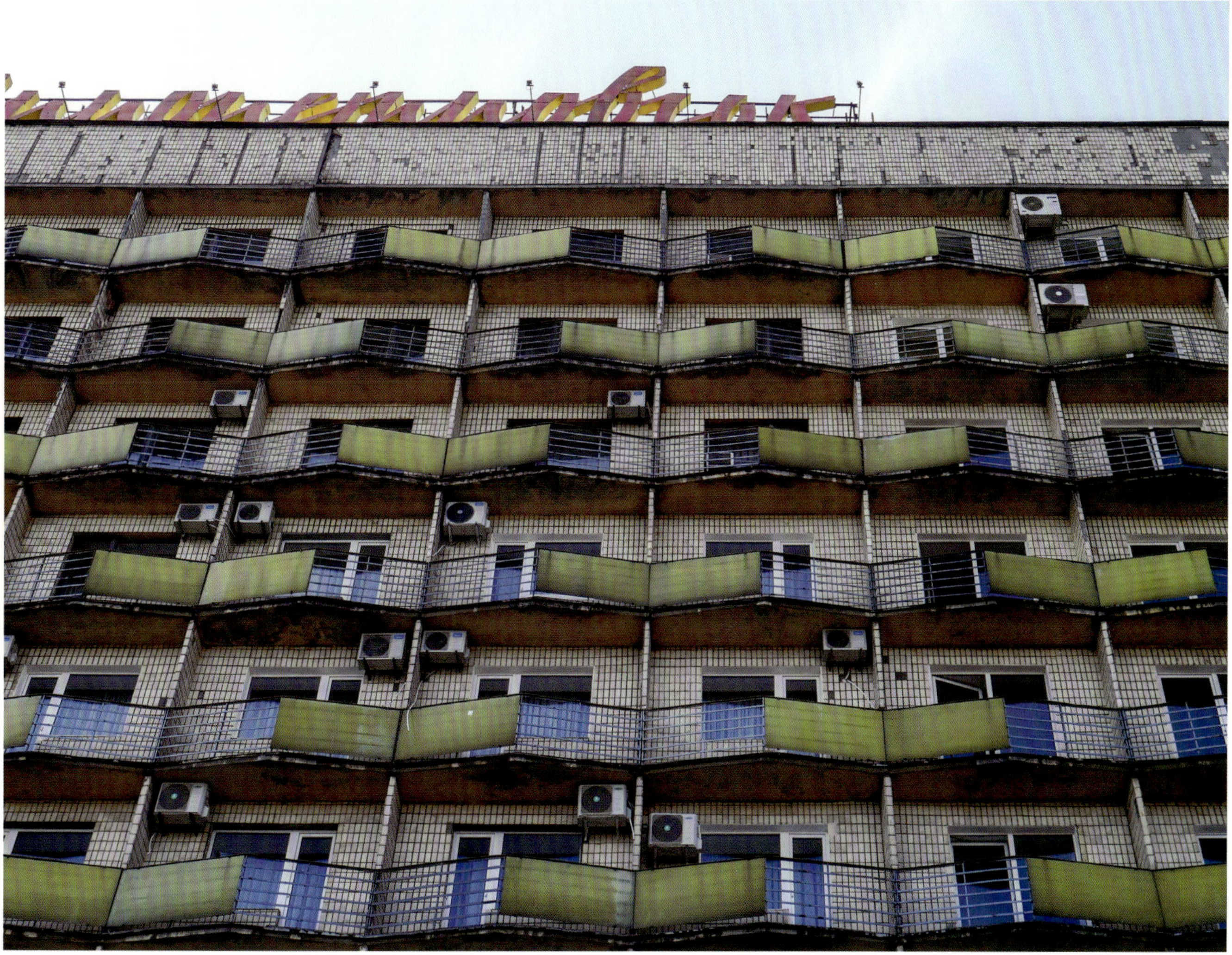

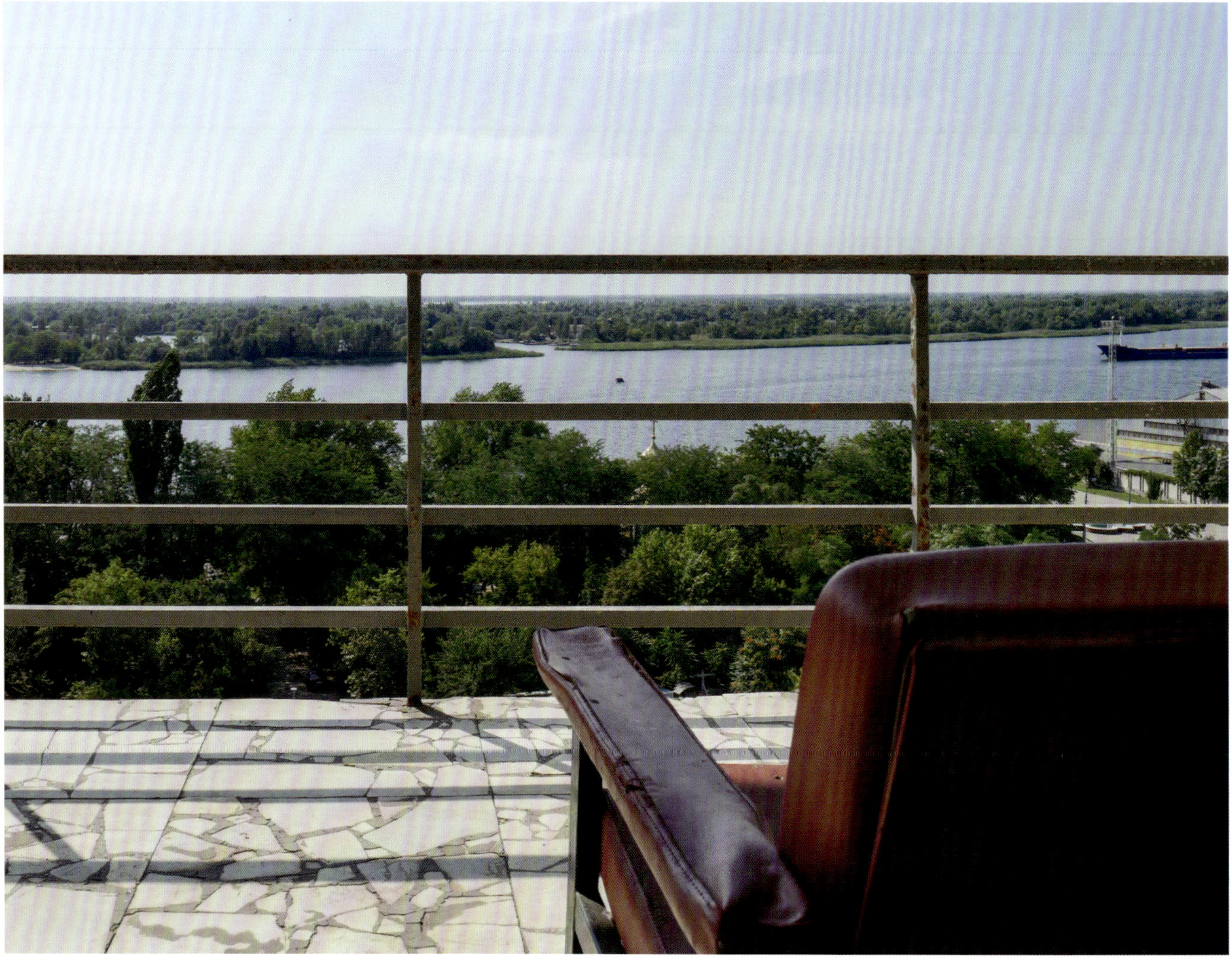

 Hotel Fregat, Kherson, Ukraine

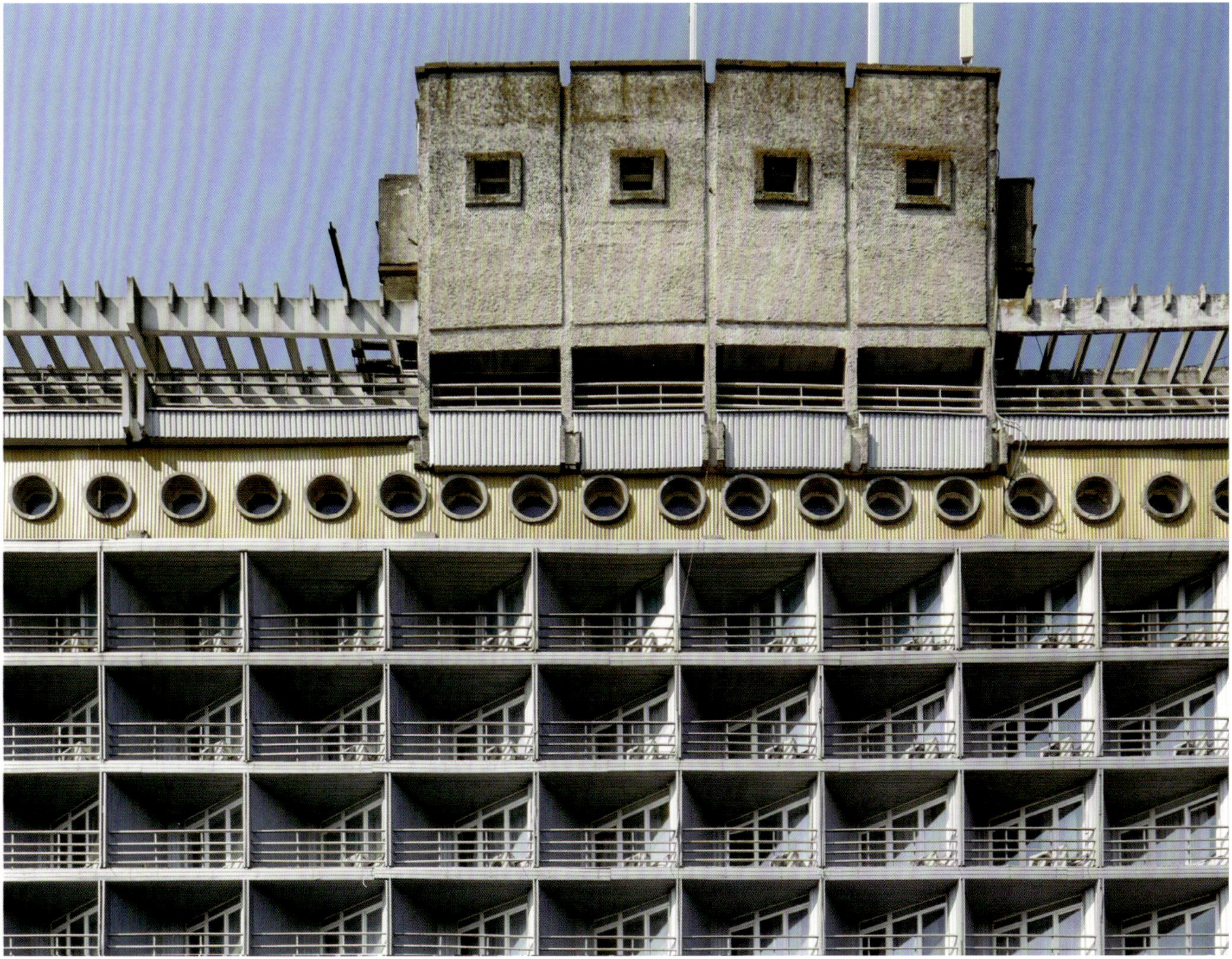

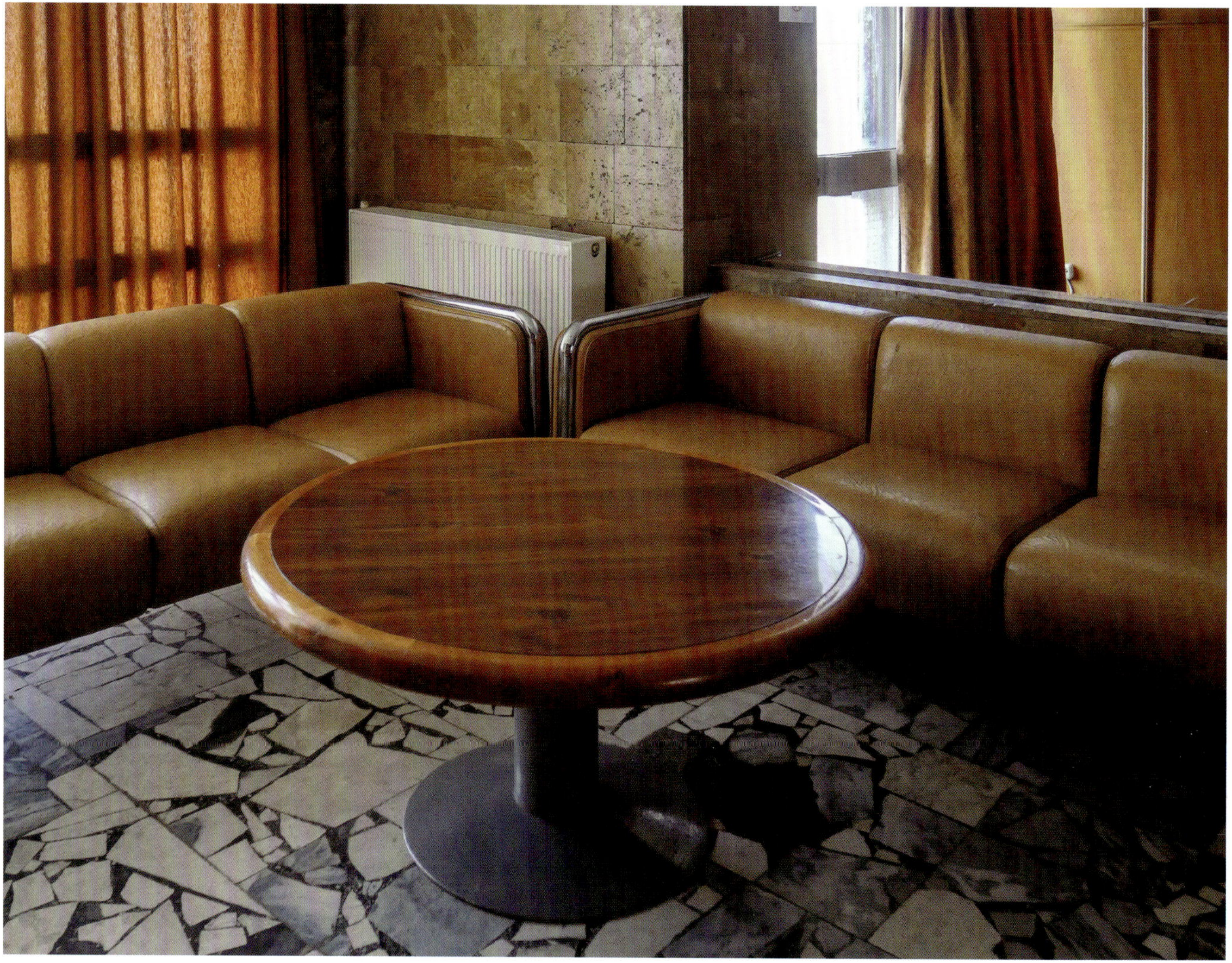

 Hotel Fregat, Kherson, Ukraine

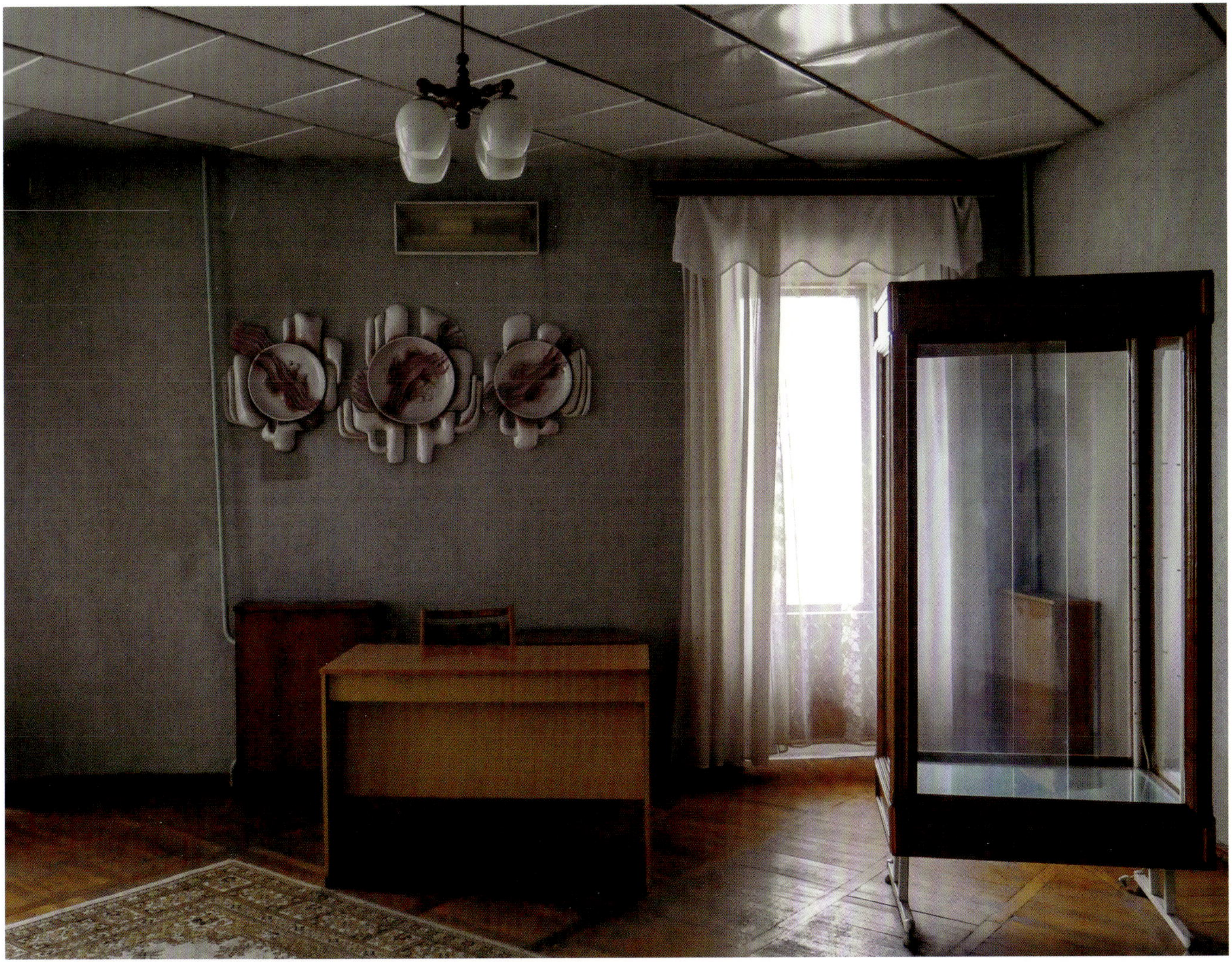

Hotel Evropa, Kropyvnytskyi, Ukraine

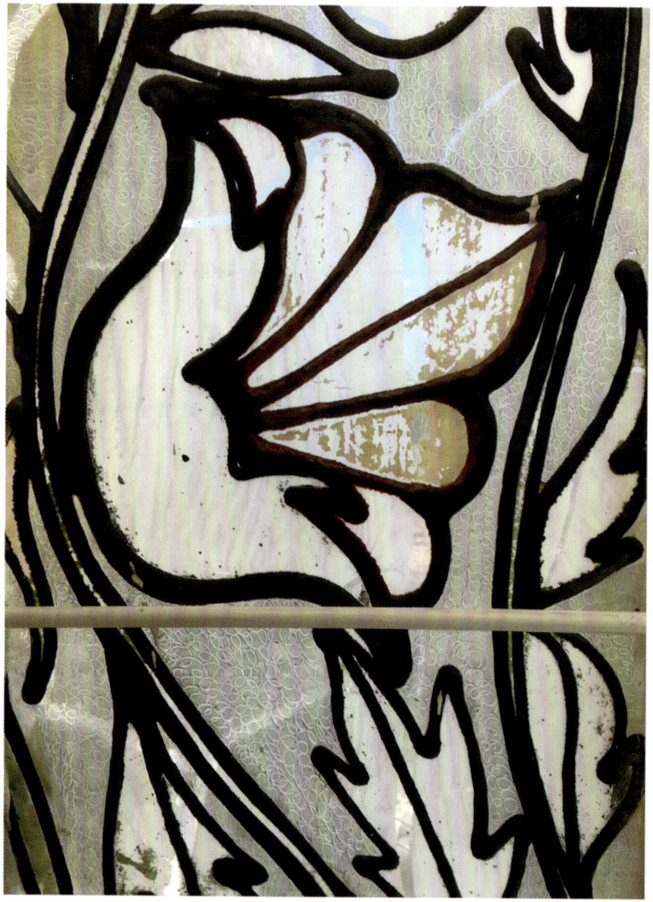

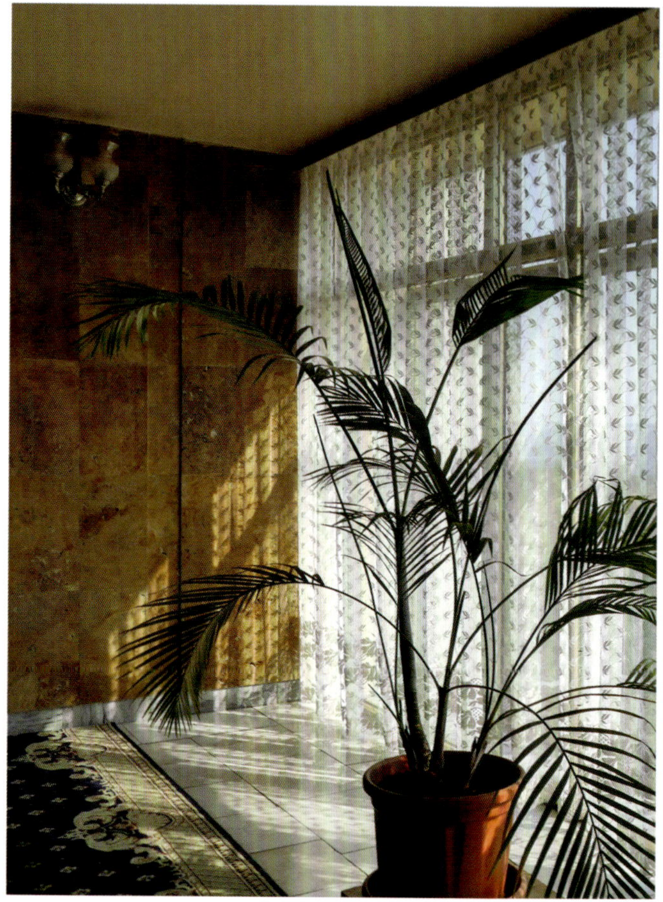

 Hotel Ukraina (former Hotel Moskva), Kyiv, Ukraine

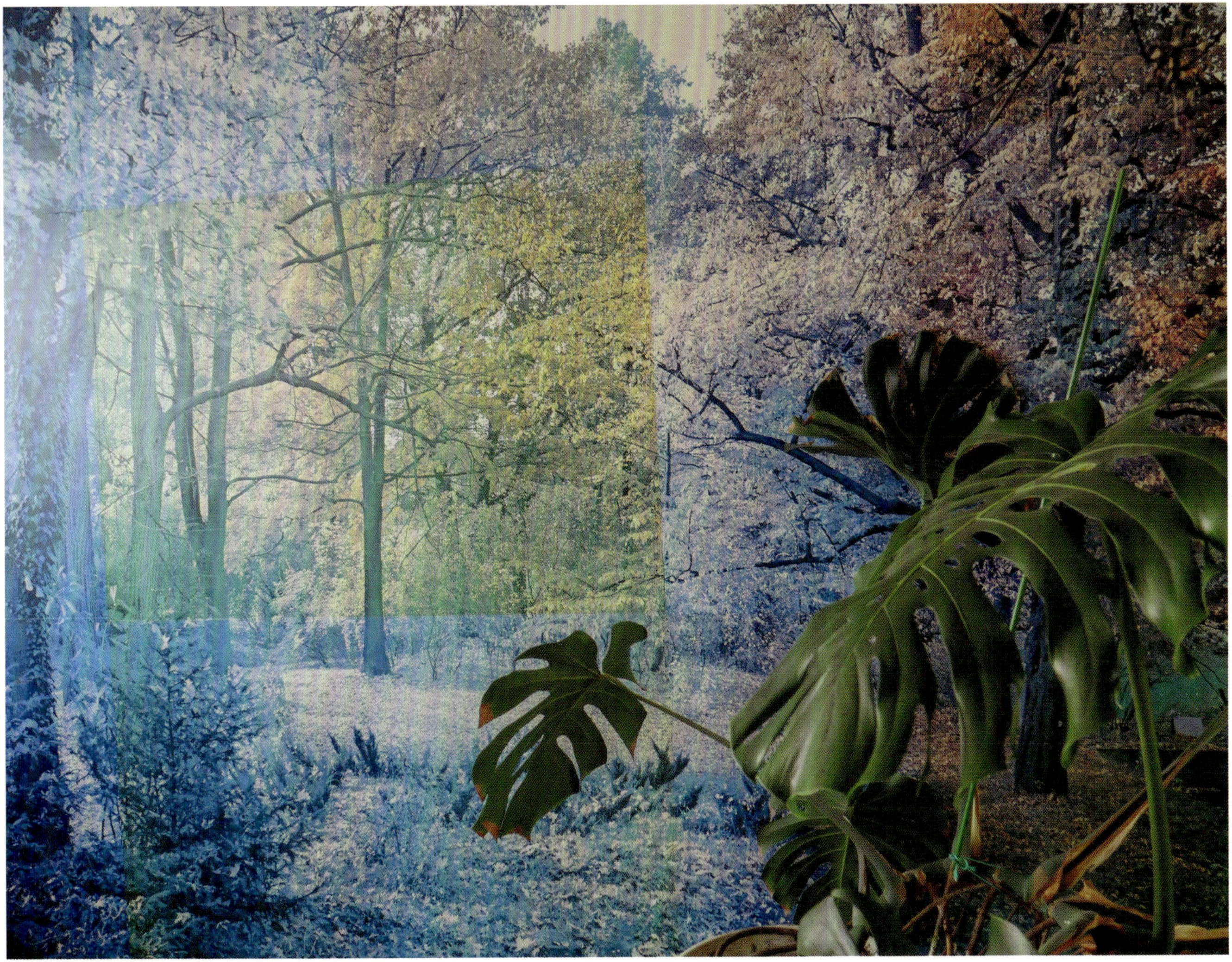

Hotel Dnipro (former Accommodation for Government Employees), Cherkasy, Ukraine

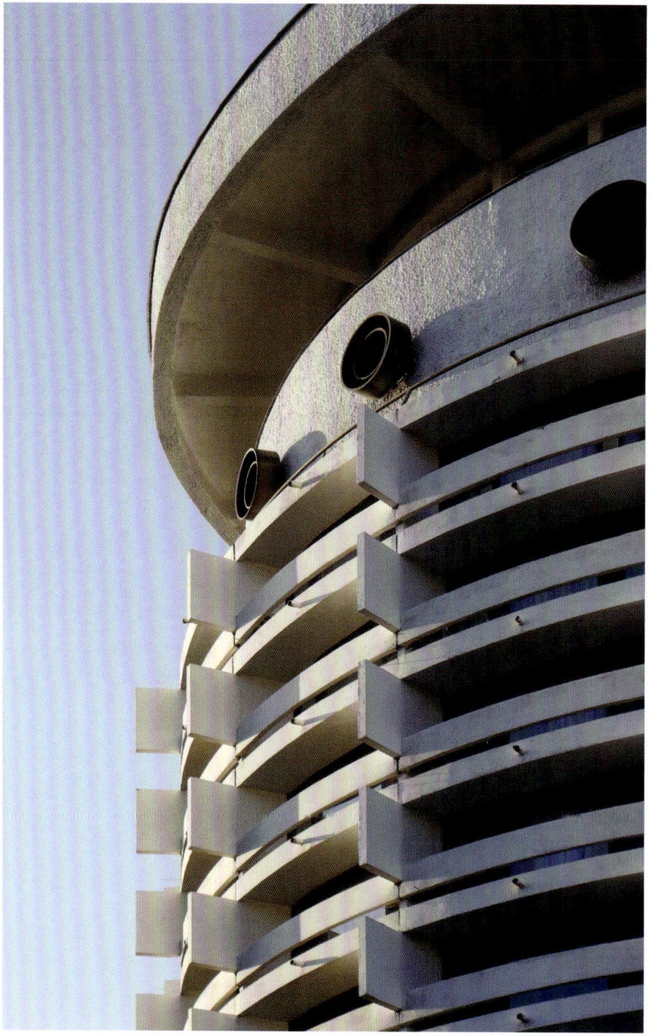

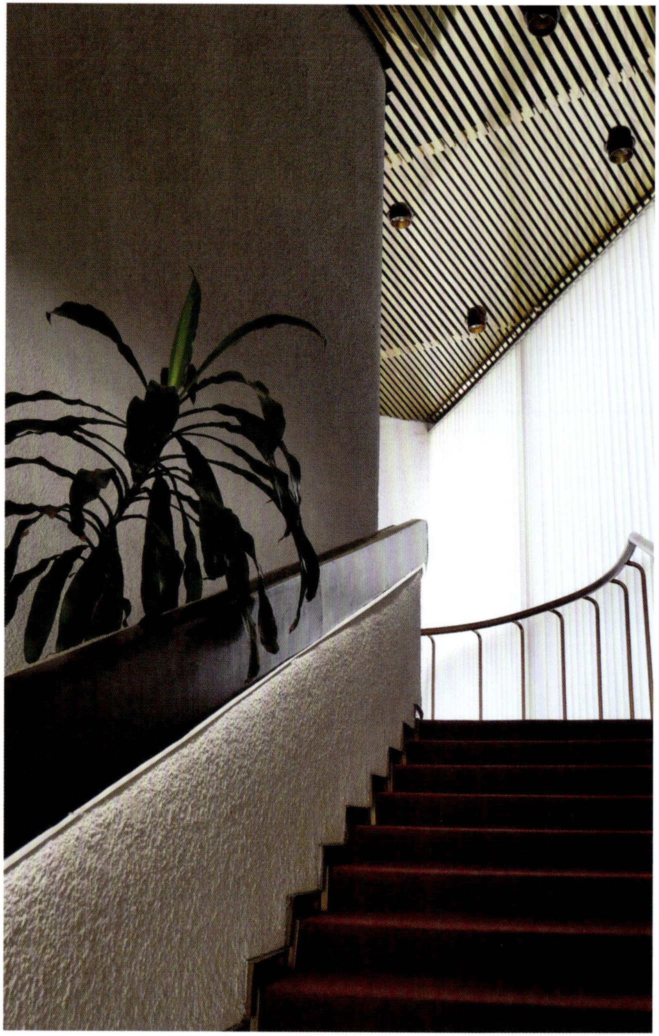

 Hotel Salyut, Kyiv, Ukraine

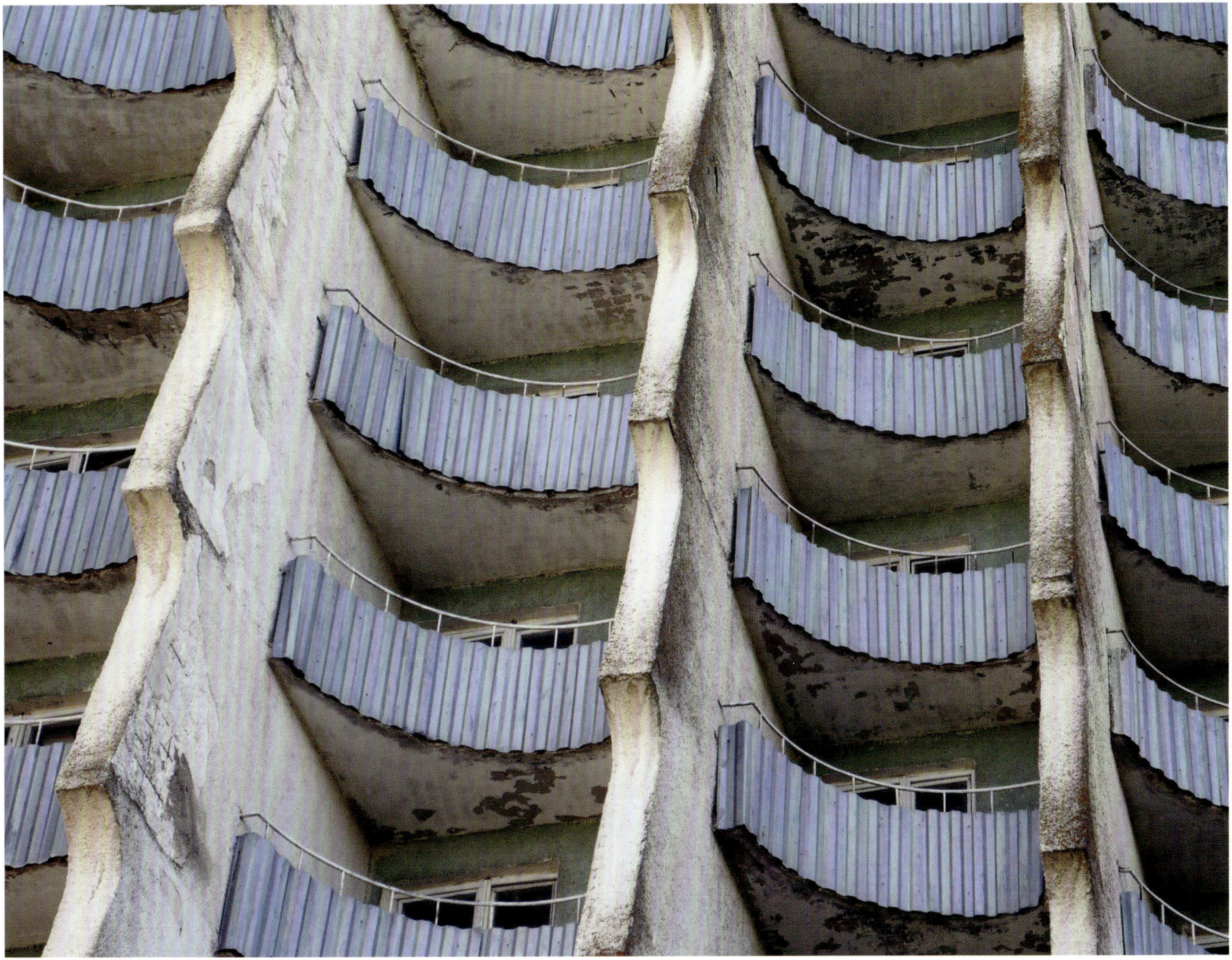

Hotel Yuzhny, Odessa, Ukraine

UZBEKISTAN

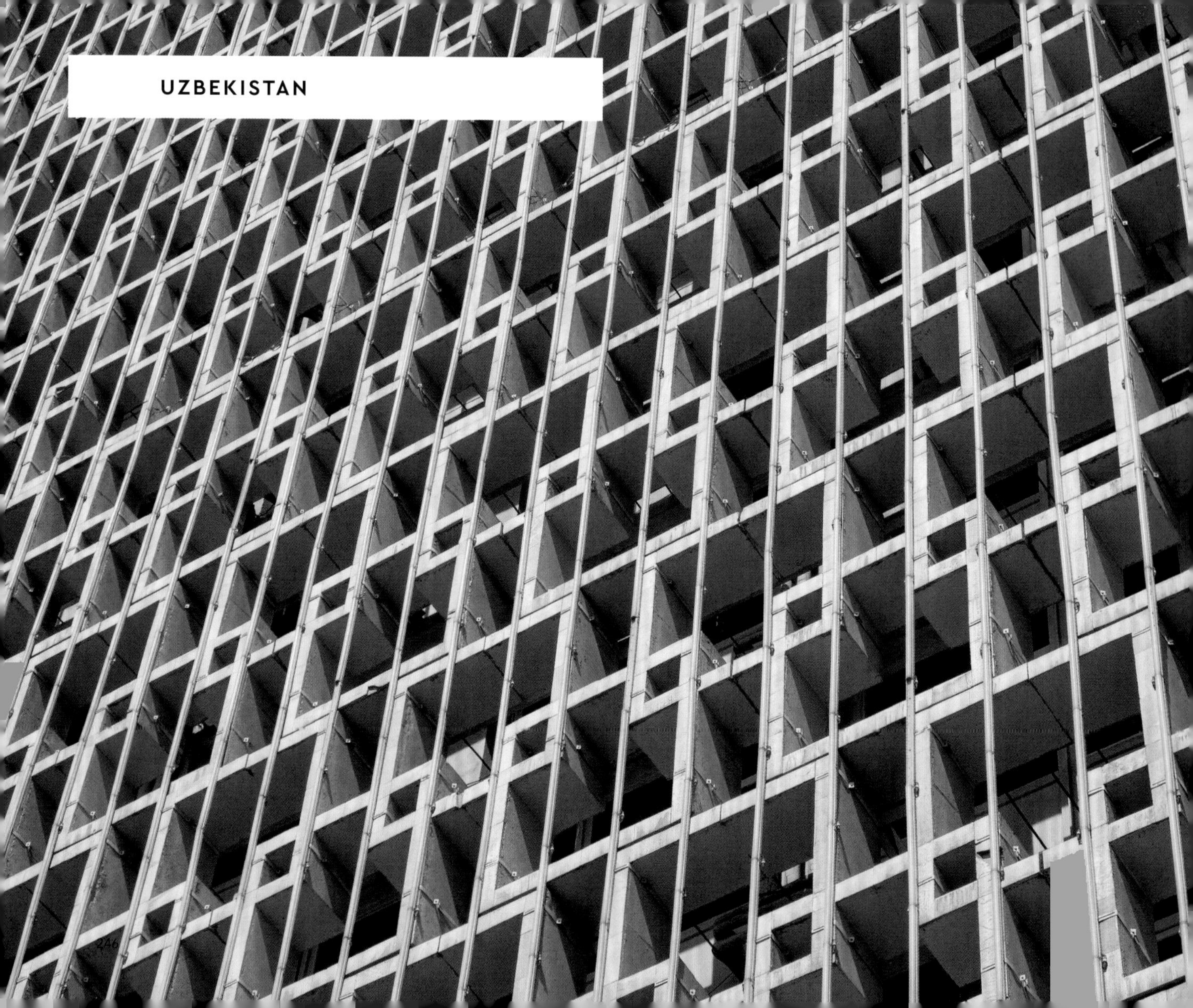

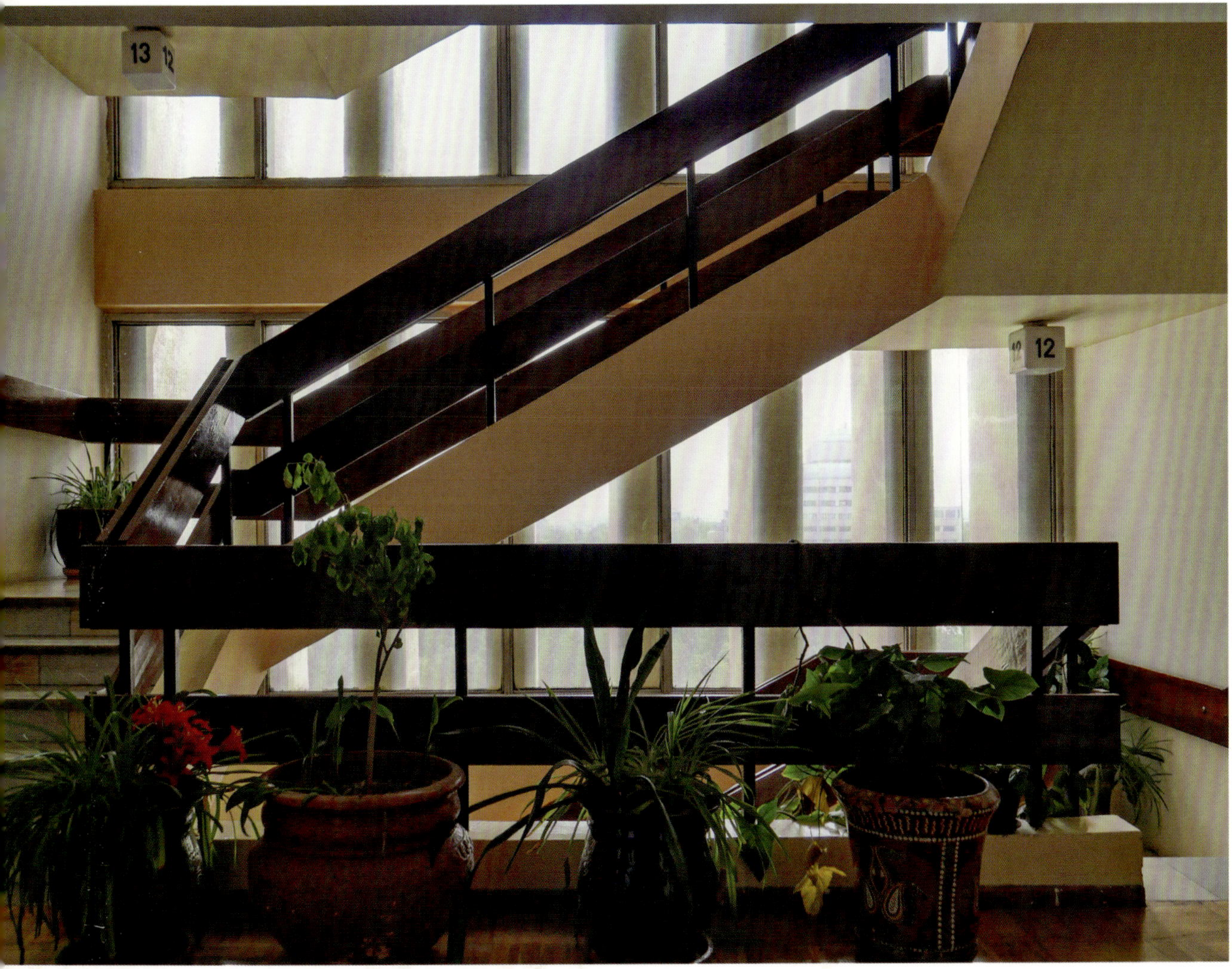

Hotel Uzbekistan, Tashkent, Uzbekistan

Elena Amabili is a Berlin-based photographer and researcher, having grown up in a hotel. Her work explores the fading legacy of socialism. With *Socialist Hotels*, she documents modernist holiday spaces, brimming with collective stories. Her typical subjects include overlooked architecture, tropical plants, and vintage patterned wallpapers, dark places and wild beaches, and all things lobster orange.

Caroline Eden is a writer contributing to the food, travel and culture pages of the *Guardian*, *Times Literary Supplement* and *Financial Times*, among other publications. Specialising on Central Asia and the Caucasus, her books have won numerous awards and she occasionally reports on the region for *From Our Own Correspondent* (BBC Radio 4).

Published in 2026

FUEL Design & Publishing
33 Fournier Street
London E1 6QE

fuel-design.com
@fuelpublishing

Designed and edited by Murray & Sorrell FUEL

Distribution by Thames & Hudson / D. A. P.
ISBN: 978-1-0682946-1-7
Printed in China

The authorised representative in the EU for product safety and compliance is: Interart S.A.R.L., 19 rue Charles Auray, 93500 Pantin, Paris, France. www.interart.fr

This book is dedicated to Giuseppe – *Great party, isn't it?*

Thanks to:
Gufo, without whom this book – and much else – would never have existed.

Mum, for tolerating me and her own nerves in equal measure. Alessandra and Luigi, who braved trips with me and never turned down a heroic breakfast. Picci – she never once said no when it came to okaying my time off. Ariel, for supporting me with Zen-like calm from the very beginning. All my friends – and the shrink as well – putting up with my meltdowns during the making. Reinder Wijnveld, who showed us around the derelict Lunik, and everyone on Instagram who happily shared clues, places and hints.

All the hotel staff, for warmly welcoming photography – and even opening closed rooms. Special thanks to the teams at Hotel Holiday, Sarajevo; Writers' House, Tsaghkadzor; Hotel Journalist, Chayka; Hotel Druzhba, Kurpaty; Hotel Krystal, Prague; Hotel Continental, Skopje; Hotel Tatry, Murzasichle; Hotel Casa Tineretului, Câmpina; Hotel Moldova, Iași; Hotel Peking and Hotel Sovietsky, Moscow; Hotel Omorika, Tara National Park; Hotel Montfort, Tatranská Javorina.

FSC
www.fsc.org
MIX
Paper | Supporting responsible forestry
FSC® C008047

Printed with non mineral ink on FSC® (Forest Stewardship Council) certified paper, from responsibly managed forests and recycled materials, ensuring sustainable forestry practices and environmental protection.